# THE SAVIOR'S
## *Final Week*

# THE SAVIOR'S
## Final Week

GETHSEMANE

GOLGOTHA

THE GARDEN TOMB

## ANDREW C. SKINNER

DESERET
BOOK

SALT LAKE CITY, UTAH

The three books in this volume were originally published by Deseret Book Company:
*Gethsemane* © 2002
*Golgotha* © 2004
*The Garden Tomb* © 2005

**Library of Congress Cataloging-in-Publication Data**

(CIP on file)
ISBN 978-1-60907-850-8

Printed in the United States of America
R. R. Donnelley, Crawfordsville, IN

10   9   8   7   6   5   4   3   2   1

*For family and friends
who have taught me so much
about the Atonement and about
God's love and who have paved
the way with dignity*

# Contents

## 1. GETHSEMANE

# 2. GOLGOTHA

# 3. THE GARDEN TOMB

# CONTENTS

# Publisher's Preface

Few other Latter-day Saint works published in recent decades provide as much depth and breadth of insight and inspiration about the Atonement as do Andrew C. Skinner's landmark books on the culminating events of the mortal life and resurrection of our Savior Jesus Christ. Deseret Book Company is therefore pleased to make available all three of those works—*Gethsemane*, *Golgotha*, and *The Garden Tomb*—in this single volume, entitled *The Savior's Final Week*.

Here, through a narrative supported by scripture and other prophetic passages, Brother Skinner shows us the Last Supper and events that transpired in Gethsemane, the garden of the winepress, where our Lord's redemptive suffering for the sins and pains of all humankind began. Next we examine the irony of the Jewish and Roman trials and the torture of the scourging, and we move onward, upward, to Golgotha, where we see the Son of God subjected to the agony and ignominy of crucifixion. Finally, we explore the miracle of the Resurrection, in which the sinless Son of Man burst the bands of death and rose from the Garden Tomb in resurrected immortality. With great insight and doctrinal clarity, Brother Skinner helps us more nearly comprehend the story of how salvation comes to the children of God through Jesus Christ, the Only Begotten Son of the Father, who "abolished death, and . . . brought life and immortality to light through the gospel" (2 Timothy 1:10).

It is hoped that by means of this combined edition, Deseret Book Company can help members of the Church as well as individuals of other faiths better understand the transformative power of the Atonement of Jesus Christ.

# Gethsemane

# Introduction

Years ago I found myself sitting behind a desk in our ward meetinghouse, a young bishop trying to figure out what the Lord wanted done and how he wanted me to do it. Across the room from me was a thirteen-year-old young woman (I'll call her Brittany) who had many physical and developmental challenges. To this day she remains in my mind's eye tiny and frail. Her parents had insisted that she be baptized, even though, in my view, she did not need baptism because of her mental disabilities—the Atonement was already operating in her life.

Thankfully, I remembered some counsel given by a Church leader about compassion, and I listened to Brittany's parents' request that she be interviewed for baptism. I say thankfully because that evening Brittany taught me the lesson of a lifetime. It was an experience I shall never forget.

The interview did not start out well, nor did it improve as the minutes passed. I asked Brittany question after question that she could not answer the way I thought she should be able to. She could not talk about the first principles and ordinances of the gospel the way all the other Primary children had been able to, at least up to that point in my short tenure as bishop. She could not tell me why baptism is performed or how one is supposed to perform it. I grew frustrated and, I think, so did she. We were both miserable. I began to feel vindicated in thinking we didn't need to be in this interview. It was, after all, eating up valuable time I could have been using to "save" those who really needed it—couples with failing marriages, teenagers with moral challenges, and a host of other problems.

As I was about to abandon the interview, out of the corner of my eye I glimpsed a picture that the previous bishop had left hanging on the office wall. It was a framed print of the Savior in Gethsemane. At that instant the thought came into my mind, *Why don't you ask her who that picture represents?*

I had sense enough to follow the impression, even though my attitude wasn't in harmony with the nature of the question. I said to Brittany, "Do you know who this is?" as I pointed to the painting of the Savior, but my tone or inflection or demeanor or something made it sound like, "I'll bet you don't even know who this is!"

In a scene that remains frozen in my mind, I saw Brittany stand on her crippled feet, shuffle across the floor on the sides of her shoes, plop her hands down on the surface of my desk, lean towards me so that her face was directly in front of mine, only inches away, and say with deliberate and careful articulation, "That's Jesus—and he loves us!" To emphasize her point, Brittany lifted one of her hands off the desk, drew a circle in the air while at the same time nodding her head and saying, "All of us!"

I sat stunned. How was Brittany able to teach such a profound lesson? Fortunately, she drew the circle big enough to include me, for it was clear to me that at that moment I did not deserve to be in the circle with her. Her words convicted me as well as lifted and blessed me, all in the same instant.

"He loves us." The meaning and message of Jesus' experience in Gethsemane are that simple: he loves us—all of us. That is precisely the reason he went to Gethsemane as well as to Golgotha: love—love for his Father, love for his Father's children, love for leaders in his Church, love for all his humble followers, love for the entire human family, and, indeed, love for each one of us as individuals. He went to Gethsemane not only to redeem Brittany from the birth defects that left her unable to explain the fine points of baptism but also to ransom me from my narrow-minded, self-important impatience and deficient behavior. He went to Gethsemane for Brittany and me and literally billions and billions of others of our Father's children.

Jesus' experience with the bitter cup that terrible night in Gethsemane changed me the night of my interview with Brittany. That night in the bishop's office, Gethsemane became very personal. Because the Savior drank the bitter cup, because he squarely faced the bitterest of experiences in Gethsemane nearly two thousand years ago, all my own bitter experiences can become sweet. That is what happened the evening of my interview with Brittany. I am persuaded that others, unseen but very real, were looking in on us.

It is fair to say that Gethsemane became a focal point of my thinking and study, one that invited me to explore its significance as explained in the scriptures. I have come to appreciate that both Gethsemane and Golgotha were critical to the Father's plan, that Gethsemane had to come before Golgotha, and that Gethsemane is a much more significant part of the Savior's atoning sacrifice than some of us might have realized. The thoughts and ideas that follow have come from my explorations in the scriptures and in the writings of latter-day prophets and apostles.

And now, behold, I will testify unto you of myself that these things are true. Behold, I say unto you, that I do know that Christ shall come among the children of men, to take upon him the transgressions of his people, and that he shall atone for the sins of the world; for the Lord God hath spoken it.

For it is expedient that an atonement should be made; for according to the great plan of the Eternal God there must be an atonement made, or else all mankind must unavoidably perish; yea, all are hardened; yea, all are fallen and are lost, and must perish except it be through the atonement which it is expedient should be made.

ALMA 34:8–9

# CHAPTER 1

# Gethsemane and the Bitter Cup

B ecause each one of us is in very deed a daughter or son of divine parents, we ought to care very much about Gethsemane. All of our Heavenly Father's planning and preparation, all of his interest in his children and all of his desires for them, all of his aims and goals for the entire universe came down to a singular moment in a specific time and place on this earth in a garden called Gethsemane. Without Gethsemane in God's eternal plan, everything else would have been a colossal waste—*everything*. Without the events involving one particular Man in that olive vineyard almost two thousand years ago, God's purposes would have been utterly frustrated. Sin, death, decay, destruction, hell, and endless torment would reign supreme forever and ever. If Gethsemane had turned out to be a place associated with suffering and failure rather than suffering and triumph, everything that went before and everything that came afterward would have been reduced to a series of meaningless events in the eternal scheme of things, for there would be no eternal life. Deterioration, disorder, and chaos would ultimately fill the vastness of the universe;

all beauty, human kindness, refinement, and acts of goodness would be forgotten as wasted energy. Truly, Gethsemane was the place where eternity hung in the balance.

## GETHSEMANE, THE ATONEMENT, AND RENEWAL

The events that occurred in Gethsemane were part of the atonement of Jesus Christ—not preparatory to it, nor secondary to it, but at the very heart of it. Without the Savior's unique and unparalleled redemptive activity in Gethsemane, there could have been no atonement, no reprieve from the relentless degenerative effects of sin, and, ultimately, no resurrection to eternal life beyond the Savior's own. Hence, physical and spiritual deterioration could never have been reversed. The pervasive, perpetual degeneration of our universe that is a result of the fall of Adam would not have been halted.

The redemption brought about by events in Gethsemane and the redemption brought about by the Resurrection fit together in complementary fashion. The Savior had "life in himself" (John 5:26) and thus power over his own death. But it was his substitutionary payment in Gethsemane for the fall of Adam and for our sins, together with his resurrection, that gave *us* lasting power over death. Gethsemane was as essential to salvation as Golgotha and the Garden Tomb. Gethsemane brought into existence the opportunity for all of Heavenly Father's children to experience spiritual rebirth, newness of life, and the renewal, rejuvenation, and cleansing of spirit bodies, just as resurrection brings about the renewal, even the re-creation, of physical bodies and establishes them as indestructible material entities. Both kinds of redemption are necessary. Golgotha and the Garden Tomb would mean nothing to us without Gethsemane.

Scientists tell us that the natural order of things in our universe is an irrevocable, steady movement toward decay: from life to death, from organization to chaos, from a condition or state of lesser degeneration to one of greater degeneration (a concept called entropy). This state of being is true for all kingdoms and creations—animals, plants, planets, stars, and other systems. Without Christ's atonement, human beings *and* the worlds on which they reside would be locked forever in the vise grip of death and dissolution. But with and through Christ's atonement, all things are made new. The process of decay is not only halted but reversed. Because of the Atonement, which includes events in Gethsemane as well as the universal resurrection, all things in the universe are empowered, renewed, and revitalized. Thus, Christ is the light and the *life* of the world.

If that godly Being named Jesus had not both lived a perfect life *and* had "life in himself," which attribute was genetically passed on to him by his Father in Heaven, he would not have had power over death, nor the physical capacity to endure the deathly horrors of Gethsemane, nor the ability to determine the time of his own decease while hanging on the cross, nor the capability to rise from the dead, nor the ability to pass on the power of regeneration to others. All men, women, and children would have remained subject to sin and its author forever. In truth, all would have become like the devil, even angels to the devil (2 Nephi 9:5–10). What the Savior *was* (the literal Son of God, having life in himself) gave him power over death for himself. What the Savior *did* (paying vicariously for the transferred sin and suffering of others in Gethsemane) gave him power over death for others.

# THE ATONEMENT AND ALL LIVING THINGS

So extensive and intensive is the atonement of Jesus Christ that this planet Earth is itself redeemed and sanctified by the same atoning power that redeems and sanctifies individual human beings. This concept has been revealed to God's prophets in all ages. Enoch testified that the earth is a living entity and requires the redemptive power of the Savior just as human beings do:

> And behold, Enoch saw the day of the coming of the Son of Man, even in the flesh; and his soul rejoiced, saying: The Righteous is lifted up, and the Lamb is slain from the foundation of the world; and through faith I am in the bosom of the Father, and behold, Zion is with me.
>
> And it came to pass that Enoch looked upon the earth; and he heard a voice from the bowels thereof, saying: Wo, wo is me, the mother of men; I am pained, I am weary, because of the wickedness of my children. When shall I rest, and be cleansed from the filthiness which is gone forth out of me? When will my Creator sanctify me, that I may rest, and righteousness for a season abide upon my face? (Moses 7:47–48)

The patriarch Abraham learned that the fall of Adam and Eve was so powerful that when our first parents fell, the earth also fell, or moved—from its position near Kolob, which is "nigh unto the throne of God" (Abraham 3:9) to its present location in our solar system (Abraham 5:13). But the atonement of Christ is infinitely more powerful than the Fall, and the earth will someday be physically moved back into the presence of God by the power of God (the Atonement). The Prophet Joseph Smith said, "This earth will be rolled back into the presence of God, and crowned with celestial glory" (*Teachings of the Prophet Joseph Smith*, 181).

President Brigham Young was even more detailed in his description of the physical fall and the redemption of this earth:

> When the earth was framed and brought into existence and man was placed upon it, it was near the throne of our Father in heaven. . . . But when man fell, the earth fell into space, and took up its abode in this planetary system, and the sun became our light. When the Lord said—"Let there be light," there was light, for the earth was brought near the sun that it might reflect upon it so as to give us light by day, and the moon to give us light by night. This is the glory the earth came from, and when it is glorified it will return again unto the presence of the Father, and it will dwell there, and these intelligent beings that I am looking at, if they live worthy of it, will dwell upon this earth. (*Journal of Discourses*, 17:143)

In a revelation so sublime it was designated "The Olive Leaf," Joseph Smith gave us another glimpse of just how much the atonement of Christ is tied to the physics of the universe and just how little we know about the greatest of the many powers operating in the cosmos. Because of the atonement of Christ, our earth will not only be physically changed, renewed, and receive a paradisiacal glory (Article of Faith 10) but will be crowned with celestial glory in the very presence of God the Father:

And the redemption of the soul is through him that quickeneth all things, in whose bosom it is decreed that the poor and the meek of the earth shall inherit it.

Therefore, it [the earth] must needs be sanctified from all unrighteousness, that it may be prepared for the celestial glory;

For after it hath filled the measure of its creation, it shall be crowned with glory, even with the presence of God the Father;

That bodies who are of the celestial kingdom may possess it forever and ever; for, for this intent was it made and created, and for this intent are they sanctified. (D&C 88:17–20)

In other words, because of the incomprehensible power of the Atonement not only is the earth redeemed and sanctified but it is destined to become the eternal abode and inheritance of all people who are similarly redeemed and sanctified by the very same atoning power of Jesus Christ. Thus, the Atonement connects people and planets in a seamless web of creation and redemption. In fact, every creature which fills the measure of its creation is likewise blessed by the power of the Atonement to inherit the kingdom of the Father's glory. Of the different beasts portrayed in the book in the Bible entitled The Revelation of St. John the Divine (Revelation 4:6–9; 5:13), the Prophet Joseph Smith said they were examples of the many varied creatures in heaven redeemed by God:

I suppose John saw beings there of a thousand forms, that had been saved from ten thousand times ten thousand earths like this,—strange beasts of which we have no conception: all might be seen in heaven. . . . John learned that God glorified Himself by saving all that His hands had made, whether beasts, fowls, fishes or men; and He will glorify Himself with them.

Says one, "I cannot believe in the salvation of beasts." Any man who would tell you that this could not be, would tell you that the revelations are not true. John heard the words of the beasts giving glory to God, and understood them. God who made the beasts could understand every language spoken by them. The four beasts were four of the most noble animals that had filled the measure of their creation, and had been saved from other worlds. (*Teachings of the Prophet Joseph Smith*, 291–92)

The atonement of Christ is so great in its effects and so far-reaching in its consequences that it easily qualifies as the most important occurrence in time or in all eternity. Nothing ever has or ever will surpass it in significance. Nothing is greater in the entire universe or in the history of created things than Christ's atonement. In Hebrew, the word *atonement* is rendered as *kippur* (as in *Yom Kippur*, "Day of Atonement"), which derives from the root *kaphar*, meaning "to cover." This is an apt connotation, for the atonement of Christ "covers" all things. "When the prophets speak of an *infinite* atonement, they mean just that. Its effects cover all men, the earth itself and all forms of life thereon, and reach out into the endless expanses of eternity" (McConkie, *Mormon Doctrine*, 64).

Thus, the atonement of Christ is infinite in time, space, and quantity—infinite in scope and eternal in duration. All death is answered; every creature under the Savior's dominion is resurrected. All sin is compensated for; every combination of sins is covered. The Atonement goes beyond personal sin to include disappointment, sorrow, and suffering caused by the sins of others. It even extends to the sicknesses and infirmities we must bear just because we are mortal (Alma 7:11–12). It was made by a being who was God before he came to earth, who was the Son of God on earth, and who will be God eternally and endlessly.

## THE ATONEMENT AND THE UNIVERSE

Most stunning of all, the infinite atonement of Christ, worked out on this earth, extends to all worlds which Christ created under the direction and tutelage of God the Father—and that includes "worlds without number" (Moses 1:33). This sweeping aspect of the infinite atonement was revealed to the Prophet Joseph Smith and recorded in Doctrine and Covenants 76, a revelation so powerful and profound it is called simply the Vision. In this revelation the Prophet and Sidney Rigdon bear ultimate and irrefutable witness of the Savior's reality as well as his expansive *creative* power:

> And now, after the many testimonies which have been given of him, this is the testimony, last of all, which we give of him: That he lives!
>
> For we saw him, even on the right hand of God; and we heard the voice bearing record that he is the Only Begotten of the Father—
>
> That by him, and through him, and of him, the worlds are and were created, and the inhabitants thereof are begotten sons and daughters unto God. (D&C 76: 22–24)

Next they describe the extent of his *redeeming* power:

> That he came into the world, even Jesus, to be crucified for the world, and to bear the sins of the world,

and to sanctify the world, and to cleanse it from all unrighteousness;

That through him *all* might be saved whom the Father had put into his power and made by him. (D&C 76:41–42; emphasis added)

From the panoramic vision given to Moses, we begin to glimpse the magnitude and meaning of the statement that *all* are saved which the Father put into the Savior's power and made by him: "And *worlds without number* have I created; and I also created them for mine own purpose; and by the Son I created them, which is mine Only Begotten" (Moses 1:33; emphasis added). Remember how the Prophet Joseph Smith described it: "ten thousand times ten thousand earths like this [one]."

The doctrine of the all-encompassing nature of the Atonement was taught by Joseph Smith as part of his poetic rendering of Doctrine and Covenants 76. He reworked it into a poem which he composed in response to a poem penned by his friend W. W. Phelps. The portion of the Prophet's inspired rendition that corresponds to verses 22 through 24 reads as follows:

> And I heard a great voice, bearing record
>     from heav'n,
> He's the Saviour and only begotten of God—
> By him, of him, and through him, the worlds
>     were all made,
> Even all that career in the heavens so broad.
>
> Whose inhabitants, too, from the first to the
>     last,
> Are sav'd by the very same Saviour of ours;

And, of course, are begotten God's daughters
and sons,
By the very same truths, and the very same
pow'rs.
(*Times and Seasons* 4 [1 February 1843]: 82–83)

The Prophet Joseph Smith's singular witness of the Lord's living reality, his divine Sonship, and his creative workmanship also implies that the Creation is still going on. Joseph Smith learned what God revealed to Moses: "For behold, there are many worlds that have passed away by the word of my power. And there are many that now stand, and innumerable are they unto man; but all things are numbered unto me, for they are mine and I know them" (Moses 1:35). The Atonement covers all these worlds; Gethsemane was ordained that they might be redeemed. The power and wisdom exercised by Jesus are beyond the grasp of mortals. The written declarations of prophets about the creation and redemption of millions of earths by Christ through the same power that is held by the Father is testimony enough of Jesus' stature before his birth as the mortal Messiah. But such testimony is made visual when one stands outdoors on a clear, cloudless night to gaze into the star-filled heavens and realize that the vast expanse of the visible universe is only a small part of the Savior's realm.

Astronomers tell us that our solar system is located in a spiral arm of the Milky Way Galaxy, a flat, disc-shaped cluster of stars approximately 100,000 light years across at its widest point. A light year is the distance light travels in one year. Moving at the speed of 186,000 miles per second, a beam of light traverses 5.7 trillion miles in 365 days! The size of our galaxy in miles is a staggering 5.7 trillion times 100,000, and it is estimated to contain 200 billion stars, 50 percent of which (100 billion) possess solar systems like our own. The next closest galaxy is Andromeda, a galaxy much like our own Milky Way, that is approximately 2.2 million light years away from us. Furthermore, our best telescopes can probe outward into space to a distance of approximately 5 billion light years and view about 500 million galaxies, each of which possesses billions of stars. And these galaxies are only the ones we can detect with the present state of our technology. Truly, the observation made by Enoch the seer is one of the grandest *understatements* of all time: "And were it possible that man could number the particles of the earth, yea, millions of earths like this, it would not be a beginning to the number of thy creations; and thy curtains are stretched out still" (Moses 7:30).

The Savior redeems all that he creates. Such are the sweeping and incomprehensible powers of Jesus, the Victor of Gethsemane. And what's more, these creations are maintained and renewed continually by the very same power possessed by their creator, for

> he that ascended up on high, as also he descended below all things, in that he comprehended all things, that he might be in all and through all things, the light of truth;
>
> Which truth shineth. This is the light of Christ . . .
>
> Which light proceedeth forth from the presence of God to fill the immensity of space—
>
> The light which is in all things, which giveth life to all things, which is the law by which all things are governed, even the power of God who sitteth upon his

throne, who is in the bosom of eternity, who is in the midst of all things. (D&C 88:6–13)

## THE ATONEMENT AND THE BITTER CUP

All that the Atonement was and is, all that it put into effect or operation, all that it set in motion, all that it touches in the vastness of space for time and eternity centers on a moment in this earth's temporal history at the spot called Gethsemane. It is true that the Atonement involved both Gethsemane and Golgotha, but the agony of redemption began in Gethsemane. Prophets have taught that the Savior's greatest suffering was in Gethsemane. President Joseph Fielding Smith said:

> [Christ's] greatest suffering was in Gethsemane. We speak of the passion of Jesus Christ. A great many people have an idea that when he was on the cross, and nails were driven into his hands and feet, that was his great suffering. His great suffering was before he ever was placed upon the cross. It was in the Garden of Gethsemane that the blood oozed from the pores of his body: "Which suffering caused myself, even God, the greatest of all, to tremble because of pain, and to bleed at every pore, and to suffer both body and spirit—and would that I might not drink the bitter cup, and shrink."
>
> That was not when he was on the cross; that was in the garden. That is where he bled from every pore in his body. Now I cannot comprehend that pain. (*Doctrines of Salvation*, 1:130)

And so it was that by divine decree and ordination, all laws were poised for this greatest of events we sometimes refer to simply as Gethsemane. All things pointed to it. God the Father's great plan of happiness was created around it. It was the Father's will that such a thing take place. Jesus was the perfectly innocent but willing volunteer. And thereby hangs the tale, for the Savior consistently and repeatedly in scripture referred to the events in Gethsemane as "the bitter cup."

To every disciple of every dispensation, Gethsemane was and is the sweetest of victories: "From the terrible conflict in Gethsemane, Christ emerged a victor" (Talmage, *Jesus the Christ*, 614). That victory means everything to us as mortals. Because of it, every human being who seeks God's love receives not only that love but hope as well. Yet, to the Sinless One himself, a being of infinite goodness and perfect sensitivity, Gethsemane was the ultimate torture, the darkest hour, the starkest terror. His most extreme distress had little to do with the thought of physical death, even the hideous kind of death brought on by crucifixion. Rather, to that one being in all the universe who was personally and completely undeserving of the horrible, infinite punishments inflicted, Gethsemane was the bitterest anguish, the greatest contradiction, the gravest injustice, the bitterest of cups to drink. Yet, the will of the Father was that the bitter cup be swallowed—drained to its dregs. And drained it was, swallowed to the last drop by Christ. Thus it would be said, in ultimate irony, that the will of the Son was "swallowed up in the will of the Father" (Mosiah 15:7).

Irony and contradiction are two of the best descriptors of Gethsemane's bitter cup, causing thoughtful disciples to reflect on the nature of tests and trials in mortality and how the lessons of the bitter cup can have profound meaning in their lives. The Prophet Joseph Smith taught that the Savior "descended in suffering below that which man can suffer; or, in other

17

words, suffered greater sufferings, and was exposed to more powerful contradictions than any man can be" (*Lectures on Faith*, 59). Perhaps the greatest trials are those which seem the most unfair, but the faithful may take comfort in knowing that there is One who understands with perfect empathy. In Gethsemane, the contradictions that constitute the bitter cup are seen with crystal clarity. He who was the Son of the Highest descended below all things. He who was sinless was weighed down by the crushing sins of everyone else. He who was the light and the life of the world was surrounded by darkness and death. He who was sent to earth out of love and who was characterized as Love suffered the effects of enmity, or hatred, toward God. He who was the essence of loyalty was the object of betrayal and disloyalty. He who did nothing but good suffered evil. He who was the Righteous One was buffeted by the enemy of all righteousness. And from it all, he emerged victorious.

That Latter-day Saints are different from almost all other Christians in placing so much emphasis on Gethsemane is evidenced in our expanded and expansive canon of scripture. The events of Gethsemane are a focal point of Latter-day Saint scripture, which testifies of its profundity. The experience of the bitter cup seems to have had such an effect on the Savior himself that he discussed it not only in Gethsemane but during his ministry to the Nephites after his resurrection and in his revelations of the latter days. It affected Jesus to the very core of his being. By studying the bitter cup, we can see, really see, how the bitterest agony for One opened the door to the sweetest ecstasy for all.

My young friend Brittany did not know about the doctrine of the bitter cup. But she did know the most important thing of all—Jesus did what he did out of love. She knew of his love for her, and she loved him. On this point she was as articulate and clear as the scriptures she could not read. Jesus endured the suffering of the bitter cup out of love. He endured the bitter cup so that we don't have to. As the apostle John said, "We love him, because he first loved us" (1 John 4:19). By studying the bitter cup, we can have a guide and support to help make sense of life's trials, sorrows, suffering, and contradictions. We can know of a surety that God's love is as deep and profound as the Savior's suffering. We can learn the precious price of redemption.

And when the hour was come, he sat down, and the twelve apostles with him.

And he said unto them, With desire I have desired to eat this passover with you before I suffer. . . .

And he took bread, and gave thanks, and brake it, and gave unto them, saying, This is my body which is given for you: this do in remembrance of me.

Like wise also the cup after supper, saying, This cup is the new testament in my blood, which is shed for you.

LUKE 22:14–20

When Jesus had spoken these words, he went forth with his disciples over the brook Cedron, where was a garden, into the which he entered, and his disciples.

And Judas also, which betrayed him, knew the place: for Jesus oft-times resorted thither with his disciples.

JOHN 18:1–2

# CHAPTER 2

# The Preparation for the Bitter Cup

The Savior's preparation for the awful events of Gethsemane began to take shape several months before his actual experience in the garden, as he tried to fortify his apostles against the coming suffering and rejection he knew he would have to endure at Jerusalem. The authors of all three synoptic Gospels (Matthew, Mark, and Luke) indicate that immediately after his experience on the Mount of Transfiguration with Peter, James, and John, the Savior began to teach his disciples about his impending death. Matthew says: "From that time forth began Jesus to shew unto his disciples, how that he must go unto Jerusalem, and suffer many things of the elders and chief priests and scribes, and be killed, and be raised again the third day" (Matthew 16:21). Mark points out the rejection of Jesus as a separate aspect of his suffering: "And he began to teach them, that the Son of man must suffer many things, *and* be rejected of the elders, and of the chief priests, and scribes" (Mark 8:31; emphasis added).

## REJECTION OF JESUS

The rejection Jesus experienced his whole life, but which intensified as he neared the end, actually centered in his own family long before the last six months of his ministry. John records, "Neither did his brethren believe in him" (John 7:5). His "brethren," or half brothers James, Joses, Simon, and Judas (Matthew 13:55) chided and goaded him over his messianic claims, undoubtedly seeking to mock and chastise him (John 7:2–4, 7). Thus it may be said, colloquially but fairly, that Jesus himself, the great Jehovah come to earth, was the product of a part-member family, thereby showing his followers that not even he was exempt from the heartache and rejection sometimes inflicted by those whom we most wish could be our greatest supporters.

How this must have stung! In the Savior's case, this suffering and rejection from family members was but a prelude to even greater and more intense anguish he had to endure at the end of his life. It demonstrates that the prophecies uttered by Isaiah began to be fulfilled in a most exacting and all-encompassing manner long before the culminating events of Gethsemane. Truly, in every way Jesus was "despised and rejected of men; a man of sorrows, and acquainted with grief" (Isaiah 53:3). Thus, his disciples in our day may take comfort in knowing that because of his own experience, Jesus comprehends every kind of pain, sorrow, and rejection. He therefore is able to be both a perfect advocate and a perfect nurturer for those who suffer, even those who suffer deep pain from the actions and cruelty of others through no fault of their own.

However great they were, the apostles of ancient times little understood what Jesus was telling them about his suffering (current and impending) as well as his approaching and inevitable redemptive sacrifice. In fact, President Wilford Woodruff said that the apostles of the meridian dispensation had as little idea that Jesus was going to suffer death and be taken from them as had the early apostles of our own dispensation that Joseph Smith was going to suffer a martyr's fate. He said: "I remember very well the last charge that Joseph gave to the Apostles. We had as little idea that he was going from us as the Apostles of the Savior did that He was going to be taken from them. Joseph talked with us as plainly as did the Savior to His Apostles, but we did not understand that he was about to depart from us any more than the Apostles understood the Savior" (*Collected Discourses*, 188).

Reasons for their failing to understand are undoubtedly complex, but Jesus' rebuke of Peter for "savour[ing] not the things that be of God, but the things that be of men" (Mark 8:33) may indicate that the apostles were expecting that, in the end, Jesus would be the same kind of Messiah the rest of the Jewish people were looking for: a towering military conqueror and political deliverer.

As the Savior's mortal life moved unalterably closer to the final week when his prophesied and nearly unbearable suffering would explode upon him, his fame spread, his popularity waxed and waned, opposition toward him increased among Jewish leaders, and plots to take his life fomented beneath the surface of a society whose leaders contemptuously conspired against him. On the last Sunday of his mortal existence, the Savior made his triumphal entry into Jerusalem, just as the long awaited King-Messiah was expected to do and as other kings of Israel had done (1 Kings 1:38–39). He rode upon a donkey, symbolic of royalty and in fulfillment of prophecy (Matthew

21:4–5), rather than upon a horse, symbolic of war and conquest. In ironic fulfillment of Jewish messianic expectation, when Jesus comes again he will be riding a white horse as the ultimate conqueror of all—only this will be his great and terrible second coming (Revelation 19:11–16).

Messianic fervor and expectation reached a feverish pitch as Jesus made his triumphal entry into Jerusalem the last Sunday of his mortal existence. Matthew testified of this when he reported that

> a very great multitude spread their garments in the way; others cut down branches from the trees, and strawed them in the way.
>
> And the multitudes that went before, and that followed, cried, saying, Hosanna to the Son of David: Blessed is he that cometh in the name of the Lord; Hosanna in the highest.
>
> And when he was come into Jerusalem, *all the city was moved*, saying, Who is this?
>
> And the multitude said, This is Jesus the prophet of Nazareth of Galilee. (Matthew 21:8–11; emphasis added)

It is likely that some were expecting Jesus, as the long-awaited King-Messiah-Deliverer-Conqueror, to enter the Jerusalem Temple via the Eastern, or Golden, Gate, turn toward the Antonia Fortress, drive the Roman overlords from the land of Israel, and, in fulfillment of Davidic expectation, establish an idyllic messianic kingdom, much as King David had done when he conquered Jerusalem in 1004 B.C. and set up an unrivaled domain (2 Samuel 5:6–10). Jesus did enter the Temple complex, but instead of going to the Antonia Fortress where Roman sentries were barracked, he went to the Temple courtyard and drove out the money changers. This action dashed the hopes of those who thought their political deliverer-warrior had actually come, and it further angered Jewish leaders, who began looking in earnest for a way to rid themselves of the prophet from Nazareth, who was disrupting the flow of economic traffic at the center of Jewish life—the Temple (Matthew 21:15). The apostle John summarizes the attitude of two groups of leaders, the chief priests and the Pharisees, who were, strangely enough, at that moment in alignment over Jesus: "If we let him thus alone, all men will believe on him: and the Romans shall come and take away both our place and our nation" (John 11:48). Elements of Jewish leadership from all quarters of society, even those from opposite ends of the political-religious spectrum, were now irreversibly set against the Savior. His fate was sealed.

## THE PASSOVER PLOT COMPLETED

So it was that a couple of days after his triumphal entry, and two days before the Passover celebration, perhaps Tuesday of the last week of the Savior's mortal life, Luke tells of the Passover conspiracy being completed:

> Now the feast of unleavened bread drew nigh, which is called the Passover.
>
> And the chief priests and scribes sought how they might kill him; for they feared the people.
>
> Then entered Satan into Judas surnamed Iscariot, being of the number of the twelve.
>
> And he went his way, and communed with the chief priests and captains, how he might betray him unto them.

And they were glad, and covenanted to give him money.

And he promised, and sought opportunity to betray him unto them in the absence of the multitude. (Luke 22:1–6)

A more chilling description than this one can hardly be imagined. Luke tells of Satan entering "into Judas surnamed Iscariot" (Luke 22:3) and the latter covenanting and promising to betray the Master in the absence of the multitude. We might be tempted to ascribe Luke's description to hyperbole except that John (whose Gospel is not one of the synoptic Gospels and is therefore a good source of corroboration) also tells us that Satan entered into Judas during the evening of the Last Supper (John 13:27).

At this point, we might ask if such a thing is really possible. Could Satan really have entered Judas, a member of the Twelve? "Perhaps," wrote Elder Bruce R. McConkie, "for Satan is a spirit man, a being who was born the offspring of God in pre-existence, and who was cast out of heaven for rebellion. He and his followers have power in some cases to enter the [physical] bodies of men" (*Doctrinal New Testament Commentary*, 1:701–2).

Though such a circumstance is almost too terrifying to contemplate, we have the assurance of a modern prophet that Satan can have no power over a person unless he is granted it by the individual: "All beings who have bodies have power over those who have not. The devil has no power over us only as we permit him" (Smith, *Teachings of the Prophet Joseph Smith*, 181).

Whether or not Satan literally entered into Judas on this occasion, Judas "had sold himself to the devil" well before he sold Jesus into the hands of evil men (Talmage, *Jesus the Christ*, 592). The agreed-upon price of betrayal was thirty pieces of silver, which was the price of a slave in Jesus' day, as foreseen in prophecy (Exodus 21:28–32; Zechariah 11:12). The chief priests with whom Judas communicated were those very leaders who later actively "sought for witness against Jesus to put him to death" (Mark 14:55) and incited the multitudes to reject their King (John 19:6, 15). It appears that the "captains" whom Luke describes as covenanting with Judas (Luke 22:4) were officers of the temple guard, chosen mostly from the Levites. They were also with the chief priests shouting, "Crucify him, crucify him" when Jesus was arraigned before the Roman governor, Pontius Pilate (John 19:6).

## THE PASSOVER MEAL

After Judas' preparations had been completed and the plot was in place, the Savior's own preparation for Gethsemane culminated in the "cup after supper," the sacrament, which involved the ordinance of the washing of the feet. That is, before Jesus endured the "bitter cup," as he himself called his experience in Gethsemane, he fortified himself and his apostles against the coming spiritual onslaught by instituting the sacrament of the Lord's Supper only hours before the fury in Gethsemane was unleashed.

The sacrament itself required some preparation, for it had been celebrated the previous twelve hundred years or so as the traditional Passover, or Seder, meal of the people of Israel. The Hebrew word *seder* means "order, or arrangement" and evokes images of elaborate preparation of special foods to be eaten in a prescribed order as well as specific teachings and scriptures to be recited in proper sequence throughout the evening.

Passover commemorated the night in Egypt when the angel of death, sent by Jehovah, passed over the homes of the children of Israel and spared the lives of their firstborn, providing they had sacrificed an unblemished male lamb, eaten the roasted meat, and daubed the blood of the lamb on the lintel and doorposts of their houses (Exodus 12:5, 7, 13, 22–23, 27).

It was a night of judgment, but the substitutionary death of the Passover lamb brought forgiveness to God's people, Israel. It washed away 430 years of Egypt's contamination. The blood of the lamb protected them from the wrath of the Almighty. Its roasted flesh nourished their bodies with strength for the long, perilous journey ahead. They ate in haste, loins girded, staff in hand, shoes on their feet, prepared to leave at any moment at God's command. In that awe-filled night of waiting, they experienced Jehovah's loving protection, even in the midst of the unleashing of His fierce judgment. (Rosen and Rosen, *Christ in the Passover*, 23–24)

The English word *Passover* is a translation of the Hebrew *pesach*, which means "to skip over, to hop" and also carries the connotation of "protecting." *Passover* can be used to mean either the sacrificial ceremony or the actual lamb itself, as in Luke 22:7: "Then came the day of unleavened bread, when *the passover* must be killed" (emphasis added).

The Greek equivalent of *pesach* is *pascha*, hence the term "paschal lamb," which was sacrificed as part of the annual Passover ceremony so that Israel would always remember the Lord's power and protection. The meaning of the practice has been summarized in the following way: "The slain lamb, the sheltering behind its blood and the eating of its flesh, constituted the *pesach*, the protection of God's chosen people beneath the sheltering wings of the Almighty. . . . It was not merely that the Lord passed by the houses of the Israelites, but that He stood on guard, *protecting* each blood-sprinkled door! [The Lord . . . will not suffer the destroyer to come in (Exodus 12:23b)]" (Rosen and Rosen, *Christ in the Passover*, 22–23).

During Jesus' time, the Passover lambs used in the feast were killed on the fourteenth day of the month of Nissan, and the meal was eaten between sundown and midnight, in conformity with Exodus 12:6. Because the Jewish day began at sundown, the Passover feast itself took place on the fifteenth of Nissan. The Feast of Unleavened Bread followed the Passover feast and lasted seven more days (Exodus 12:15–20; 23:15; 34:18; Deuteronomy 16:1–8).

The special foods and other items of the first Passover, as well as their arrangement, were highly symbolic, although most Jewish people today do not recognize or acknowledge the Christ-centered symbolism of those elements. The following is a summary of the most important elements of the first Passover:

1. Just as "the firstborn in the land of Egypt [would] die" (Exodus 11:5), so Jesus, the Firstborn of the Father (D&C 93:21), would die.

2. Just as the Passover sacrifice was a male lamb "without blemish" (Exodus 12:5), so Jesus was "as of a lamb without blemish" (1 Peter 1:19) and was called the Lamb of God (1 Nephi 11:21).

3. Just as no bone of the Passover lamb was to be broken

# THE PASSOVER THROUGH THE AGES

| THE ORIGINAL PASSOVER IN THE TIME OF MOSES | THE TRADITIONAL PASSOVER AT THE TIME OF CHRIST | THE JEWISH PASSOVER AS PRACTICED TODAY |
|---|---|---|
| *EXODUS 12* | *THE SEDER (Luke 22)* | *THE SEDER Today* |
| 1. A MALE LAMB<br>• Slain as a sacrifice<br>• Blood on doorpost<br>• Lamb eaten | 1. A MALE LAMB<br>• Slain at temple altar<br>• Blood on doorpost<br>• Lamb eaten | 1. SHANK BONE of a lamb |
| 2. UNLEAVENED BREAD<br>• At the meal and for 7 more days<br>• Symbolized haste in leaving Egypt | 2. UNLEAVENED BREAD | 2. UNLEAVENED BREAD (matzos) |
| 3. BITTER HERBS Symbolized the bitterness of bondage in Egypt | 3. BITTER HERBS | 3. HORSERADISH (bitter herb) |
| | 4. FOUR CUPS OF WINE<br>• Cup of blessing (telling of the story)<br>• Cup before eating (eating of the food)<br>• Cup after supper (songs of thanks)<br>• Cup of Elijah | 4. FOUR CUPS OF WINE |
| | 5. OTHER FOODS FOR FEAST | 5. PARSLEY (spring) |
| | | 6. SALT WATER (Red Sea) |
| | | 7. AN EGG (new life) |
| | | 8. "HAROSET"–reddish fruit salad (representing brick mortar) |
| | | 9. MEAL–main course of turkey, chicken, etc. |
| | | 10. GEFILTE FISH |
| Note what the sacrificial lamb symbolized. | Note what elements of the Passover Jesus gave as a new way to remember him. | Note how modern Passover services omit the symbolism of the Messiah. |
| *Future sacrifice of Jesus Christ* | *Bread and wine (cup after supper; Luke 22:19–20)* | *There is NO LAMB* |

(Exodus 12:46), so no bone of Jesus was broken during his atoning sacrifice (John 19:36).

4. Just as no stranger was to eat of the Passover lamb (Exodus 12:43), so, too, no stranger (one who is estranged from God through unworthiness) is to eat of the emblems of the sacrifice of the Lamb of God—the sacrament (3 Nephi 18:28–30).

5. Just as hyssop was associated with the Passover sacrifice (Exodus 12:22), so hyssop was associated with the crucifixion of the great and last sacrifice of the Lamb of God (John 19:29).

6. Just as the blood of the Passover lamb caused death to pass by the believers (Exodus 12:13), so the blood of the Lamb of God causes the effects of sin or spiritual death to pass by the believers (John 1:29; Alma 7:14; 11:40–43).

The special foods to be prepared and eaten for the Passover meal changed over the twelve hundred years between the original Passover in Moses' day (Exodus 12–13) and the Passover meal at the time of Jesus. Nevertheless, the three most important elements in Jesus' day continued to be the unleavened bread, the wine, and the male lamb without blemish or spot.

This information, summarized on the accompanying chart, is valuable for several reasons. First, it helps us understand the unstated historical and cultural background that Jesus and his apostles, all of them observant Jews, brought to the last Passover of Jesus' mortal life. It helps us see meaning in the absence of a lamb in the modern observances: the Jewish people lack a knowledge of their Redeemer, the Messiah who has come and gone but will return. Most important, it helps us recognize a connection between the Passover meal and the sacrament of the Lord's Supper. We see what elements of the Passover meal Jesus emphasized in order to help us remember him: the bread and the wine (water).

A significant but sometimes overlooked doctrinal principle is involved here as well. Just as the Atonement itself had been foreshadowed before the coming of Jesus Christ in the flesh, so too the sacrament had been foreshadowed as early as Melchizedek's and Abraham's day. We remember that Abraham had made a covenant with God, the terms of which included the promises of land, posterity, priesthood, and salvation through the Messiah. Abraham's spiritual leader was Melchizedek, the very same man who was translated because of his righteousness and his work in pointing his people to the coming of Jesus Christ through participation in the ordinances of God (JST Genesis 14:25–36; Alma 13:14–19). Thus, after Abraham's return from war with the kings, the following scene unfolded: "And Melchizedek, king of Salem, brought forth bread and wine; and he break bread and blest it; and he blest the wine, he being the priest of the most high God, and he gave to Abram, and he blessed him, and said, Blessed Abram, thou art a man of the most high God, possessor of heaven and of earth" (JST Genesis 14:17–18).

The Joseph Smith Translation makes it clear that the bread and wine were more than just a snack after a hard day on the battlefield—a point lost in other versions of the Bible. Melchizedek broke the bread and blessed it and blessed the wine precisely *because* he was the priest of the Most High God and had the authority to administer the ordinances of God. We are further convinced by Elder Bruce R. McConkie's observation that the ordinance of the sacrament was purposely foreshadowed and prefigured "some two thousand years before its formal institution among men, when 'Melchizedek, king of Salem, brought forth bread and wine; and he brake bread and blest it, and he blest wine, he being priest of the most high God.' . . . It will be administered after the Lord comes again, to all the faithful of all ages, as they in resurrected glory assemble before him" (*Promised Messiah*, 384).

## IN THE UPPER ROOM

We know that the Savior was aware of the need to prepare for the Passover feast because on the day when the Passover lamb was traditionally killed, he sent the apostles Peter and John to the home of someone who was himself a disciple so that they could make the necessary preparations. We know the man to whom the apostles were sent was a disciple of Jesus because Jesus told the apostles to tell the homeowner that the Master was requesting the use of his furnished upper room (Luke 22:7–12). That is, Jesus was the homeowner's Master as well.

On the afternoon of the appointed day when the Passover lambs were to be killed, while Jesus and his apostles were making their preparations for the Passover feast, thousands of paschal lambs were being slain within the precincts of the Jerusalem temple by representatives of families getting ready to participate in their own Passover feasts. A portion of blood from each of the Passover lambs was sprinkled at the foot of the great altar by one of a large number of priests on duty for the occasion. The Jewish historian Josephus indicates that the lambs had to be slain between the ninth and eleventh hours of the day, that is, between 3 and 5 P.M. Some authorities hold that during the time of Jesus, two nights were devoted to the Passover observance and the lamb could be eaten during either of the two days. This accommodation was made because the greatly increased population in Jerusalem during Passover seasons of the meridian dispensation necessitated the ceremonial slaughtering of more lambs than could be sacrificed on a single day (Talmage, *Jesus the Christ*, 618). According to Josephus, the number of Passover lambs slain at a single Passover season during this period was 256,500 (*Wars*, 6.9:3).

With preparations completed, Jesus sat down with his apostles in the upper room of one of Jerusalem's more expensive houses to participate in the last Passover of his mortal life. What emotion must have choked the atmosphere of this significant occasion as Jesus said to the assembled group, "With desire I have desired to eat this passover with you before I suffer" (Luke 22:15). Or, as the New International Version of the Bible translates this passage, "I have eagerly desired to eat this Passover with you before I suffer" (Luke 22:15). The very Being who instituted the first Passover more than twelve hundred years before now expressed his yearning to be with his closest friends to show them how everything about the Passover pointed to himself.

We have every reason to believe that the Seder meal on this special night followed the traditional manner of presentation—up to a point. Though the critical, most significant elements of the Passover had been revealed by Jehovah in Old Testament times, by the time of Christ some elements had been borrowed from Roman custom. One of these was the kind of table used. Called a *triclinium*, this table was low to the floor and composed of three sections configured in a U shape. Both the table and the room in which it was set were called the triclinium. Known from historical texts, actual specimens of tricliniums have been found in modern times through archaeological excavation in the Holy Land at Herodium, Nablus, Sepphoris, and the modern Jewish Quarter of the Old City of Jerusalem.

Rabbinic and New Testament sources tell us that diners reclined around the table, resting on their left elbows, heads toward the table, feet pointed away, reaching and eating with their right hands, which were free. This form of dining imitated the practice of the free, wealthy, and aristocratic members of Roman Hellenistic society. According to Jewish tradition, all who participate in the Passover are regarded as kings before God during this special time, which celebrates liberty and protection of the once oppressed.

The seat on the outside edge of the triclinium, second in from the end, was reserved for special guests, dignitaries, or learned teachers. It is possible that Jesus sat here as he led the Passover service. The Gospel of John helps us further visualize the seating arrangements at the triclinium, specifically, who was seated in front of, or to the right side of, Jesus. "Now there was leaning on Jesus' bosom one of his disciples, whom Jesus loved" (John 13:23). That is, as Jesus reclined with feet away from the table, John (the "beloved" disciple) was situated so he could lean back and rest his head and shoulder against the chest of Jesus.

## THE NEW ORDINANCE INSTITUTED

The order of events probably unfolded according to recognized custom. The first cup of wine was blessed and drunk. Hands were washed as a blessing was recited. Bitter herbs, symbolic of the bitterness of Egyptian bondage, were eaten—dipped in sour broth made of vinegar and bruised fruit, both messianic symbols. Because of the composition of the group (there being no youngest son to ask questions about why this night was different from all other nights), the origins of Passover were likely recounted by the leader of the Seder service—who was, in this instance, Jesus. The lamb was then placed on the table or, if already on the table, it was acknowledged, and the first parts of the Hallel (Psalms 113 and 114) were sung. The second cup of wine was blessed and drunk.

But then something extraordinary happened. According to the Gospel of Luke, instead of breaking the unleavened bread of Passover and reciting the traditional blessing appropriate at this juncture, Jesus "took bread, and gave thanks, and brake it, and gave unto them, saying, This is my body which is given for you: this do in remembrance of me" (Luke 22:19). The disciples must have sat in stunned silence as they struggled to eat a piece of the bread and then consume a fragment of the lamb, as was the custom. Such a thing as this had never been done before. Such a comment as Jesus had made would have been totally inappropriate—unless, of course, the commentator really was the Messiah.

From this point, a typical Passover dinner usually proceeded at a leisurely pace until everything was eaten and the atmosphere of celebration increased. But the apostles of the Lamb had just eaten a piece of bread and a fragment of lamb, not in remembrance of the events of the first Passover (Exodus 12:8) but in remembrance of the Bread of Life and the Lamb of God, just as Jesus had intimated they would when he had delivered his Bread of Life discourse months earlier. It seems likely that the apostles would have remembered at that moment in the upper room the words Jesus had uttered on the earlier occasion. That event had been momentous not only because it immediately followed the miracle of the loaves and fishes in feeding the five thousand but also because the words Jesus spoke were themselves so unusual, even astonishing:

I am that bread of life.

Your fathers did eat manna in the wilderness, and are dead.

This is the bread which cometh down from heaven, that a man may eat thereof, and not die.

I am the living bread which came down from heaven: if any man eat of this bread, he shall live for ever: and the bread that I will give is my flesh, which I will give for the life of the world.

The Jews therefore strove among themselves, saying, How can this man give us [his] flesh to eat?

Then Jesus said unto them, Verily, verily, I say unto you, Except ye eat the flesh of the Son of man, and drink his blood, ye have no life in you.

Whoso eateth my flesh, and drinketh my blood, hath eternal life; and I will raise him up at the last day. (John 6:48–54)

Now, on this night of nights, the apostles were actually doing in symbolic fashion the very thing Jesus had described—eating the lamb, both literally and symbolically. But more surprises were yet to come. As is still well known in modern times, ordinarily after the dinner portion of the Seder celebration has been completed, the third cup of wine, the "cup after supper"—what the rabbis also called "the cup of blessing"—was mixed with water, and then blessed and drunk, again in an atmosphere of celebration. The Gospel of Luke, however, describes the scene in the upper room with solemn brevity and poignancy: "Likewise also the cup after supper, saying, This cup is the new testament in my blood, which is shed for you" (Luke 22:20).

Though the apostles would not fully appreciate the symbolism of mixing water with the third cup of wine until after the crucifixion, when the Savior's pierced side yielded blood *and water* (John 19:34–35), they could not have mistaken the revolutionary change that had been enacted during their time together that night in what had started out as a traditional Passover celebration. Nor could they have missed much of its meaning and significance. The ordinance of Passover now centered squarely on Jesus of Nazareth. Instead of remembering the Exodus from Egypt, a slaughtered pastoral animal (the lamb), and escape from the physical and mental bondage of slavery, now and forever more, followers of Jesus were to remember him who established the Passover, remember him who was the true king over the children of Israel, remember him who was the lamb slain from before the foundations of the world, remember him who saves from all types of bondage—physical, mental, emotional and spiritual—indeed, remember him always. In what is probably the earliest recorded account of the events of the Last Supper we read: "For as often as ye eat this bread, and drink this cup, ye do shew the Lord's death till he come" (1 Corinthians 11:26, which is perhaps the apostle Paul's earliest letter).

The new ordinance now known as the sacrament replaced the old system of animal sacrifice in which a priest ritually slaughtered an offering on behalf of the covenantor. The sacrament of the Lord's Supper raised to a new height the level and intensity of individual commitment and interaction with God. Instead of communal involvement and interaction with a priest at the Temple in Jerusalem, it demanded a more direct and intimate communion with Deity. It did away with any priestly intermediary as well as almost all outward aspects of the old system of blood sacrifice. What the Savior said explicitly to the Nephites he said by inference to the apostles during the Last Supper: "And ye shall offer up unto me no more the shedding of blood; yea, your sacrifices and your burnt offerings shall be done away, for I will accept none of your sacrifices and your burnt offerings. And ye shall offer for a sacrifice unto me a broken heart and a contrite spirit" (3 Nephi 9:19–20).

These verses are connected to both the sacrament and Gethsemane in a startling way. The same two aspects of sacrifice that the Lord commanded the Nephites to offer in place of animals are the same two aspects of sacrifice he asks each of us to offer. And these two offerings we are required to make as we partake of the sacrament are the very things Jesus, the Lamb of God, experienced during his agony in the Garden of Gethsemane and on the cross at the moment he died: Jesus experienced a contrite ("crushed") spirit in the garden and a broken heart on the cross. For each of us, the broken heart and contrite spirit lead to newness of life through repentance. President J. Reuben Clark Jr., a counselor in the First Presidency, said, "Under the new covenant that came in with Christ, the sinner must offer the sacrifice out of his own life, not by offering the blood of some other creature; he must give up his sins, he must repent, he himself must make the sacrifice . . . so that he would become a better and changed man" (*Behold the Lamb of God*, 107–8).

Truly, the "cup after supper," which was transformed into the sacrament of the Lord's Supper, was important preparation for the "bitter cup" of which the Savior partook. It serves as our tangible link with the Savior as well as with the historical events in the upper room, in the Garden of Gethsemane, and on the cross.

The cup after supper fortified the Savior spiritually and emotionally to face burdens and agonies such as no other being will
ever bear. It satisfied his yearning to share the true significance
of the Passover with the original Twelve, and it provides all disciples everywhere with physical emblems by which to remember
him and his atonement. Jesus could go to Gethsemane knowing
he had done all to prepare the Twelve to face their own special burdens brought on by the bitter cup that only he would
consume but which they would also have to partake of in certain ways. The cup after supper prepared the disciples for future
events by providing them one last, profound witness that Jesus
was not only the Messiah but the very God who had instituted
the Passover more than twelve hundred years before.

## THE LAST SUPPER ENDS

If the activities of the evening had concluded with only the
establishment of the sacrament, the night would still have been
far spent. It would have left the apostles emotionally and physically drained, not to mention mentally awash in a sea of new
and profound ideas, as they tried to internalize the monumental
happenings of the evening as well as the monumental feelings
that accompanied those events. But, as it turned out, the evening was far from over.

Actually, it was not then nor is it now uncommon for
serious-minded, observant Jews to linger around the Passover
table for hours singing and discussing the Passover. This
night, however, as Jesus and his apostles remained together
after the meal, another powerful ordinance was instituted by
the Savior—the washing of the feet—and many powerful and
important teachings were also delivered by the Master. Jesus
concluded his final teaching moments on this night of nights by

offering what has come to be known as the great high priestly prayer, or the great intercessory prayer. All of these key events after the Last Supper, along with their accompanying doctrines and concepts, are uniquely recorded in the New Testament by John for the benefit of Church members in these latter days (John 13–17). In fact, we could make a good case that John was really writing for seasoned and valiant members of the Lord's true Church. This truth becomes apparent when we consider the uniqueness of John's expressions in both his Gospel and his Apocalypse (the book of Revelation). It is particularly significant that John speaks of Jesus' instruction about the Second Comforter (John 14:16–23; Smith, *Teachings of the Prophet Joseph Smith*, 150), the nature of eternal life as knowing personally God and his Son Jesus Christ (John 17:3; D&C 132:24), and the Savior's work to make "us kings and priests unto God and his Father" (Revelation 1:6).

Jesus instituted the ordinance of the washing of the feet as "a holy and sacred rite, one performed by the saints in the seclusion of their temple sanctuaries," according to Elder Bruce R. McConkie (*Doctrinal New Testament Commentary*, 1:708). It appears to be an ordinance of ultimate approbation by the Lord and, in a fascinating way, stands in direct contrast to the ordinance of the dusting off of the feet, which seems to be the ultimate earthly ordinance of condemnation by the Lord, which is performed only by his authorized servants.

That Jesus performed the ordinance of the washing of the feet for his closest friends is another indication of his attempts to prepare them for the coming spiritual onslaught in Gethsemane as well as to teach them further about his role in fulfilling of the law of Moses. As the Joseph Smith Translation summarizes, "He that has washed his hands and his head, needeth not save to wash his feet, but is clean every whit; and ye are clean, but not all. Now this was the custom of the Jews under their law; wherefore, Jesus did this that the law might be fulfilled" (JST John 13:10).

John's Gospel further tells us that after the washing of the feet, Jesus said to his apostles: "Now is the Son of man glorified, and God is glorified in him. If God be glorified in him, God shall also glorify him in himself, and shall straightway glorify him. Little children, yet a little while I am with you. Ye shall seek me: and as I said unto the Jews, Whither I go, ye cannot come. . . . Simon Peter said unto him, Lord, whither goest thou? Jesus answered him, Whither I go, thou canst not follow me now; but thou shalt follow me afterwards" (John 13:31–36).

Here Jesus speaks as though his looming agony in Gethsemane and the suffering on the cross are a foregone conclusion and his glorification of the Father already a living reality. Thus, where he is about to go and what he is about to accomplish have already been foreseen by himself and his Father. The apostles cannot yet follow him, but they soon will, even in the manner of their own deaths, in some cases. With the perspective afforded by hindsight, this prophecy clearly appears to be an important foreshadowing directed to Peter: "Whither I go, thou canst not follow me now; but thou shalt follow me afterwards." According to tradition, Peter was later crucified head downward for the cause of his Master because he felt unworthy to die in the exact manner of the Lord (Eusebius, *Ecclesiastical History* 3.1.2).

## THEY SANG A HYMN

We do not know at what moment Judas left the Passover dinner to consummate his act of betrayal; the four Gospel accounts are not clear on this point (Talmage, *Jesus the Christ*, 619). We only know that he left sometime after the Savior identified him as the betrayer, though that identification was not recognized by all present. Elder James E. Talmage has written: "The others understood the Lord's remark as an instruction to Judas to attend to some duty or go upon some errand of ordinary kind, perhaps to purchase something for the further celebration of the Passover, or to carry gifts to some of the poor, for Judas was the treasurer of the party and 'had the bag.' But Iscariot understood. His heart was all the more hardened by the discovery that Jesus knew of his infamous plans, and he was maddened by the humiliation he felt in the Master's presence" (*Jesus the Christ*, 598).

Moreover, we do not know at what moment Jesus and the apostles left the upper room to proceed to the Garden of Gethsemane. John 14:31 reports Jesus saying to the group after his instruction on the two Comforters, "Arise, let us go hence." Indeed, the opening content of John 15, Jesus' discourse on the True Vine, suggests an outdoor setting because of the readily visible images of vines or vineyards outside Jerusalem's city walls. Others have been less definitive in assigning a location to all the teachings found in John 14, 15, 16, and 17. However we view the sequence of scenes, though, we know that at some point before the end of their Passover experience together, they concluded by singing together. "And when they had sung an hymn, they went out into the mount of Olives" (Mark 14:26). Likely, this hymn was the last part of the great Hallel, that magnificent set of messianic psalms (Psalms 115–18) whose thinly veiled meanings testify of Jesus Christ. Though the Hallel was ordinarily sung as part of the Passover service or dinner, it seems most significant that at this most solemn and eventful

moment in the Lord's mortal ministry, he and his anointed servants concluded their time together by singing a sacred hymn.
On this point, Elder Boyd K. Packer has commented: "There
are many references in the scriptures, both ancient and modern, that attest to the influence of righteous music. The Lord,
Himself, was prepared for His greatest test through its influence, for the scripture records: 'And when they had sung an
hymn, they went out into the mount of Olives.' (Mark 14:26.)"
(*Ensign*, January 1974, 25).

I have been in meetings when hymns have lifted, blessed,
built, and taught the worshipers more than anything else could
have. A few years ago, I sat in a sacrament meeting in a room
overlooking the Old City of Jerusalem. I had been privileged
to take in that scene many times before, but on this Sabbath
day the sacrament hymn was "O Savior, Thou Who Wearest
a Crown." The moment we began singing, something struck
me powerfully—the words, the scene before me, the spiritual
power of the Atonement itself, or perhaps, a combination of all
of these. Against the backdrop of the very place where the last
hours and acts of the Savior's life unfolded, we sang these lyrics:

> O Savior, thou who wearest
> A crown of piercing thorn,
> The pain thou meekly bearest,
> Weigh'd down by grief and scorn.
> The soldiers mock and flail thee;
> For drink they give thee gall;
> Upon the cross they nail thee
> To die, O King of all.
>
> No creature is so lowly,
> No sinner so depraved,

> But feels thy presence holy
> And through thy love is saved.
> Though craven friends betray thee,
> They feel thy love's embrace;
> The very foes who slay thee
> Have access to thy grace.
>
> (*Hymns*, no. 197)

At that moment I was dumbfounded. I heard nothing else in the meeting for a long time afterward. It had never occurred to me that the words of that hymn were teaching doctrine and articulated the essence of the Atonement: "The very foes who slay thee / Have access to thy grace." This concept changed me forever, capturing as it did the arresting power of Christ's love and his atoning sacrifice. This sacred hymn taught the point of doctrine that is at the heart of our Heavenly Father's plan: Christ "inviteth them *all* to come unto him and partake of his goodness; and he denieth none that come unto him" (2 Nephi 26:33; emphasis added). I realized in that instant that "all" means *all!*

Perhaps, in some similar way, the apostles had a spiritual experience as they sang a hymn and then went out into the Mount of Olives.

## INTO THE GARDEN

John records the arrival of the group at the Garden of Gethsemane as occurring immediately following the great high priestly prayer, when the Savior of the world gave a personal and tender report to his literal Father, our Father in Heaven, about his earthly ministry. "When Jesus had spoken these words, he went forth with his disciples over the brook Cedron,

where was a garden, into the which he entered, and his disciples. And Judas also, which betrayed him, knew the place: for
Jesus ofttimes resorted thither with his disciples" (John 18:1–2).

The Garden of Gethsemane is on the lower half of the western slope of the Mount of Olives, directly opposite the Temple
Mount. In ancient times it was part of an olive vineyard (*vineyard* is preferred over *orchard*). Jesus and his apostles would have
reached it by leaving Jerusalem through one of the city gates,
descending the slope of the Temple Mount, crossing the little
brook in the narrow Kidron Valley, and entering the lower,
western end of the garden. Gethsemane was near the Jerusalem
cemetery, well used from the tenth century B.C. onward. A full
moon would have been shining brightly that evening, owing
to the time of the month when Passover occurs each year. It
is quite possible, as some have suggested (assuming no cloud
cover), that the full moon cast the shadow of the Temple over
the garden near the graveyard. Jesus and the apostles thus made
their way to Gethsemane in the shadow of the Temple by a
place of death. Such a scene could not have done other than
serve as a foreboding reminder to the Savior of his impending
fate and infuse the atmosphere with increasing gloom.

John 18:1–2 discloses two important details about the
Garden of Gethsemane. First, Judas Iscariot, who was not with
the apostles because he was with the armed force coming to
make the arrest, knew the place. Thus, he would know where to
find Jesus at that hour of the night. Second, Judas knew about
Gethsemane because Jesus had gone there many times before
with the Twelve, as Luke confirms (Luke 22:34). We might
speculate that when Jesus was in Judea he went to Gethsemane
because it was a place of refuge and reflection for him. It is
even possible that he went there often because he knew or

sensed that this place would be connected to his most important actions in mortality. In his last general conference address, Elder Bruce R. McConkie commented on Gethsemane's significance for Jesus and the disciples:

> Two thousand years ago, outside Jerusalem's walls, there was a pleasant garden spot, Gethsemane by name, where Jesus and his intimate friends were wont to retire for pondering and prayer.
>
> There Jesus taught his disciples the doctrines of the kingdom, and all of them communed with Him who is the Father of us all, in whose ministry they were engaged, and on whose errand they served.
>
> This sacred spot, like Eden where Adam dwelt, like Sinai from whence Jehovah gave his laws, like Calvary where the Son of God gave his life a ransom for many, this holy ground is where the Sinless Son of the Everlasting Father took upon himself the sins of all men on condition of repentance. (*Ensign*, May 1985, 9)

With Jesus and his apostles in the Garden of Gethsemane, history was now poised for the very event for which the God of heaven and earth, the Great Jehovah, had come into the world as a mortal. The condescension of God was about to be completely fulfilled. The preparation of the cup after supper was about to give way to the bitter cup. And no one could stop this imminent ordeal except the very Being himself who would later say that this was the ultimate reason for his birth, "To this end was I born, and for this cause came I into the world" (John 18:37).

And they came to a place which was named Gethsemane: and he saith to his disciples, Sit ye here, while I shall pray.

And he taketh with him Peter and James and John, and began to be sore amazed, and to be very heavy;

And saith unto them, My soul is exceeding sorrowful unto death: tarry ye here, and watch.

And he went forward a little, and fell on the ground, and prayed that, if it were possible, the hour might pass from him.

And he said, Abba, Father, all things are possible unto thee; take away this cup from me: nevertheless not what I will, but what thou wilt.

MARK 14:32–36

CHAPTER 3

# The Shock of the Bitter Cup

The word *Gethsemane*, a combination of the two Hebrew terms *gath* and *shemen*, means "oil press." Situated on the lower half of Olivet, or the Mount of Olives, the Garden of Gethsemane was a lovely area and the site of the production of olive oil in ancient times. The traditionally accepted location of the garden still boasts olive trees that have been reputably dated by Hebrew University botanists to be between eighteen hundred and twenty-three hundred years old. What stories these gnarled and venerable living wonders could tell! When Holy Land tour guides, generally inveterate romantics, try to convince their listeners that some of the trees sheltered Christ—they may be right (*Biblical Archaeologist*, May 1977, 14). That this area has been used for the production of both olive oil and wine is confirmed by the remnants of a very old winepress still visible today in the garden area.

When Jesus and his special witnesses approached the entrance to the garden, Jesus instructed the others to sit and pray so as to "enter not into temptation" (Luke 22:40). Matthew and Mark indicate that he took the chief apostles— Peter, James, and John, who were the First Presidency of the

Church in that day—and went a little farther into the garden. But immediately Jesus began to feel very heavy. Matthew adds that He was "exceeding sorrowful even unto death" (Matthew 26:38), and Mark explicitly states that He felt "sore amazed" (Mark 14:33).

Many of us can readily understand what caused the Savior to feel heavy, weighed down, and so depressed as to think of death. Some have wrestled with the kind of hopelessness that can push a person to the brink of destruction, and thus they can further appreciate the mental and spiritual trauma that afflicted Jesus on this darkest of all nights. In his case, however, the trauma was of a kind and degree that no human being could ever experience. For Jesus was weighed down with the sin, sorrow, and suffering of the entire human family. It was an experience that only a God could withstand and not succumb to death. We might correctly suppose that the sins alone of all humankind would produce in the Savior the feelings described by the Gospel writers. But that is not all there is to it.

## HE BECAME US

To be sure, the Savior's heaviness in Gethsemane was caused by all the sins and all the transgressions committed knowingly by everyone who has ever lived on this earth. But his redemption also included payment for all laws and commandments violated in ignorance. Thus, the Savior suffered in Gethsemane for the most wicked actions of the vilest sinners as well as the unwitting transgressions of the meekest of souls. The spiritual and physical feelings brought about by these transgressions, as well as the full effects of all sins and violent acts ever committed, were literally placed upon the Savior and suffered by him on behalf of those who would repent and *allow* the Savior to be the proxy, or substitute, sufferer for their misdeeds. The apostle Paul taught that God "hath made him [Christ] to be sin for us, who knew no sin; that we might be made the righteousness of God in him" (2 Corinthians 5:21).

In other words, in Gethsemane Jesus became *us*, each one of us, and we became him. Our sins were transferred to Jesus. His perfection was transferred to us. He was a substitute recipient for our pain and punishment. He acted in our place to take the consequences and sorrows of wicked behavior, which each of us deserves, so that we could be free from the devastating effects of sin. The scriptures of the Restoration teach that the Savior took to himself the full force of the punishment deserved by each of us. He suffered God's wrath in our place. Elder Neal A. Maxwell observed that "Jesus always deserved and always had the Father's full approval. But when He took our sins upon Him, of divine necessity required by justice He experienced instead 'the fierceness of the wrath of Almighty God' (D&C 76:107; 88:106)" (*Lord, Increase Our Faith*, 13).

The fierceness of the wrath of Almighty God is a terrifying thing to contemplate. In Gethsemane Jesus took the full force of God's overwhelming and retributory punishment. Justice demanded it, and we, who are sinners, deserve it. According to the rules framing the universe, the full consequences of transgressed laws cannot be dismissed or overlooked. They must be borne by someone—the sinner or the substitute. Jesus was that substitute for all of us who will allow him to be so. Elder Boyd K. Packer testified that "upon Him was the burden of all human transgression, all human guilt. . . . By choice, [Christ] accepted the penalty . . . for brutality, immorality, perversion, and corruption, for addiction, for the killings and torture and terror—for all of it that ever had been or all that ever would be enacted upon this earth" (*Ensign*, May 1988, 69).

This act of pure grace gave our Savior the right to act as our advocate with the Father and to invoke the law of mercy on our behalf. One of the most powerful scenes in all of scripture allows us to part the curtains of heaven and witness the scene of the Savior's pleadings for us:

> Listen to him who is the advocate with the Father, who is pleading your cause before him—
>
> Saying: Father, behold the sufferings and death of him who did no sin, in whom thou wast well pleased; behold the blood of thy Son which was shed, the blood of him whom thou gavest that thyself might be glorified;
>
> Wherefore, Father, spare these my brethren that believe on my name, that they may come unto me and have everlasting life. (D&C 45:3–5)

## PAIN AND SORROW AHEAD OF SIN

Suffering for our sins was a monumental act of love, an incomprehensible gift unmerited by anything we can do. Lehi taught that the Holy Messiah "offereth himself a sacrifice for sin, . . . [for] there is no flesh that can dwell in the presence of God, save it be through the merits, and mercy, and grace of the Holy Messiah" (2 Nephi 2:7–8). But that is not all.

The scriptures also teach that the Savior's suffering was for far more than our sins alone. The prophet Alma taught clearly that the Savior suffered first and foremost for the sorrow, suffering, and sickness of the Lord's people, as well as for their sins. Thus, the Atonement is far more expansive in its reach and far more comprehensive in its effects than we can possibly fully comprehend. Here are Alma's powerful words:

> And he shall go forth, suffering pains and afflictions and temptations of every kind; and this that the word might be fulfilled which saith he will take upon him the pains and the sicknesses of his people.
>
> And he will take upon him death, that he may loose the bands of death which bind his people; and he will take upon him their infirmities, that his bowels may be filled with mercy, according to the flesh, that he may know according to the flesh how to succor his people according to their infirmities.
>
> Now the Spirit knoweth all things; nevertheless the Son of God suffereth according to the flesh that he might take upon him the sins of his people, that he might blot out their transgressions according to the power of his deliverance; and now behold, this is the testimony which is in me.
>
> Now I say unto you that ye must repent, and be born again; for the Spirit saith if ye are not born again ye cannot inherit the kingdom of heaven; therefore come and be baptized unto repentance, that ye may be washed from your sins, that ye may have faith on the Lamb of God, who taketh away the sins of the world, who is mighty to save and to cleanse from all unrighteousness. (Alma 7:11–14)

The Savior's heaviness in Gethsemane, then, was caused not just by our sins but the weight of all the sickness, sorrow, suffering, injustice, and unfairness that everyone on this earth has ever experienced. He suffered for all the heartaches and sorrows caused by broken homes, marital infidelity, abuse of every kind, children gone astray, disloyalty on the part of trusted friends, crises of health, depression, sickness, pain, lost opportunities, loneliness resulting from the death of a loved one, and psychological scars left by horrible events of which some of us cannot even conceive.

An example or two may illustrate the redemptive power the Savior's suffering in Gethsemane can bring to us. A woman whose husband broke his marriage vows by being unfaithful said, "He broke my heart into a million pieces." But she also said that Jesus' substitutionary suffering helped her and her children work through the unmitigated anguish brought on by the hurtful act of a once-trusted husband and father. The Savior *can* change feelings and bind up broken hearts. Knowing that he has perfect empathy because of his knowledge of our feelings and infirmities is helpful. But knowing he can replace our anguish with feelings of peace—again, because of his substitutionary suffering—is truly miraculous. Another woman, in a similar situation, said with great conviction, "Because of the Savior, I have a place to put the hurt."

Another friend has spoken of her wrestle with "the black hole of depression" that comes when she is expecting a child. Rather than being a time of happiness, this becomes for her a time when energy, emotional stability, spirituality, even a portion of life itself are drained out of her. She is confined to her bed for most of the nine months. She described her mental fog and the dark feelings of hopelessness that come in the face of desiring to do the right things—hold family home evenings, teach her young children the value of prayer and how to pray, have family scripture study, make her home a place of peace rather than of dread and desperation—but ultimately being unable to function, unable to provide a mother's love and guidance. The depression completely overwhelms her. "The thing that helped make a difference this last time," she said, "was realizing that the Savior suffered for these things, suffered for me, paid for the things I didn't do but was supposed to do. The Atonement gave me some glimmer of hope because it made up for my inability to do all the things I knew I needed to do but simply could not do. The Atonement was for me."

Indeed, the Atonement, the Savior's suffering in the Garden of Gethsemane, was undertaken for each one of us, for all of our shortcomings as well as lost opportunities. Gethsemane is not just personal and individual but tailor-made for our differing and changing needs. But that is not all.

## THE WEIGHT OF WORLDS

In Gethsemane Jesus took upon himself not only the sorrows and sins of every person who will ever live on this earth but also all the suffering, sorrows, and sins of every being who will ever live on any of the millions and millions of earths in the vast universe which he helped to create under the direction of our Father in Heaven. The Prophet Joseph Smith bore record of his infinite atoning power:

> That by him, and through him, and of him, the worlds are and were created, and the inhabitants thereof are begotten sons and daughters unto God. . . .
>
> That he came into the world, even Jesus, to be crucified for the world, and to bear the sins of the world, and to sanctify the world, and to cleanse it from all unrighteousness;

That through him all might be saved whom the Father had put into his power and made by him. (D&C 76: 24, 41–42)

We glimpse the magnitude of all those creations that "the Father had put into his power and made by him" by reviewing a few verses the Lord revealed to the ancient prophets Moses and Enoch:

And behold, the glory of the Lord was upon Moses, so that Moses stood in the presence of God, and talked with him face to face. And the Lord God said unto Moses: For mine own purpose have I made these things. Here is wisdom and it remaineth in me. . . .

And worlds without number have I created; and I also created them for mine own purpose; and by the Son I created them, which is mine Only Begotten. (Moses 1:31–33)

And were it possible that man could number the particles of the earth, yea, millions of earths like this, it would not be a beginning to the number of thy creations; and thy curtains are stretched out still; and yet thou art there, and thy bosom is there; and also thou art just; thou art merciful and kind forever. (Moses 7:30)

Thus, the Savior has redeemed through his payment in Gethsemane, and later on the cross, all that he has created. In the same revelation to Enoch that speaks of millions of earths like this one, the Lord indicated why Jesus experienced the Atonement on this earth rather than on one of the millions of other earths: "Wherefore, I can stretch forth mine hands and hold all the creations which I have made; and mine eye can pierce them also, and among all the workmanship of mine hands there has not been so great wickedness as among thy brethren" (Moses 7:36).

We may now begin to appreciate why Jesus immediately began to feel very heavy and exceedingly sorrowful unto death. It was no less than the fall of Adam on this earth combined with all the effects of the Fall (including general sorrow, suffering, sickness, tribulation, and sin), combined with the individual sorrows and sins of every inhabitant of our earth, combined with all the sorrows and sins of the inhabitants of all the millions of earths like this one, combined with the fallen condition of every creature on this and all the other worlds, that caused the Savior to be pressed down by a weight such as no other being will ever experience.

Our finite mortal minds cannot grasp the tremendous load borne by the Savior in Gethsemane. But we begin to comprehend what this means in practical terms by remembering that this earth alone has had some 60 to 70 billion people live upon it during its temporal history. Each one of these 60 to 70 billion people has committed sin: "All have sinned and come short of the glory of God," Paul said (Romans 3:23). Multiply the sins, sorrows, heartaches, and injustices of these 60 to 70 billion souls by the millions of earths that the Savior created and redeemed, and we may begin to view the term "infinite atonement" in a different light. Gethsemane paid for all these things plus an infinitely possible combination of these things—even before they happened to us who live in modern times. Such is "the awful arithmetic of the Atonement," as Elder Neal A. Maxwell once said (*Ensign*, May 1985, 73). But even that is not all.

## SORE AMAZED

The Gospel of Mark is clear that Jesus felt something else in Gethsemane besides heaviness and sorrow. The King James Version translates the Greek *ekthambeisthai* as "sore amazed" (Mark 14:33). It is often rendered as "awestruck" or "astonished." One respected New Testament scholar says that this word is best rendered as "terrified surprise" (Murphy-O'Connor, "What Really Happened at Gethsemane," 36). What could possibly cause the Creator and Savior of worlds without number to feel surprised? It is difficult to conceive of something that the Savior did not know and hence would have been surprised over.

Yet, for all the things the Savior knew, there was one thing he did not know, and, in fact, could not know because of what he was. The scriptures declare with absolute certainty that Jesus was perfect, without sin. Paul testified, "For we have not an high priest which cannot be touched with the feeling of our infirmities; but was in all points tempted like as we are, yet without sin" (Hebrews 4:15).

Being perfect, Jesus did not and could not know what sin felt like. He did not have the experience of feeling the effects of sin—neither physically, spiritually, mentally, nor emotionally. Not until Gethsemane, that is. Now, in an instant, he began to feel all the sensations and effects of sin, all the guilt, anguish, darkness, turmoil, depression, anger, and physical sickness that sin brings. All of this the Savior felt and much, much more.

The shock to the Savior at this moment in his existence must have been overwhelming. Because he was perfect, he was also perfectly sensitive to all the effects and ramifications of sin on our mental, emotional, and physical makeup. His makeup was such that it could not tolerate sin or its effects, just as our systems cannot tolerate poison, disease, extreme heat, cold, dehydration, or a hundred other harmful substances and conditions. More significantly, as Mark describes for us, the experience Jesus had of finally comprehending sin as well as the feelings that issue from sin were absolutely surprising to him. He had never before experienced these sensations. Not only did it surprise him but it terrified him. For the first time in his eternal existence, the God of heaven and earth was experiencing the terrifying feelings associated with sin. Imagine! Jesus, the Eternal God of Old Testament times learned something in Gethsemane he had never known before. Perhaps that is the full meaning of Alma's words that the Son of God, the Messiah, would be born as a mortal so that "he may know *according to the flesh* how to succor his people" (Alma 7:12; emphasis added). Elder Maxwell summarizes this point: "Imagine, Jehovah, the Creator of this and other worlds, 'astonished'! Jesus knew cognitively what He must do, but not experientially. He had never personally known the exquisite and exacting process of an atonement before. Thus, when the agony came in its fulness, it was so much, much worse than even He with his unique intellect had ever imagined!" (*Ensign*, May 1985, 72–73).

Jesus Christ was a perfect God, a sinless God, but now he was also one who knew what sin felt like—even though he himself had committed no sin and even though his substitutionary experience with sin was terrifyingly surprising to him. Remember, he had before chided his apostles because they had been terrified and exhibited a lack of faith (Mark 4:40). Now, he himself knew terror. But in so discovering these new feelings, he became perfectly equipped to support and comfort each one of us in our moments of terrified surprise.

## He Cried, "Abba"

Under the crushing weight of sin, sorrow, and suffering—all of which were originally ours but now had become his—and in a state of shock and terrified surprise, the Savior cried out in distress to his Father, just as a child might cry out for the comfort offered by a loving parent. The only relief the Savior could hope for might be found in prayer "that, if it were possible, the hour might pass from him" (Mark 14:35). Thus, in the most anguished cry of his life, the Savior pleaded, "Abba . . . all things are possible unto thee; take away this cup from me" (Mark 14:36).

To miss the significance of the word *Abba* at this point in the story of Gethsemane is to miss the true relationship that existed between Jesus and his Father. The word *Abba* is an Aramaic word meaning "Papa" or "Daddy." It is a form of address signifying the close, intimate, loving, and special bond that develops between some fathers and their children. The Gospel of Mark preserves a number of Aramaic words, it being the language of common discourse in Jesus' day, even among the learned rabbis.

I remember the first time I heard the word used in actual conversation. One of my Jewish studies professors in graduate school had invited some of us to attend synagogue services with his family. He had reserved a small classroom off to the side of the synagogue assembly hall to answer our questions after the service was over. His young daughter, four or five years old, was in the room with us. It was obvious that she was the apple of her father's eye, for when she kept interrupting his explanations, always beginning with "Abba," he would stop talking and rivet his attention on her—and always with a smile. Afterward,

I asked him what *Abba* meant (although I was sure I knew). He answered with pride, "Why, *Daddy*, of course."

In Gethsemane, on that terrible but glorious night, in a scene so personal as almost to dissuade us from listening in, Jesus cried out in shockingly familiar tones, "Daddy (Papa), all things are possible for you. Please take this experience away—it is worse than even I thought it would be. Nevertheless, I will do what you desire and not what I desire."

It is important to remember that this plea was not theatrics. This petition really happened between a son and his father. It is a privileged communication, but we have been extended the privilege of learning about it because of God's love for us and his trust that we will hold it in reverence.

## TAKE AWAY THIS CUP

That Jesus reached the point where he wished not to partake of the bitter cup and asked his Father in intensely intimate, forthright terms to remove it, is evidenced in at least three ways.

First, Jesus' speech is reported essentially the same way in all three synoptic Gospels: "take away," "remove," "let this pass." The Greek word translated as "cup" (*potērion*) also means "a person's lot" (as in lot in life) or even "dispensation." Three of the four Gospels unequivocally tell us that, frankly, things got so bad that Jesus was asking for any alternative to his unalterable course of suffering, any less horrible way to accomplish his Father's plan and purposes.

Second, the prophet Abinadi taught that in the atoning process the Savior subjugated his personal desires to his Father's desires, "the will of the Son being swallowed up in the will of the Father" (Mosiah 15:7). In this supreme act of meekness, he again set the example for us, showing us that subjecting our wills to the will of the Father is the monumental test of mortality. The Greek term for "will" used in Mark 14:36 ("nevertheless not what I *will*, but what thou *wilt*") is *thelo*, which means "to be willing, to desire, to prefer." Abinadi teaches us the true doctrine that Jesus' personal desires or preferences were brought into submission to the Father's desires. This is what Isaiah means when he says, "It pleased [the Father] to bruise him" (Isaiah 53:10). One gospel teacher put it this way:

> Begotten of an immortal Father and a mortal mother, Jesus possessed *two natures* (one divine, one human) and, therefore, *two wills* (that of the Father, and that of the Son). He could manifest either nature "at will." . . . The atonement required the subjection and sacrifice of the fleshly will of the "Son" to the spiritual will of the "Father." . . . The *Son* willed to let the cup pass; the *Father* willed that it should be drunk to its dregs. Abinadi described Jesus' submission as "the will of the Son being swallowed up in the will of the Father." . . . In a sense, it was not the Son *as* Son, but the Father *in* the Son who atoned. That is, Jesus not only did the will of his Father *in heaven*, but the will of the Father *in himself*. (Jackson, *1 Nephi to Alma 29*, 245)

Third, in his personal testimony about Gethsemane to the Prophet Joseph Smith, the Savior said that he "would [rather] . . . not drink the bitter cup" (D&C 19:18). Nevertheless, he did partake, and he finished his work on behalf of all humanity.

Rather than diminishing the Savior's accomplishment in Gethsemane by mentioning his personal preference to avoid suffering, we actually magnify it. When we acknowledge that

Jesus' submission to the Father's will was made in the face of having thought about other ways of accomplishing the Father's plan, we also acknowledge that he experienced every human emotion, every human thought, indeed, he descended below every human thought and every human desire. He demonstrated the human impulse to look for ways out of the horrors and agonies that constituted Gethsemane. The Savior's human nature wrestled with his divine nature. Yet, he was perfectly obedient. Most impressively, his obedience was informed obedience, not blind submission. There is no greater attribute than complete commitment with complete knowledge.

Will there not come a time—or many times—in our life when we will wrestle with conflicting impulses? Will there not come a time when each one of us will consciously have to choose to be obedient, to subjugate our desires and preferences to the will of God, to yield our agency to Deity? Our agency, our personal decision-making power, is really the only thing that is truly our private possession and domain—the only thing we "own" in mortality. To yield this ultimately personal possession to God is the greatest act of Christlike behavior we can engage in. Elder Neal A. Maxwell has said:

> The submission of one's will is really the only uniquely personal thing we have to place on God's altar. The many other things we "give," brothers and sisters, are actually the things He has already given or loaned to us. However, when you and I finally submit ourselves, by letting our individual wills be swallowed up in God's will, then we are really giving something to Him! It is the only possession which is truly ours to give!

Consecration thus constitutes the only uncondi-
tional surrender which is also a total victory! (*Ensign*,
November 1995, 24)

In Gethsemane Jesus also demonstrated perfect meekness,
for in the end he took what was thrust upon him without blam-
ing other people or circumstances. Meekness may be thought
of as poise under pressure, patience in the face of provocation.
In another of his sermons, Elder Maxwell has provided us an
example of the kind of meekness Jesus possessed in all its perfection:

> We even tend to think of a meek individual as
> being used and abused—as being a doormat for others.
> However, Moses was once described as being the most
> meek man on the face of the earth (see Num. 12:3), yet
> we recall his impressive boldness in the courts of Pharaoh
> and his scalding indignation following his descent from
> Sinai.
>
> President Brigham Young, who was tested in many
> ways and on many occasions, was once tried in a way
> that required him to "take it"—even from one he so
> much adored and admired. Brigham "took it" because
> he was meek. Yet, surely, none of us sitting here would
> think of Brigham Young as lacking in boldness or firm-
> ness! However, even President Young, in the clos-
> ing and prestigious days of his life, spent some time in
> courtrooms being unjustifiably abused. When he might
> have chosen to assert himself politically, he "took it"—
> meekly. (*Ensign*, March 1983, 71)

We are told that each of us must cultivate the godly
attribute of meekness. Meekness is not weakness. Rather, it is

one of the clearest reflections of how closely our personality or makeup emulates the Savior's.

Thus, we return to two statements made by Paul in the book of Hebrews and marvel at the full, complete, and absolute truth the apostle teaches. Jesus confronted the full range of experiences, challenges, and decisions which all mortals face in this life. Yet, he remained our perfect exemplar and, thus, our perfect nurturer:

> Wherefore in all things it behoved him to be made like unto his brethren, that he might be a merciful and faithful high priest in things pertaining to God, to make reconciliation for the sins of the people.
>
> For in that he himself hath suffered being tempted, he is able to succour them that are tempted. (Hebrews 2:17–18)

> For we have not an high priest which cannot be touched with the feeling of our infirmities; but was in all points tempted like as we are, yet without sin.
>
> Let us therefore come boldly unto the throne of grace, that we may obtain mercy, and find grace to help in time of need. (Hebrews 4:15–16)

When it comes to describing the human condition, or our experience as frail mortals, nothing more profound has ever been spoken than the words, "Jesus knows what it's like!" He experienced it all for our sakes. The infinite and eternal God, who created the heavens and the earth, chose to come down to the earth to help us get back to heaven. He chose to become man so that we could become like God. He is able to show us the way to God because he knows the way of humans.

*And he came out, and went, as he was wont, to the mount of Olives; and his disciples also followed him.*

*And when he was at the place, he said unto them, Pray that ye enter not into temptation.*

*And he was withdrawn from them about a stone's cast, and kneeled down, and prayed,*

*Saying, Father, if thou be willing, remove this cup from me: nevertheless not my will, but thine, be done.*

*And there appeared an angel unto him from heaven, strengthening him.*

*And being in an agony he prayed more earnestly: and his sweat was as it were great drops of blood falling down to the ground.*

LUKE 22:39–44

# CHAPTER 4

# The Agony of the Bitter Cup

The Gospel writer Luke gives us a unique perspective on Gethsemane. Luke was apparently not a member of the Quorum of the Twelve Apostles nor an eyewitness to the events of our Savior's life and ministry. He was a convert who received the apostolic witness with faith and magnified that witness in his own writings and in his missionary service. A lifelong companion to the apostle Paul (2 Timothy 4:11), Luke undoubtedly knew the other apostles and thus spoke of testimonies handed down to him by those who were "eyewitnesses, and ministers of the word" from the beginning (Luke 1:2).

Luke followed up his Gospel with a remarkable sequel, the Acts of the Apostles, which details in a powerful fashion the work of the Church leaders after the Savior's resurrection and ascension. But perhaps the real jewel in Luke's magnificent treasure trove of writings is Luke 22, particularly his description of the Savior's agony in Gethsemane. This is not because of any sensationalistic quality (I think we actually recoil from such graphic descriptions of God's sufferings) but rather because of its unique details and singular lesson on what the Atonement cost—what price was paid. In fact, reading Luke 22 prompts us to cry out, "If a being who is all-powerful suffers that much, what hope is there for any of us? It looks like no one is immune from suffering!"

That is precisely the point. No one *is* immune from the trials, tribulations, and sufferings of mortality. But because Jesus did suffer so much, we don't have to.

## AN ANGEL FROM HEAVEN—MIGHTY MICHAEL

In describing Jesus' experience in Gethsemane, Luke confirms many details found in the other three Gospels. Jesus left the upper room and went "as he was wont, to the mount of Olives" (Luke 22:39). Jesus was accustomed to going to Gethsemane, as John indicates (John 18:1–2). There Jesus instructed the apostles on guarding against temptation (Matthew 26:41) and then moved into the garden a stone's throw farther distant, at which point he began to petition the Father to remove the bitter cup (Mark 13:35).

But his pleadings were tempered by his stated commitment to obey the Father's will. Undoubtedly, the author of Hebrews 5:8–9 had in mind this very moment in Gethsemane when he wrote: "Though he were a Son [meaning God's literal Son who occupied a special position], yet learned he obedience by [or because of] the things which he suffered. . . . and . . . he became the author of eternal salvation unto all them that obey him."

This passage portrays the doctrinal essence of Gethsemane. Just as Jesus became the author of eternal salvation by obeying the Father, all of us must obey Jesus if we want to partake of that salvation and become like the Father.

Luke's narrative also includes a stunning detail not found

anywhere else in the New Testament. An angel appeared to the Savior for the express purpose of strengthening him in his extremity.

Who cannot be moved by this scene? Under extreme duress, Jesus pleads with his Father to remove the bitter cup. This Son is the Well Beloved Son. He has never done anything wrong, never! He is perfect and has always sought to honor his Father, to do everything right and good and compassionate.

But the one thing the Father cannot now do for his perfect Son is the very thing his Well Beloved Son has suggested—remove the bitter cup. He must watch his Son go through all this agony and more. Perhaps it is no exaggeration to say that at that fateful moment in the Garden of Gethsemane almost two thousand years ago, two divine Beings suffered and sacrificed to bring about an eternity's worth of possibilities for you and me and billions upon billions of others.

Latter-day Saint author Edwin W. Aldous has said: "The Father himself witnessed the intense physical and spiritual agony of his Only Begotten Son in Gethsemane and on the cross. And, just as he can remove our pain, he could have spared his Son that agony; indeed, he had the power to remove the bitter cup from the Savior, but the consequences were unacceptable" ("Reflection on the Atonement's Healing Power," 13). Brother Aldous also mentions a well-known statement by Elder Melvin J. Ballard of the Quorum of the Twelve Apostles, which is one of the grandest insights into this moment in Gethsemane that has ever been written:

> In that moment when he might have saved his Son,
> I thank him and praise him that he did not fail us, for
> he had not only the love of his Son in mind, but he also

had love for us. I rejoice that he did not interfere, and that his love for us made it possible for him to endure to look upon the sufferings of his Son and give him finally to us, our Savior and our Redeemer. Without him, without his sacrifice, we would have remained, and we would never have come glorified in his presence. And so this is what it cost, in part, for our Father in Heaven to give the gift of his Son unto men. (Hinckley, *Sermons and Missionary Services of Melvin Joseph Ballard*, 154–55)

If the scene in Gethsemane plays on our emotions, if it tugs at our heartstrings, that is well and good. It ought to, for it is at the very heart of who we are and what we can become.

Another apostle, Elder Jeffrey R. Holland, in a more recent day also spoke to the issue of our Heavenly Father not removing the bitter cup from his Only Begotten Son. In an Easter general conference address on 3 April 1999, Elder Holland began:

I wish to thank not only the resurrected Lord Jesus Christ but also His true Father, our spiritual Father and God, who, by accepting the sacrifice of His firstborn, perfect Son, blessed all of His children in those hours of atonement and redemption. Never more than at Easter time is there so much meaning in that declaration from the book of John which praises the Father as well as the Son: "For God so loved the world, that he gave his only begotten Son, that whosoever believeth in him should not perish, but have everlasting life." (John 3:16)

I am a father, inadequate to be sure, but I cannot comprehend the burden it must have been for God in His heaven to witness the deep suffering and

Crucifixion of His Beloved Son in such a manner. His every impulse and instinct must have been to stop it, to send angels to intervene—but He did not intervene. He endured what He saw because it was the only way that a saving, vicarious payment could be made for the sins of all His other children, from Adam and Eve to the end of the world. I am eternally grateful for a perfect Father and His perfect Son, neither of whom shrank from the bitter cup nor forsook the rest of us who are imperfect, who fall short and stumble, who too often miss the mark. (*Ensign*, May 1999, 14)

Our Heavenly Father could not, would not, take away the bitter cup. Thankfully, he did not shrink from the bitter cup, just as his Son did not shrink from it. But our Heavenly Father did send needed help in the form of an angel to minister to his Son.

Undoubtedly, many have wondered about the identity of that angel sent from the heavenly courts. Elder Bruce R. McConkie believed it to have been Michael, or Adam, the Ancient of Days and the father of the human family on this earth (*Ensign*, May 1985, 9).

Why Michael? Why would our Heavenly Father choose him, or why would he have been allowed to perform so noble a task? Choosing Michael makes perfect sense. Besides the sins of all humankind, for whose single, separate, and unique transgression was Jesus paying the debt owed to justice?

The apostle Paul taught, "For since by man came death, by man came also the resurrection of the dead. For as in Adam all die, even so in Christ shall all be made alive" (1 Corinthians 15:21–22). That is to say, the Savior's atoning work in

Gethsemane is directly linked to Adam's transgression, which brought about the fall of man. The Creation, the Fall, and the Atonement are inextricably linked as the three pillars of eternity, the three central events upon which the Father's plan rests. Who better than Adam to aid and assist the Savior during his time of extreme distress than he whose actions had brought about mortality? Who better to thank the Savior for paying the debt that his actions had introduced (sin, suffering, and the other myriad effects of the Fall) than Adam himself? Who better to strengthen the Great Creator than he who, as one of the gods, assisted the Savior in laying the foundations of the very planet where the Savior himself, as well as all the children of Adam, would someday reside? Who better to minister to the mortal Jesus than one of his own mortal ancestors, for Adam was in very deed a forefather of the Savior's mother, Mary.

## JESUS LEFT ALONE

All of these reasons and others help us to understand why the Father could have sent mighty Michael to stand in his own stead and minister to his Only Begotten Son. He could not remove the bitter cup from his Son because that was the very reason his Son had been sent into the world—to redeem the entire family of God (John 18:37). Nor could the Father himself come to the aid of his Son, for that would not have given the Son the complete victory he needed to have over sin, sorrow, suffering, hell, and the effects of the Fall. The Father is pure, glorified, unadulterated life, and in Gethsemane the Savior had to experience *all* things, even descend *below* all things, to satisfy the demands of justice. The things he had to experience included spiritual death, the withdrawal of the Father and the removal of his immediate influence (which experience later returned to the Savior as he hung on the cross)—in truth, the atmosphere of hell itself.

In Gethsemane, Jesus was left alone by the Father. He was engulfed in darkness, spiritual death, and the agony of hell. He descended below the level of anything ever experienced by any man or woman. All mortals possess a measure (to a greater or lesser degree) of the Lord's Spirit. But Jesus possessed the Spirit in its fulness (John 3:34; JST John 3:34). The shock of the Spirit's withdrawal, the withdrawal of light and life, was over-whelmingly traumatic and plunged Jesus into hell. His victory over all things demanded it.

The Book of Mormon prophet Jacob taught that "spiritual death is hell" (2 Nephi 9:12). The Prophet Joseph Smith learned that spiritual death comes when man is separated from God's presence and influence (D&C 29:40–41). "For Jesus to take upon Himself the consequences of sin required that he suffer spiritual death for all men" (Andrus, *God, Man, and the Universe,* 424).

Thus, our Father in Heaven left his Beloved Son alone to suffer the pains of hell, and out of that wrenching crucible, Jesus gained the victory. Elder James E. Talmage said:

> From the terrible conflict in Gethsemane, Christ emerged a victor. Though in the dark tribulation of that fearful hour He had pleaded that the bitter cup be removed from His lips, the request, however oft repeated, was always conditional; the accomplishment of the Father's will was never lost sight of as the object of the Son's supreme desire. The further tragedy of the night, and the cruel inflictions that awaited Him on the morrow, to culminate in the frightful tortures of

the cross, could not exceed the bitter anguish through which He had successfully passed. (*Jesus the Christ*, 614)

The Father could not assist his Son directly, but he sent an angel to strengthen him. The human family was saved by one of its own, and the Saving One was strengthened by one of his own—his many times over great-grandfather Adam.

## HE PRAYED MORE EARNESTLY

From Luke's inspired description, we begin to comprehend that the Savior's anguish and suffering was unrelenting. In fact, it increased and increased—more pressure, more torture, more agony. "And being in an agony he prayed more earnestly" (Luke 22:44). Here the Savior of the universe teaches us through his experience that all prayers are not alike, nor are they expected to be. A greater need, a more intense life circumstance, calls forth from us more earnest, faith-filled petition and pleading.

I remember hearing as a young deacon a priesthood lesson on prayer given by a man that I and the other members of my quorum were very fond of. He talked about the need for profound respect when approaching God in prayer and spoke of several other important matters relative to prayer, including the how's and why's. And then he said, "But I'll tell you a little secret. It's when you are in the middle of a crisis that you really learn about prayer."

He told us about a time when his infant son became sick and then died, how his prayers were different because he and his wife pleaded with such intensity, and about how it felt to really talk with our Father in Heaven. His counsel had a great effect. It is not the words we speak or the language we use that is important. What really matters is getting down to admitting with all our hearts that we need God's help.

Since those days of my youth, I have come to appreciate what our deacons quorum leader meant and how such experiences help us understand the lessons in Luke's description of the Savior's more earnest pleadings. Not all prayers are alike. As with the Savior, so with us. Some prayers will be more earnest than others.

President Joseph F. Smith also taught that it is intensity of spirit much more than eloquence of language that constitutes sincere prayer:

> It is not such a difficult thing to learn how to pray. It is not the words we use particularly that constitute prayer. . . . True, faithful, earnest prayer consists more in the feeling that rises from the heart and from the inward desire of our spirits to supplicate the Lord in humility and in faith, that we may receive his blessings. It matters not how simple the words may be, if our desires are genuine and we come before the Lord with a broken heart and contrite spirit to ask him for that which we need. (*Gospel Doctrine*, 219)

President Smith's counsel links our prayers with those of the Savior's experience in Gethsemane. A "broken heart and contrite spirit" were displayed by the Savior as he worked out the infinite and eternal atonement. We must acquire the same characteristics.

President Harold B. Lee taught something about prayer that strikes a responsive chord as we seek to comprehend the Savior's experience in Gethsemane: "The most important thing you can do is to learn to talk to God. Talk to Him as you would talk to your father, for He is your Father, and He wants you to talk to Him" (*Church News,* 3 March 1973, 3).

The scriptures are full of examples of people who, like the Savior, talked with God as their Father in an intimate way and found that a greater need calls forth a more earnest, intense, and yearning prayer. Moses, Hannah, Solomon, Hezekiah, Lehi, Nephi, Enos, and Zechariah, the father of John the Baptist, are just a few examples.

## GREAT DROPS OF BLOOD

So intense did Jesus' agony in Gethsemane become that he began to sweat great drops of blood. Some scholars have suggested that the Savior's sweating blood was not an actual occurrence (because some of these verses do not appear in the earliest manuscripts of Luke's Gospel) or that a later editor of Luke's record intended to convey that his sweat was so profuse that it fell to the ground in the same way drops of blood fall to the ground, or even that this portion of Luke's story is entirely allegorical. Latter-day Saints, however, have been spared any doubt about the essential truth of Luke's description because the Savior himself has given us his own testimony of the reality of his exquisite agony (Mosiah 3:7; D&C 19:16–19). Likewise, the Joseph Smith Translation of these verses in Luke testify of their validity. Truly, Jesus bled from every pore in Gethsemane.

Such a condition as Jesus experienced is not unknown. A remarkable article in the *Journal of the American Medical Association* discusses the rare phenomenon called hematidrosis (bloody sweat) as the very real condition described by Luke. It has been known to occur in persons with bleeding disorders, or, more significantly, in persons experiencing extreme distress and highly emotional states. As a result of extreme stress and pressure, the small blood vessels just under the skin hemorrhage. Blood mixes with perspiration, and the skin becomes fragile and tender. Thus, in the cold night air, this condition may have also produced chills in Jesus. Some have further suggested that the hematidrosis suffered by Jesus also produced hypovolemia, or shock due to excessive loss of bodily fluid (Edwards, Gabel, and Hosmer, "On the Physical Death of Jesus," 1455–56).

That Luke alone in the New Testament preserves the scene of the Savior's bloody trauma in Gethsemane becomes all the more noteworthy when we realize that he was a physician (Colossians 4:14). It is only natural that he be interested in the physical effects of Gethsemane on the Savior's body. Luke, in fact, preserves a number of observations about trauma, healing, and the physical body in his writings, precisely because he was a physician and well trained in observing disorders of the human body. With respect to Jesus, Luke would have us know without equivocation that "no other man, however great his powers of physical or mental endurance, could have suffered so; for his human organism would have succumbed, and syncope would have produced unconsciousness and welcome oblivion" (Talmage, *Jesus the Christ*, 613).

## JESUS AND THE OLIVE

That Jesus bled from every pore in Gethsemane is significant in two ways. First, the literal significance is that he shed his blood for us twice: in the garden and on the cross. His atoning blood in Gethsemane was no less important than his atoning blood on the cross. Thus, Jesus approached death twice: in the garden and on the cross—which is where he finally yielded up his life. But Gethsemane was also slow agony—death by degrees—and the results of Jesus' trauma in Gethsemane came back to torment him during his trial. When he was stripped of his clothing before he was crucified (Matthew 27:26–28), the dried blood from his pores would have been pulled away from the tender flesh and inflicted even more pain.

Second, the symbolic significance of Jesus shedding his blood in Gethsemane has to do with the very place where it all happened. Gethsemane, the garden of the "oil press" on the Mount of Olives, is where olives were crushed to harvest their oil. Under extreme weight and pressure, the olives yielded their valuable fluid. Under extreme weight and pressure, Jesus bled from every pore. In Gethsemane, not only did Jesus become us but he became the olive. In the garden of the oil press, where olives were pressed out, Jesus himself was pressed out.

This symbolic correspondence is no accident, and there are many parallels between Jesus and the olive and between the Atonement and the pressing process that are not mere coincidences. In ancient Israel, the olive tree was supreme among all others, as reflected in scripture. First mentioned in connection with the Great Flood, the dove released by Noah returned to the ark with an olive leaf in her mouth, signifying that the waters were abating (Genesis 8:11). Thus, by the appearance together of these two symbolic objects, the dove and olive leaf, the promise of continuing life on earth and peace with Deity was assured. Later in the Pentateuch, olive trees are mentioned in the early descriptions of Canaan, signifying both that the land was a holy land of promise given by Deity to Israel and that the olive tree itself was a gift from God:

> And it shall be, when the Lord thy God shall have
> brought thee into the land which he sware unto thy

fathers, to Abraham, to Isaac, and to Jacob, to give thee great and goodly cities, which thou buildedst not,

And houses full of all good things, which thou filledst not, and wells digged, which thou diggedst not, vineyards and olive trees, which thou plantedst not; when thou shalt have eaten and be full. (Deuteronomy 6:10–11)

Jeremiah 11:16 indicates that even Israel itself was called by Jehovah "a green olive tree, fair, and of goodly fruit." Later rabbinic commentary expounded on that symbolism: "Israel was called 'an olive tree, leafy and fair' because they [Israel] shed light on all" (*Shmot Raba* 36.1). This imagery undoubtedly came from the coloration of the olive leaf itself as well as the fact that the oil was burned for light.

It is not simple happenstance that when Gideon's youngest son, Jotham, climbed Mount Gerizim and proclaimed a parable to the citizens of Shechem, the olive tree was given pride of place:

And when they told it to Jotham, he went and stood in the top of mount Gerizim, and lifted up his voice, and cried, and said unto them, Hearken unto me, ye men of Shechem, that God may hearken unto you.

The trees went forth on a time to anoint a king over them; and they said unto the olive tree, Reign thou over us.

But the olive tree said unto them, Should I leave my fatness, wherewith by me they honor God and man, and go to be promoted over the trees?

And the trees said to the fig tree, Come thou, and reign over us.

But the fig tree said unto them, Should I forsake my

sweetness, and my good fruit, and go to be promoted over the trees? (Judges 9:7–11)

One reason the olive tree was foremost among all others was that it was used to worship God as well as to sustain the life of mankind. The olive tree and its oil were unequivocally regarded as a necessity of life. In fact, nothing from the olive tree went unused in the daily life of Israel. The oil from the fruit—the olives—was used for cooking, lighting, medicine, lubrication, and anointing. Olives not crushed and pressed were pickled in brine and spices and then eaten. The wood of the olive tree was used in constructing buildings and carved into furniture, ornaments, and tools, including the shepherd's crook, or staff. We may truly say that the olive tree was (and continues to be) a staff of life in the Middle East.

Olive trees were even more abundant in the Holy Land in Jesus' day than they are today. In fact, the olive tree was anciently both a religious and a national symbol for the people of Israel, and its fruit was an important domestic and exported product in the biblical period. In Old Testament times, virtually every village and even most houses had a small oil press to supply families with the necessities of life deriving from olive cultivation. By New Testament times, olive crushers made of stone and lever presses were quite plentiful throughout the land.

Techniques of olive production in modern times suggest the way olives were cultivated, harvested, and processed in ancient times. Olive trees do not mature quickly, and the best yields come only after twelve or more years of patient care—a circumstance that requires a certain degree of settlement and peace. But with only a little attention, an adult olive tree will continue to produce heavily, usually every other year, for hundreds of years. Yield from a good tree was expected to run anywhere from ten to fifteen gallons each season.

Production of olive oil anciently was a time-consuming undertaking. It consisted of six basic steps or procedures:

1. *Harvesting* the olives. Some, of course, were left for the poor, the fatherless, the widow, or the sojourner, as scripture required (Deuteronomy 24:19–21; Leviticus 19:9–10; Ruth 2:2–3). Olives in ancient times were harvested during the period from September to late October, right after the first rains, which signaled the time for the harvest to begin. Growers in the Holy Land today still follow this timetable.

2. *Separating* the olives into two groups. Olives for pickling were separated from those to be crushed for oil.

3. *Crushing* the olives intended for oil. Crushing the olives—pits and all—produced a pasty, oily mash, or pulp. In Old Testament times, the crushing was done with a millstone or by pounding from human feet in a rock-hewn press, even a winepress (Deuteronomy 33:24; Micah 6:15). By New Testament times, olives were crushed in a specially carved rock basin called a *yam*. A crushing wheel made of stone was fitted snugly inside the stone basin and either pushed around the interior of the basin by a strong man or pulled around it by a beast of burden.

4. *Gathering* the crushed pulp from the *yam*. The pulp was collected and placed in flat, round, woven baskets. The baskets, usually about two feet in diameter and three to four inches high, were stacked two or three high under one of two traditional kinds of presses—a lever press or a screw

press. The lever press consisted of a long heavy wooden beam with huge stone weights attached to the end of the beam opposite the woven baskets. Use of the lever press can be dated to the early Iron Age, around the tenth century before Christ. The screw press was not used until the late Hellenistic period, beginning about the first century before Christ. It consisted of a giant wooden screw carved from a large piece of olive wood with a handle attached to its top so it could be turned. The screw was held in place by a large frame. Turning the screw applied increasing pressure to the baskets containing the olive mash.

5. *Pressing* the olive pulp. Pressure applied to the olive mash in the baskets stacked under the press caused oil to ooze out of the baskets and run down a shallow channel into a collection pit. Hot water could be poured over the baskets being squeezed to increase the flow of oil. Unlike modern processes involving hydraulic presses, the pressing procedure in ancient times took many hours, even days, with pressure constantly being increased.

6. *Refining* the oil by allowing it to sit for several days in the collection pit. When the oil flowed into the collection basin, it consisted of two liquids: the pure olive oil and a heavier, watery, sediment-filled liquid called the dregs. When the two liquids were allowed to set up, or settle, the pure oil rose to the top and was either skimmed off by hand or allowed to spill over into another collecting vat, where the settling process was repeated to further refine the oil.

This cultural and historical background helps us to more fully understand the profoundly symbolic relationship between the olive, the Savior, and the Atonement. We appreciate the symbolic significance of Jesus' experience in Gethsemane all the more when we remember that—

1. Just as olives are one of seven native fruits indigenous to the Holy Land (Deuteronomy 8:8), so was Jesus a native of the Holy Land. Moreover, the ancient rabbis likened Judah, the lineage of Jesus, to the olive tree (Babylonian Talmud, Menahoth, 53b).

2. Just as at least one strand of Jewish tradition identifies the tree of life as the olive tree, so does the Book of Mormon equate Jesus Christ with the tree of life and identify his atonement as the reality behind the symbol of the *fruit* of the tree of life in Lehi's dream (Ginzberg, *Legends of the Jews*, 1:93; 2:119; 1 Nephi 11:21–22, 25–33).

3. Just as in Jewish tradition the olive tree is called the tree of light (*Shmot Raba* 36.1) and a symbol of "light to the world" (*Tankhuma Tzave* 5.1), so too is Jesus the "Light of the World" (John 1:4–5; 8:12; 9:5; D&C 11:28). Anciently, the Temple *menorah* ("candlestick") was lit with "'pure oil of pounded olives'—not with walnut oil or radish [seed] oil, but only with olive oil which is a light unto the world.' However, it is not only the olive oil which gives forth light, but also the olive tree itself" (Hareuveni, *Nature in Our Biblical Heritage*, 134). In addition, in ancient times only pure olive oil could be used for the Sabbath lamps (Mishnah, *Shabbat* 26a).

4. Just as the olive branch has been regarded as a universal symbol of peace from earliest times, so too is Jesus the Prince of Peace whose recognition will someday be universal (Romans

14:11). This is the message of Doctrine and Covenants 88, which "was designated by the Prophet as the 'olive leaf . . . plucked from the Tree of Paradise, the Lord's message of peace to us'" (headnote to D&C 88).

5. Just as olives are best picked individually so as not to damage the tree (ideally, the olives are not stripped from the branches), so too is Christ's love individual. If alternative methods of harvesting the olives, such as stripping the branches or beating the tree (Deuteronomy 24:20) are used to finish the harvest more quickly, the tree may be damaged. As with olives, so too with souls; it takes time and effort on an individual basis to effectively harvest both. But even the process of "beating" the tree is itself symbolic of the atoning act of the Savior (Isaiah 53:4–5); perhaps that is why the scriptures permit this method of harvest.

6. Just as the connection is literal between the meaning of the word *Gethsemane* ("oil press") and what was done there agriculturally, so is the connection profoundly symbolic between *Gethsemane* and what Jesus did there in the last hours of his mortal life.

7. Just as the life fluid of the olives was pressed out by the intense pressure of the crushing stone rolling over them in the stone basin, so too was the goodness and perfection of Jesus' life "harvested" in Gethsemane. There he was "bruised," as Isaiah prophesied (Isaiah 53:5), and there his life fluid, his blood, was pressed out by the crushing weight of sin and the extreme pressure of spiritual agony.

8. Just as the bitter taste of the olive pulp is removed in the pressing process (olives straight from the tree are exquisitely

bitter) and the remaining oil actually has a kind of sweet flavor, so too is the bitterness of mortal life, brought on by sin and the other effects of the fall of Adam, removed or "pressed out" by Christ's atonement (D&C 19:16–19). For example, nothing was so "sweet" to Alma as his joy over being redeemed through the atonement of Christ (Alma 36:21).

9. Just as the color of the oil from the best olives at first runs red in the crusher at the beginning of each pressing season, so too was the perspiration of the best, finest, purest Being on earth turned red as he bled from every pore (Luke 22:44). Pure, fresh olive oil is the perfect symbol of Christ's blood. Such imagery turns our thoughts not just to the Savior's first coming but also to his second coming, as taught in the scriptures:

> And it shall be said: Who is this that cometh down from God in heaven with dyed garments; yea, from the regions which are not known, clothed in his glorious apparel, traveling in the greatness of his strength?
>
> And he shall say: I am he who spake in righteousness, mighty to save.
>
> And the Lord shall be red in his apparel, and his garments like him that treadeth in the wine-vat. . . .
>
> And his voice shall be heard: I have trodden the wine-press alone, and have brought judgment upon all people; and none were with me. (D&C 133:46–50)

The connection in ancient times between oil presses and winepresses was a real one. Winepresses were sometimes used as oil presses to crush olives when they were trodden out with the feet (Micah 6:15), and thus the presses were regarded as interchangeable.

10. Just as the pressure on the olives under the press became more intense with each passing moment and the olives exuded more of their oil as more pressure was applied, so too did the pressure on the Savior in the garden become more intense over time and put him under greater stress the longer he was in Gethsemane, the place called the "oil press" (Luke 22:39–44; Matthew 26:36–45).

11. Just as pure olive oil was used as a healing agent for the physical body in the ancient world—a concept taught by the parable of the good Samaritan (Luke 10:34)—so too the Atonement, the product of the pressing process in Gethsemane, is the greatest healing agent in all the universe, "worlds without number" (Moses 1:33; D&C 76:42–43). Christ is truly the "balm in Gilead" (Jeremiah 8:22).

12. Just as the olive-pressing process yields the purest and brightest burning of vegetable oils—a fact known in ancient Israel (Exodus 27:20)—so too the pressing process in Gethsemane involved the purest and brightest burning, in terms of eternal glory, of the Father's children.

13. Just as the refined product of bruised, crushed, and pressed olives—the pure olive oil—is consecrated and set apart for healing of the sick, so too the purest of God's children was consecrated and set apart in premortality to be bruised, crushed, and pressed for our "sicknesses" and "pains" as well as our sins (Alma 7:11) so that we can be healed both physically and spiritually.

14. Just as pure olive oil was used in the temple in ancient times for anointing (Leviticus 8:6–12), so is it similarly used today in the Lord's temples, those buildings in which we learn the most about the Anointed One. Every aspect of temple worship centers on, is grounded in, and points us to the Savior and his atonement.

15. Just as in ancient times Israel anointed her prophets, priests, and kings with olive oil (Exodus 30:30; 2 Samuel 2:4; 1 Kings 19:16), so was Jesus anointed to become the Redeemer (D&C 138:42). In fact, the anointing of Israel's prophets, priests, and kings was done as a type and shadow of the Anointed One to come (Hebrew, *mashiach*; English, *Messiah*). The Anointed One is the true Prophet, Priest, and King of all eternity, as testified of in the hymn: "I know that my Redeemer lives. . . . He lives, my prophet, priest, and king" (*Hymns*, no. 136).

16. Just as Deuteronomy 21:23 foreshadowed the death of the Messiah upon a "tree," so history teaches that the Roman crosses used for crucifixions in Palestine were often solidly rooted olive trees with most of their branches removed and a crossbar attached. This image is presented by the apostle Paul in his epistle to the Galatians on the merits and mercies of Christ (Galatians 3:13). Ironically, he describes Jesus, who is symbolized by the olive tree, as being crucified on an olive tree.

17. Just as in ancient times the anointing with olive oil and even the horn in which the oil was kept were linked to the Messiah, so the anointing with olive oil and its container are linked to Jesus. In ancient times, olive oil was

kept in a horn, the well-recognized repository for the anointing agent (1 Samuel 16:13). The Hebrew idiom "horn of salvation" signified the Messiah's great power to judge and save (1 Samuel 2:10; 2 Samuel 22:3; Psalm 18:2; 132:17). Likewise is Jesus symbolized by the horn of oil, which represents his power. Zacharias said of Jesus, the Messiah, at the time his own son, John the Baptist, was born: "Blessed be the Lord God of Israel; for he hath visited and redeemed his people. And hath raised up an *horn* of salvation for us in the house of his servant David" (Luke 1:68–69).

18. Just as we cannot anoint and consecrate ourselves with olive oil to perform ordinances on ourselves (we can only anoint and consecrate others), so too only another, the Anointed One, could make an infinite and eternal atonement on our behalf (Alma 34:9–15). As we serve others by anointing them, we imitate the Messiah, who served not himself but us by consecrating his life.

19. Just as the prophets Zenos and Jacob (like Paul in his epistle to the Romans) depict the scattering and gathering of Israel through the imagery of the tame and the wild olive trees, so the Book of Mormon teaches that the scatterer and gatherer of Israel is Jesus Christ himself: "All the people who are of the house of Israel, will *I* gather in, saith the Lord, according to the words of the prophet Zenos" (1 Nephi 19:16; emphasis added). Israel is gathered first and foremost to Jesus Christ.

20. Just as putting oil in the lamp was a common, everyday necessity in the ancient world, so has "oil in the lamp"

become a powerful metaphor signifying faithfulness and readiness for the time of the Anointed One's second coming (Matthew 25:1–13). "Wherefore, be faithful, praying always, having your lamps trimmed and burning, and oil with you, that you may be ready at the coming of the Bridegroom" (D&C 33:17; 45:56–57).

Other symbolism of this kind can surely be enumerated, but there is one emblem to which my mind returns again and again. The pure olive oil that priesthood holders use to anoint the sick and that temple officiators, both men and women, use to anoint those being endowed is, without doubt, the supreme symbol of the Savior's blood and his atoning sacrifice offered in Gethsemane. We use this emblem, symbolic of the True Healing Agent, to demonstrate our faith in his ability to heal the sick in mortality as well as consecrate the pure in heart in our temples.

## GETHSEMANE AND A MODERN EXPERIENCE

As a student of the Savior's experience in Gethsemane, I had a profound experience which will forever remain etched in my memory. Brigham Young University maintains a study center on the Mount of Olives, overlooking the very places of our Lord's ministry. Three olive presses are situated on the grounds, where they serve both as object lessons and as invitations to explore ancient olive culture.

One fall semester I supervised the students at the BYU Jerusalem Center as they participated in their own olive harvest and pressing activity. The olives were placed in the *yam*, or rock basin, and the crushing stone was pushed around and around the basin until the olives began to ooze their oil. When the oil began to run down the lip of the limestone basin, it had the distinctive red color characteristic of the first moments of the new pressing each year.

At that instant an audible gasp came from the 170 students who surrounded the olive press to witness our re-creation of the ancient pressing process. It was a stunning, even chilling, minute until the oil turned back to its usual golden color. I believe everyone in that group had the same thought as we watched this happen. It was more than just an amazing confirmation of the symbolism we had discussed. This was, right before our very eyes, a real-life reflection of Gethsemane.

As those who have lived in or visited the Holy Land know, a person cannot escape the image of the olive tree. Olive vineyards and ancient olive presses seem to be everywhere, and visitors' hearts and minds become acutely attuned to their existence. Especially after witnessing an olive harvest, visitors never look at olive trees the same way again. They never regard them as they might have in the past, never view them as being common or an ordinary part of the landscape.

Olive trees are extraordinary trees in an extraordinary land. They are part of the landscape of belief. It is not by accident that we anoint those seeking a blessing with olive oil. Olive trees and the oil derived from their fruit are the most powerful and plentiful symbols in the Holy Land of Jesus Christ, the Master Healer, who was born into a land with abundant reminders of his divinity.

Olive trees are witnesses of his and his Father's love. Just as olive trees and olive oil are gifts from God (Deuteronomy 6:10–11; 11:14), so too is the Savior our great gift from God (John 3:16), and the effects which flow from his atonement—eternal life—"is the greatest of all the gifts of God" (D&C 14:7). In the place called the "oil press," Gethsemane, the Savior was pressed in our behalf as he wrought for all mankind the infinite and eternal atonement. Just as the olive tree and olive oil may sustain our lives temporally, so does the Savior sustain our lives eternally.

And he went a little further, and fell on his face, and prayed, saying, O my Father, if it be possible, let this cup pass from me: nevertheless not as I will, but as thou wilt.

And he cometh unto the disciples, and findeth them asleep, and saith unto Peter, What, could ye not watch with me one hour?

Watch and pray, that ye enter not into temptation: the spirit indeed is willing, but the flesh is weak.

He went away again the second time, and prayed, saying O my Father, if this cup may not pass away from me, except I drink it, thy will be done.

And he came and found them asleep again: for their eyes were heavy.

And he left them, and went away again, and prayed the third time, saying the same words.

Then cometh he to his disciples, and saith unto them, Sleep on now, and take your rest: behold, the hour is at hand, and the Son of man is betrayed into the hands of sinners.

Rise, let us be going: behold, he is at hand that doth betray me.

MATTHEW 26:39–46

# CHAPTER 5

# The Intensity of the Bitter Cup

Matthew, who was also known as Levi (Matthew 9:9; Mark 2:14), was a member of the Quorum of the Twelve Apostles and a powerful witness of the Lord's atoning sacrifice. His Gospel, according to the early Church historian Eusebius (ca. A.D. 340), was written and preserved in Aramaic, the very language in which Jesus prayed in Gethsemane.

Matthew was a gifted writer who wanted the Jews to see that Jesus was the promised King-Messiah, the singular prophet of whom Moses had prophesied (Deuteronomy 18:18) and, thus, the new Moses, the very One whose life followed the pattern of the life of the Old Testament lawgiver and deliverer.

Matthew's testimony of the Savior's suffering in Gethsemane helps us more fully understand his experience in the garden and rounds out our picture of the intensity of his agony. We sense that Matthew tells the story with real feeling.

## HE PRAYED THE THIRD TIME

Unique to Matthew's report of Gethsemane is the observation that Jesus prayed three times, "saying the same words"
(Matthew 26:44). This fact is confirmed in a remarkable vision
beheld by Orson F. Whitney (1855–1931) several years before
he was ordained an apostle. Brother Whitney regarded this singular event as the turning point in his life and traced all future
success to this vision:

> I seemed to be in the Garden of Gethsemane, a
> witness of the Savior's agony. I saw Him as plainly as
> ever I have seen anyone. Standing behind a tree in
> the foreground, I beheld Jesus, with Peter, James and
> John, as they came through a little . . . gate at my right.
> Leaving the three Apostles there, after telling them to
> kneel and pray, the Son of God passed over to the other
> side, where He also knelt and prayed. It was the same
> prayer with which all Bible readers are familiar: "Oh my
> Father, if it be possible, let this cup pass from me; never-
> theless not as I will, but as thou wilt."
>
> As He prayed the tears streamed down his face,
> which was toward me. I was so moved at the sight that
> I also wept, out of pure sympathy. My whole heart went
> out to him; I loved him with all my soul, and longed to
> be with him as I longed for nothing else.
>
> Presently He arose and walked to where those
> Apostles were kneeling—fast asleep! He shook them
> gently, awoke them, and in a tone of tender reproach,
> untinctured by the least show of anger or impatience,
> asked them plaintively if they could not watch with
> him one hour. There He was, with the awful weight

of the world's sin upon his shoulders, with the pangs of every man, woman and child shooting through his sensitive soul—and they could not watch with him one poor hour!

Returning to his place, He offered up the same prayer as before; then went back and again found them sleeping. Again he awoke them, readmonished them, and once more returned and prayed. Three times this occurred. (*Through Memory's Halls*, 82)

We can scarcely fail to be moved by so tender a description: the tears of the Savior himself, his anguish and feelings of being alone, the tears of Brother Whitney, and, above all, the impression of relentless agony.

This description, like Matthew's, paints the picture of a man coming apart; a man unraveling or breaking down physiologically and mentally; a man trying to find some respite from a true physical and spiritual ordeal; a man looking for any kind of relief after prayers, one after the other, that did not yield any relief; a man seeking relief from the weight of sin, sorrow, suffering—even if only for a moment—by getting up to check on trusted associates and to seek some support. No relief was to be found for those intense moments—how long they lasted we do not know. There would be no relief until justice had been satisfied, and that was only until all the agony returned as Jesus hung on the cross on Calvary's hill.

Elder Whitney's description brings to mind a phrase to depict Gethsemane: blood, sweat, and tears—all belonging to Jesus. The New Testament does not mention tears, but Elder Whitney is our confirming witness that tears of sorrow and suffering mingled with Jesus' blood and sweat. In reading his description, our own tears become mingled with Elder Whitney's and with the Savior's. Jesus' compassionate act moves us to compassion for him.

I know of a man, a genuinely good and compassionate man, a saintly soul and one of the great religious educators of our day, whose life was cut short by a brain tumor. He suffered considerable pain, and his family and friends felt much sorrow because of his relatively young age. In the midst of his suffering, the kind that comes with terminal cancer, he was asked by a colleague about his experience.

Through his tears he told of the difficult times but, more important, of the things he was learning through his suffering. He said that one of the great blessings that had come to him was the understanding he had gleaned about the Savior's suffering, especially the realization that if the Savior suffered as much as he did because he loved us, that was an awful lot of love.

When Brother West Belnap died, his example was extolled by Church leaders at the funeral. Today his picture hangs in one of the buildings on the Brigham Young University campus to remind those who know his story that the Savior does comprehend all the tears we weep because he wept them first. The Savior indeed descended below all things.

Another person I know was afflicted with a truly miserable condition that caused excruciating dizziness, nausea, and headaches and affected his ability to perform even the routine tasks of life. It was the type of malady that brings with it a special kind of emotional trauma—a longing for release, even through death, when the symptoms get really severe. There were times when he prayed for relief but felt none was forthcoming. What is worse, his suffering took on a spiritual dimension because he felt no Divine ear was listening.

Along with consulting doctors, the man also sought a priesthood blessing. In the midst of his suffering, my friend's father-in-law asked him if he had been administered to. Yes, was the reply.

The next question was, What did the blessing tell you? The man responded that the blessing told him that if he were patient, the illness would diminish, but more important, it would teach him lessons about the Savior's experience in Gethsemane that could be taught in no other way. His father-in-law, a man of great faith and wisdom, replied that that is what would indeed happen.

And so it has. Though the man at times felt like he was coming apart and would not want anyone to have to endure the malady he has endured, he knows through experience that pain and suffering are special teachers. As a result of his affliction, he now can say he has a deeper insight into what the Savior went through for all of Heavenly Father's children. The Savior went through that kind of suffering—and more—for he descended below all things.

As we contemplate our own trials and suffering, perhaps we can better appreciate another dimension of the Savior's experience in Gethsemane as he prayed the same prayer three times. Though he was the Father's Well Beloved Son, though the Father loved him with a perfect love, and though he prayed more earnestly each successive time, as Luke describes (Luke 22:44), there seemed to be no satisfactory answer. Each successive pleading with yet more intensity yielded no hoped-for result.

How like life for us this seems to be! I would be very

surprised to learn of someone who has never had at least one disappointment when it comes to the way prayers have been answered. And thus how grateful we ought to be for this dimension of the Savior's experience in Gethsemane—showing us again just how well he understands our plight. Doubt and disappointment come to all of us. I am told that President Hugh B. Brown used to say that no one comes to the position of authentic assurance without first having served an apprenticeship in doubt. Through his own experience, the Savior comprehends our mortal struggles and strivings.

Elder Rex D. Pinegar of the Seventy has summarized the lesson that emerges from Gethsemane about the need for patience in our prayers as we seek to follow the Lord's will in the midst of our trials:

> We can only try to imagine the anguish the Savior felt when we read in the Gospels that He was "sore amazed and very heavy" (Mark 14:33) that He "fell on his face" and prayed not once, but a second time, and then a third. (Matthew 26:39, 42, 44.) "Father, if thou be willing remove this cup from me: nevertheless not my will, but thine, be done." (Luke 22:42.). . . .
>
> Sometimes, when our prayers are not answered as we desire, we may feel the Lord has rejected us or that our prayer was in vain. We may begin to doubt our worthiness before God, or even the reality and power of prayer. That is when we must continue to pray with patience and faith and to listen for that peace. (*Church News*, 19 June 1999, 14)

## WITHDRAWAL OF LIGHT AND LIFE

Pain and suffering are powerful teachers. A wise man once said to me, "I learn the most when I hurt the worst!" Individuals among us have special empathy for the pain and suffering of others as well as the suffering experienced by the Savior because the pain they have endured has become a special teacher of divine principles.

Still, there is a huge difference between Jesus in Gethsemane and any other being on the earth, for the things any of us endure will never, ever compare to the Savior's sufferings or be compounded by the complete withdrawal of our Heavenly Father's Spirit and all heavenly influences from our lives, as was the Savior's lot. The withdrawal of the Father was a critical dimension of the Savior's incomprehensible agony in Gethsemane.

John 5:26 teaches that Jesus was a different kind of being from any of us. He had the powers, attributes, and characteristics of eternal life in the same way that our Heavenly Father possesses them. We are totally dependent upon Jesus Christ for these powers, but Jesus possessed them independently, having received them from his Father as part of his genetic makeup, as it were.

One gospel scholar has explained the ordeal in Gethsemane this way: "In order to satisfy the demands of divine justice and redeem fallen man, Christ sacrificed the attributes and powers of both physical and eternal life which He possessed on earth. In this way, Jesus made an 'infinite and eternal'—not merely a sinless human—sacrifice. To this end, the powers of eternal life or glory which He possessed were withdrawn, by His consent,

99

as He commenced His great ordeal" (Andrus, *God, Man and the Universe*, 417).

His great ordeal commenced in Gethsemane. So great became this ordeal that Jesus pleaded with his Father three times to remove the cup. Brigham Young states that it was the withdrawal of our Heavenly Father from his Son, and hence the withdrawal of the spiritual powers of light and life in Gethsemane, that caused Jesus to sweat blood. President Young said, "If he [Jesus] had had the power of God upon him, he would not have sweat blood; but *all* was withdrawn from him, and a veil was cast over him" (*Journal of Discourses* 3:205–6; emphasis added).

Two conditions resulted from the withdrawal of the Father's power and influence and the powers of light and life from Jesus. First, he was engulfed by spiritual death and hell. Second, he became completely vulnerable to the powers of Satan.

## SATAN'S PRESENCE IN GETHSEMANE

The prophet Amulek warns us that when we fail to repent of our sins, we "become subjected to the spirit of the devil, and he doth seal you his; therefore, the Spirit of the Lord hath withdrawn from you, and hath no place in you, and *the devil hath all power over you*" (Alma 34:35; emphasis added).

Because we know that the power of God withdrew from Jesus, that he experienced the pains and sins of *all* people (Alma 7:11–13; D&C 18:11), and that he descended below *all* things and comprehends *all* things (D&C 88:6), we know that he faced the full power and rage of the devil, as Amulek said. Even Jesus, the greatest of all, did not escape Satan's wrath. Perhaps it would be more accurate to say *especially* Jesus did not escape Satan's wrath. In other words, in Gethsemane Jesus became fully subject to the powers of Satan.

The experience of the Prophet Joseph Smith in the Sacred Grove helps us to understand, in small measure, what Jesus was subjected to and what he withstood in full measure in Gethsemane. The life of the one serves as a model or pattern for the other:

> After I had retired to the place where I had previously designed to go, having looked around me, and finding myself alone, I kneeled down and began to offer up the desires of my heart to God. I had scarcely done so, when immediately I was seized upon by some power which entirely overcame me, and had such an astonishing influence over me as to bind my tongue so that I could not speak. This darkness gathered around me, and it seemed to me for a time as if I were doomed to sudden destruction.
>
> But, exerting all my powers to call upon God to deliver me out of the power of this enemy which had seized upon me, and at the very moment when I was ready to sink into despair and abandon myself to destruction—not to an imaginary ruin, but to the power of some actual being from the unseen world, who had such marvelous power as I had never before felt in any being—just at this moment of great alarm, I saw a pillar of light exactly over my head, above the brightness of the sun, which descended gradually until it fell upon me.
>
> It no sooner appeared than I found myself delivered

from the enemy which held me bound. (Joseph Smith–
History 1:15–17)

Joseph Smith learned that the powers of darkness and
Satan's control over the elements, as well as his attempts to
control the physical bodies of mortals, are real. Jesus endured
these same powers but to an even greater degree—in fact, the
greatest degree possible. In the case of Jesus, however, unlike
that of Joseph Smith, there was no ultimate deliverance by
heavenly beings from Satan's complete fury. Of the Savior's
experience, President Boyd K. Packer said: "He, by choice,
accepted the penalty for all mankind for the sum total of all
wickedness and depravity. . . . In choosing, He faced the awesome power of the evil one who was not confined to flesh nor
subject to mortal pain. That was Gethsemane" (*Ensign*, May
1988, 69).

Thus, we may say with perfect accuracy as well as irony that
while (or maybe because) our Heavenly Father was not present
in the Garden of Gethsemane that awful night almost two
thousand years ago, we know that someone else was—Satan.
He was there, hurling at Jesus every horror of which he was
capable, trying to force the Savior to retreat from, renounce,
and forfeit his redemptive mission.

The truth is chilling. Unspeakable horror was at work that
night in Gethsemane, when eternity hung in the balance. But
Jesus came off conqueror against the evil one, whose presence
was very real. Elder Talmage has penned the scene for us in
memorable language:

> Christ's agony in the garden is unfathomable by
> the finite mind, both as to intensity and cause. . . . He
> struggled and groaned under a burden such as no other

being who has lived on earth might even conceive as possible. It was not physical pain, nor mental anguish alone, that caused Him to suffer such torture as to produce an extrusion of blood from every pore; but a spiritual agony of soul such as only God was capable of experiencing. No other man, however great his powers of physical or mental endurance, could have suffered so; for his human organism would have succumbed, and syncope would have produced unconsciousness and welcome oblivion. In that hour of anguish Christ met and *overcame all the horrors that Satan, "the prince of this world" could inflict* [John 14:30]. The frightful struggle incident to the temptations immediately following the Lord's baptism was surpassed and overshadowed by this supreme contest with the powers of evil. (*Jesus the Christ*, 613; emphasis added)

The unimaginable happened in Gethsemane. Jesus Christ, the greatest of all, the one perfect Being who walked the earth, the all-powerful God of the Old Testament, was turned over to the buffetings of Satan. Truly, he descended below all things.

## TEMPTATION

From all that has been written in scripture and taught by prophets, it appears that Gethsemane entailed risk. The Savior's experience in the garden was not without danger. One of Satan's roles is the great tempter. And he unleashed all his power on Jesus.

To those who may think Jesus' station prevented him from being able to experience real risk, real temptation, we simply point out King Benjamin's prophecy: "And lo, he shall suffer temptations, and pain of body, hunger, thirst, and fatigue, even more than man can suffer, except it be unto death; for behold, blood cometh from every pore, so great shall be his anguish for the wickedness and the abominations of his people" (Mosiah 3:7).

Here we have it. The omnipotent God of the universe would, for a time, shed his status and power and condescend to come to earth. He would, as the word *condescend* literally means, "come down with" the people to suffer far more than any human could withstand and not succumb to death—including temptations of every kind. He would experience these temptations to such an extent that justice could not say, "You really didn't know what it means to be human."

We are indebted to C. S. Lewis (1899–1963) for providing us with a most magnificent insight into the Savior's temptation and atoning experience:

> No man knows how bad he is till he has tried very hard to be good. A silly idea is current that good people do not know what temptation means. This is an obvious lie. Only those who try to resist temptation know how strong it is; after all, you find out the strength of the German army by fighting against it, not by giving in. You find out the strength of a wind by trying to walk against it, not by lying down. A man who gives into temptation after five minutes simply does not know what it would have been like an hour later.
>
> That is why bad people in one sense know very little about badness. They've always lived a sheltered life by always giving in. We never find out the strength

of the evil impulse inside us until we try to fight it: and Christ, because he was the only man who never yielded to temptation, is also the only man who knows to the full what temptation means—the only complete realist. (*Mere Christianity*, 126)

This is a stunning revelation, not to mention an irony of staggering proportions. Jesus was severely tempted—tested to the limit because he was the greatest of all. For him, as for us, some of his greatest tests came as he was tempted: on the Mount of Temptation east of the Jericho Valley, on the pinnacle of the Temple in Jerusalem, and in the Garden of Gethsemane on the Mount of Olives. For him, as for us, the tests and temptations are all part of Heavenly Father's plan and purposes. As finite beings we cannot know the mind of God in all things, but we can pay attention to his prophets, who give us glimpses of the eternal perspective.

President Brigham Young knew something of the tests and temptations Jesus faced relative to the tests and temptations all of us face. Jesus was tempted and tested and had to confront the enemy of all righteousness in direct proportion to the light and truth he possessed. President Young said:

> Is there a reason for men and women being exposed more constantly and more powerfully, to the power of the enemy, by having visions than by not having them? There is and it is simply this—God never bestows upon His people, or upon an individual, superior blessings without a severe trial to prove them, to prove that individual, or that people to see whether they will keep their covenants with Him, and keep in remembrance what He has shown them. Then the greater the vision,

the greater the display of the power of the enemy. And when such individuals are off their guard they are left to themselves, as Jesus was. (*Journal of Discourses,* 3:205–6)

Jesus was tempted in direct proportion to the light and life given him. Each of us is similarly tested and tempted. But that is good news. As one man expressed in the midst of life's trials, "The Lord allows it because he thinks you're worth it."

In light of King Benjamin's prophecy, C. S. Lewis's insight, and President Young's comment, I believe it is possible to resist the less noble impulses inside us and the greater temptations that surround us. That is, we can "overcome by faith" (D&C 76:53), or, more specifically, overcome temptation through our faith in Jesus Christ (Alma 37:33).

Jesus knows our challenges. He understands them even better than we do, precisely because he resisted the tempter to the very end. Our sons and daughters must know from us that it is possible for them to call upon a true Friend and find help in time of need. They can resist the evil impulses planted in their hearts by the evil one. We may expect it of them because of their standing and station and because of our confidence in them after they have been properly taught.

Apostles and prophets have taught that members of the house of Israel living in this last dispensation are spirit children of our Father in Heaven who have been reserved to be born at this time because of their strength and talents.

Speaking to members of the Church, President Gordon B. Hinckley said, "You are a great generation. . . . I think you are the best generation who have ever lived in this Church"

(*Church News*, 14 February 1998, 4). Elder Neal A. Maxwell noted that

> there is the increasing presence of choice and talent-laden spirits sent now because of what each can add to the symphony of salvation. President George Q. Cannon said these were reserved because they would have "the courage and determination to face the world" and because they would "honor" God "supremely" and would be "fearless" and "obedient" to God "under all circumstances." I am impressed, deeply impressed, with the youth and young adults in the Church, collectively. President Cannon's statement simply underscores, prophetically, what so many of us see and feel in this regard (*Deposition of a Disciple*, 63–64).

## EFFECT ON THE APOSTLES

We know from Matthew's account that Jesus was concerned for the welfare of his special witnesses during the entire time they were with him in the Garden of Gethsemane. At least twice he went to them to instruct them to watch and pray so as not to enter into temptation (Matthew 26:40–44). We also know that his concern was well founded. It was not just because of his own personal experience with Satan in the garden that he was concerned. Rather, as we come to learn, Satan was already filling the minds of the apostles with doubt, anger, and frustration over Jesus' actions in the garden.

In the Joseph Smith Translation of Mark 14:36–38, which is significantly different from the King James Version, we see how Satan had already begun his work among the apostles:

And they came to a place which was named Gethsemane, which was a garden; and the disciples began to
be sore amazed, and to be very heavy, and to complain
in their hearts, wondering if this be the Messiah.

And Jesus knowing their hearts, said to his disciples,
Sit ye here, while I shall pray.

And he taketh with him, Peter, and James, and
John, and rebuked them, and said unto them, My soul
is exceeding sorrowful, even unto death; tarry ye here
and watch.

From this passage we understand that the apostles had
begun to question whether Jesus really was the Messiah. We
may imagine that the more Jesus suffered, the more the apostles
doubted his messianic identity. After all, *the* King-Messiah, in
the minds of most Jews, was not supposed to suffer, not supposed to fail in restoring the great Davidic kingdom of ancient
times, not supposed to collapse under the weight of spiritual distress nor retreat in the face of expectations of great demonstra-
tions of power, signs, and wonders.

Obviously, the apostles did not fully comprehend the
true and varied roles of the real Messiah. In their minds
he was supposed to be the unfailing and triumphant
warrior-conqueror-deliverer who would restore again the
kingdom of Israel—an expectation the apostles still held even
at the time of the Savior's ascension (Acts 1:6). And this
was their Achilles' heel, so to speak, which Satan worked on.
That is why the Savior was so concerned for their welfare that
night in Gethsemane and why he repeatedly asked them to
pray and watch so as not to enter into temptation, or rather,
even greater temptations.

Joseph Smith's translation of Mark 14 does not contradict the truth of the King James Version, which tells us that *Jesus* began to be sore amazed and very heavy. But the Joseph Smith Translation rendering does give us a more complete perspective on Gethsemane. It shows us what was happening in the minds and hearts of the apostles (they were, in a very limited sense, suffering with their Master), while the King James Version tells us what was happening at the same time to the Savior in the garden as a result of the great turmoil and spiritual onslaught that engulfed him. Both the Joseph Smith Translation account and the King James Version account are true. Both are incredibly valuable. Both teach us what happened in Gethsemane.

## TOWARD GOLGOTHA

After Jesus had wrestled for some time (exactly how long we do not know) with the forces of evil and the onslaught of pain, sin, sorrow, and suffering and after he had descended below *all* things, the intensity of his experience seems to have subsided somewhat. He finished praying for the third time that his Father would remove the bitter cup, but coming to know with absolute certainty that his Father's will was otherwise, he drank the cup he was given and then returned to his apostles, who were sound asleep: "Then cometh he to his disciples, and saith unto them, Sleep on now, and take your rest: behold, the hour is at hand, and the Son of man is betrayed into the hands of sinners" (Matthew 26:45).

In Gethsemane, the ancient prophecies of the Savior's solitary suffering were fulfilled. As the psalmist noted a thousand years before the actual events of Gethsemane occurred, the Savior would find no support from his apostolic associates as he suffered: "Reproach hath broken my heart; and I am full of heaviness: and I looked for some to take pity, but there was none; and for comforters, but I found none" (Psalm 69:20).

Even though we have been made aware of the apostles' weaknesses, it is still wise for us to regard them with the highest respect and deference. These were great men, among the very best on the earth at that or any other time in history. They were *special* witnesses. They had given up everything in pursuit of their Master's call to follow him. In some cases, they had consecrated a significant amount. By the time they reached Gethsemane that awful night, they had been awake for many hours straight, and, above all, they were mortals subject to all the influences and frailties of mortality as brought on by the Fall.

They were also leaders in transition. Nothing like the events they had witnessed and participated in had ever happened before, nor would the events that followed over the course of the next three days find any precedent in the history of our universe. All the events of the meridian dispensation were as new to the members of the Quorum of the Twelve then as the events of this final dispensation were to Joseph Smith and his associates. We ought therefore to increase our gratitude for the strength and power demonstrated by Jesus' original Quorum of the Twelve rather than seek to multiply their shortcomings.

For Jesus, there was more to be endured. By his own admission, the bitter cup was not yet finished. The arrest in the garden, the arraignment before Jewish as well as Roman leaders, the suffering, torture, scourging, and mockery at the hands of wicked and ignorant men, and ultimately crucifixion itself—all these lay ahead of Jesus after he finished that special ordeal that was Gethsemane. Not surprisingly, the very same apostles who had been infected by doubt tried to keep him from the suffering that lay ahead. Jesus rebuked them by reminding them that the bitter cup had not yet been completely consumed. Would they now intervene to try to prevent the final acts from unfolding as God the Father desired? "Then said Jesus unto Peter, Put up thy sword into the sheath: the cup which my Father hath given me, shall I not drink it?" (John 18:11).

The final act was played out. Jesus drained the dregs of the bitter cup, and the eternal possibilities of Heavenly Father's children were safely secured.

*Therefore I command you to repent—repent, lest I smite you by the rod of my mouth, and by my wrath, and by my anger, and your sufferings be sore—how sore you know not, how exquisite you know not, yea, how hard to bear you know not.*

*For behold, I, God, have suffered these things for all, that they might not suffer if they would repent;*

*But if they would not repent they must suffer even as I;*

*Which suffering caused myself, even God, the greatest of all, to tremble because of pain, and to bleed at every pore, and to suffer both body and spirit—and would that I might not drink the bitter cup, and shrink—*

*Nevertheless, glory be to the Father, and I partook and finished my preparations unto the children of men.*

<small>DOCTRINE AND COVENANTS 19:15–19</small>

# CHAPTER 6

# The Savior's Testimony of the Bitter Cup

S ignificantly, it was not his arrest, trial, or crucifixion that Jesus recounted to others with vivid recollection after his resurrection. It was the bitter cup in Gethsemane. President Joseph Fielding Smith helps us to understand why this is so:

> It is understood by many that the great suffering of Jesus Christ came through the driving of nails in His hands and in His feet, and in being suspended upon a cross, until death mercifully released Him. That is not the case. As excruciating, as severe as was that punishment, . . . yet still greater was the suffering which He endured in carrying the burdens of the sins of the world—my sins, and your sins, and the sins of every living creature. This suffering came before He ever got to the cross, and it caused the blood to come forth from the pores of His body, so great was the anguish of His soul, the torment of His spirit that He was called upon to undergo. (Conference Report, April 1944, 50)

Gethsemane seems to have so affected the Savior that he reminded his audiences of it when he spoke to them at the beginning of two new dispensations after his resurrection. The first was in the Americas in A.D. 34, and the next was also in the Americas, when the Savior spoke to Joseph Smith in March 1830 (D&C 19).

The Book of Mormon records the feelings of the twenty-five hundred Nephites assembled at the temple in Bountiful and then the powerful words of the Savior to them:

> And it came to pass, as they understood they cast their eyes up again towards heaven; and behold, they saw a Man descending out of heaven; and he was clothed in a white robe; and he came down and stood in the midst of them; and the eyes of the whole multitude were turned upon him, and they durst not open their mouths, even one to another, and wist not what it meant, for they thought it was an angel that had appeared unto them.
>
> And it came to pass that he stretched forth his hand and spake unto the people, saying:
>
> Behold, I am Jesus Christ, whom the prophets testified shall come into the world.
>
> And behold, I am the light and the life of the world; and I have drunk out of that bitter cup which the Father hath given me, and have glorified the Father in taking upon me the sins of the world, in the which I have suffered the will of the Father in all things from the beginning. (3 Nephi 11:8–11)

Thus the Savior reminds his disciples, then and now, that his consumption of the bitter cup was indeed the fulfillment of his promise made to the Father long ago, in the very beginning, that he would suffer the will of the Father in *all* things. We are reminded of the Great Council in Heaven, held during our premortal existence, when the Firstborn said, "Father, thy will be done, and the glory be thine forever" (Moses 4:2). Gethsemane and Calvary are the two places where Jesus fulfilled his promise and accomplished the will of the Father.

Just as the Savior remembers Gethsemane, so should we always remember it. It has remained a focal point of his self-identification. But neither of Christ's postresurrection accounts of the bitter cup (3 Nephi 11; D&C 19) was given to scare us into submission nor to force our obedience. Rather, I think a very earnest Savior is trying to tell us just exactly what it cost to ransom us from the grasp of justice, what price was paid to secure our freedom from death, hell, and the devil.

## THE PRICE OF REDEMPTION

Occasionally mortals indulge in "what if . . ." speculations about certain events. "What if this would have happened instead of that?" Sometimes the answers are useless. But there are other times when the conjured possibilities can teach profound lessons. In the case of the Savior's redemptive acts, a prophet in the Book of Mormon helps us to see the frightening truth about our human plight if there had been no Gethsemane and no Calvary. Without the Savior's atoning sacrifice, we would have had no escape from the awful grasp of death, hell, and the devil. In fact, without both Gethsemane and Calvary, each of us would have become devils, just like Lucifer himself in his irredeemable condition. Jacob says:

Wherefore, it must needs be an infinite atonement—

save it should be an infinite atonement this corruption could not put on incorruption. Wherefore, the first judgment which came upon man must needs have remained to an endless duration. And if so, this flesh must have laid down to rot and to crumble to its mother earth, to rise no more.

O the wisdom of God, his mercy and grace! For behold, if the flesh should rise no more our spirits must become subject to that angel who fell from before the presence of the Eternal God, and became the devil, to rise no more.

And our spirits must have become like unto him, and we become devils, angels to a devil, to be shut out from the presence of our God, and to remain with the father of lies, in misery, like unto himself; yea, to that being who beguiled our first parents, who transformeth himself nigh unto an angel of light, and stirreth up the children of men unto secret combinations of murder and all manner of secret works of darkness. (2 Nephi 9:7–9)

In declaring the explicit cost of our redemption from the throes of sin as well as the devil, the Savior's personal testimony in Doctrine and Covenants 19:18 is without parallel. God himself, the greatest of all, one of three all-knowing and all-powerful Gods in the entire universe, *trembled* because of pain, *bled* at every pore, suffered *body and spirit* to rescue us. The pain that he suffered was "the pain of all men" (D&C 18:11). When he said he "suffered these things for all" he was not exaggerating. He meant it. He suffered the consequences of *every* sin committed by Adam and by all of Adam's posterity. He suffered both physically and spiritually. He suffered to the very limits of possibility. There is no way or manner in which he did not suffer. He suffered everything imaginable. He suffered for billions and billions of lifetimes of sin and sorrow. There is not anyone for whom he did not suffer. "The Savior's Atonement is stunningly inclusive," said Sister Sheri L. Dew. "Come one, come all, the Lord has invited. The gospel of Jesus Christ is for every man and woman, boy and girl. He doesn't change the rules for the rich or the poor, the married or unmarried, the Portuguese or the Chinese. The gospel is for *every one* of us, and the spiritual requirements and rewards are universal. In matters pertaining to salvation, '*all* are alike unto God' (2 Ne. 26:33, emphasis added)" (*Ensign*, May 1999, 66).

## SUFFERING AND CONTRADICTION

Though the Savior's suffering is for all individuals, ironically he suffered alone. He said on several occasions, "I have trodden the wine-press alone, and have brought judgment upon all people; and none were with me" (D&C 133:50; D&C 76:107; 88:106; Revelation 14:20). The metaphor of the wine-press is appropriate because the image it conjures up takes us immediately to the Garden of Gethsemane where, still today, we can see remnants of ancient winepresses.

Anciently, winepresses and olive presses were sometimes used interchangeably. Several people would get into the press, a rock-lined pit with a mosaic or plaster floor, and, holding onto one another, smash the grapes or olives with their feet until the fruit turned into a thick pulp. Unless one held onto others in the press, it was almost impossible to lift one's feet in the thick sludge to tromp the grapes into juice. It also became very slippery, and without others in the press to hang onto for support, it was very easy to fall. Thus, when the Savior says he trod the winepress alone, he means that at a certain point in Gethsemane no one was there to help him through his ordeal. Ironically, in a place named for an activity that required several participants, one Man suffered for all men—the greatest contradiction in the history of created things.

From what has been revealed to us, we cannot help but believe that a significant source of Jesus' great spiritual agony stemmed from the total contradiction of the situation. In Gethsemane, God, the greatest of all, suffered the greatest contradictions of all. As we have said, the Prophet Joseph Smith taught that Jesus Christ "descended in suffering below that which man can suffer; or, in other words, suffered greater sufferings, and was exposed to *more powerful contradictions* than any man can be. But, notwithstanding all this, he kept the law of God, and remained without sin, showing thereby that it is in the power of man to keep the law and remain without sin" (*Lectures on Faith*, 5:2). This has to be one of the great principles of mortality. We, like Jesus, suffer contradictions as part of our probation on this earth; there is no doubt of that. It is what we do in the face of those contradictions, how we react, that demonstrates our commitment to God and thus determines our place in eternity.

All of the noble and great leaders among our Father's children have experienced such contradictions in their lives. Perhaps the most notable, besides the Savior, is Abraham. He was commanded to offer Isaac, his long-promised son, as a human sacrifice, even though Isaac was the son through whom Abraham believed he was to receive God's promises of innumerable posterity and an everlasting line of priesthood holders. Moreover, God abhorred human sacrifice, and Abraham himself had been rescued from becoming a human sacrifice under his own father's hand by the very same Deity who then turned around and commanded Abraham to sacrifice his son (Abraham 1:5–16).

As Abraham learned, the contradictions of mortality serve a great purpose. Not only do they act as the Lord's refining fire but they precede great and marvelous blessings. Said Moroni, a prophet who knew a great deal about trials, tribulations, and contradictions: "Ye receive no witness until after the trial of your faith" (Ether 12:6). We can state the principle in another way: the greater the contradiction, faithfully endured, the greater the blessing enjoyed afterward.

Again, Abraham is a good example. Because of Abraham's faithfulness, God made good on every promise to him, and more. His son Isaac has the honor of being one of only two individuals designated "only begotten son" (Hebrews 11:17). The other is Jesus Christ. Because of Abraham's faithfulness, his experience with Isaac on Mount Moriah is held up as *the* earthly model of the relationship that existed between God the Father and his Only Begotten Son. "Behold, they believed in Christ and worshiped the Father in his name, and also we worship the Father in his name. And for this intent we keep the law of Moses, it pointing our souls to him; and for this cause it is sanctified unto us for righteousness, even as it was accounted unto Abraham in the wilderness to be obedient unto the commands of God in offering up his son Isaac, *which is a similitude of God and his Only Begotten Son*" (Jacob 4:5; emphasis added). And ultimately, because of Abraham's faithfulness, he and his sons "have entered into their exaltation, according to the promises, and sit upon thrones, and are not angels but are gods" (D&C 132:37).

Every disciple of the Lord and true follower of Abraham

will face the kind of tests, trials, and contradictions the great patriarch faced. These will be different for every person, but they will come! The Lord has said, "They [those who profess discipleship] must needs be chastened and tried, even as Abraham, who was commanded to offer up his only son. For all those who will not endure chastening, but deny me, cannot be sanctified" (D&C 101:4–5).

Abraham is the standard. He was true and faithful to Jehovah, and his life became a powerful witness of the principle that "after much tribulation . . . cometh the blessing" (D&C 103:12).

So it is for each one of us. We remember that the Lord said "after *much* tribulation cometh the blessing," not a little difficulty or a small challenge here and there. President John Taylor said, "You will have all kinds of trials to pass through. And it is quite as necessary for you to be tried as it was for Abraham and other men of God. . . . God will feel after you, and He will take hold of you and wrench your very heart strings, and if you cannot stand it you will not be fit for an inheritance in the Celestial Kingdom of God" (*Journal of Discourses*, 24:197).

All such tests are calculated to allow us the opportunity to demonstrate our loyalty just as Abraham demonstrated his. God doesn't want anything but our minds, our hearts, and all that we possess! He does not want much—he wants everything. And he desires with all his soul to give us back everything he possesses. We are asked to give up all in order to receive an infinitely greater all.

The magnitude of the promise is almost incomprehensible and the unevenness of the offer staggering: everything we possess in exchange for everything God possesses! Why would any of us be unwilling to sacrifice all we have been given, all that is not even ours to begin with? I treasure the words of President George Q. Cannon:

> There is no sacrifice that God can ask of us or His servants whom He has chosen to lead us that we should hesitate about making. In one sense of the word it is no sacrifice. We may call it so because it comes in contact with our selfishness and our unbelief; but it ought not to come in contact with our faith. . . .
>
> Why did the Lord ask such things of Abraham? Because, knowing what his future would be and that he would be the father of an innumerable posterity, he was determined to test him. God did not do this for His own sake for He knew by His foreknowledge what Abraham would do; but the purpose was to impress upon Abraham a lesson and to enable him to attain unto knowledge that he could not obtain in any other way. That is why God tries all of us. It is not for His own knowledge, for He knows all things beforehand. He knows all your lives and everything you will do. But he tries us for our own good, that we may know ourselves; for it is most important that a man should know himself. He required Abraham to submit to this trial because He intended to give him glory, exaltation and honor. He intended to make him a king and a priest, to share with Himself the glory, power and dominion which He exercised. (*Gospel Truth*, 89)

With regard to the principle of contradictions, as in all things, Jesus is our greatest exemplar, particularly in that awful night in Gethsemane. When it comes to contradiction, Abraham on Mount Moriah and Jesus in Gethsemane are like each other, but Gethsemane involved so much more. The Jewish people refer to Mount Moriah as the place of infinite resignation, because Abraham resigned himself to follow God's will even in the face of overwhelming contradiction. It can be justly said that Gethsemane was the night of infinite resignation, infinite suffering, *and* infinite contradiction.

Perhaps it was the night of infinite suffering *because* of infinite contradiction. Though Jesus was the Son of the Highest, in Gethsemane he descended below all things. Though he was sent out of love (John 3:16) and though he was characterized as the embodiment of love (1 John 4:8), in Gethsemane he was surrounded by hate and betrayal. Though he was the light and life of the world, in Gethsemane he was subjected to darkness and spiritual death. Though he was sinless, in Gethsemane he was weighed down by monumental sin and iniquity. Though he gave no offense in anything (2 Corinthians 6:3), in Gethsemane he suffered for the offenses of all. In Gethsemane, the sinless One became the great sinner (2 Corinthians 5:21), that is, he experienced fully the plight of sinners. Though he was fully deserving of the Father's love and the Father's glory, in Gethsemane he suffered the wrath of Almighty God.

Is it any wonder, then, that the Savior said to Joseph Smith that unrepentant sinners would be smitten by his own wrath, by his anger, by sufferings so sore, exquisite, and hard to bear they could not be comprehended? He himself had suffered these things, and if individuals will not accept his suffering, then they must suffer those same things themselves.

The contradictions of Gethsemane filled the bitter cup. In contemplating them, how can we fail to be moved to tears of gratitude because the Savior drank the cup to its dregs and made it possible for us to escape the kind of suffering demanded by the exacting requirements of justice? But there is another reason for gratitude.

We know that even with the benefits of the Atonement fully operating in our lives, mortality still entails some suffering and some contradictions for each of us. Yet, because the Savior endured perfectly his staggering contradictions, we will be recompensed for our own faithful endurance of life's contradictions, injustices, and flat-out unfair circumstances. That is, through the Atonement, all of life's contradictions, all injustices, and all unfair circumstances will be made up to us, all unfair disadvantages will be made right in the eternal scheme of things. In an ironic twist, because of Christ's atonement, because of his supreme act of mercy which rescues us from the demands of justice, justice ultimately becomes our friend by making up to us all of the things in life that weren't fair and right. All unfair circumstances and contradictions will be put right—if we remain faithful to the Savior.

## LIFE'S TUTORS

President Spencer W. Kimball was a man acquainted with many of life's trials, contradictions, and injustices. I appreciate his counsel because he lived it. He intimated that if mortality were the absolute beginning and end of our existence, then sorrow, suffering, pain, unfairness, injustice, and failure would be the greatest calamities. But mortality is only a very small fraction of eternity. In Gethsemane and on the cross, the Savior turned sorrow, pain, and injustice into the ultimate blessing for us by making possible eternal life. In fact, the Savior's experience in Gethsemane showed us how suffering can become one of our great tutors. President Kimball said (in *Tragedy or Destiny*, 3):

Being human, we would expel from our lives physical pain and mental anguish and assure ourselves of continual ease and comfort, but if we were to close the doors upon sorrow and distress, we might be excluding our greatest friends and benefactors. Suffering can make saints of people as they learn patience, long-suffering, and self-mastery. The sufferings of our Savior were part of his education. "Though he were a Son, yet learned he obedience by the things which he suffered; And being made perfect, he became the author of eternal salvation unto all them that obey him" (Hebrews 5:8–9).

I love the verse of "How Firm a Foundation"—

When through the deep waters I call thee to go,
The rivers of sorrow shall not thee o'erflow
For I will be with thee, thy troubles to bless,
And sanctify to thee thy deepest distress.
(*Hymns*, [1985, no. 85])

The Savior is a true friend, and because of his experience in Gethsemane, our trials and contradictions also turn out to be our friends and special tutors. His atonement makes eternal existence, bathed in a fulness of joy, a reality. Our own experiences, the enjoyable as well as the distasteful, become the foundation of our quest for knowledge and help us to become more like our Heavenly Parents. As Elder Orson F. Whitney said:

No pain that we suffer, no trial that we experience is wasted. It ministers to our education, to the development of such qualities as patience, faith, fortitude and humility. All that we suffer and all that we endure, especially when we endure it patiently, builds up our characters, purifies our hearts, expands our souls, and makes us more tender and charitable, more worthy to be called the children of God . . . and it is through sorrow and suffering, toil and tribulation, that we gain the education that we come here to acquire and which will make us more like our Father and Mother in heaven. (In Kimball, *Tragedy or Destiny*, 4)

Each of us experiences something of Gethsemane in our own lives. We suffer contradictions and injustices and feel pain for others as well as experience pain because of the actions of others. Sometimes we may even feel we are having to endure our own Gethsemane. But the Savior is able to cure all the hurt and heal all the bruises and in the process transforms our trials, tribulations, and sufferings into sacred experiences.

President James E. Faust, a counselor in the First Presidency, gave this instructive counsel:

> At times I have stumbled and been less than I should have been. All of us experience those wrenching, defining, difficult decisions that move us to a higher level of spirituality. They are the Gethsemanes of our lives that bring with them great pain and anguish. Sometimes they are too sacred to be shared publicly. They are the watershed experiences that help purge us of our unrighteous desires for the things of the world. As the scales of worldliness are taken from our eyes, we see more clearly who we are and what our responsibilities are concerning our divine destiny. (*Ensign*, November 2000, 59)

Our obedience and sacrifice in the face of trials and tribulations allow us to come to know God in a more intimate way than we could have known him without our sufferings. The historian George Bancroft, when reflecting upon a low point for George Washington and the patriots during the American Revolution, wrote words that apply to all of us: "The spirit of the Most High dwells among the afflicted, rather than the prosperous; and he who has never broken his bread in tears knows not the heavenly powers" (in Dibble, "Delivered by the Power of God," 48).

Indeed, righteous persons who seem to have suffered the most also seem to appreciate their suffering the most and learn what God wants his children to learn from their sacrifice and suffering in obedience. In addition to Abraham and other scriptural figures are individuals from Latter-day Saint history who allowed their sacrifices and sufferings to tutor them. A powerful lesson was taught by one of the survivors of the Martin handcart company when, years later, he heard criticism leveled against Church leaders for allowing the handcart company to take its journey in such adverse conditions. In a session of general conference, Elder James E. Faust recounted that the man said:

> "I ask you to stop this criticism. You are discussing a matter you know nothing about. Cold historic facts mean nothing here, for they give no proper interpretation of the questions involved. Mistake to send the Handcart Company out so late in the season? Yes. But I was in that company and my wife was in it and Sister Nellie Unthank whom you have cited was there, too. We suffered beyond anything you can imagine and many died of exposure and starvation, but did you ever hear a survivor of that company utter a word of criticism? *Not one of that company ever apostatized or left the*

*Church, because every one of us came through with the absolute knowledge that God lives for we became acquainted with him in our extremities.*

"I have pulled my handcart when I was so weak and weary from illness and lack of food that I could hardly put one foot ahead of the other. I have looked ahead and seen a patch of sand or a hill slope and I have said, I can go only that far and there I must give up, for I cannot pull the load through it. . . .

"I have gone on to that sand and when I reached it, the cart began pushing me. I have looked back many times to see who was pushing my cart, but my eyes saw no one. I knew then that the angels of God were there.

"Was I sorry that I chose to come by handcart? No. Neither then nor any minute of my life since. *The price we paid to become acquainted with God was a privilege to pay, and I am thankful that I was privileged to come in the Martin Handcart Company.*" (*Relief Society Magazine*, Jan. 1948, p. 8.)

Here then is a great truth. In the pain, the agony, and the heroic endeavors of life, we pass through a refiner's fire, and the insignificant and the unimportant in our lives can melt away like dross and make our faith bright, intact, and strong. In this way the divine image can be mirrored from the soul. It is part of the purging toll exacted of some to become acquainted with God. In the agonies of life, we seem to listen better to the faint, godly whisperings of the Divine Shepherd. (*Ensign*, May 1979, 53)

Sacrifice and obedience to God's will in the face of trials, tribulations, and suffering are the price we pay to know God! We are never more like the Savior than when we offer our obedience in the face of affliction. Even the sacrifices we think we are making for righteousness' sake are rewarded with the blessings of eternal life and everlasting happiness precisely because of the Savior's own sacrifice in Gethsemane and on the cross of Calvary. Everything we suffer and sacrifice for righteousness' sake will be made up to us because of the Savior's suffering and sacrifice. The Prophet Joseph Smith taught: "All your losses will be made up to you in the resurrection; provided you continue faithful. By the vision of the Almighty I have seen it" (*Teachings of the Prophet Joseph Smith*, 296).

I am reminded that our English word *sacrifice* derives from a combination of two Latin words, *sacer* ("sacred") and *facere* ("to make"), thus meaning "to make sacred." Of course, *sacred* means "set apart for or dedicated to Deity." Does the Savior's sacrifice in Gethsemane and at Golgotha mean, then, that we are set apart for God's use, for his purposes? Or that we have been dedicated and singled out to become like God? Or does it mean something else? Any way we look at it, Jesus' experience in Gethsemane has something to do with the answer. His life is bound up with ours, inescapably.

## WHAT HE ASKS OF US

Ultimately, the Savior's personal testimony regarding the bitter cup seems strikingly simple in its intention—to help us understand what it cost him to remove the burden of our sins and to teach us what is required for us to be able to enjoy his rich gift. Repentance! Of all things he could have asked, he asks us to repent. He asks us to change, to turn to him, to leave our sins and misdeeds behind and commit to trying with all our hearts to live good and decent lives. He wants to spare us the suffering he experienced. He desires only *our* welfare.

In an early revelation of this dispensation, the Lord instructed his servants Joseph Smith, Oliver Cowdery, and others to "say nothing but repentance unto this generation" (D&C 6:9). Interestingly, the Lord followed his own counsel when he bore witness of his experience in Gethsemane, as recorded in Doctrine and Covenants 19:15–19, for there he too focused on repentance.

Repentance is sometimes misunderstood. In a powerful address at Brigham Young University, Elder Theodore M. Burton explained the doctrine of repentance in a most helpful fashion:

> Just what *is* repentance? Actually it is easier for me to tell you what repentance is *not* than to tell you what repentance *is*.
>
> My present assignment as a General Authority is to assist the First Presidency. I prepare information for them to use in considering applications to readmit transgressors into the Church and to restore priesthood and/or temple blessings. Many times a bishop will write: "I feel he has suffered enough!" But suffering is not repentance. Suffering comes from *lack* of complete repentance. A stake president will write: "I feel he has been punished enough!" But punishment is not repentance. Punishment *follows* disobedience and *precedes* repentance. A husband will write: "My wife has confessed everything!" But confession is not repentance. Confession is an admission of guilt that occurs *as* repentance begins. A wife will write: "My husband

is filled with remorse!" But remorse is not repentance. Remorse and sorrow continue because a person has *not* yet fully repented. But if suffering, punishment, confession, remorse, and sorrow are not repentance, what *is* repentance? ("Meaning of Repentance," 96)

Elder Burton explained that repentance is a doctrine discussed with clarity in the Old Testament. *Repentance* is the English word used to translate the Hebrew word *shuv*, which means "to turn, return, or turn back." Elder Burton then quoted Ezekiel:

> "When I say unto the wicked, O wicked man, thou shalt surely die; if thou dost not speak to warn the wicked from his way, that wicked man shall die in his iniquity; but his blood will I require at thine hand.
>
> "Nevertheless, if thou warn the wicked of his way to [*shuv*; or] turn from it; if he do not [*shuv*; or] turn from his way, he shall die in his iniquity; but thou hast delivered thy soul.
>
> "Therefore, O thou son of man, speak unto the house of Israel; Thus ye speak, saying, If our transgressions and our sins be upon us, and we pine away in them, how should we then live?
>
> "Say unto them, As I live, saith the Lord God, I have no pleasure in the death of the wicked; but that the wicked [*shuv*; or] turn from his way and live: [*shuv, shuv!*] turn ye, turn ye from your evil ways; for why will ye die, O house of Israel?" (Ezek. 33:8–11)

I know of no kinder, sweeter passage in the Old Testament than those beautiful lines. Can you hear a kind, wise, gentle, loving Father in Heaven pleading with you to [*shuv*] or turn back to him, to leave unhappiness, sorrow, regret, and despair behind and now turn back to your Father's family where you can find happiness, joy, and acceptance among his other children? In the Father's family, you are surrounded with love and affection. That is the message of the Old Testament, and prophet after prophet writes of [*shuv*], which is that turning back to the family of the Lord [is] where you can be received with joy and rejoicing. . . .

People must somehow be made to realize that the true meaning of repentance is that we do not require people to be punished or to punish themselves, but to change their lives so they can escape eternal punishment. If they have this understanding, it will relieve their anxiety and fears and become a welcome and treasured word in our religious vocabulary. ("Meaning of Repentance," 96–97)

True repentance requires that we turn to God, change our sinful ways, confess our sins, renew our pledge or covenant with the Lord, repay our debt, serve others, and never return to our iniquity. To the Prophet Joseph Smith, the Lord said: "Behold, he who has repented of his sins, the same is forgiven, and I, the Lord, remember them no more. By this ye may know if a man repenteth of his sins—behold, he will confess them and forsake them" (D&C 58:42–43).

One element of repentance that we sometimes overlook is the necessity of time. Elder Burton said:

It takes time for repentance to be final. An injury to the soul is similar to an injury to the body. Just as it takes time for a wound in the body to heal, so it also takes time for a wound of the soul to heal. The deeper the cut in the body, the longer it takes to heal, and if broken bones are involved, that healing process is extended. If I cut myself, for example, the wound will gradually heal and scab over. But as it heals, it begins to itch, and if I scratch at the itching scab it will take longer to heal, for the wound will open up again. But there is a greater danger. Because of the bacteria on my fingers as I scratch the scab, the wound may become infected and I can poison the wound and can lose that part of my body and eventually even my life!

Allow injuries to follow their prescribed healing course or, if serious, see a doctor for skilled help. So it is with injuries to the soul. Allow the injury to follow its prescribed healing course without scratching it through vain regrets. If it is serious, go to your bishop and get skilled help. It may hurt as he disinfects the wound and sews the flesh together, but it will heal properly that way. Don't hurry or force it, but be patient with yourself and with your thoughts. Be active with positive and righteous thoughts and deeds. Then the wound will heal properly and you will become happy and productive again. ("Meaning of Repentance," 100)

Why does the Lord command us to repent? Not to punish us, not to humiliate us, not to impress upon us who is boss, and certainly not to make us miserable. The Savior asks of us true repentance because we are worth more to him and his Father than we can possibly comprehend:

Remember the worth of souls is great in the sight of God;

For, behold, the Lord your Redeemer suffered death in the flesh; wherefore he suffered the pain of all men, that all men might repent and come unto him.

And he hath risen again from the dead, that he might bring all men unto him, on conditions of repentance.

And how great is his joy in the soul that repenteth! (D&C 18:10–13)

I used to look at these verses in Doctrine and Covenants 18 regarding the worth of souls as "missionary" verses. I look at them a little differently now. The worth of souls is great in the sight of God because an infinite price has been paid for the redemption of all souls—for mine and for yours. We are not our own; each of us owes an infinite debt; we are bought with a tremendous price (1 Corinthians 6:19–20; 7:23). The price was paid out of love.

Jesus went to Gethsemane out of love. Jesus asks us to repent out of love—a deep and abiding love for each one of us, a love that continues even during those times when we are not so lovable.

*But behold, an awful death cometh upon the wicked; for they die as to things pertaining to things of righteousness; for they are unclean, and no unclean thing can inherit the kingdom of God; but they are cast out, and consigned to partake of the fruits of their labors or of their works, which have been evil; and they drink the dregs of a bitter cup.*

ALMA 40:26

# CHAPTER 7

# The Bitter Cup Ignored

As we have seen, the Savior himself gave us important insights into the nature of his supreme act of mercy in Gethsemane (D&C 19:15–19). He testified that he experienced exquisite, unbearable, and unimaginable suffering for all (D&C 18:11). The pain of all mankind was transferred to him, and he was able to act as the single substitutionary sufferer for everyone. Yet, for that vicarious suffering to work its power in our lives, each one of us must exercise faith in Jesus Christ and repent of our sins. If we do not, we will suffer exactly as the Savior did. The Savior provided an important illustration when he warned: "Wherefore, I command you again to repent, lest I humble you with my almighty power; and that you confess your sins, lest you suffer these punishments of which I have spoken, of which in the smallest, yea, even in the least degree you have tasted at the time I withdrew my Spirit" (D&C 19:20).

Martin Harris tasted such suffering and punishment when he lost the first 116 pages of manuscript that Joseph Smith had translated from the Book of Mormon plates (the book of Lehi).

Joseph also experienced the agony and torture that resulted from the withdrawal of the Lord's Spirit on that occasion. Lucy Mack Smith described as best she could, as well as mortal language is capable of describing, the feelings her son and other family members endured for only a short period:

> I well remember that day of darkness, both within and without. To us, at least, the heavens seemed clothed with blackness, and the earth shrouded with gloom. I have often said within myself, that if a continual punishment, as severe as that which we experienced on that occasion, were to be inflicted upon the most wicked characters who ever stood upon the footstool of the Almighty—if even their punishment were no greater than that, I should feel to pity their condition. (*History of Joseph Smith by His Mother*, 132)

According to the Savior himself, the anguish experienced by the Prophet Joseph Smith and Martin Harris was only a small sample (in fact, he said it was the smallest sample or least degree) of the suffering he experienced in Gethsemane. Such severe suffering is also only the smallest sample or least degree of suffering that each of us will experience if we do not repent once we come to a knowledge of God's plan for his children. This is the awful fate that awaits the wicked if they choose to ignore the Savior's atoning sacrifice.

## OTHERS LEARNED OF THE BITTER CUP

At least one other Book of Mormon prophet, King Benjamin, was familiar with the imagery of the bitter cup, which he very well may have seen in vision, considering all the other things that were revealed to him about the Messiah's ministry and mission. In the same magnificent discourse wherein he prophesied events of Jesus' life and death, King Benjamin also described the ultimate fate of the wicked, those who have rebelled against God by rejecting the call to repent and ignoring the command to exercise faith in the Lord Jesus Christ (Mosiah 3:12). He declared:

> And if they be evil they are consigned to an awful view of their own guilt and abominations, which doth cause them to shrink from the presence of the Lord into a state of misery and endless torment, from whence they can no more return; therefore they have drunk damnation to their own souls.
>
> Therefore, they have *drunk out of the cup of the wrath of God*, which justice could no more deny unto them than it could deny that Adam should fall because of his partaking of the forbidden fruit; therefore, mercy could have claim on them no more forever. (Mosiah 3:25–26; emphasis added)

King Benjamin's prophetic reference to "the cup of the wrath of God" that the wicked must consume is powerful in its vividness. The Savior himself reemphasized in our own dispensation the terrible nature of this cup when he spoke of having experienced the "fierceness of the wrath of Almighty God" (D&C 76:107; 88:106). The cup of the fierce wrath of Almighty God symbolizes God's abhorrence of sin of any kind and his retributive justice for it. When this cup was consumed by the Savior, it caused him to shrink (D&C 19:18). Likewise, those who rebel against the Savior and do not repent will drink the dregs of the bitter cup, or the cup of wrath, and shrink from the presence of God into a state of misery and endless torment.

By consuming the bitter cup in Gethsemane, Jesus shrank into a state of misery and torment, and being an infinite God, he experienced in that compacted time frame in Gethsemane the feelings that come to those who know their state or condition is one of "endless torment." Remember, the Savior descended below all these things (D&C 122:8).

King Benjamin was not only a mighty prophet and master teacher but also a model minister and amazing leader. When he had finished instructing his people, he followed up by checking to see if they understood his teachings and then had them commit themselves to living the doctrines and principles he had expounded (Mosiah 5:1–2). It was in this context that Benjamin's people internalized the message of the bitter cup:

> And we are willing to enter into a covenant with our God to do his will, and to be obedient to his commandments in all things that he shall command us, all the remainder of our days, that we may not bring upon ourselves a never-ending torment, as has been spoken by the angel, that we may not drink out of the cup of the wrath of God. (Mosiah 5:5)

The message of the Savior, King Benjamin, Alma, Joseph Smith, and others regarding the Savior's suffering and sacrifice in Gethsemane and on the cross is quite clear. No one who learns of the Atonement is free to ignore it. Justice demands commitment to Jesus Christ and his gospel, or else individuals must themselves suffer the fierceness of the wrath of Almighty God. C. S. Lewis observed: "You must make your choice. Either this man was, and is, the Son of God: or else a madman or something worse. You can shut Him up for a fool, you can spit at Him and kill Him as a demon; or you can fall at His feet and call Him Lord and God" (*Mere Christianity*, 56).

Once we have learned about Gethsemane, we cannot ignore it: "He has not left that open to us. He did not intend to" (Lewis, *Mere Christianity*, 56).

Elder Marion G. Romney has explained what that means in practical terms: "The gospel *requires* us to believe in the Redeemer, accept his atonement, repent of our sins, be baptized by immersion for the remission of our sins, receive the Gift of the Holy Ghost by the laying on of hands, and continue faithfully to observe, or do the best we can to observe, the principles of the gospel all the days of our lives" (Conference Report, October 1953, 36; emphasis added). That seems pretty simple and clear.

## ALL SORROW IS NOT FROM SIN

Another profound reason for embracing the Savior, his suffering and sacrifice in Gethsemane, is that all sorrow in life is not from sin. The Savior's own experience in Gethsemane helps us to see in a stunning way that not all sorrow and adversity are the result of someone having broken the commandments. Not every trial is caused by our deficient action, foolishness, or carelessness. The Savior not only knows this but appreciates it because of his experience in mortality: "Wherefore in all things it behoved him to be made like unto his brethren, that he might be made a merciful and faithful high priest" (Hebrews 2:17).

Brother Roy Doxey has written: "The Prophet Joseph Smith taught that it is a false idea to believe that the saints will escape all the judgments—disease, pestilence, war, etc.— of the last days; consequently, it is an unhallowed principle to say that these adversities are due to transgression. . . . President

Joseph F. Smith taught that it is a feeble thought to believe that
the illness and affliction that come to us are attributable either
to the mercy or the displeasure of God" (*Doctrine and Covenants
Speaks*, 2:373).

Some trials, some tribulation and suffering, come to each of
us just because of the nature of mortal life. Simply living in a
fallen world produces tests, trials, pain, sickness, and affliction.

## LETTING HIM TAKE OUR BURDENS

Whatever the sources of our suffering, we know with assurance that our Father in Heaven never intended to leave us to
ourselves, to let us flounder when life gets tough. As the designated substitute sufferer for us (a designation made before
the foundations of this world were laid), Jesus has taken upon
himself our sorrow and suffering caused by a myriad of other
things besides sin. He is able to make those things work for our
good, if we will let him. To the prophet Moroni, the Savior
said: "And if men come unto me I will show unto them their
weakness. I give unto men weakness that they may be humble;
and my grace is sufficient for all men that humble themselves
before me; for if they humble themselves before me, and have
faith in me, then will I make weak things become strong unto
them" (Ether 12:27).

Jesus Christ can make our weaknesses into strengths. He
can change our minds and hearts. He can change our views and
attitudes. He can change our appetites and refine our passions.
He can change feelings that we sometimes can't help feeling
if we are left on our own without another perspective. He can
cause us to see things in new and different ways. He can heal
emotional wounds as well as psychological trauma and spiritual
scars. If we will pray for it and work for it, just as we pray and

work when we repent, there is no heart he cannot heal. There is no problem he cannot solve. There is no sickness he cannot cure. There is no wound he cannot bind up.

Our Lord knows all things. He has all power. He has foreseen every contingency. He is not a grand cosmic laboratory experimenter who might have to run back and check the books to figure out an answer if he bumps up against a problem he has not confronted before. We can pray to him in absolute trust and confidence knowing that he is able to answer our prayers without equivocation. We can and should go to him to find help in time of need.

Indeed, the Savior desires to help us with all our concerns and challenges, all sin, sorrow, suffering, trials, and tribulations. He himself bids us to seek his help: "Come unto me, all ye that labour and are heavy laden, and I will give you rest. Take my yoke upon you, and learn of me; for I am meek and lowly in heart: and ye shall find rest unto your souls. For my yoke is easy, and my burden is light" (Matthew 11:28–30). The word *rest*, of course, has multiple meanings. The Savior can give us rest from the weariness that life's challenges bring on, and he also lifts our vision to see that he brings rest in its greatest sense—the fulness of God's glory (D&C 84:24). He could have also said, "Come unto me, all ye that labour and are heavy laden . . . for your burdens will be light."

We come to appreciate that Jesus can deliver what he promises because he does not work in the same way other agents or influences in the world work. His ways are not our ways, and his thoughts are not our thoughts (Isaiah 55:8–9). President Ezra Taft Benson taught this general principle when he said:

The Lord works from the inside out. The world

works from the outside in. The world would take people out of the slums. Christ takes the slums out of people, and then they take themselves out of the slums. The world would mold men by changing their environment. Christ changes men who then change their environment. The world would shape human behavior, but Christ can change human nature. (*Ensign*, November 1985, 6)

Of course, a danger we face when we acknowledge the Savior's omnipotence and consuming desire to help us is the temptation to believe that prayer will give us a quick fix, that our coming to him will magically solve all our problems. Just as with overcoming sin and its effects, however, so every other challenge we face, every other sorrow, trial or pain, takes time and effort to cure or overcome. The Savior removes from us the stain of sin, but we must do the repenting. The Savior removes from us sorrow and suffering, but we must pray for it and work for it. Neither sin or tribulation go away automatically or instantaneously, at least not usually. Both involve a process.

President Benson spoke of the process of repentance and spiritual progress in a way that can serve as a model for the way in which the Lord helps us through our sorrow, suffering, and pain, and eventually removes them. He said:

We must be careful, as we seek to become more and more godlike, that we do not become discouraged and lose hope. Becoming Christlike is a lifetime pursuit and very often involves growth and change that is slow, almost imperceptible. The scriptures record remarkable accounts of men whose lives changed dramatically, in an instant, as it were: Alma the Younger,

Paul on the road to Damascus, Enos praying far into the night, King Lamoni. Such astonishing examples of the power to change even those steeped in sin give confidence that the Atonement can reach even those deepest in despair.

But we must be cautious as we discuss these remarkable examples. Though they are real and powerful, they are the exception more than the rule. For every Paul, for every Enos, and for every King Lamoni, there are hundreds and thousands of people who find the process of repentance much more subtle, much more imperceptible. Day by day they move closer to the Lord, little realizing they are building a godlike life. They live quiet lives of goodness, service, and commitment. They are like the Lamanites, who the Lord said were baptized with fire and with the Holy Ghost, *and they knew it not.* (3 Ne. 9:20; italics added.) . . .

Finally, we must remember that most repentance does not involve sensational or dramatic changes, but rather is a step-by-step, steady, and consistent movement toward godliness. (*Ensign,* October 1989, 26)

I believe the pattern President Benson describes is the pattern for the way the Lord helps us through sorrow, pain, trials, and suffering. Sometimes there is immediate deliverance, but most of the time, the results are less dramatic. We must take smaller steps of persistent, continual growth and progress. The Lord is at the helm and knows what is best for us—how to help us through our trials while accomplishing his purposes. He will get us safely home with the greatest blessing and advantage to us. We must not lose hope or confidence in our Master.

Life in the Lord is a refiner's fire. Elder James E. Faust said: "For some, the refiner's fire causes a loss of belief and faith in God, but those with eternal perspective understand that such refining is part of the perfection process" (*Ensign*, May 1979, 53).

There is another important parallel, which we cannot ignore, between repentance, or the removal of our sins, and the removal of other kinds of sorrow, suffering, pain and anguish thrust upon us from causes other than our sins. Christ removes the stain of our sins and extends forgiveness to us with the requirement that we forgive others. Likewise, other kinds of hurt, trauma, sorrow and suffering will not go away until we have extended forgiveness to others, including those who have offended us. Joseph Smith experienced the bitter cup, or the "cup of gall," as he referred to it, many times in his life—most of them not of his own making. He knew better than most the contradictions and unfairness of life. He sought to do the Lord's will but was met with horrible treatment. Yet, like the Savior, the Prophet was quick to extend mercy and forgiveness to those who sought it, even if they had caused significant injury and harm to himself and the Lord's work.

One example is the treacherous betrayal of the Prophet and the Saints in Missouri by W. W. Phelps. Nonetheless, Joseph extended his sincere forgiveness when the penitent Phelps came around. In language recalling images of the Savior in Gethsemane, the Prophet wrote to Brother Phelps to welcome him back to the fold. And in so doing, Joseph allowed us a window of insight into how close to the Savior he really was, how much he truly understood Gethsemane, and how much he had internalized what transpired there. Following is part of Joseph's letter to Brother Phelps:

Dear Brother Phelps:—I must say that it is with no ordinary feelings I endeavor to write a few lines to you in answer to [your letter]; at the same time I am rejoiced at the privilege granted me.

You may in some measure realize what my feelings, as well as Elder Rigdon's and Brother Hyrum's were, when we read your letter—truly our hearts were melted into tenderness and compassion when we ascertained your resolves. . . .

It is true, that we have suffered much in consequence of your behavior—the cup of gall, already full enough for mortals to drink, was indeed filled to overflowing when you turned against us. . . .

However, the cup has been drunk, the will of our Father has been done, and we are yet alive, for which we thank the Lord. And having been delivered from the hands of wicked men by the mercy of our God, we say it is your privilege to be delivered from the powers of the adversary, be brought into the liberty of God's dear children, and again take your stand among the Saints of the Most High, and by diligence, humility, and love unfeigned, commend yourself to our God, and your God, and to the Church of Jesus Christ.

Believing your confession to be real, and your repentance genuine, I shall be happy once again to give you the right hand of fellowship, and rejoice over the returning prodigal. . . .

"Come on, dear brother, since the war is past,
For friends at first, are friends again at last."
(*History of the Church*, 4:162–64)

We must become like Jesus. We must follow the example of Joseph Smith.

## GRATITUDE FOR GETHSEMANE

None of us in this life will escape sin, trials, tribulations, pain, or suffering. To whom, then, shall we turn for the help we so desperately need? Who possesses the kind of power to fulfill all the promises of redemption and exaltation made in the scriptures? It is Jesus Christ. In him we are secure in our hope for help.

Through his experience in Gethsemane, the Savior extends his mercy to sinners and his comfort and help to the forlorn and forsaken. He can never forget us nor forsake us. I believe it is simply not in his makeup to be able to do so or even to think of doing so. What Jesus said to ancient Israel in his role as Jehovah is more applicable than ever because it describes his relationship to us: "Can a woman forget her sucking child, that she should not have compassion on the son of her womb? yea, they may forget, yet will I not forget thee" (Isaiah 49:15).

The words of the apostle Paul are equally reassuring. He too was a man who had significant acquaintance with suffering stemming from his sins as well as his actions for righteousness' sake. He said: "Who shall separate us from the love of Christ? shall tribulation, or distress, or persecution, or famine, or nakedness, or peril, or sword?" (Romans 8:35).

Because of Gethsemane, Jesus is able to be our Great Consoler. Elder Orson F. Whitney described the purpose of trials and suffering in a way that links us with the Savior's experiences in Gethsemane and on the cross: "Is not this God's purpose in causing his children to suffer? He wants them to become more like himself. God has suffered far more than man ever did or ever will, and is therefore the great source of sympathy and consolation" (*Improvement Era*, November 1918, 7).

Why would anyone choose to ignore the bitter cup? Why would anyone choose not to embrace the Savior's atonement? Why would anyone think it more advantageous to go it alone in the world or think it advisable to try to pay for one's own mistakes and sins? President Joseph Fielding Smith flatly stated that if we are rebellious and ignore the Atonement, "we will have to pay the price ourselves" (*Doctrines of Salvation*, 1:131).

But more than that, there is an infinite difference between mere repayment and complete redemption. The Savior's experience in Gethsemane not only satisfies the demands of justice by returning us to the level of non-sinfulness required for entrance into God's kingdom but actually makes justice our friend. The Savior's atonement is able to bring us back into a right relationship with God—which we call the doctrine of justification—and set us on the path of sanctification until we actually become like God. Because of Gethsemane, all of life's unfair circumstances will be made up to us. Because of Gethsemane, Jesus is able to be a merciful God and also a just and perfect God as well. Because of Gethsemane, Jesus is able to lift us to new heights and a new way of life, able to empower us, build us, and put all things right for us.

The Savior's power is of staggering, even infinite, proportions in its ability to change us and make us into something we could not otherwise become. The Savior's experience in Gethsemane removes the effects of the Fall, the bitterness of life, and allows us to glimpse heaven. Stephen Robinson put it this way:

All the negative aspects of human existence brought about by the Fall, Jesus Christ absorbed into himself. He experienced vicariously in Gethsemane all the private griefs and heartaches, all the physical pains and handicaps, all the emotional burdens and depressions of the human family. He knows the loneliness of those who don't fit in, or who aren't handsome or pretty. He knows what it's like to choose up teams and be the last one chosen. He knows the anguish of parents whose children go wrong. He knows these things personally and intimately because he lived them in the Gethsemane experience. Having personally lived a perfect life, he then chose to experience our imperfect lives. In that infinite Gethsemane experience, in the meridian of time, the center of eternity, he lived a billion billion lifetimes of sin, pain, disease, and sorrow.

God has no magic wand with which to simply wave bad things into nonexistence. The sins that he remits, he remits by making them his own and suffering them. The pain and heartache that he relieves, he relieves by suffering them himself. These things can be transferred, but they cannot be simply wished or waved away. They must be suffered. Thus, we owe him not only for our spiritual cleansing from sin but for our physical, mental and emotional healings as well, for he has borne these infirmities for us also. All that the Fall put wrong, the Savior in his atonement puts right. It is all part of his infinite sacrifice—of his infinite gift. (Religious Education prayer meeting, 12 February 1992)

When I wonder how and why Jesus did what he did in

148

Gethsemane, when I try to take it all in, to absorb the infinite, I am reduced to inadequate expressions. To use Elder Neal A. Maxwell's phrase, Gethsemane was "enormity multiplied by infinity" (*Ensign*, May 1985, 78). I cannot succinctly explain the how and why. And then I realize that no more profound words were probably ever spoken than by my little friend Brittany: "That's Jesus, and he loves us. All of us!"

# Golgotha

# Introduction

Golgotha is a necessary sequel to Gethsemane, for what began in the Garden of Gethsemane was completed on the cross of Golgotha and ultimately in the Garden Tomb. In Gethsemane Jesus of Nazareth absorbed to himself all of the sins, sorrows, sufferings, and heartaches of the whole human family—those living on this earth and on countless others like it. In Gethsemane he confronted horrors the likes of which most of us may glimpse but not really comprehend. In Gethsemane Jesus became us, so to speak, each one of us, so that we can become like him (2 Corinthians 5:21). In Gethsemane Jesus consumed the bitter cup so that we will not have to. But Gethsemane was not the end of the bitter cup. At Golgotha the bitter cup was refilled and drunk again. In the economy of the universe, Golgotha had to follow Gethsemane. Without Golgotha Gethsemane would have been incomplete. As Elder Bruce R. McConkie noted, "In some way, incomprehensible to us, Gethsemane, the cross, and the empty tomb join into one grand and eternal drama, in the course of which Jesus

1

abolishes death, and out of which comes immortality for all and eternal life for the righteous" (*Mortal Messiah*, 4:224).

The essence of Golgotha for the Savior was abandonment in the face of treachery and malicious treatment. The lesson of Golgotha for us is meekness and character—the pure, unadulterated, unparalleled personality and makeup of our Lord. Golgotha is as profound a story of unsurpassed concern for others in the face of violence and vileness as will ever be found. Even in the throes of death, when he was experiencing the greatest suffering and most undeserved treatment ever known, the Savior of the universe was thinking of others—his family, his associates, all of us, and his literal Father (our Father in Heaven). In my lifetime I have both seen and heard of the kind of character possessed by the Savior, who took what was meted out solely for the sake of others and the kingdom of God. Those modern examples have helped me to understand more clearly what was truly accomplished on a far greater scale at Golgotha.

Years ago, as a full-time missionary for The Church of Jesus Christ of Latter-day Saints, I was told by a trustworthy source about a man who had been called to serve a mission in the Southern States many decades before. He arrived in the mission field only to find out from the president that his companion's arrival would be delayed. Therefore, he was asked to go alone to a certain town and do what he could until a companion could join him. (Things were a little less formal in those days.) He accepted the assignment, went to the town (which had not seen missionaries for a long time), and began to look for odd jobs or community service projects. He hoped that by doing so he could create some goodwill in the community and thereby establish a foundation of relationships upon which he and his future companion could build.

A few days passed, and still no companion arrived. Word began to spread that the Mormons were in town—and they were not welcome. When this elder returned to his lodgings at night, usually without having found any townsfolk interested even in free labor, he began to be accosted in the back streets and alleyways by the local bullies. He defended himself as best he could—sometimes even admirably (he had been a boxer before he entered the mission field)—but he could not fend off three or four opponents at a time. He became discouraged and felt completely abandoned. To be beaten up every night was depressing and painful. But to suffer unjust punishment for something good he was trying to accomplish, something that had been asked of him by Church leaders, was truly demoralizing and a challenge to his faith.

Nevertheless, he hung on and prayed every day that the Lord would hurry and send him a companion. Years later he said that he had told the Lord he didn't care one bit if the companion knew anything about the gospel, "just let him be a fighter!"

The message of this missionary's deeds had a powerful and profound effect on me, who many decades later was trying to muster enough gumption and maturity to go forth and be a powerful servant like the one in the story. I did not immediately make any connection with the Savior or Golgotha. The missionary in the story was purely a hero to me then. But in the years that have followed, I have come to see that this missionary was more like the Savior than I fathomed at the time. I had not yet read Doctrine and Covenants 138, Joseph F. Smith's 1918 vision of the redemption of the dead, because it was not at that time part of our official canon (it was adopted as part of the standard works in 1976). Since then, however, I have come to see the connection between the Savior's enduring sacrifice and the sacrifice of the missionary in the story—and, in fact, the connection between the Savior on the cross at Golgotha and the sacrifices of all the righteous in any age who offer their best in the face of malicious treatment, feelings of being abandoned by God, depression, demoralizing challenges, destitution, hardship, or other tribulations. The missionary in the story was an illustration of, indeed a similitude of, Jesus' experience at Golgotha. As President Joseph F. Smith saw in vision:

> There were gathered together in one place an innumerable company of the spirits of the just, who had been faithful in the testimony of Jesus while they lived in mortality;
>
> And who had offered sacrifice in the similitude of the great sacrifice of the Son of God, and had suffered tribulation in their Redeemer's name. (D&C 138:12–13)

Ultimately, the circumstances of the missionary in the story did come to some resolution. One day he received a telegram from the mission president indicating that he was to meet a companion at the train station at such and such a time. He went to the station with some hope, but that feeling changed back to hopelessness as passenger after passenger filed off the train without any sign of a missionary companion. As the last of the passengers departed, he was turning away in despair when out of the corner of his eye, he caught a glimpse of something shiny. He turned to see what it was. Staring him in the face was the biggest belt buckle he had ever seen in his life. Filling the doorframe of the railroad car was the figure of a six-foot-six-inch-tall cowboy from Wyoming—his new companion. Immediately things began to look up (in more ways than one)!

I do not recall hearing that the set of missionaries had any success in that place, at least as success is measured by baptisms. I do remember hearing that the missionaries "began to clean up the town." As it turned out, the missionary from Wyoming had grown up on a ranch, roping and wrestling cattle. A few town bullies did not intimidate him. I remember thinking at the time that God always hears and answers the prayers of his servants. I still have a conviction that such a doctrine is true, but I have also come to know that storybook endings do not always occur in mortality. Rather, God honors and rewards the sacrifices of those who love him, whether in this life or in the next. He is able to do so precisely because of the infinite sacrifice of his Beloved Son, who, after experiencing Gethsemane, did not shrink from Golgotha but saw it through to its end and thus was willing to forgo a happy ending in mortality to ensure a happy ending in eternity.

Ultimately, all of our hopes, dreams, and righteous desires come down to the meekness and character of Christ. I hope that the story of Golgotha as told in the following pages will increase our appreciation for the meekness and character of the sinless Son of God. The story of Golgotha leaves us with the lasting impression that all things truly testify of Christ, for all of Israelite history, prophecy, ritual, symbolism, and religious institutions pointed to the Savior and were fulfilled in him.

---

And while he yet spake, lo, Judas, one of the twelve, came, and with him a great multitude with swords and staves, from the chief priests and elders of the people.

Now he that betrayed him gave them a sign, saying, Whomsoever I shall kiss, that same is he: hold him fast.

And forthwith he came to Jesus, and said, Hail, master; and kissed him.

And Jesus said unto him, Friend, wherefore art thou come? Then came they, and laid hands on Jesus, and took him.

And, behold, one of them which were with Jesus stretched out his hand, and drew his sword, and struck a servant of the high priest's, and smote off his ear.

MATTHEW 26:47–51

---

# CHAPTER 1

# Betrayal and Arrest

We do not know how long Jesus endured the agony of Gethsemane, but surely its toll is to be measured in intensity rather than simply length. The noted English theologian and biographer of Christ, Frederic Farrar, called Gethsemane "a grief beyond utterance, a struggle beyond endurance, a horror of great darkness. . . . how dreadful was that paroxysm of prayer and suffering through which He passed" (*Life of Christ*, 553).

From a purely human perspective, it must have looked as though the bloodied and tear-stained Son of God suffered nothing more than the tragedy and disgrace of emotional breakdown. After all, the Messiah was supposed to be a conqueror, not a sufferer, and the apostles knew it—else why would they "be sore amazed, and . . . be very heavy, and . . . complain in their hearts, wondering if this be the Messiah" (JST Mark 14:36).

But the Savior was not out to impress either onlookers or associates. He was focused singly on doing his Father's will, even when it meant that divine wrath had to be poured out on the Son because he was absorbing for us the eternal punishments deserved for every law mankind has ever broken. "Jesus always deserved and always had the Father's full approval. But when He took our sins upon Him, of divine necessity required by justice He experienced instead 'the fierceness of the wrath of Almighty God' (D&C 76:107; 88:106)" (Maxwell, *Lord, Increase Our Faith*, 13). In Gethsemane Jesus suffered the wrath of God—the wrath of divine justice—so that we do not have to. He suffered the wrath and ravages of spiritual death and hell so that you and I can escape it. As President Joseph Fielding Smith said:

> Jesus did come into the world to ransom it. Through his atonement we were bought from death and hell. Death and hell were paid—paid in full—and Christ was the only one who could pay that debt. . . .
>
> . . . He carried, in some way that I cannot understand and you cannot understand, the burden of the combined weight of the sins of the world. It is hard enough for me to carry my own transgressions, and it is hard enough for you to carry yours. . . . I have seen [people] cry out in anguish because of their transgressions—just one individual's sins. Can you comprehend the suffering of Jesus Christ when he carried, not merely by physical manifestation but in some spiritual and mental condition or manner, the combined weight of sin? . . .
>
> . . . This extreme suffering—which was beyond the power of mortal man either to accomplish or endure—was undertaken because of the great love which the Father and the Son had for mankind. (*Doctrines of Salvation*, 1:125, 129–30, 131)

Sin brings divine wrath because God cannot tolerate sin or look upon it with the least degree of allowance (D&C 1:31), nor can sin be tolerated in a universe framed by the perfect, pure, and fair law of justice. God's physical makeup, his holiness and purity, make it impossible for him to tolerate or withstand any kind of sinful environment. Christ's atonement removes from us the intolerable taint or stain of sin.

From an eternal perspective, we know that when Jesus had finished praying the same prayer three times in Gethsemane, he had gained a victory of monumental, unequaled proportions. He had fulfilled perfectly his Father's will up to that point, knowing even then that he had yet to face the agony of the cross and drain again the dregs of the bitter cup refilled.

## The Kiss of Betrayal

The Gospel writers tell us that as Jesus addressed his sleeping apostles for the final time in the Garden of Gethsemane after he had finished praying, he was met by a multitude of chief priests and elders—the police force of the Jerusalem Temple—brandishing weapons and led by none other than Judas Iscariot, one of the Twelve Apostles, who was to identify Jesus by the prearranged signal of a kiss (Matthew 26:48). So began a series of exhausting events after an already long night, events that culminated in the Crucifixion, events that provide us with a profound lesson in loyalty.

John's unique account of events that occurred after Jesus concluded his time in Gethsemane reminds us that Judas knew where to find Jesus during those wee hours of the morning because "Jesus ofttimes resorted thither with his disciples" (John 18:2). In other words, Jesus had gone often to Gethsemane on several occasions *before* his atoning act, and

Judas knew it. Even more significant, John alone describes the remarkable scene that indicates Judas's kiss was not the sole mark of identification but that Jesus proactively initiated an exchange between himself and his stalkers:

> Jesus therefore, knowing all things that should come upon him, went forth, and said unto them, Whom seek ye?
>
> They answered him, Jesus of Nazareth. Jesus saith unto them, *I am* he. And Judas also, which betrayed him, stood with them.
>
> As soon then as he had said unto them, *I am* he, they went backward, and fell to the ground.
>
> Then asked he them again, Whom seek ye? And they said, Jesus of Nazareth.
>
> Jesus answered, I have told you that *I am* he: if therefore ye seek me, let these go their way:
>
> That the saying might be fulfilled, which he spake, Of them which thou gavest me have I lost none.
>
> Then Simon Peter having a sword drew it, and smote the high priest's servant, and cut off his right ear. The servant's name was Malchus. (John 18:4–10; emphasis added)

The tone of this episode seems to indicate that in Gethsemane's dark shadows Jesus was not immediately recognized, hence the response of the arresting mob to Jesus' question about whom they were seeking. They do not say, "It is you we are seeking." They say, "Jesus of Nazareth." In the darkness Jesus did not immediately look appreciably different from the apostles surrounding him. But Jesus was no shy or retiring leader. Neither did he fear his captors. He boldly identified himself to the mob by using language that equated him with God—"I Am." That is the very name of Deity as revealed to Moses (Exodus 3:13–14). The translators of the King James Version of the Bible added the word *he* after each use of the phrase "I Am" in this passage, believing it rounded out the translation. Without that added word, however, we can understand more readily why the chief priests and elders responded as they did, for when they heard Jesus utter those words, they fell backward to the ground—as might anyone who has had the wind knocked out of him because God himself has just responded to his inquiry. To say that Jesus' words were shocking to the chief priests and elders is an understatement of greatest proportion. We suppose that it was not only *what* Jesus said but *how* he said it. That is, the force of Jesus' response, indeed his very presence and power of personality, had a stunning effect on the armed mob: Jesus spoke with heavenly power.

Elder Parley P. Pratt witnessed a similar scene when he was incarcerated in Richmond, Missouri, with Joseph Smith. Like Jesus, the Prophet had been betrayed into the hands of enemies by a trusted associate. One evening in the jail, Elder Pratt saw the Prophet Joseph speak with the same kind of power that had caused Jesus' captors to fall backwards in stunned silence, overcome by the force of Jesus' words. Elder Pratt described his experience:

> In one of those tedious nights we had lain as if in sleep till the hour of midnight had passed, and our ears and hearts had been pained, while we had listened for hours to the obscene jests, the horrid oaths, the dreadful blasphemies and filthy language of our guards . . . as they recounted to each other their deeds of rapine,

murder, robbery, etc., which they had committed among the "*Mormons*" while at Far West and vicinity. They even boasted of defiling by force wives, daughters, and virgins, and of shooting or dashing out the brains of men, women and children.

I had listened till I became so disgusted, shocked, horrified, and so filled with the spirit of indignant justice, that I could scarcely refrain from rising upon my feet and rebuking the guards; but had said nothing to Joseph, or anyone else, although I lay next to him and knew he was awake. On a sudden he arose to his feet, and spoke in a voice of thunder, or as the roaring lion, uttering, as near as I can recollect, the following words:

'SILENCE, *ye fiends of the infernal pit. In the name of Jesus Christ I rebuke you, and command you to be still. I will not live another minute and bear such language. Cease such talk, or you or I die THIS INSTANT!*'

He ceased to speak. He stood erect in terrible majesty. Chained, and without a weapon; calm, unruffled and dignified as an angel, he looked upon the quailing guards . . . whose knees smote together, and who, shrinking into a corner, or crouching at his feet, begged his pardon, and remained quiet till a change of guards.

I have seen ministers of justice, clothed in magisterial robes, and criminals arraigned before them, while life was suspended on a breath, in the Courts of England; I have witnessed a Congress in solemn session to give laws to nations; I have tried to conceive of kings, of royal courts, of thrones and crowns; and of emperors assembled to decide the fate of kingdoms; but dignity and majesty have I seen but *once*, as it stood in chains, at midnight, in a dungeon in an obscure village of Missouri. (Pratt, *Autobiography*, 262–63)

*Dignity* and *majesty* are words that truly describe the Savior on the night of his arrest, even though he was in his extremity, suffering incomprehensibly, and surrounded by armed assailants, just as the Prophet Joseph Smith would be.

The synoptic Gospels report that Judas did step forward and verify the identity of his Master by kissing him, but they make no mention of Jesus' identifying himself to the armed mob as the Gospel of John does. Nonetheless, Judas's kiss has become the hallmark event of the night of betrayal. That there is exact and pointed agreement among the synoptic gospels regarding Judas's position as a member of the Quorum of the Twelve Apostles perhaps reflects the shock and intensity with which that moment was felt by those disciples present. Surely the fact that Judas held the keys of the apostleship, along with the other special witnesses, added to the Savior's grief as Judas singled him out. After all, do we not learn that in all dispensations of time loyalty to one's brethren always was and always will be essential? (Proverbs 6:16, 19; John 17:11; D&C 38:27). There seem to be few things that the Lord abhors more than disloyalty. Conversely, there are few things as highly prized as loyalty and true friendship. The Prophet Joseph Smith said on one occasion:

> I don't care what a man's character is; if he's my friend—a true friend, I will be a friend to him, and preach the Gospel of salvation to him, and give him good counsel, helping him out of his difficulties.
>
> Friendship is one of the grand fundamental principles of 'Mormonism'; [it is designed] to revolutionize and

civilize the world, and cause wars and contentions to cease and men to become friends and brothers. . . .

It is a time-honored adage that love begets love. Let us pour forth love—show forth our kindness unto all mankind, and the Lord will reward us with everlasting increase; cast our bread upon the waters and we shall receive it after many days, increased to a hundredfold. (*Teachings of the Prophet Joseph Smith*, 316)

The great kiss of betrayal evokes an irony matched by few other episodes. By New Testament times, a kiss in public was a symbol both of distinction and of elevation. Among the ancient Israelites, a kiss often signified reconciliation between separated or estranged parties, as when Esau ran to Jacob after a long and wrenching conflict and "embraced him, and fell on his neck, and kissed him: and they wept" (Genesis 33:4). After years of separation, Joseph "kissed all his brethren, and wept upon them: and after that his brethren talked with him" (Genesis 45:15). When the Lord sent Aaron to meet Moses, he found him "in the mount of God, and kissed him" (Exodus 4:27).

Among the later Jews, a kiss was a token of respect with which pupils or disciples greeted their great rabbis or teachers. Among Christians, a kiss was a demonstration of fellowship and brotherhood. When he was visiting Simon the Pharisee's house, the Savior rebuked Simon, saying, "Thou gavest me no kiss" (Luke 7:45). The apostle Paul counseled early Church brethren to "greet all the brethren with an holy kiss" (1 Thessalonians 5:26). In our own day, one recalls that President Spencer W. Kimball was fond of greeting some of his associates and friends with a kiss on the cheek. I vividly remember a teenage friend telling me of walking along a street in downtown Salt Lake

City with his father several years before. All of a sudden there was a flurry of activity as an energetic old man came running across the street, stopping traffic, walking up to his father, and greeting him with a kiss on the cheek. Much to my friend's surprise, he found himself staring at President Kimball. My friend's father had been called as a stake president several years earlier by then-Elder Kimball, and they had remained close friends. President Kimball's kiss was a tangible sign of his respect and affection.

The custom of greeting special friends with a kiss is still current in certain Middle Eastern countries. A few years ago, I was with a group of American students in Egypt, waiting for a guide who would take us to some archaeological sites. As it turned out, the guide assigned to us that day was a wonderful man who had become a friend through the years. Therefore, when he arrived, he immediately walked over to me and kissed me on both cheeks, much to the surprise of the students gathered in the parking lot of our Cairo hotel.

Proverbs 27:6 thus becomes even more poignant as we reflect on the episode involving Judas Iscariot in the Garden of Gethsemane that awful Thursday night: "Faithful are the wounds of a friend: but the kisses of an enemy are deceitful." How the kiss from Judas must have stung the Savior as he remembered the verse from Proverbs. And how Judas must have been taken aback by the Savior's rejoinders: "*Friend*, wherefore are thou come?" (Matthew 26:50; emphasis added) and "Betrayest thou the Son of Man with a kiss?" (Luke 22:48). Could a greater indictment of guilt have been leveled at Judas than with the single word *friend?* Or could there have been a greater expression of devastated disappointment uttered than the question, "You're betraying me with a *kiss?*"

The Greek word Matthew used to describe Judas's kiss, *kataphileo*, means "to kiss earnestly, intensely." It is used elsewhere in certain stories in the Gospels to imply a deep, affectionate, reverential worship of Jesus. That Judas betrayed the guileless Son of God while pretending deep and earnest affection for him makes Judas's deed all the more despicable.

## THE ARREST AND THE TEMPLE CONNECTION

The composition of the group that came to arrest Jesus is significant. Luke indicates the mob included "the chief priests, and captains of the temple, and the elders" (Luke 22:52)—all associated with the Temple. The chief priests preserved spiritual order by performing the ordinances of Aaronic Priesthood temple worship (the Temple at Jerusalem was not a Melchizedek Priesthood temple), the captains of the Temple kept physical order on the Temple Mount, and the elders were spiritual and social leaders who taught in the Temple. Some scholars have even suggested that the elders came from the ranks of the priests, who, of course, had responsibility to serve in the Temple. (The term *elder* in Judaism of the first century after Christ is not to be confused with the Melchizedek Priesthood office.) The "captains of the temple" were officials known from Old Testament times.

The arresting party was essentially the same group of conspirators responsible for planning the seizure and execution, indeed the premeditated murder, of Jesus just a couple of days earlier, as Matthew had reported:

And it came to pass, when Jesus had finished all these sayings, he said unto his disciples,

Ye know that after two days is the feast of the passover, and the Son of man is betrayed to be crucified.

Then assembled together the chief priests, and the
scribes, and the elders of the people, unto the palace of
the high priest, who was called Caiaphas,

And consulted that they might take Jesus by sub-
tilty, and kill him. (Matthew 26:1–4; Mark 14:1)

Additionally, Luke comments that "the captains" of the
Temple were among Judas's initial contacts with whom he
worked out the details of the betrayal and, thus, were among
the conspirators (Luke 22:4).

The irony is that the Temple was supposed to be the
house of the Lord, meaning the home of both our Father in
Heaven and his Son Jesus Christ. At the first cleansing of the
Temple, at the beginning of his ministry, Jesus had referred to
the Temple as "my Father's house" (John 2:16). And at the
second cleansing, at the end of his ministry, he had referred
to the Temple as "my house" (Matthew 21:13). The Temple
was supposed to be the place of supreme sanctity. In reality it
had become the habitation of the wicked. Little wonder that
when Jesus uttered his last lament over Jerusalem just a couple
of days before his arrest, he implied that the Divine Presence
had altogether abandoned the Temple structure: "Behold, *your*
house is left unto *you* desolate" (Matthew 23:38; emphasis
added). Because those responsible for the care of the Temple
were also responsible for the Savior's premeditated murder, the
Temple was ripe for destruction. That destruction came a few
decades later (A.D. 70) at the hands of the very Romans who
helped with the arrest and execution of the Lord.

The Gospel of John implies that the arresting band

contained Roman soldiers as well. The word *band* in the King James Version (John 18:3) is translated from the Greek word for *cohort*, a subdivision of the Roman army. Presumably, Roman leadership at some level was persuaded to help with the arrest, though they probably were not in on the actual conspiracy to take Jesus' life. Having Roman soldiers in the group of Temple officers who went to arrest Jesus would have given Jewish leaders and conspirators the cloak of official business and government power to hide behind. They feared the Savior's power and his popularity with the people. Mark makes this clear: "And the scribes and chief priests heard it, and sought how they might destroy him: for they feared him, because all the people was astonished at his doctrine" (Mark 11:18). Thus, the conspirators insisted that the arrest not take place during the feast of the Passover in order to avoid a possible riot (Matthew 26:4–5). Luke adds that they extracted a promise from Judas that he would betray Jesus "in the absence of the multitude" (Luke 22:6).

## PETER AND THE HIGH PRIEST'S SERVANT

All of the Gospels report that as Jesus was being arrested, a scuffle ensued. The chief apostle was at the center of it. Peter showed no hesitation in defending the life of his Master by force in the face of overwhelming odds, though only the Gospel of John mentions Peter by name. He drew his short sword, the kind Galilean fishermen used, and cut off the ear of Malchus, the servant of the high priest (John 18:10). That action, in turn, drew a stern rebuke from the Savior to put away the sword. Those who live by the sword are destined to die by the sword, and Jesus did not want anything to happen to his chief apostle, the future earthly head of the Church.

In fact, Jesus likely averted combat between the apostles and the armed mob with a comment he had made earlier, in the upper room. When trying to teach his apostles that he would shortly be arrested, tried, and "reckoned among the transgressors," and that they needed to be prepared for what lay ahead, the apostles misunderstood the kind of preparation he meant, and they said, "Lord, behold, here are two swords." Jesus answered, "It is enough," meaning, that was enough of such foolish talk (Luke 22:37–38). Had the apostles tried to arm themselves more fully, a real blood bath might have ensued at the arrest of Jesus. As it was, Judas's kiss, combined with the mob's initial overtures to arrest Jesus, evoked from the apostles a question about whether or not to retaliate: "Lord, shall we smite with the sword?" (Luke 22:49). Before Jesus could respond, Peter acted out his misplaced determination to defend his Master.

In rebuking Peter for his attack on Malchus, Jesus asked if Peter didn't realize that he could immediately summon more than twelve legions of angels from God the Father to defend himself? (Matthew 26:53). In first-century Roman Judea, the chief subdivision of the imperial army was a legion, a unit composed of up to six thousand foot soldiers, plus cavalry. What an army of angelic warriors that would have been! Twelve legions of angels—seventy-two thousand heavenly warriors with incomprehensible power at their disposal. It will be remembered that one angel of the Lord in a single night slew 185,000 Assyrian warriors when they threatened the city of Jerusalem in 701 B.C. (2 Kings 19:35). The people in Jesus' day knew very well the structure and power of the Roman military, and such an image would not have been lost on any who heard the Savior's question that night.

The Savior's rebuke of Peter included a reminder to all the other apostles that the ordeal of the bitter cup was not yet finished and that the remaining ordeal was the Father's will. Jesus asked them, "The cup which my Father hath given me, shall I not drink it?" (John 18:11). Certainly the Savior had unlimited power at his disposal. But his purpose that night was to bless, not to destroy. He was now unalterably committed to carry out the supreme saving mission of the Father and thus fulfill the scriptures. He was loyal to the Father at all costs.

Peter's seemingly impulsive action adds yet another confirming witness to our understanding of the chief apostle's unwavering sense of loyalty. His action against Malchus is in perfect harmony with the consistent portrayal in the Gospels of a chief apostle who acted fearlessly to keep Jesus out of harm's way by any means at his disposal. Malchus could very well have been a high-ranking servant of the high priest because he was in the front of the mob, leading the enforcement of the Temple conspirators' wishes. It is likely that Peter was aiming not for Malchus's ear but rather his head and that Malchus was fortunate to lose only his ear by means of deft maneuvering. Remarkably, Jesus healed the man's ear on the spot, but even that miraculous act apparently gave no one pause to consider who it was they were arresting (Luke 22:51). This is another of the great ironies of this whole drama that demonstrate, again and again, the unsurpassed character and meekness of the Master. Poise in the face of provocation, concern for others despite personal tribulation and hardship—these are characteristics of the kind of meekness the Savior displayed, and these characteristics are a true measure of just how closely we mirror Christlike behavior in our own lives.

The healing of Malchus's ear is the last of the Savior's

recorded miracles in mortality, before the occurrence of the greatest miracle of all time: the Resurrection. It seems significant that only Luke—the physician interested in physiological matters, the disciple whose Gospel contains the only biblical description of the Savior's bloody sweat in Gethsemane, the writer who preserves the account of the Savior's compassionate act of raising the widow's son from death—he alone describes the healing of Malchus by the mortal Son of God, who was experiencing his own greatest distress. From this account we see again Luke's interest in the workings of the physical body and, even more, in the Savior's unwavering compassion, which are hallmarks of his Gospel record.

---

*Then said Jesus unto him, Put up again thy sword into his place: for all they that take the sword shall perish with the sword.*

*Thinkest thou that I cannot now pray to my Father, and he shall presently give me more than twelve legions of angels?*

*But how then shall the scriptures be fulfilled, that thus it must be?*

*In that same hour said Jesus to the multitudes, Are ye come out as against a thief with swords and staves for to take me? I sat daily with you teaching in the temple, and ye laid no hold on me.*

*But all this was done, that the scriptures of the prophets might be fulfilled. Then all the disciples forsook him, and fled.*

MATTHEW 26:52–56

*Then the band and the captain and officers of the Jews took Jesus, and bound him.*

JOHN 18:12

*And there followed him a certain young man, having a linen cloth cast about his naked body; and the young men laid hold on him:*
*And he left the linen cloth, and fled from them naked.*

MARK 14:51–52

---

# CHAPTER 2

# Prophecy Fulfilled in the Arrest

With the miracle of healing accomplished and Malchus made whole, Jesus was seized by the police force and "led away with a rope around his neck, as a common criminal, to be judged by the arch-criminals who as Jews sat in Aaron's seat" (McConkie, "Purifying Power of Gethsemane," 9). Of all those who have written about Jesus' arrest, Elder Bruce R. McConkie alone describes a rope around the Savior's neck, an insight that cannot be ascribed to anything other than the visionary gift of a modern apostolic witness.

The irony, the contradiction inherent in this situation, is overwhelming: arch-criminals judging the Sinless One, who was forced to play the role of a base criminal. With a noose around his neck, Jesus fulfilled the symbolism of the scapegoat in the Israelite sacrificial system—the animal upon whose head the sins of the people were laid on the Day of Atonement and who was led away to be released into the wilderness to perish bearing those sins (Leviticus 16:21–22).

## JESUS AND ISAAC

Jesus' arrest and seizure fulfilled Old Testament symbolism in another powerful way. John tells us that "the band and the captain and officers of the Jews took Jesus, and *bound* him" (John 18:12; emphasis added). The perfect foreshadowing of the Master's binding was the binding of Isaac by Abraham, or what the Jews call the *Akedah*, the Binding of Isaac. "And they came to the place which God had told him of; and Abraham built an altar there, and laid the wood in order, and bound Isaac his son, and laid him on the altar upon the wood" (Genesis 22:9). Just as Isaac meekly submitted to God's will and his father's intent to offer him as a sacrifice, so too Jesus meekly submitted to God's will and his Father's intent to offer him as the great and last sacrifice in order to bring salvation to those who believe on his name (Alma 34:14–15).

Undoubtedly that is why the Book of Mormon prophet Jacob taught that "it was accounted unto Abraham in the wilderness to be obedient unto the commands of God in offering up his son Isaac, which is a similitude of God and his Only Begotten Son" (Jacob 4:5). Not only did the binding of Isaac point to and correspond with the binding of Jesus but the general locations where each event occurred pointed to and corresponded with each other. Perhaps that is the reason God commanded Abraham to go to Moriah for the sacrifice of Isaac. What happened to Isaac and where it happened foreshadowed the very thing that would happen to Jesus and where it would happen to him, as Abraham himself came to understand: "And Abraham called the name of that place Jehovah-jireh [literally, "Jehovah will be seen"]: as it is said to this day, In the mount of the Lord it shall be seen" [or, "In a mount the Lord shall be manifest"] (Genesis 22:14). The Savior would be seen in the place where Isaac once was.

Jewish teachings about the *Akedah,* or the Binding of Isaac, speak of the "ashes of Isaac," as though Abraham had actually completed the sacrifice because Abraham's unwavering intention was to complete it. In other words, God regarded the intent of Abraham's heart to follow through with the sacrifice the same as if he had actually sacrificed Isaac. This principle is both noble and true. God judges us not only by our actions but by the righteous desires of our hearts (D&C 137:9). That is very good news, because sometimes our desires turn out to be much nobler than our actions. As Christians we believe that Abraham could possess that kind of single-minded intent to go through with the sacrifice of his son because of his faith in God's power "to raise him up, even from the dead" (Hebrews 11:19). Thus, Abraham's sacrifice of Isaac is also tied to the Resurrection and to his prophetic belief in it. Furthermore, the King James Version of the Bible emphasizes the parallel between the sacrifice of Jesus and the sacrifice of Isaac by referring to Isaac as Abraham's only begotten son, in similitude of God's Only Begotten Son: "By faith Abraham, when he was tried, offered up Isaac: and he that had received the promises offered up his only begotten son" (Hebrews 11:17). Jesus and Isaac are the only two beings in the King James Version of the Bible to whom the title "only begotten son" is applied.

But for Latter-day Saints there is another, even more remarkable, dimension of Abraham's sacrifice that makes his story much more than just a theological parallel to, or literary foreshadowing of, the sacrifice of Jesus Christ. Each one of us is called by the Savior to participate in the kind of sacrifice made by Abraham and, therefore, made by the Savior. The Savior declared to the Prophet Joseph Smith through revelation: "Therefore, they must needs be chastened and tried, even as Abraham, who was commanded to offer up his only son. For all those who will not endure chastening, but deny me, cannot be sanctified" (D&C 101:4–5). Of Abraham's sacrifice and God's requirement that each of us pass through the same experience, the Prophet Joseph further said, "The sacrifice required of Abraham in the offering up of Isaac, shows that if a man would attain to the keys of the kingdom of an endless life; he must sacrifice all things" (*Teachings of the Prophet Joseph Smith*, 322).

None of us knows when or what kind of Abrahamic tests we will pass through. But we may take heart in knowing that our experience actually parallels the experience of both Abraham and the Lord Jesus Christ. God is not only mindful of us in our trials but will aid us because he wants to exalt us. Like the Savior, we will triumph over all our foes (D&C 121:8), including the most menacing ones: sin, death, sorrow, and heartache. The binding of Isaac and the binding of Jesus teach profound lessons about the meekness to submit and the character to endure. Perhaps at some point in our lives we may feel bound by circumstances beyond our control. If we submit patiently and endure faithfully, we will receive the blessings of Abraham and the Savior—all that the Father himself possesses—so that as it was said of Abraham and Isaac, so it will be said of us: "They have entered into their exaltation, according to the promises, and sit upon thrones, and are not angels but are gods" (D&C 132:37).

President John Taylor once said that the Prophet Joseph Smith taught that eternal life cannot be gained in any other way except by being tried and proven as was Abraham but that in the testing comes a closeness to God that cannot be enjoyed in any other way: "You will have all kinds of trials to pass through. And it is quite as necessary for you to be tried as it was for Abraham and other men of God. . . . God will feel after you, and He will take hold of you and wrench your very heart strings, and if you cannot stand it, you will not be fit for an inheritance in the Celestial Kingdom of God" (*Journal of Discourses*, 24:197).

## ONE FINAL QUESTION

Standing helplessly by, as Jesus was about to be led away from Gethsemane in bondage, the disciples heard their Master ask one final, penetrating question. It pointedly reminded all those present of the connection between the members of the mob and their leadership roles in the Jerusalem Temple:

> Then Jesus said unto the chief priests, and captains of the temple, and the elders, which were come to him, Be ye come out, as against a thief, with swords and staves?
>
> When I was daily with you in the temple, ye stretched forth no hands against me: but this is your hour, and the power of darkness. (Luke 22:52–53; Matthew 26:55; Mark 14:48–49)

In one stroke, Jesus emphasized to his captors their hypocrisy as well as their depravity. He was saying, in effect, "You were in the Temple every day, in that holiest of places. I was also there, yet you didn't have the courage to arrest me openly, while I was teaching in your midst. Instead, you have come after me as though I were a thief in the night, precisely because *you* are the ones ruled by the power of darkness." The Greek original of the last clause of Luke 22:53 is actually stronger than the translation in the King James Version and might be rendered: "But this is your hour and the authority of darkness." Jesus left no doubt in the minds of the chief priest and captains of the Temple that he knew they were operating under the authority of Satan, the prince of darkness. Again, we see in Jesus remarkable teaching skills: boldness, thorough knowledge of his audience, and precision of language. We are reminded of what others have said about great teachers: They teach their audiences what they need to hear, not what they want to hear.

## THE DISCIPLES FLED

At this point, Matthew's record links the arrest and seizure of Jesus with the fulfillment of prophecy: "But all this was done, that the scriptures of the prophets might be fulfilled" (Matthew 26:56). Then there immediately follows the wrenching declaration that as Jesus was being led away, "all the disciples forsook him, and fled" (Matthew 26:56; Mark 14:50). The Savior of the world was abandoned by his closest friends. Here the heart of every modern disciple goes out to him, because most of us know in some small measure the feelings that come from being left alone. Though it is tempting to view this situation in its harshest light, regarding it as an example of supreme disloyalty, it appears that there were mitigating circumstances and that we should temper our judgment of the eleven special witnesses.

First of all, as Elder James E. Talmage observed, once the armed police force showed up, resistance to the arrest of Jesus was useless. He also noted that the apostles were in real jeopardy themselves:

The eleven apostles, seeing that resistance was useless, not only on account of disparity of numbers and
supply of weapons but chiefly because of Christ's determination to submit, turned and fled. . . . That they were
really in jeopardy is shown by an incident preserved by
Mark alone. An unnamed young man, aroused from
sleep by the tumult of the marching band, had sallied
forth with no outer covering but a linen sheet. His
interest in the arrest of Jesus and his close approach
caused some of the guardsmen or soldiers to seize him;
but he broke loose and escaped leaving the sheet in
their hands. (*Jesus the Christ*, 617)

This story of the young man fleeing is one of the strangest
in the Gospels; it is presented only in Mark 14:51–52. It cannot be referring to one of the apostles because they had all fled,
and we know nothing else about it from scripture; however, an
apocryphal document called *The Secret Gospel of Mark*, which
claims to be a fuller account of Mark's Gospel, indicates that
the man in the linen cloth was a disciple of the Master who
had come to Gethsemane to receive from the Savior special
teachings related to the mysteries of the kingdom. Such an idea
resonates with Latter-day Saints because of its obvious connection to temple ordinances. And such a concept about Jesus
initiating his disciples into the mysteries of the kingdom is sub-
stantiated in the writings and traditions of the early Church,
including the apocryphal Acts of John and Eusebius's *History
of the Church*. Be that as it may, we do not know the identity of
the young man in Mark's story, though one tradition holds that
it was Mark himself.

A second reason for tempering our view toward the fleeing

apostles that awful night comes from the testimony of John the Beloved. He takes pains to report in different portions of his Gospel how protective Jesus was of his apostles, perhaps even to the point of suggesting or encouraging their flight or dispersal from the garden, because he did not want any harm to come to them. For example, from the Savior's great high priestly prayer, we read this petition on behalf of the apostles:

> I pray for them: I pray not for the world, but for them which thou hast given me; for they are thine. . . .
>
> And now I am no more in the world, but these are in the world, and I come to thee. Holy Father, keep through thine own name those whom thou hast given me, that they may be one, as we are. . . .
>
> I have given them thy word; and the world hath hated them, because they are not of the world, even as I am not of the world.
>
> I pray not that thou shouldest take them out of the world, but that thou shouldest keep them from the evil. (John 17:9, 11, 14–15)

Finally, the Savior tried to protect his apostles and ensure their safety at the moment he was being arrested by the mob. "Then asked he them again, Whom seek ye? And they said, Jesus of Nazareth. Jesus answered, I have told you that I am he: if therefore ye seek me, let these go their way: That the saying might be fulfilled, which he spake, Of them which thou gavest me have I lost none" (John 18:7–9).

Given all we know about the dangers ready to befall the apostles at the time of Jesus' arrest, perhaps it is more instructive to think of the episode of their fleeing as a scattering caused by external forces. This seems to be the sense in which the prophet Zechariah prophesied of the event: "Awake, O sword, against my shepherd, and against the man that is my fellow, saith the Lord of hosts: smite the shepherd, and the sheep shall be scattered: and I will turn mine hand upon the little ones" (Zechariah 13:7). Certainly the Good Shepherd was struck or smitten, the sheep scattered, and the hand of the smiter turned against the little ones, or apostles.

There is no question that Jesus knew beforehand and foretold these events affecting the apostles, including the prophecy of Zechariah. When Jesus and the Quorum of the Twelve finished the Last Supper, Mark records: "And when they had sung an hymn, they went out into the mount of Olives. And Jesus saith unto them, All ye shall be offended because of me this night: for it is written, I will smite the shepherd, and the sheep shall be scattered. But after that I am risen, I will go before you into Galilee" (Mark 14:26–28). Let me emphasize that even though the apostles would be scattered, Jesus ends this prophecy on a note of optimism, saying, in effect, "Even though you're going to be scattered, we will meet again in Galilee after I am resurrected."

With the scattering of the apostles as their Master was being arrested, the die was cast. Prophecy was fulfilled. Irrevocable forces were set in motion. There was no turning back from the final events of the Savior's remaining ordeal—from the final swallows of the bitter cup.

And led him away to Annas first; for he was father in law to Caiaphas, which was the high priest that same year. . . .

The high priest then asked Jesus of his disciples, and of his doctrine.

Jesus answered him, I spake openly to the world; I ever taught in the synagogue, and in the temple, whither the Jews always resort; and in secret have I said nothing.

Why askest thou me? ask them which heard me, what I have said unto them: behold, they know what I said.

And when he had thus spoken, one of the officers which stood by struck Jesus with the palm of his hand, saying, Answerest thou the high priest so?

Jesus answered him, If I have spoken evil, bear witness of the evil: but if well, why smitest thou me?

Now Annas had sent him bound unto Caiaphas the high priest.

JOHN 18:13, 19–24

Now the chief priests, and elders, and all the council, sought false witness against Jesus, to put him to death.

. . . at the last came two false witnesses,

And said, This fellow said, I am able to destroy the temple of God, and to build it in three days.

MATTHEW 26:59–61

# CHAPTER 3

# Arraignment before the High Priests

I n the dark hours of the night or the early morning, Jesus was marched away from Gethsemane under armed guard to be interrogated by Caiaphas, the high priest who held judicial power over the Jewish people and ruled at the pleasure of Roman authorities. John tells us, however, that Jesus was first taken to a man named Annas, father-in-law to Caiaphas (John 18:13).

## ANNAS, THE POWER BROKER

Annas wielded great influence and seems to have been the real power operating behind the scenes. He himself had ruled as high priest during the days of Jesus' youth (A.D. 7–15) but had been deposed by the Romans, though he was still referred to by the title high priest (John 18:19, 22), much as Latter-day Saints often continue to refer to a man as bishop even though he is not currently officiating in the office. That Annas remained a person of tremendous influence in the Sanhedrin is attested by the fact that his son-in-law, five of his sons, and a grandson became high priest. It seems reasonable to assume that when Annas gave his approval of an action, it was carried out.

Standing before Annas, Jesus was in dreadful physical condition. By this time the Savior had already been awake for an entire day and night. He had experienced the bloody agony in Gethsemane and been forced to cross the Kidron Valley, marching up its steep western slope to the residence of Annas on the western hill of Jerusalem where the wealthy and powerful lived. Ancient stone steps still mark the likely path. Jesus stood before Annas in bloody garments. He was suffering from severe emotional and mental trauma, loss of blood, shock brought on by loss of fluids from his body, and chills from the cold night air passing over his damp body (blood mixed with sweat). Such physiological distress would have caused collapse in most mortals. But the Savior's physical ordeal was far from over in those early morning hours of what the Christian world calls Good Friday.

Responding to Annas's inquiries about his doctrine, Jesus indicated that everything he had said and done was an open record seen and heard by the Jews in their synagogues and their Temple in Jerusalem (John 18:20). It should be remembered that when he was arrested, he had also proclaimed that he had "sat daily . . . teaching in the temple" (Matthew 26:55). Jesus suggested to Annas that he personally ask those who had heard Jesus teach just what the nature of His doctrine was all about (John 18:21). This suggestion was intended to keep fresh in the minds of Annas and the others associated with the interrogation the link between Jesus, the Temple, and all those who were responsible for the Savior's arrest and later crucifixion. In one way or another, everyone associated with the conspiracy to kill Jesus was connected to the Temple. Remember, Matthew identifies the *planners* of the plot as the chief priests, scribes, and elders of the people, who served or taught in the Temple (Matthew 26:3–5). And Luke describes those sent to *arrest* Jesus as "the chief priests, and captains of the temple, and the elders" (Luke 22:52).

The uncomfortably direct connection Jesus pointed out between Temple and conspirators did not go unnoticed. For his comments Jesus received the first of several abusive slaps in the face, intended both to humiliate and to inflict physical pain. Perhaps it was retaliation for the high priest's own embarrassment. Slaves and servants in hellenistic society were liable to being buffeted by slaps with the open hand.

Jesus knew that Annas knew that He had spoken the truth and asked the high priest to produce evidence to the contrary (John 18:23). But Annas chose to further the predetermined, premeditated aims of the conspirators to get rid of Jesus "by craft" (Mark 14:1). He therefore "sent [Jesus] bound unto Caiaphas the high priest" (John 18:24). Though the tone of John's comment implies a separate location for the next phase of Jesus' arraignment before the Jews, it has been suggested that the residences of Annas and Caiaphas shared a common courtyard, the place where Peter awaited his Master's fate (Matthew 26:69). It is also important to note that this is the second mention of the binding of Jesus in John's Gospel. John must have been deeply affected by the Savior's having been shackled.

## BEFORE CAIAPHAS AND THE COUNCIL

In the early morning hours of the most fateful Friday the universe has ever known, the chief priests and scribes came together to judge Jesus in their council meeting (Matthew 26:59). The high priest was in charge (Matthew 26:62–66).

Caiaphas, or Joseph ben Caiaphas, served as high priest from A.D. 18 to A.D. 36. The high priest during Old Testament times was the primary official of the Israelite religious system. After the Exile (586–538 B.C.) and the construction of Zerubbabel's Temple, or the Second Temple (520–515 B.C.), the high priest became the supreme authority in Judaism, acquiring, generally speaking, the prestige and power formerly held by the Israelite kings. During the period of Maccabean consolidation, from about 141 to 63 B.C., the high priest was the unquestioned religious and political head of the independent nation of Israel.

With the coming of Roman overlordship in 63 B.C., the high priests were appointed and deposed at the pleasure of the Romans. Herod the Great, vassal king in the land of Israel (37–4 B.C.), diminished the high priestly office to almost nothing. But after his death, the Roman procurators, or governors, gave the office of high priest greater power in local affairs and strengthened its prestige considerably, especially with the pro-Roman family of Annas and Caiaphas. This close connection between the Roman rulers and the high priestly office made the family of its holders, including Annas, Caiaphas, and their successors, very suspicious of anyone who seemed to oppose Roman rule or who was likely to upset the status quo.

The Gospel of John confirms the general picture of Caiaphas and other Jewish leaders as being far more concerned with keeping peace with the Romans by getting rid of Jesus than with the righteousness of their nation or the recognized identity of the Messiah. "If we let him thus alone, all men will believe on him: and the Romans shall come and take away both our place and nation" (John 11:48; see also vv. 47–51). In addition, they sought to destroy the undeniable evidence of Jesus' great power by killing Lazarus. The raising of Lazarus from the dead had been the final straw, so to speak, in Jesus' actions. The leaders became unalterably motivated to get rid of both the prophet from Galilee and his friend Lazarus. "Much people of the Jews therefore knew that he was there: and they came not for Jesus' sake only, but that they might see Lazarus also, whom he had raised from the dead. But the chief priests consulted that they might put Lazarus also to death; Because that by reason of him many of the Jews went away, and believed on Jesus" (John 12:9–11). It seems that the wickedness of the chief priests knew no bounds. They were consummately evil men.

There also seems to have been another reason behind the determination to eliminate Jesus: he had interfered with economic traffic on the Temple Mount (John 2:14–16; Matthew 21:12–13). The high priestly family was in charge of such commerce and had grown wealthier because of it. They saw it as a necessary (and welcome) part of activities at the house of the Lord. But Jesus had called all of this into question when he referred to the Temple as a house of merchandise and a den of thieves (John 2:16; Matthew 21:13). The Gospel of Mark makes the direct connection between Jesus' actions in this regard and the culmination of plots to take his life: "And he taught, saying unto them, Is it not written, My house shall be called of all nations the house of prayer? but ye have made it a den of thieves. And the scribes and chief priests heard it, and sought how they might destroy him" (Mark 11:17–18).

It is no small thing to say that economic issues were at the heart of the conspiracy to murder Jesus. From nearly the dawn of creation on this earth, getting gain has been one of the foundation stones of wickedness, if not the cornerstone itself. Cain, who slew his brother Abel over such matters, entered into a covenant with Satan to promote this activity. "And

Cain said: Truly I am Mahan, the master of this great secret, that I may murder and get gain. Wherefore Cain was called Master Mahan, and he gloried in his wickedness" (Moses 5:31). Murder to get gain! This is still a moving force in the world today. Wars have been fought because of it. Nations have fallen due to it. Untold individual human misery has resulted from it.

Is it any wonder then that when God himself came to earth as a mortal, and the great forces of righteousness and wickedness did battle face to face, he would ultimately confront the "great secret," the Mahanic principle, and lose his life over it?

## WHICH COUNCIL?

It is impossible to know exactly which group of Jewish leaders, led by Caiaphas, interrogated Jesus after his examination by Annas. In the New Testament the Greek word *synedrion*, "Sanhedrin," is used for judicial courts in general and is sometimes conflated with *presbyterion*, "council of elders." Theoretically, the high priest presided over the supreme judicial and legislative court in Jerusalem, called the Great Sanhedrin. It had seventy-one members and met in the Chamber of Hewn Stone in the Temple complex. Our information about this council, however, comes in part from the later codification of Jewish oral law and tradition called the Mishnah (ca. A.D. 200). We do not know whether this information about the Great Sanhedrin and associated legal regulations reflects third-century practice, or Second Temple reality, or an idealized conceptualization projected back from the third century to the first century, or a combination of these.

Additionally, in the Mishnah, the word *Sanhedrin* is also used for law courts of twenty-three members that decided capital cases. Was the council before whom Jesus stood this lesser Sanhedrin? To further complicate matters, the Jewish historian Josephus (born A.D. 37) speaks of many local and national councils (*synedria*, or Sanhedrins) whose powers and composition changed with political circumstances. Therefore, we conclude with Elder James E. Talmage that the size of the judicial body involved in Jesus' arraignment is uncertain and of small importance compared to the monumental nature of the whole atoning act (*Jesus the Christ*, 623).

One thing is certain, however, and that is that Jesus' arraignment before Caiaphas and the other Jewish authorities was neither legal nor fair. Perhaps the most sinister aspect of the whole business is best reported by Matthew: "Now the chief priests, and elders, and *all* the council, sought false witness against Jesus, to put him to death; but found none: yea though many false witnesses came, yet found they none" (Matthew 26:59–60; emphasis added; see also Mark 14:55). Thus, we are also sure that the Jewish council that morning could not have been made up of the full complement of seventy-one Sanhedrists because, as Matthew and Mark testify, the whole council present that morning was guilty of suborning perjury and at least two members of the Sanhedrin, Joseph of Arimathaea and Nicodemus, were righteous men who were not associated with the conspiracy. Nicodemus defended the Savior during his ministry (John 7:50–53), and Joseph of Arimathaea was "a rich and faithful Israelite who took no part in the condemnation of our Lord" (LDS Bible Dictionary, 717). These two men were later involved in the burial of their Master.

Deuteronomy 17:6 states, "At the mouth of two witnesses, or three witnesses, shall he that is worthy of death be put to death; but at the mouth of one witness he shall not be put to death." That *all* the council would scrupulously adhere to this law of witnesses as outlined in the law of Moses by seeking more than one witness but then wholeheartedly endorse false witnesses and the suborning of perjury is testimony enough to the thorough and murderous corruption of Jewish leadership in Jerusalem at the time. These hypocrites would not dare violate the outward forms of the law for fear of the people, but they had no qualms about secretly manipulating, even destroying, the moral underpinnings of their society in order to ensure the fulfillment of their plan of premeditated murder. Elder Talmage comments:

> In the Sanhedrin, every member was a judge; the judicial body was to hear the testimony, and, according to that testimony and nought else, render a decision on every case duly presented. . . . But in the so-called trial of Jesus, the judges not only sought witnesses, but specifically tried to find false witnesses. Though many false witnesses came, yet there was no "witness" or testimony against the Prisoner, for the suborned perjurers failed to agree among themselves; and even the lawless Sanhedrists hesitated to openly violate the fundamental requirement that at least two concordant witnesses must testify against an accused person, for, otherwise, the case had to be dismissed. (*Jesus the Christ*, 623)

Surely this is one of the moments the Lord had in mind anciently when he spoke with Enoch the seer about the inhabitants of this earth: "Wherefore, I can stretch forth mine hands and hold all the creations which I have made; and mine eye can pierce them also, and among all the workmanship of mine hands there has not been so great wickedness as among thy brethren" (Moses 7:36). The Savior's arraignment before

Jewish leaders must also have been part of Jacob's visionary understanding when he said: "Wherefore, as I said unto you, it must needs be expedient that Christ—for in the last night the angel spake unto me that this should be his name—should come among the Jews, among those who are the more wicked part of the world; and they shall crucify him—for thus it behooveth our God, and there is none other nation on earth that would crucify their God" (2 Nephi 10:3).

## The Savior's Crime

At last the Jewish leaders produced two false witnesses, though their respective testimonies did not agree with one another in details (Mark 14:59). The strength of the warning against false witnesses in the Mosaic law helps us to understand just how badly these leaders wanted Jesus eliminated. Perjurers were liable to the same punishment intended for the accused (Deuteronomy 19:16–19). Ultimately, the accusation against Jesus centered on the Jerusalem Temple: "And there arose certain, and bare false witness against him, saying, We heard him say, I will destroy this temple that is made with hands, and within three days I will build another made without hands" (Mark 14:57–58).

The exact nature of the crime here is difficult to ferret out. Elder Talmage sees this initial accusation as focusing on sedition: "The plan of the conspiring rulers appears to have been that of convicting Christ on a charge of sedition, making Him out to be a dangerous disturber of the nation's peace, an assailant of established institutions, and consequently an inciter of opposition against the vassal autonomy of the Jewish nation, and the supreme dominion of Rome" (*Jesus the Christ*, 624–25). This interpretation accords well with the later scene reported by Luke, in which the charge that was leveled against Jesus by "the whole multitude of them that arose and led him unto Pilate" was officially registered as "perverting the nation" (Luke 23:1–2).

The flurry of activity occurring immediately after the accusation by the false witnesses helps us to see that the charge of sedition, which would lead to Jesus' conviction by the Romans, was coupled with blasphemy, the high crime in Jewish society, which would ensure Jesus' conviction among the Jews. Matthew's account tells us what happened after the perjured testimony had been accepted:

> And the high priest arose, and said unto him, Answerest thou nothing? what is it which these witness against thee?
>
> But Jesus held his peace. And the high priest answered and said unto him, I adjure thee by the living God, that thou tell us whether thou be the Christ, the Son of God.
>
> Jesus saith unto him, Thou hast said: nevertheless I say unto you, Hereafter shall ye see the Son of man sitting on the right hand of power, and coming in the clouds of heaven.
>
> Then the high priest rent his clothes, saying, He hath spoken blasphemy; what further need have we of witnesses? behold, now ye have heard his blasphemy.
>
> What think ye? They answered and said, He is guilty of death. (Matthew 26:62–66)

Throughout this pretense of a proper hearing, Jesus stood before his accusers calm and quiet, refraining from comment on the scurrilous charges (Matthew 26:63). In those moments of silence, Isaiah's unparalleled messianic prophecy was fulfilled: "He was oppressed, and he was afflicted, yet he opened not his mouth: he is brought as a lamb to the slaughter, and as a sheep before her shearers is dumb, so he openeth not his mouth" (Isaiah 53:7). In an action reminiscent of high courtroom drama, Caiaphas then arose from his seat and forced Jesus to respond to his interrogation by placing him under oath, "I adjure thee by the living God, that thou tell us whether thou be the Christ, the Son of God" (Matthew 26:63). There is something disturbing in the vehement tone that comes through the written words of Matthew's text. We also note that Caiaphas seems to have equated the title "Christ" (Messiah) with the title "Son of God" (v. 63). Here the Gospel of Mark uses "Son of the Blessed" instead of the more jarring "Son of God." In responding to the high priest's direct question about his identity, Jesus again left no room for doubt. As he did when he was arrested, Jesus identified himself by using the divine name "I am" (Mark 14:62). "It was an unqualified avowal of divine parentage, and inherent Godship," wrote Elder Talmage (*Jesus the Christ*, 626). In this Jesus was guilty of nothing except telling the truth.

Caiaphas tore his clothes when he heard Jesus answer. Likely, from the high priest's perspective, this was the hoped-for self-incrimination. The tearing of one's clothing anciently was done to convey shock, outrage, or grief—and to signify the death of a member of one's family or community (Genesis 37:34; Numbers 14:6; 2 Samuel 1:11). Perhaps Caiaphas did it to register his outrage dramatically, pretended though it was, and to signal Jesus' death as a foregone conclusion. Yet, the high priest was not supposed to tear his clothes, according to divine rules for priestly behavior (Leviticus 21:10). He was now the one who was actually guilty of breaking the laws of God—not Jesus—but he and his associates had the pretext they needed to move forward with their premeditated plan of murder. With only a few more words, Caiaphas forestalled any verdict other than guilty: "He hath spoken blasphemy; what further need have we of witnesses? . . . What think ye?" (Matthew 26:65–66). To Caiaphas's carefully orchestrated manipulations, the entire council responded, "He is guilty of death" (v. 66).

These final irregularities encapsulate the entire proceedings. The members of the Sanhedrin, judges of Israel, were supposed to vote on the verdict one by one, yet they spoke in unison. More important, a unanimous verdict of guilt pronounced on the same day as the trial constituted an automatic acquittal and the defendant was supposed to be set free (Mishnah Sanhedrin 4:1). Why? Because such proceedings, according to ancient rabbinic law, smacked of collusion. "If you're tried and everybody in the room is against you, then there must be a conspiracy, because that many people can't all agree on one thing" (Kofford, "Trial of Christ," 15). Ironically, the very thing Jewish law was structured to prevent—conspiracy—was the very thing that made the law of no effect in the case of Jesus of Nazareth.

Having accomplished their unwavering goal of convicting Jesus, the council took advantage of the opportunity to vent their anger openly against him whom they regarded as their arch-enemy: the sinless Son of God. Matthew reports that they spat in His face, buffeted (battered) Him, and slapped Him with open palms. Mark and Luke add that they blindfolded Him and then struck Him. This is implied in Matthew's account as well because each of the three synoptic Gospels indicate that as the members of the council struck Jesus, they also taunted him by commanding him to "prophesy unto us, thou Christ, Who is he that smote thee?" (Matthew 26:68). It is not hard to see the sarcasm dripping from the phrase "thou Christ."

In another of the many powerful ironies of Jesus' situation, Luke tells us that the Jewish council spoke "many other things *blasphemously*" to Jesus (Luke 22:65; emphasis added). The Savior was the one convicted of the charge, but the chief priests were the ones guilty of it.

The Savior of the world bore this horrible abuse with quiet dignity and majesty. Much later the chief apostle testified of his Master's composure in this setting and encouraged us to follow His example: "For even hereunto were ye called: because Christ also suffered for us, leaving us an example, that ye should follow his steps: . . . Who, when he was reviled, reviled not again; when he suffered, he threatened not; but committed himself to him that judgeth righteously" (1 Peter 2:21–23).

Jesus bore his tribulation with patience. He suffered his indignity with dignity. He endured scorn and physical abuse by himself. No one was with him. No man defended him. No one spoke on his behalf. No one protected him. He trod the winepress alone. He was rejected of men, truly "a man of sorrows, and acquainted with grief" (Isaiah 53:3). There is nothing anyone can tell him about loneliness or the unfairness of life. He is able to have perfect empathy for each one of us because he experienced all things, even descended below all things.

Though condemned to death by evil conspirators and premeditating murderers under the most unfair circumstances, the Holy One of Israel willingly surrendered himself in an attitude of perfect meekness. And still the bitter cup was not yet empty.

---

Now Peter sat without in the palace: and a damsel came unto him, saying, Thou also wast with Jesus of Galilee.

But he denied before them all, saying, I know not what thou sayest.

And when he was gone out into the porch, another maid saw him, and said unto them that were there, This fellow was also with Jesus of Nazareth.

And again he denied with an oath, I do not know the man.

And after a while came unto him they that stood by, and said to Peter, Surely thou also art one of them; for thy speech bewrayeth thee.

Then began he to curse and to swear, saying, I know not the man. And immediately the cock crew.

And Peter remembered the word of Jesus, which said unto him, Before the cock crow, thou shalt deny me thrice. And he went out, and wept bitterly.

MATTHEW 26:69–75

---

# Peter's Denial

At the same time the tragic drama of the Savior's inquisition unfolded inside the palace of the high priest, another drama was being played out outside the palace. There the apostle Peter endured an inquisition of his own.

When the other disciples fled as Jesus was being arrested, Peter followed his Master and the arresting party "afar off unto the high priest's palace" (Matthew 26:58). This palace seems to have housed the residences of both Caiaphas and Annas, before whom Jesus was arraigned first. In keeping with his presentation of unique details, John adds that Peter "followed Jesus, and so did another disciple" who "was known unto the high priest." This disciple went into the palace with Jesus and eventually "spake unto her that kept the door, and brought in Peter" (John 18:15–16). It is not known who this other disciple was, but some scholars have suggested it was John himself.

Given that Matthew and Mark clearly state that at some point Peter "sat without in the palace" (Matthew 26:69), or "Peter was beneath in the palace" (Mark 14:66), it is likely that

Peter was first admitted to Jesus' arraignment before Annas and later sat out in the courtyard while his Master's next hearing, before Caiaphas, took place in another part of the palace complex. This surmise accords well with the archaeological evidence of a courtyard set down the hill below the main palace complex.

The traditional, and probably accurate, location of the high priest's palace is high above the Hinnom Valley on the western hill of Jerusalem, then inside the city walls, and later known as Mount Zion. A fourth-century traveler to Jerusalem, nicknamed the Pilgrim of Bordeaux, said: "In the same valley of Siloam you go up to Mount Sion and you see the site where the house of Caiaphas stood" (*St. Peter "in Gallicantu,"* 2). In the fifth century after Christ, a church was built on this site, and the Crusaders later named it *Gallicantus*, "the cock-crow." In modern times, a dungeon, scourging room, courtyard, artifacts, and a Hebrew inscription have been unearthed on the site that are consistent with expectations associated with the residence and judicial functions of the high priest.

## ACCUSATIONS

As Peter sat beside a fire in the palace courtyard, awaiting word regarding the ultimate fate of Jesus, one of the servants of the high priest's household approached him. Mark's account of the scene is similar to that of the other synoptic Gospels:

> And when she saw Peter warming himself, she looked upon him, and said, And thou also wast with Jesus of Nazareth.
> But he denied, saying, I know not, neither understand

I what thou sayest. And he went out into the porch; and the cock crew.

And a maid saw him again, and began to say to them that stood by, This is one of them.

And he denied it again. And a little after, they that stood by said again to Peter, Surely thou art one of them: for thou art a Galilaean, and thy speech agreeth thereto.

But he began to curse and to swear, saying, I know not this man of whom ye speak.

And the second time the cock crew. And Peter called to mind the word that Jesus said unto him, Before the cock crow twice, thou shalt deny me thrice. And when he thought thereon, he wept. (Mark 14:67–72)

John's account, through shorter, adds an interesting detail:

One of the servants of the high priest, being his kinsman whose ear Peter cut off, saith, Did not I see thee in the garden with him? Peter then denied again: and immediately the cock crew. (John 18:26–27)

Apparently, this kinsman was an eyewitness both to Peter's attack on his relative, Malchus, and to Peter's intimate association with Jesus in the garden.

To fully appreciate the significance of the exchange between Peter and his accusers, we need to go back to events of the Last Supper several hours before. In the upper room the Savior described to his apostles their reaction to events that were about to burst forth upon them: "All ye shall be offended because of me this night." Peter protested, "Though all men shall be offended because of thee, yet will I never be offended" (Matthew 26:31, 33).

Jesus' specific response to Peter teaches us profound lessons, especially in light of the confidence Jesus had in Peter's faithfulness and the potential he knew Peter possessed: "Simon, Simon, behold, Satan hath desired to have you, that he may sift you as wheat: but I have prayed for thee, that thy faith fail not: and when thou art converted, strengthen thy brethren" (Luke 22:31–32).

The thought that any prayer offered by the Savior would not come to pass, nor any prediction of his not be fulfilled, is unthinkable. Peter's faith would not fail, though he had a deeper conversion yet to experience. The texts of all four Gospels indicate that even up to that point, Peter still did not fully comprehend the earth-shaking events soon to overtake the Savior and the early Church. Again the Savior patiently tried to teach Peter of things that must shortly come to pass:

> Simon Peter said unto him, Lord, whither goest thou? Jesus answered him, Whither I go, thou canst not follow me now; but thou shalt follow me afterwards.
>
> Peter said unto him, Lord, why cannot I follow thee now? I will lay down my life for thy sake.
>
> Jesus answered him, Wilt thou lay down thy life for my sake? Verily, verily, I say unto thee, The cock shall not crow, till thou hast denied me thrice. (John 13:36–38)

Peter was never one to shrink from danger, and we cannot doubt that at that moment, and all the moments before it and after it, Peter would have forfeited his life for his Master's. But that was precisely the problem. Peter might recklessly have laid down his life for Jesus when something different was needed and intended by the Savior.

After the Last Supper concluded, events moved along unalterably as the apostles followed Jesus to the Garden of Gethsemane. When the Savior finished praying the same prayer for the third time, the police force of the Jerusalem Temple appeared, ready to arrest Jesus. Peter drew his sword and became embroiled in the events we have already discussed. It important to remember that Peter's selfless act of protection was done in the face of an armed mob who could have easily overwhelmed the chief apostle. That action is in complete harmony with everything else we know about Peter. Even when all the other disciples fled at Jesus' arrest, Peter followed afar off and ended up confronting the two women and the man who accused him of associating with Jesus.

What gives us pause at this point is consideration of Peter's motivation for denying that he knew his Master. Why did he deny Him? The reasons usually given range from fear of personal harm, to weakness, to embarrassment, to pride, to indecision, or to some other flaw or weakness in Peter's character. Yet these reasons seem to contradict everything else we have read about the chief apostle in the New Testament, including his bold, unequivocal confession of the Savior's Sonship at Caesarea Philippi, when a diverse set of opinions regarding Jesus was floating about the land, and his single-minded resolve not to allow anyone to harm the Savior.

In every instance when the impending arrest or death of Jesus had come to Peter's attention, he had been both quick and forceful to say that he would not let such a thing happen (Matthew 16:21–23), and he would protect Jesus at all costs, even at the peril of his own life, which is what happened in Gethsemane when the armed forces of the chief priests could not intimidate a chief apostle who was ready to do battle with all of them (John 18:7–12). Now we are to believe that in the face of a challenge initially put forward by a slave girl, the most unimportant person imaginable in Jewish society, Peter denied even knowing Jesus for fear of being exposed as a follower? (The word *damsel* used in Matthew 26:69 does not convey the lowly position of Peter's first interrogator, but the footnote to that verse in the LDS edition of the Bible approaches it.)

## PRESIDENT SPENCER W. KIMBALL'S REFLECTIONS

Years ago President Spencer W. Kimball invited us to reevaluate our understanding of Peter's actions in a magnificent address entitled *Peter, My Brother*. Speaking of his model and mentor, this modern-day apostle asked penetrating questions: Do we really know Peter's mind and heart? Are we sure of his motives? Do we understand the circumstances of Peter's denial as well as we think we do? President Kimball began his discussion with this admission:

> Some time ago a newspaper in a distant town carried an Easter Sunday religious editorial by a minister who stated that the presiding authority of the early-day church fell because of self-confidence, indecision, evil companions, failure to pray, lack of humility, and fear of man. . . .
>
> As I read this, I had some strange emotions. I was shocked, then I was chilled, then my blood changed its temperature and began to boil. I felt I was attacked viciously, for Peter was my brother, my colleague, my example, my prophet, and God's anointed. I whispered

to myself, "That is not true. He is maligning my brother." (*Peter, My Brother*, 488)

President Kimball discussed the tremendous strength, power, faithfulness, and other apostolic attributes of Peter, including his boldness. Then he said:

> Much of the criticism of Simon Peter is centered in his denial of his acquaintance with the Master. This has been labeled "cowardice." Are we sure of his motive in that recorded denial? He had already given up his occupation and placed all worldly goods on the altar for the cause. . . .
>
> Is it conceivable that the omniscient Lord would give all these powers and keys to one who was a failure or unworthy? . . .
>
> If Peter was frightened in the court when he denied his association with the Lord, how brave he was hours earlier when he drew his sword against an overpowering enemy, the night mob. Later defying the people and state and church officials, he boldly charged, "Him [the Christ] . . . ye have taken, and by wicked hands have crucified and slain." (Acts 2:23.) To the astounded populace at the healing of the cripple at the Gate Beautiful, he exclaimed, "Ye men of Israel . . . the God of our fathers, hath glorified his Son Jesus; whom ye delivered up, and denied him in the presence of Pilate. . . . ye denied the Holy One. . . . And killed the Prince of life, whom God hath raised from the dead; whereof we are witnesses." (Acts 3:12–15.)
>
> Does this portray cowardice? Quite a bold assertion for a timid one. Remember that Peter never denied the

divinity of Christ. He only denied his association or acquaintance with the Christ, which is quite a different matter. . . .

Is it possible that there might have been some other reason for Peter's triple denial? Could he have felt that circumstances justified expediency? When he bore a strong testimony in Caesarea Philippi, he had been told that "they should tell no man that he was Jesus the Christ." (Matthew 16:20.) (*Peter, My Brother*, 488–89)

To what, then, might we attribute Peter's denial? Perhaps it could be attributed to Jesus himself—to a request or command he made that Peter should deny knowing him, not to deny his divinity but to deny knowing him as the religious rebel the Jewish leaders saw him to be. Why? To ensure Peter's safety as chief apostle and to ensure the continuity and safety of the Quorum of the Twelve.

Some may object that God would never command any of his children to do such a thing, but we do not know all that God knows, nor do we know all that went on in this situation. Moreover, we find interesting contradictions, or seeming contradictions, in other scriptural passages that put this episode in a different light. For example, God commanded Abraham that his wife, Sarah, should tell the Egyptians that she was Abraham's sister so that he would be protected, just as Jesus wanted the apostles protected (Abraham 2:23–25). We also remember Deity commanding Nephi to slay Laban in order to keep a whole nation safe spiritually and to bring forth God's righteous purposes (1 Nephi 4:13). The Prophet Joseph Smith taught:

But we cannot keep all the commandments without

first knowing them, and we cannot expect to know all, or more than we now know unless we comply with or keep those we have already received. That which is wrong under one circumstance, may be, and often is, right under another.

God said, "Thou shalt not kill;" at another time He said, "Thou shalt utterly destroy." This is the principle on which the government of heaven is conducted—by revelation adapted to the circumstances in which the children of the kingdom are placed. Whatever God requires is right, no matter what it is, although we may not see the reason thereof till long after the events transpire. If we seek first the kingdom of God, all good things will be added. So with Solomon: first he asked wisdom, and God gave it him, and with it every desire of his heart, even things which might be considered abominable to all who understand the order of heaven only in part, but which in reality were right because God gave and sanctioned by special revelation. (*Teachings of the Prophet Joseph Smith*, 256)

Remember, by the time of his arrest, Jesus was protective of his apostles, and the safety of the Quorum had become a major concern for him. As we have indicated, in his great high priestly prayer, the Savior prayed for the safety of the apostles. "I pray not that thou shouldest take them out of the world, but that thou shouldest keep them from the evil" (John 17:15). When he was arrested in the garden, he said to the mob, "I have told you that I am he: if therefore ye seek me, let these go their way" (John 18:8). Jesus did not want anything to happen to those who were ordained to take over the earthly leadership of the Church. He had already averted wholesale slaughter in Gethsemane when first, in the upper room, he restricted to two the number of swords carried by the apostles (Luke 22:38). Later, while being arrested, he told Peter to put away his sword, "for all they that take the sword shall perish with the sword" (Matthew 26:52). It will be remembered that some of the apostles asked, "Lord, shall we smite with the sword?" (Luke 22:49) while Peter went ahead and lopped off Malchus's ear without waiting for an answer.

Jesus had told Peter at the Last Supper that He had prayed that Peter's faith would not fail—and it did not. As President Kimball stated: "Peter was under fire; all the hosts of hell were against him. The die had been cast for the Savior's crucifixion. If Satan could destroy Simon now, what a victory he would score. *Here was the greatest of all living men.* Lucifer wanted to confuse him, frustrate him, limit his prestige, and totally destroy him. However, this was not to be, for he was chosen and ordained to a high purpose in heaven, as was Abraham" (*Peter, My Brother,* 488–89; emphasis added).

Matthew tells us that Peter went to the high priest's palace "to see the end" (Matthew 26:58). The implication is that Peter went as a witness of the last events associated with the life of the mortal Messiah. Had Peter been inclined to cowardice, it seems likely he would not have gone to the palace and put himself in harm's way. How grateful we are to have had Peter there as an eyewitness of that part of the atoning sacrifice.

In sum, it is apparent that Jesus knew of Peter's fearlessness in defending him. He had seen several manifestations of Peter's unswerving, almost reckless, commitment to prevent any physical harm to the Savior. And this was something Jesus knew could get Peter into trouble if it were not tempered. It would put the chief apostle in grave physical danger. Therefore, it is possible that when Jesus told Peter he would deny him thrice before the cock crowed twice, it was not a prediction—it was a command. This is, in fact, a possible reading of the synoptic texts, according to the grammatical rules of Koine Greek, which is the language in which early manuscripts of the New Testament were written. In their accounts of this episode, Matthew (26:34, 75), Mark (14:30, 72), and Luke (22:34, 61) all use the same verb and verb form, *aparnēse*, which can be read either as an indicative future tense or as an imperative (command) tense. One Latter-day Saint scholar of classical languages arrived at the following conclusion:

> When the Lord had informed the eleven who remained with Him to finish the Last Supper that they would soon be scattered, Peter protested that he would never abandon the Savior, but sooner go to his death. Tradition portrays Christ as then prophesying of the three-time denial of Peter to come that very night (Matthew 26:31–35; Mark 14:27–31; Luke 22:31–34; John 13:36–38). However, close examination of the original Greek of John's account (John 13:38) reveals that the phrase "till thou hast denied me thrice" is structured around the verb ἀρνήσῃ [arnēse], a second person singular future indicative verb form. Virtually the same verb ἀπαρνήσῃ [aparnēse], in the same second person singular future indicative form, appears in Matthew (26:34), Mark (14:30), and Luke (22:34). Although the tense is future, and may accurately be construed as indicating a prediction or prophecy of Peter's future behavior, it is possible that such a rendering is not at all

the meaning of Christ's statement. In Greek, a future tense verb in the second person can also be construed to express a command, just as if it were an imperative form of the verb. This usage is given the grammatical term of the "jussive future." It occurs not infrequently in both classical and *koine* Greek. Accordingly, if the future in these passages is interpreted as a jussive future, then Christ would seem actually to be giving Peter a command to deny knowing Him, and Peter's protestation would seem to reflect his dissatisfaction about such an instruction. This rendering appears very much in keeping with Peter's natural courage. Restraint would test Peter's faith so much more, for he was being refused permission to expose himself to the tribulations that Christ must undertake alone. . . .

When Christ was taken, instead of acting impulsively, Peter did demonstrate great restraint both in not trying to interfere in the process of Jesus' death and in protecting himself that he might live to fulfill his mission. How he must have wanted to wield his sword and free the Savior! How he must have desired to proclaim Jesus as the Christ to those assembled in the courtyard! Although Peter never denied the divinity of Christ, he must have been in tremendous turmoil not to be able to admit to his friendship with Jesus, and could even have felt as if this practically constituted a denial of his friend. Each time Peter was questioned as to his association with Jesus and compelled to deny it, seemingly contradicting his own pledge of loyalty unto death, what faith was put into the charge Christ had given him for the future! Peter was neither impetuous, nor did he lack faith. Quite the opposite. The man who had fearlessly struck with his sword at Gethsemane, was the same man who evidenced fearless and faithful restraint in the courtyard of the high priest. John's telling of the account shows Peter's faith, not his fear. (Hall, *New Testament Witnesses of Christ*, 65–66)

Some might ask, "Why then did Peter weep bitterly after his denial?" Isn't it possible that those were tears of frustration and bitter sorrow in the realization that he was powerless to change the Lord's fate? He had done what needed to be done, but every impulse inside him was to act differently—to prevent the suffering of the Savior. That must have been a bitter pill for Peter to swallow. He wept tears of frustration precisely because he was obedient and also because he was fully aware that he was going to lose his Master to the inevitability of death. In my view, Peter's denial, far from detracting from his stature, greatly adds to it. How grateful we are to a modern prophet and apostle, Spencer W. Kimball, for helping us to look at events in the New Testament differently with the aid of prophetic interpretation.

All the chief priests and elders of the people took counsel against Jesus to put him to death:

And when they had bound him, they led him away, and delivered him to Pontius Pilate the governor.

Then Judas, which had betrayed him, when he saw that he was condemned, repented himself, and brought again the thirty pieces of silver to the chief priests and elders,

Saying, I have sinned in that I have betrayed the innocent blood. And they said, What is that to us? see thou to that.

And he cast down the pieces of silver in the temple, and departed, and went and hanged himself.

And the chief priests took the silver pieces, and said, It is not lawful for to put them into the treasury, because it is the price of blood.

And they took counsel, and bought with them the potter's field, to bury strangers in.

Wherefore that field was called, The field of blood, unto this day.

Then was fulfilled that which was spoken by Jeremy the prophet, saying, And they took the thirty pieces of silver, the price of him that was valued, whom they of the children of Israel did value;

And gave them for the potter's field.

MATTHEW 27:1–10

# CHAPTER 5

# Pontius Pilate and Judas Iscariot

Having convinced themselves that Jesus of Nazareth was guilty of blasphemy and sedition ("they *all* condemned him to be guilty of death"; Mark 14:64; emphasis added), the Jewish leaders made ready to deliver him to Pontius Pilate. All of the safeguards put into place in the Mosaic law and rabbinic tradition to ensure that the innocent were not made scapegoats or railroaded into conviction—no one-day trials resulting in capital punishment, no self-incrimination or confession without corroborating witnesses who agreed with each other, no hearing before the Sanhedrin in the house of the high priest—all these elements seem to have been deliberately ignored in the case of Jesus.

## IRONIES AND CONTRADICTIONS

The ironies—indeed, the contradictions—of Jesus' separate arraignments before Annas and Caiaphas are stunning. Though he was convicted as a result of the testimony of false witnesses, Jesus Christ was and is the *"faithful* witness" (Revelation 1:5; emphasis added). Though the Sanhedrin spoke blasphemously

61

to him, Jesus was truly God. Though he rightly spoke as God, he was convicted of blasphemy against God (Mark 14:62–63). Though he stood before Annas and Caiaphas, who held the title of high priest, Jesus is the true High Priest, the "High Priest of our profession" (Hebrews 3:1).

Everything those false high priests were not, Jesus Christ is—"an high priest . . . who is holy, harmless, undefiled, separate from sinners, and made higher than the heavens" (Hebrews 7:26). Though he was forced to stand before two high priests who considered themselves to be important because they supervised the daily sacrifices in the Temple and entered the Holy of Holies once a year on the Day of Atonement, Jesus himself was the very author of the sacrificial system as well as the great and last sacrifice under the Mosaic law, the fulfillment of the whole system of sacrifice (Alma 34:13–14). The book of Hebrews explains the ways in which Jesus fulfilled the role of the Israelite high priest as well as the system of animal sacrifice, which was a pattern of Jesus' sacrifice:

> Who needeth not daily, as those high priests, to offer up sacrifice, first for his own sins, and then for the people's: for this he did once, when he offered up himself.
>
> It was therefore necessary that the patterns of things in the heavens should be purified with these; but the heavenly things themselves with better sacrifices than these.
>
> For Christ is not entered into the holy places made with hands, which are the figures of the true; but into heaven itself, now to appear in the presence of God for us:

Nor yet that he should offer himself often, as the high priest entereth into the holy place every year with blood of others;

For then must he often have suffered since the foundation of the world: but now once in the end of the world hath he appeared to put away sin by the sacrifice of himself. (Hebrews 7:27; 9:23–26)

Many more ironies and contradictions would be added to the list of the Savior's tribulations in Jerusalem on the eve of Passover. But enough have been discussed already to allow a deeper appreciation of the Prophet Joseph Smith's statement that Jesus Christ "descended in suffering below that which man can suffer; or, in other words, suffered greater sufferings, and was exposed to *more powerful contradictions* than any man can be. But, notwithstanding all this, he kept the law of God, and remained without sin, showing thereby that it is in the power of man to keep the law and remain also without sin" (*Lectures on Faith*, 5:2; emphasis added). If ever a statement applied to Jesus' arraignments in front of Jewish leaders, this one does.

## PONTIUS PILATE

With poignant brevity Matthew reports what happened to Jesus after he endured the long night of suffering, accusation, and abuse, which culminated in his being condemned to death by Caiaphas and the council of unrelenting Jewish leaders. "When the morning was come, all the chief priests and elders of the people took counsel against Jesus to put him to death: And when they had bound him, they led him away, and delivered him to Pontius Pilate the governor" (Matthew 27:1–2).

Jesus had prophesied his arraignments in front of Pilate as well as the Jewish council several days before that fateful Friday. As he made his way to Jerusalem for the last time, Jesus warned the Twelve that "the Son of man shall be delivered unto the chief priests, and unto the scribes; and they shall condemn him to death, and *shall deliver him to the Gentiles*" (Mark 10:33; emphasis added). The Savior knew full well what lay ahead before he ever made his triumphal entry into Jerusalem and before he was brought to stand in front of Pilate, one of the Gentiles of whom he spoke.

Pontius Pilate was the Roman governor of Judea from A.D. 26 to 36. Technically, his title was *Praefectus Iudaeae*, "prefect of Judea," according to an inscription found at Caesarea Maritima on the Mediterranean coast. The Passion (from Latin, *passus*, "to suffer") narratives in the Gospels portray him as something of a well-meaning but weak ruler who attempted to shift responsibility for the execution of Jesus from himself to others.

The truth is, Pilate was extremely powerful when he began his rule; he was also cruel and arrogant. When the Roman emperor appointed a governor over an imperial province such as Judea, he invested the appointee with full authority to administer the territory economically, politically, and militarily. In judging Jesus, Pilate was free to decide His guilt or innocence, to adopt or reject the Sanhedrin's decision, or to consult with anyone he wished. The problem was that Pilate had so inflamed his Jewish subjects that he had used up all the goodwill, respect, and political capital he needed to set Jesus free. Ultimately, he chose political expediency. He chose to wash his hands of the situation and not to take the stand he could have taken to free Jesus. He chose not to act on his knowledge and impressions of the Savior's innocence. Ironically, he chose not to oppose the Jewish opinion makers in this instance, although he had done so plenty of other times.

Nonbiblical sources describe Pilate's problems with the Jews, characterizing him as insensitive, offensive, corrupt, irrational, and cruel. Josephus reports that Pilate deeply offended the people and violated Mosaic law when he attached graven images of the emperor to Roman standards within Jerusalem's sacred precincts. He incited a deadly riot when he appropriated funds from the Temple treasury to finance an aqueduct that brought water into the Temple, even though it was needed. According to Philo, the Jewish philosopher-theologian, Pilate incensed the Jews when he installed shields bearing the emperor's name in Herod's former palace in Jerusalem. He was recalled to Rome in A.D. 36 after a massacre of the Samaritans and never again appointed to an important government post.

## SUICIDE OF JUDAS

Before describing the Savior's arraignment in front of Pilate, Matthew inserts a unique note regarding the fate of Jesus' betrayer. When Judas saw that Jesus had been condemned by the Jewish council and was being transferred to the Roman governor to secure capital conviction, the gravity of the situation caused a change of heart. He tried to reverse his betrayal and return the paltry sum of thirty pieces of silver, the price of a slave. To his co-conspirators, the chief priests, he confessed his self-realized grievous sin of betraying innocent blood. But they would have none of it—a witness of the truth from the Savior's very betrayer was turned away. Justice and truth were ignored. Distraught, Judas cast the money into the Temple and went out and hanged himself (Matthew 27:3–5).

At some point the chief priests, ever observant of the smallest legal issues when it served their purposes, decided it was not lawful to deposit Judas's blood money in the Temple treasury (never mind that it had originated with them). So, magnanimously, they purchased the potter's field as a cemetery for strangers and in so doing fulfilled another Old Testament prophecy, which Matthew attributed to Jeremiah but which can now be found only in Zechariah: "And I said unto them, If ye think good, give me my price; and if not, forbear. So they weighed for my price thirty pieces of silver. And the Lord said unto me, Cast it unto the potter: a goodly price that I was prised at of them. And I took the thirty pieces of silver, and cast them to the potter in the house of the Lord" (Zechariah 11:12–13).

No definite explanation can be found about why Matthew attributes this prophecy to Jeremiah. Perhaps it was once found in Jeremiah's writings, or perhaps an oral tradition once ascribed its origin to Jeremiah. Whatever its source, however, its impressive fulfillment cannot be denied.

Some scholars have pitted Matthew's version of Judas's death against the apostle Peter's version, which states that Judas, "falling headlong, he burst asunder in the midst, and all his bowels gushed out" (Acts 1:18). The Joseph Smith Translation of Matthew 27:6 indicates that both occurred: "And he . . . went, and hanged himself on a tree. And straightway he fell down, and his bowels gushed out, and he died."

Great questions remain about Judas's motives for betraying the Savior. Various theories favorable to Judas have been proffered about why he betrayed his Master. Perhaps, they say, Judas was attempting to get Jesus to display his messianic powers and authority to hasten the overthrow of the Romans, and so forth. In other words, these theories suggest, Judas was not wicked; he just misunderstood the kind of Messiah Jesus was. It must be remembered, however, that the Gospels of both Luke and John refer to Satan entering "into" Judas—not just influencing him (Luke 22:3; John 13:27). And the Prophet Joseph Smith taught that "the devil has no power over us only as we permit him. The moment we revolt at anything which comes from God, the devil takes power" (*Teachings of the Prophet Joseph Smith,* 181). Certainly, the devil took control of Judas's life at some point.

Similarly, questions remain concerning Judas's ultimate situation in eternity. Some students of the New Testament adhere strictly to the text of the Savior's high priestly prayer as they argue that Judas was guilty of the unpardonable sin. In that prayer Jesus refers to having lost none of those whom the Father had given to him, except "the son of perdition" (John 17:12). It is true that Judas is not liked very much in the Gospels—especially in John (see, for example, John 12:6, in which Judas is referred to as a "thief"). Nonetheless, modern prophets, who possess extraordinary doctrinal acumen, have been cautious in their assessments. President Joseph F. Smith observed:

> Now, if Judas really had known God's power, and had partaken thereof, and did actually "deny the truth" and "defy" that power, "having denied the Holy Spirit after he had received it," and also "denied the Only Begotten," after God had "revealed him" unto him, then there can be no doubt that he "will die the second death."
>
> That Judas did partake of all this knowledge—that

these great truths had been revealed to him—that he had received the Holy Spirit by the gift of God, and was therefore qualified to commit the unpardonable sin, is not at all clear to me. To my mind it strongly appears that not one of the disciples possessed sufficient light, knowledge nor wisdom, at the time of the crucifixion, for either exaltation or condemnation; for it was afterward that their minds were opened to understand the scriptures, and that they were endowed with power from on high; without which they were only children in knowledge, in comparison to what they afterwards become under the influence of the Spirit. (*Gospel Doctrine*, 433)

In harmony with the teachings of President Joseph F. Smith, Elder Bruce R. McConkie wrote: "Only Judas has been lost; and even he, though a son or follower of Satan . . . is probably not a son of perdition in the sense of eternal damnation" (*Mortal Messiah*, 4:112–13).

Whatever Judas's ultimate destiny, we learn important lessons from his situation about the need for constant vigilance against Satan's attempts to influence us and drive a wedge between us and our Master. Judas was a member of the Quorum of the Twelve Apostles, worthy to hold that honored position when he was first chosen by the Savior. But something happened along the way to allow the devil to take control of his life. Constant vigilance against Satan's influence is the price we must pay for spiritual power. The life of Judas teaches us that no one is exempt, not even a member of the Quorum of the Twelve. We also learn from the example of Judas that great personal sorrow inevitably follows wicked actions—sometimes leading to a compounding of personal tragedy (in Judas's case, suicide). As with Judas's, our own actions hardly ever affect just ourselves. Often they affect other people, sometimes even great numbers of others.

One last lesson we learn from Judas's actions is that we may not always be able to explain why once-worthy, faithful, and trusted associates end up doing deceitful, despicable things. President Harold B. Lee taught that

> some of the greatest of our enemies are those within our own ranks. It was the lament of the Master, as he witnessed one of those chosen men, who under inspiration he chose as one of the Twelve, betray him with a kiss. . . . And Jesus could only explain that of the Twelve, meaning Judas, he had a devil.
>
> When we see some of our own today doing similar things, some who have been recognized and honored in the past as teachers and leaders who later fall by the wayside, our hearts are made sore and tender. But sometimes we have to say just like the Master said, "The devil must have entered into them." (Conference Report, October 1973, 166)

And the whole multitude of them arose, and led him unto Pilate.

And they began to accuse him, saying, We found this fellow perverting the nation, and forbidding to give tribute to Caesar, saying that he himself is Christ a King.

And Pilate asked him, saying, Art thou the King of the Jews? And he answered him and said, Thou sayest it.

Then said Pilate to the chief priests and to the people, I find no fault in this man.

And they were the more fierce, saying, He stirreth up the people, teaching throughout all Jewry, beginning from Galilee to this place.

When Pilate heard of Galilee, he asked whether the man were a Galilaean.

And as soon as he knew that he belonged unto Herod's jurisdiction, he sent him to Herod, who himself also was at Jerusalem at that time.

And when Herod saw Jesus, he was exceeding glad: for he was desirous to see him of a long season, because he had heard many things of him; and he hoped to have seen some miracle done by him.

Then he questioned with him in many words; but he answered him nothing.

And the chief priests and scribes stood and vehemently accused him.

And Herod with his men of war set him at nought, and mocked him, and arrayed him in a gorgeous robe, and sent him again to Pilate.

And the same day Pilate and Herod were made friends together: for before they were at enmity between themselves.

Luke 23:1–12

# CHAPTER 6

# Arraignment before Pilate and Herod

T he decision of the Jewish council to take Jesus to
Pilate at an early hour on Friday morning bespeaks the
urgency with which the chief priests and the Jewish
council wanted Jesus disposed of. Perhaps they figured the early
hour would also impress Pilate that the situation was extremely
dangerous and needed to be acted upon immediately. It was
probably well before 6 A.M.—considered the first hour of the day
in most eastern Mediterranean cultures—when the contingent
arrived with their prisoner. John provides the setting: "Then led
they Jesus from Caiaphas unto the hall of judgment: and it was
early; and they themselves went not into the judgment hall, lest
they should be defiled; but that they might eat the passover.
Pilate then went out unto them, and said, What accusation
bring ye against this man?" (John 18:28–29).

Because Galilean Jews reckoned their days from sunrise to
sunrise, Jesus and the apostles had already eaten their Passover
meal Thursday evening. But Jews in Judea counted their days
from sundown to sundown and had not yet celebrated their
Passover dinner, which they expected to do later that Friday

(MacArthur, *Murder of Jesus*, 163). Therefore, as John points out, the members of the council taking Jesus to Pilate felt they could not, according to rabbinic law, enter a Gentile residence without becoming ceremonially unclean and therefore unable to eat the Passover meal. Thus, they met Pilate outside his Jerusalem residence.

There is some debate over the location of Pilate's judgment hall. Roman prefects usually lived in Caesarea Maritima, west of Jerusalem, on the Mediterranean coast (Acts 23:35) and also had an official residence, or praetorium, in Jerusalem. Two buildings, both built by Herod the Great (died 4 B.C.), are candidates for having been Pilate's judgment hall. Some scholars argue vigorously for the Antonia Fortress. It was like a palace, according to Josephus, and occupied the northwest corner of the Temple Mount, overlooking the sanctuary and the courtyard of the Temple. Literary evidence, on the other hand, points to the other building, Herod's Palace, as the place where Pilate was living, even though it is not the traditional location. It was newer and more opulent than the Antonia Fortress and situated on the western side of the walled city, in what is now the Armenian Quarter of the Old City. Philo, in one of his writings, tells us plainly that "on the occasion of a Jewish feast Pilate was residing in 'Herod's Palace in the Holy City,' which he describes as 'the residence of the prefects'" (Wilkinson, *Jerusalem As Jesus Knew It*, 140). Thus, He who was regarded as the lowliest of prisoners was marched in shackles from the opulent palace of Caiaphas the high priest to the opulent palace of Pilate the Roman prefect, although in reality He was the King of the universe.

The case against Jesus likely proceeded with Pilate standing or sitting on a *bema*, or raised platform, in front of the accused and his accusers. We know that Pilate's final sentence was also delivered from the *bema* (Matthew 27:19), or in other words, from "the judgment seat in a place that is called the Pavement [in Greek, *lithostroton*], but in the Hebrew, Gabbatha" (John 19:13). The two words used here have different meanings: *Lithostroton* is a Greek term meaning "stone pavement"; *Gabbatha* is actually an Aramaic term meaning "raised place." We may therefore assume that "the regular procedure at the Palace was to use a raised outdoor paved area nearby, on which the resident Palace official set up a platform for his public appearances. This guess is made considerably more probable by our knowledge that Josephus tells us of two prefects who addressed angry crowds in Jerusalem from a platform: Pilate in about A.D. 30 and Florus in A.D. 66" (Wilkinson, *Jerusalem as Jesus Knew It*, 141).

Pilate undoubtedly knew something of Jesus' difficulties, if for no other reason than Roman soldiers were almost certainly involved in the arrest. But in that early hour on Friday morning when Jesus was standing in front of him, Pilate asked the accompanying Jewish council: "What accusation bring ye against this man?" (John 18:29). Luke implies that the entire council that had been in on the second Jewish arraignment (involving Caiaphas) began to accuse Jesus of sedition, or treason, saying, "We found this fellow perverting the nation, and forbidding to give tribute to Caesar, saying that he himself is Christ a King" (Luke 23:2). Their charge was not truthful, for just a few days earlier Jesus had taught: "Render therefore unto Caesar the things which are Caesar's" (Matthew 22:21). They did not press the charge of blasphemy, although the term *Christ*, or *Messiah*, might have had political or military connotations.

## Jesus' Innocence versus Jewish Vehemence

The Jewish assembly knew that reference to blasphemy would do nothing to elicit the approval they desired for Jesus' execution. The Romans had many gods, each to be given its due, and they knew nothing of blasphemy in the sense that the Jews meant it. But the Jewish leaders did use circular reasoning to try to force Pilate to agree to their request, saying, "If he were not a malefactor [criminal], we would not have delivered him up unto thee" (John 18:30). The arrogance of their argument is really quite stunning. They were saying, in effect, "Look, the fact that we're bringing him to you should be evidence enough to convict him. Don't ask any questions. Just do what we're telling you!"

Knowing what the Jewish leaders wanted, Pilate told them to take Jesus "and judge him according to your law" (John 18:31). He saw no reason to become embroiled in what he perceived to be an internal dispute among a people he cared little about. As a politician he did not want any part of a situation that could only make him look bad. The response of the Jewish leaders to Pilate's proposal is also significant: "It is not lawful for us to put any man to death" (John 18:31).

This scene is amazing. Here was Pontius Pilate, the most powerful man in Judea, offering the Jewish council a free hand, giving them the opportunity to deal with Jesus on the basis of their own customs and laws. But they were not satisfied. They wanted, even demanded, a Roman execution. Reasons for this are probably complex, but among the most important is surely the Jewish leaders' desire for a shield to hide behind. They feared the people and feared public opinion about Jesus (Matthew 26:5). If Pilate acceded to their wishes, they could attribute the death of Jesus to Roman decisions and Roman action. Also, if the Jews were to put Jesus to death, they would stone him, but the Romans would crucify him. Therefore, if the Romans could be made to take responsibility for the execution of Jesus within the Jewish leaders' self-imposed time constraints, they could avoid violating the Jewish regulations that would declare them ritually defiled because they had stoned someone just before the celebration of Passover. Whatever the Jews' reasons for wanting the Romans to execute Jesus, one more thing is certain. Their demands guaranteed the crucifixion of the Savior and fulfilled his own prophecy "which he spake, signifying what death he should die" (John 18:32).

Jesus' ultimate fate was no surprise to himself or to God the Father. Both Jesus and his Father knew that he would die by crucifixion. That had been prophesied by seers long before Jesus was born. Around 600 B.C. Nephi declared that he saw the Messiah "lifted up upon the cross and slain for the sins of the world" (1 Nephi 11:33). And King Benjamin testified: "And he shall be called Jesus Christ, the Son of God, the Father of heaven and earth, the Creator of all things from the beginning; and his mother shall be called Mary. And lo, he cometh unto his own, that salvation might come unto the children of men even through faith on his name; and even after all this they shall consider him a man, and say that he hath a devil, and shall scourge him, and shall crucify him" (Mosiah 3:8–9). Even more significantly, during the first year of his public ministry, Jesus himself said that the already ancient episode of Moses raising the brass serpent in the wilderness was a symbol of his forthcoming crucifixion: "And as Moses lifted up the serpent in the wilderness, even so must the Son of man be lifted up" (John 3:14).

Thus, Jesus walked in the shadow of the cross his whole life, knowing ahead of time how he would die. As Elder Neal A. Maxwell reminds us, prophecy "springs from very exact knowledge in the mind of the Lord Jesus Christ and God the Eternal Father, and it is surely very exacting in our lives as we experience its fulfillment" (*All These Things Shall Give Thee Experience,* 22). It was certainly proving to be very exacting for the Savior.

As with the Savior, so with us. There are no surprises to God when it comes to our lives. He knows all things that shall befall us, from the beginning to the end (Helaman 8:8). He knows where and when and under what circumstances each one of his spirit sons and daughters will be born and under what conditions each will live (Acts 17:26). He knows how and when we will die. He knows all things because all things are present before his eyes (D&C 38:2).

And because God knows all things, has all power, wisdom, and understanding (Alma 26:35), we may exercise unbounded confidence in him, in his love for us, and in his power to bring to pass all that is in our best interests. The Prophet Joseph Smith taught:

> Without the knowledge of all things God would not be able to save any portion of his creatures; for it is by reason of the knowledge which he has of all things, from the beginning to the end, that enables him to give that understanding to his creatures by which they are made partakers of eternal life; and if it were not for the idea existing in the minds of men that God had all knowledge it would be impossible for them to exercise faith in him.
>
> And it is not less necessary that men should have the idea of the existence of the attribute power in the Deity; for unless God had power over all things, and

was able by his power to control all things, and thereby deliver his creatures who put their trust in him from the power of all beings that might seek their destruction, whether in heaven, on earth, or in hell, men could not be saved. But with the idea of the existence of this attribute planted in the mind, men feel as though they had nothing to fear who put their trust in God, believing that he has power to save all who come to him to the very uttermost. . . .

For inasmuch as God possesses the attribute knowledge, he can make all things known to his saints necessary for their salvation; and as he possesses the attribute power, he is able thereby to deliver them from the power of all enemies; and seeing, also, that justice is an attribute of the Deity, he will deal with them upon the principles of righteousness and equity, and a just reward will be granted unto them for all their afflictions and sufferings for truth's sake. (*Lectures on Faith*, 4:11–12, 17)

Coupled with God's knowledge and power is his overriding attribute of love. God is love, as we have been told starkly (1 John 4:8, 16). I take this to mean that God is so full of love, so infused with this radiating quality, that all of God's other attributes and characteristics are shaped by, influenced by, and mediated through his love. Again, from the *Lectures on Faith:*

And lastly, but not less important to the exercise of faith in God, is the idea that he is love; for with all the other excellencies in his character, without this one to influence them, they could not have such powerful dominion over the minds of men; but when the idea is planted in the mind that he is love, who cannot see the just ground that men of every nation, kindred, and tongue, have to exercise faith in God so as to obtain to eternal life? (3:24)

Because we know that all God thinks and does is influenced by his perfect love, we may also rest assured that the horror of Christ's crucifixion, and the still greater horror of Christ's knowing beforehand that he was facing the surety of crucifixion, was necessary. It was part of our Heavenly Father's plan from the beginning and was foreordained to be of supreme benefit to us. "He doeth not anything save it be for the benefit of the world; for he loveth the world, even that he layeth down his own life that he may draw all men unto him. Wherefore, he commandeth none that they shall not partake of his salvation" (2 Nephi 26:24).

## CAPITAL PUNISHMENT

How much authority the Sanhedrin possessed to carry out capital punishment has been much debated. New Testament passages, especially Acts 21 and 22, as well as certain passages in Josephus support John's statement that Jewish councils in first-century Palestine did not possess decision-making authority in capital cases. The three most significant exceptions suggesting Jewish authorities did have some authority in such cases are the stoning of Stephen (Acts 6–7), the stoning of Paul (Acts 14:19), and the well-documented evidence (both archaeological and literary) of signs in Greek and Latin on the balustrade, or walled barrier, surrounding the Temple sanctuary forbidding all Gentiles, on penalty of death, to go into restricted holy areas beyond the Court of the Gentiles in the Temple Mount courtyard.

These three exceptions might be explained on the basis of two circumstances, however. First, the Romans granted standing approval of capital punishment for certain narrowly defined and undisputed offenses committed in public view (such as Gentiles bringing upon themselves their own death by ignoring warnings of restricted areas on the Temple Mount). Second, Jewish councils or groups of people motivated by religious zeal occasionally overstepped their authority. According to well-known New Testament scholar F. F. Bruce, "the right of jurisdiction in capital cases was most jealously reserved by provincial governors; permission to provincials to exercise it was a very rare concession, conceded only to such privileged communities as free cities within the empire. Jerusalem was no free city, and a turbulent province like Judaea was most unlikely to be granted such a concession" (*New Testament History*, 200). Thus, Stephen's later execution was a mob action precisely because the Romans did reserve the right to administer capital punishment and the mob did not want to wait for Roman legal machinery to do its work.

Whatever actual powers over life and death were invested in Jewish leaders during the years Jesus of Nazareth inhabited Roman Palestine, one thing is certain: Caiaphas and his council tried to force the Roman governor to implement the death penalty by charging Jesus with sedition.

## JESUS' DIALOGUE WITH PILATE

On this Friday morning, Pilate saw through the ruse. He saw that Jesus was not a threat to Rome, after spending only a few minutes alone with the Savior. He entered the Praetorium with Jesus, leaving the Jewish assembly outside, and began with a significant question: "Art thou the King of the Jews?" (John 18:33). The exchange that followed is reported by John:

Jesus answered him, Sayest thou this thing of thyself, or did others tell it thee of me?

Pilate answered, Am I a Jew? Thine own nation and the chief priests have delivered thee unto me: what hast thou done?

Jesus answered, My kingdom is not of this world: if my kingdom were of this world, then would my servants fight, that I should not be delivered to the Jews: but now is my kingdom not from hence.

Pilate therefore said unto him, Art thou a king then? Jesus answered, Thou sayest that I am a king. To this end was I born, and for this cause came I into the world, that I should bear witness unto the truth. Every one that is of the truth heareth my voice.

Pilate saith unto him, What is truth? And when he had said this, he went out again unto the Jews, and saith unto them, I find in him no fault at all. (John 18:34–38)

In the presence of his Roman inquisitor, Jesus bore down in pure testimony regarding His divine identity and mission. Indeed, he was King of the Jews. "To this end was I born," he declared (John 18:37), which was absolutely true. "At the time of the Savior's birth, Israel was ruled by alien monarchs. The rights of the royal Davidic family were unrecognized; and the ruler of the Jews was an appointee of Rome. Had Judah been a free and independent nation, ruled by her rightful sovereign, Joseph the carpenter would have been her crowned king; and his lawful successor to the throne would have been Jesus of Nazareth, the King of the Jews" (Talmage, *Jesus the Christ*, 87). But Jesus also declared to Pilate that His real kingdom was "not of this world" (John 18:36); it was not the Roman Empire. He further indicated that his whole-souled effort centered on bearing "witness unto the truth"—meaning religious truth, or the eternal verities, of his Father's plan of redemption.

This answer must have struck a nerve with Pilate, and he likely got the philosophical import of Jesus' statement, for he responded, "What is truth?" (John 18:38). With so many religious systems in the Roman Empire and so many gods being worshiped, it is not hard to imagine Pilate asking his question in a tone of sarcastic musing. Still, Jesus evinced nothing treasonous in either his discourse or demeanor.

Surely, Pilate had to wonder why Jesus posed such a threat. To execute him as an insurrectionist would be absurd. And surely the force of Jesus' personality alone was persuasive evidence of his greatness and uniqueness. Pilate returned outside to the open-air judgment seat, having received a deposition from the Accused, the likes of which he had never before experienced. How could he not declare Jesus to be innocent?

Pilate faced the Jewish crowd and proclaimed that he found no fault in Jesus whatsoever. The Jewish reaction to Pilate's declaration of the Savior's innocence is what we might expect. They became "more fierce," more intense in their accusations, and more adamant that Jesus was a huge threat to the peace of the entire country and beyond. "He stirreth up the people," they cried, "teaching throughout all Jewry, beginning from Galilee to this place" (Luke 23:5).

## THE FELLOWSHIP OF HIS SILENCE

Noteworthy again is the vehemence of Jesus' accusers, principally the chief priests, as they continued to press for his execution. No less significant is the Savior's silence. "And the chief priests accused him of many things: but he answered nothing.

And Pilate asked him again, saying, Answerest thou nothing? behold how many things they witness against thee. But Jesus yet answered nothing; so that Pilate marvelled" (Mark 15:3–5).

The image here is stark and heart-wrenching: Jesus suffering in silence, alone, without defenders, without help. Once again Isaiah's prophecy was fulfilled: "He was oppressed, and he was afflicted, yet he opened not his mouth: he is brought as a lamb to the slaughter, and as a sheep before her shearers is dumb, so he openeth not his mouth" (Isaiah 53:7).

Even Pilate was "surprised at the submissive yet majestic demeanor of Jesus" (Talmage, *Jesus the Christ*, 633). Modern disciples also marvel at Jesus' meekness. He took what was dished out. He exercised poise in the face of provocation. He suffered silently, knowing, as many in our day know, that sometimes silence can be the only response to trials, tribulations, and hardships. Others will not, cannot, understand. Some will not care. A few might even be inclined to think we had brought on the misery ourselves. But there is One with whom we have fellowship, One who knows silent suffering, One who hurts when we hurt, because he experienced the hurt before we did. Perhaps, it is in these moments of silent suffering and submissive meekness that we come to know God best, the time when He tutors us the most. After all, did not he who knows all things make the link between silence and the knowledge of his existence and power—in two separate dispensations, in fact? "Be still, and know that I am God," he declared (Psalm 46:10; D&C 101:16). If we try as hard as we can to endure our trials well, reviling not when we are reviled, assailing not when we are assailed, rendering not evil for evil or railing for railing, suffering silently without murmuring, whining, or feeling sorry for ourselves, then God will exalt us on high (1 Peter 2:23; 3:9; D&C 121:8).

Peter, the chief apostle, who knew something about silent suffering, taught that the trial of our faith was "much more precious than of gold that perisheth, though it be tried with fire" (1 Peter 1:7). He knew we must become like the Savior and endure our trials patiently. "For this is thankworthy, if a man for conscience toward God endure grief, suffering wrongfully. For what glory is it, if, when ye be buffeted for your faults, ye shall take it patiently? but if, when ye do well, and suffer for it, ye take it patiently, this is acceptable with God" (1 Peter 2:19–20). Finally, Peter taught that once we have entered the Savior's fellowship of suffering, we must love and serve one another, helping one another through our trials (1 Peter 1:22).

No less significant than our silence in suffering is our silence in spiritual experiences. We have been counseled not to talk much about sacred things or private spiritual experiences. President Howard W. Hunter, a man well acquainted with both personal suffering and powerful spiritual experiences, counseled: "I have watched a great many of my brethren over the years and we have shared some rare and unspeakable spiritual experiences together. Those experiences have all been different, each special in its own way, and such sacred moments may or may not be accompanied by tears. Very often they are, but sometimes they are accompanied by *total silence*" ("Eternal Investments"; emphasis added).

Silent appreciation is often the most appropriate, most Christlike response to transcendent spiritual experiences, just as silence is often the best response to private trials—be they physical or spiritual. We are never more like the Savior when we override the impulse to tell others either what profound personal experiences we enjoy or to complain about what great trials we are enduring. The Lord's age-old counsel is still timely when it comes to responding to both supernal spiritual experiences and profoundly wrenching trials: "Be still, and know that I am God" (Psalm 46:10).

## JESUS BEFORE HEROD

Pilate came close to helping the Savior by defending him to his accusers. But in the end, Pilate chose a way out. Personal preservation took precedence over principle. He sought to transfer responsibility to someone else—he sought a scapegoat. "When Pilate heard of Galilee, he asked whether the man were a Galilaean. And as soon as he knew that he belonged unto Herod's jurisdiction, he sent him to Herod, who himself also was at Jerusalem at that time" (Luke 23:6–7). And so Jesus was shunted off in shackles to Herod Antipas, son of Herod the Great, tetrarch of Galilee and Perea, who was in town for the feast of the Passover. Though perhaps not as blood-thirsty a man as his father, Antipas was despicable in his own right.

Though Pilate did not like Herod Antipas, it is easy to see how political circumstances would have dictated to Pilate the prudence of involving Herod at this point. The case of the Jewish leaders versus Jesus of Nazareth was a potential political fiasco, or worse, for Pontius Pilate. He could not simply dismiss it for fear of provoking the Jews again and lending credibility to mounting doubts about his ability and fitness to rule Judea. Philo tells how Pilate "feared lest [the Jewish leaders] might in reality go on an embassy to the emperor, and might impeach him with respect to other particulars of his government, in respect of his corruption, and his acts of insolence, and his rapine, and his habit of insulting people, and his cruelty, and his continual murders of people untried and uncondemned, and his never-ending and gratuitous, and most grievous inhumanity" (*Legatio ad Gaium*, 302).

Pilate had already provoked his subjects as well as Rome over several offenses that demonstrated his insensitivity and poor judgment. He was known to be ruthless and cruel. Luke mentions an incident involving "Galilaeans, whose blood Pilate mingled with their sacrifices" (Luke 13:1), indicating perhaps that the governor had some Jews from Jesus' home region killed on the Temple Mount as they participated in one of the feasts. We know nothing else about this, except that Galilee was a noted hotbed of insurrectionists, zealots, and terrorist activity against Rome, and perhaps Pilate took extraordinary measures over some threat, perceived or real.

Perhaps the sternest rebuke Pilate had received from the emperor in Rome, Tiberius Caesar, came as a result of the "gold shields" incident. Pilate had some gilded shields made, dedicated them to Tiberius, and hung them in Herod's palace where Pilate stayed in Jerusalem. The inscription on the shields contained the traditional titles of the emperor, one of which attributed to him divine standing, or godhood. This was so offensive to Pilate's monotheistic subjects that they threatened to protest directly to the emperor. Outraged (and worried), Pilate wrote preemptively to Tiberius, putting the best possible spin he could on the volatile situation. Confirming Pilate's worst fears, Tiberius wrote a scathing letter back, as Philo reported: "Immediately, without putting any thing off till the next day, [Tiberius] wrote a letter reproaching and reviling [Pilate] in the most bitter manner for his act of unprecedented audacity and wickedness, and commanding him immediately to take down the shields and to convey them away from the metropolis of Judaea to Caesarea" (*Legatio ad Gaium*, 305). The Jewish leaders knew they could use Pilate's increasingly tenuous position with the emperor as leverage in pressing their charges against Jesus.

It is no surprise, therefore, that Pilate thought of a way to extricate himself from the ticklish business that had real potential to bring down his government. Jesus was from Galilee. Technically, Galilee lay outside Pilate's jurisdiction. If he sent Jesus to Herod, the tetrarch of Galilee, he might be able to dump the problem in Herod's lap. Not only that, but if Pilate sent Jesus to Herod, who wanted to meet the Savior (in hopes of witnessing a miracle), and Pilate could make it look as if he were showing a courtesy to the tetrarch, he might be able to mend a poor relationship that existed between them, the Roman governor and the Jewish ruler.

> And when Herod saw Jesus, he was exceeding glad: for he was desirous to see him of a long season, because he had heard many things of him; and he hoped to have seen some miracle done by him.
>
> Then he questioned with him in many words; but he answered him nothing.
>
> And the chief priests and scribes stood and vehemently accused him.
>
> And Herod with his men of war set him at nought, and mocked him, and arrayed him in a gorgeous robe, and sent him again to Pilate.
>
> And the same day Pilate and Herod were made friends together: for before they were at enmity between themselves. (Luke 23:8–12)

The vehemence of the chief priests and scribes again occupies center stage. Jesus had already stood in silent refutation of their accusations. Now he stood in silent rebuke of the tetrarch of Galilee and Perea. I believe, along with Elder James E. Talmage, that Jesus not only disliked Herod but felt utter contempt for him. He had murdered Jesus' cousin, John the Baptist, and had tried to kill Jesus himself. He deserved no response or respect from the Son of God, whose silence distinguished Herod in the annals of history, as Elder Talmage notes:

> The chief priests and scribes vehemently voiced their accusations; but not a word was uttered by the Lord. Herod is the only character in history to whom Jesus is known to have applied a personal epithet of contempt. "Go ye and tell that fox," He once said to certain Pharisees who had come to Him with the story that Herod intended to kill him. As far as we know, Herod is further distinguished as the only being who saw Christ face to face and spoke to Him, yet never heard His voice. For penitent sinners, weeping women, prattling children, for the scribes, the Pharisees, the Sadducees, the rabbis, for the perjured high priest and his obsequious and insolent underling, and for Pilate the pagan, Christ had words—of comfort or instruction, of warning or rebuke, of protest or denunciation—yet for Herod the fox He had but disdainful and kingly silence. (*Jesus the Christ*, 636)

When Herod could see that he would get nothing out of Jesus, he and his "men-at-arms" ridiculed and mocked the Savior, sarcastically dressed him in an elegant robe, sent him back to Pilate, having "found nothing in Jesus to warrant condemnation" (Talmage, *Jesus the Christ*, 636)—and, more ironic yet, Herod became friends with Pilate over the incident.

Pilate's attempt to rid himself of Jesus' case gracefully had failed. He would have to deal squarely with the God of the universe. It was, in its own way, a burden no other ruler has ever had to face.

Pilate said unto them, Whom will ye that I release unto you? Barabbas, or Jesus which is called Christ? . . .

When he was set down on the judgment seat, his wife sent unto him, saying, Have thou nothing to do with that just man: for I have suffered many things this day in a dream because of him.

But the chief priests and elders persuaded the multitude that they should ask Barabbas, and destroy Jesus.

The governor answered and said unto them, Whether of the twain will ye that I release unto you? They said, Barabbas.

Pilate saith unto them, What shall I do then with Jesus which is called Christ? They all say unto him, Let him be crucified. . . .

When Pilate saw that he could prevail nothing, but that rather a tumult was made, he took water, and washed his hands before the multitude, saying, I am innocent of the blood of this just person: see ye to it.

Then answered all the people, and said, His blood be on us, and on our children.

Then released he Barabbas unto them: and when he had scourged Jesus, he delivered him to be crucified.

Then the soldiers of the governor took Jesus into the common hall, and gathered unto him the whole band of soldiers.

And they stripped him, and put on him a scarlet robe.

And when they had platted a crown of thorns, they put it upon his head, and a reed in his right hand: and they bowed the knee before him, and mocked him, saying, Hail, King of the Jews!

And they spit upon him, and took the reed, and smote him on the head.

MATTHEW 27:17, 19–22, 24–30

# CHAPTER 7

# The Final Verdict

The meeting between Herod and Jesus must have been short, since Jesus did not speak. Undoubtedly upset by such condemning silence, Herod had the Savior mocked again, arrayed in a robe that some modern authorities suppose was white, the usual color of dress among Jewish nobility, and sent him back to Pilate—who was now forced to act (Luke 23:11). The robe Herod used was different from the purple one used later by the Roman soldiers to mock Jesus yet again after his second arraignment before Pilate (Matthew 27:27–28). White is a premier symbol of purity and divinity (John 20:12), and though Herod meant its use as a statement of irony, it rightly identified the purest of our Heavenly Father's children.

We can imagine that Pilate was surprised and frustrated when Jesus showed up again so quickly at the Praetorium, perhaps feeling that he had had more than enough of this never-ending situation. Pilate called together the Jewish leaders who constituted Jesus' original accusers as well as others who had by this time joined the ranks of what was fast becoming a mob. He declared to everyone assembled that there were now two independent witnesses—both himself and the people's own Jewish ruler, Herod—attesting the Savior's innocence of any crime worthy of death (Luke 23:13–14). Therefore, he, Pilate, would punish Jesus in Roman fashion—by whipping rather than the much more severe scourging that always preceded crucifixion—and release him in accord with a custom that was invoked at feast time.

## RELEASE OF BARABBAS

John's Gospel is clear that the custom of releasing a prisoner at Passover time was a Jewish one (John 18:39). And the Greek text of Mark 15:6 indicates it was "usually" done, meaning the custom was in place long before Jesus' situation had arisen. Pilate seems to have attempted to use the custom at this point as a last-ditch effort to get out from under the tremendous burden of Jesus' trial while saving face at the same time. He was under great pressure not just from the Jewish council but now also from his wife, Procula, whose name we learn from nonbiblical Roman texts. With rapidly increasing intensity, the Jews demanded that Jesus be executed, while Procula anxiously pressed for Pilate to leave Jesus alone! "When he was set down on the judgment seat, his wife sent unto him, saying, Have thou nothing to do with that just man: for I have suffered many things this day in a dream because of him" (Matthew 27:19). Dreams are an important source of personal revelation, and we do not doubt that Pilate's wife received some kind of witness that Jesus was an innocent man and perhaps much more than that. Because she attested to Jesus' innocence through her dream, she was later honored as a saint by the Greek Orthodox Church (*Harper's Bible Dictionary*, s.v. "Pilate, Pontius," 559).

Pilate proposed a brilliant solution. He offered the Jewish assemblage a choice for release: Jesus of Nazareth, who was reputed to be the Messiah (Matthew 27:17), whose guilt was questionable at best, and whose popularity with the common people had been demonstrated a week before during his triumphal entry (Matthew 21:1–11); or Barabbas, an evil and notorious convicted criminal (Matthew 27:16). Surely, the Jewish crowd would choose to release Jesus of Nazareth. But their leaders had been inciting the crowd: "The chief priests and elders persuaded the multitude that they should ask Barabbas, and destroy Jesus. The governor answered and said unto them, Whether of the twain will ye that I release unto you? They said, Barabbas" (Matthew 27:20–21).

The irony of Barabbas's release is so great as to need little explication, but there are ironies beyond the obvious ones:

1. The given name of Barabbas was Yehoshua, or Jesus, the same as the Savior's. An ancient variant reading of the text of Matthew 27:16–17 preserves the full name: "Jesus Barabbas." And the early church theologian Origen (died A.D. 254) implies that the full name appeared in most of the manuscripts of his day. Scholars point out that under these circumstances a much more dramatic reading of Matthew 27:17 was originally intended: "Which Jesus do you want: the son of Abba, or the self-styled Messiah?" (*Anchor Bible Dictionary*, s.v. "Barrabas," 1:607).

2. The term *Barabbas* means, literally, "son of [Aramaic, *bar*] the father [Aramaic, *abba*]." Jesus *was* the true and literal Son of the Father. The angry, stirred-up mob chose to release one Jesus, son of the father, rather than the other Jesus, Son of the Father.

3. Barabbas was guilty of sedition (Luke 23:19, 25) but was

freed; Jesus was falsely accused of sedition (Luke 23:2) but was sentenced to death.

4. Barabbas was the fulfillment of the ritual scapegoat of the sacrificial rites performed on the Day of Atonement—the animal led to the wilderness and released; Jesus was the fulfillment of the goat sacrificed on the Temple altar as the sin offering representing the guilt of the people (Leviticus 16:7–22).

5. The Greek word used in Mark 15:13 to denote the cry of the crowd for innocent Jesus' execution in preference to that of the guilty Barabbas is the same word used when the crowd greeted Jesus in messianic tones (Mark 11:9) less than a week before, during his triumphal entry into Jerusalem (Brown, *Death of the Messiah*, 1:824).

Jesus was the embodiment of everything that is good and right and just and pure, while Barabbas seems to have been the embodiment of everything that is not—he was, in fact, the opposite of everything good, right, just, and pure. And yet, the bloodthirsty crowd called for the release of Barabbas. They would have nothing less than the destruction of righteousness in the person of Jesus Christ.

Pilate was now unalterably stuck, and he knew it. Trying one more time to secure the release of Jesus while saving his own neck politically, he spoke to the crowd and uttered the most haunting and important of all questions ever asked, "What shall I do then with Jesus which is called Christ?" (Matthew 27:22). For every modern disciple, is not this the question of the ages—the question of questions? Is it not the question that everyone will someday have to answer? Is it not *the* one question no one will be able to ignore? How will each individual—every man, woman, and child, every saint, sage, and sinner who has ever lived on the earth—choose to regard Jesus of Nazareth? What shall each person do with the name of Jesus Christ? Or, as the Savior himself posed the question, "What think ye of Christ?" (Matthew 22:42).

The response of the Jewish crowd to Pilate's question is as haunting as the question itself. They *all* shouted to Pilate, "Crucify him, crucify him" (Luke 23:21; Matthew 27:22). Pilate's rejoinder to their blood-curdling cries for crucifixion should have given pause to the mob to reconsider their bloodthirsty demands and haunted them long after as well, but apparently it did not. Pilate asked simply: "Why, what evil hath he done?" (Matthew 27:23; Mark 15:14). That the crowd became even more loud and angry can only be attributed to the unrelenting influence of the prince of darkness. "And they cried out the more exceedingly, Crucify him" (Mark 15:14; Matthew 27:23; Luke 23:21). The ugly crowd was about to get its way, the Jewish leaders were about to get their way, and Satan was about to get his way. But his way is unadulterated selfishness, "for he seeketh that all men might be miserable like unto himself" (2 Nephi 2:27). Satan has absolutely no interest in the happiness, peace, or welfare of others. The angry Jewish crowd is witness enough of that.

## Hand Washing: An Ancient Connection

The voices and workings of the chief priests now prevailed without equivocation over the voices of reason and inspiration (Luke 23:23). Under the direction of the chief priests, and undoubtedly at their instigation, the volatile Jewish crowd would have none of Pilate's alternatives or counterproposals. When Pilate could see that he "could prevail nothing" (Matthew 27:24), that he would not succeed, and that he needed to placate the tumultuous crowd to prevent a riot, he gave in to their demands, released Barabbas, scourged Jesus as the official prelude to his crucifixion, and then delivered him up to his sentence of death. But not before Pilate acted out his most famous gesture. He "took water, and washed his hands before the multitude, saying, I am innocent of the blood of this just person: see ye to it. Then answered all the people, and said, His blood be on us, and on our children" (Matthew 27:24–25).

There are several examples in ancient Greek and Roman texts of washing oneself as a symbolic demonstration of absolving oneself of guilt or responsibility for the shedding of another person's blood. Educated Romans, including Pilate, would probably have been familiar with these examples. And the governor may have invoked the procedure because of this ancient practice in the classical world. The symbolism is not difficult to understand. The literal act of washing removed, metaphorically, the fault or responsibility for another person's death. But Pilate may also have had Jewish culture in mind when he performed his ceremonial hand washing, in an effort to make a dramatic impression on Jewish leaders who knew the practice from their study of the Torah. Deuteronomy prescribes ceremonial hand washing by city elders over the carcass of a sacrificed heifer as a sign that their city was not responsible for the death of a slain man: "And all the elders of that city, that are next unto the slain man, shall wash their hands over the heifer that is beheaded in the valley: And they shall answer and say, Our hands have not shed this blood, neither have our eyes seen it. Be merciful, O Lord, unto thy people Israel, whom thou hast redeemed, and lay not innocent blood unto thy people of Israel's charge. And the blood shall be forgiven them" (Deuteronomy 21:6–8).

Whether Pilate could have seen himself in the place of the Israelite city elders and Jesus in the place of the sacrificial heifer seems doubtful; however, Pilate's hand-washing ceremony that

Friday morning in Jerusalem does seem to be a partial fulfill-
ment of the reason the Mosaic prescription was first instituted.
From ancient times it had pointed to a specific episode in
Christ's life, whether the Israelites knew it or not.

The retort of the multitude after Pilate symbolically
absolved himself of responsibility for Jesus' death is chilling
indeed. In fact, it is the opposite of the expected response of
the people as outlined in Deuteronomy 21:8. Instead of saying,
"Be merciful, O Lord, unto thy people Israel, whom thou has
redeemed, and lay not innocent blood unto thy people . . . ,"
the crowd called for the responsibility for the blood of Jesus to
be laid upon them and their children! Was this a calculated
and purposeful contradiction to the verses in Deuteronomy,
which had to have been known to at least some of the Jews
in the crowd? Was their answer suggested by the chief priests?
We do not know. But the irony here is twofold: Jesus was the
very Lord and Redeemer of Israel spoken of in the passage in
Deuteronomy. And, tragically, generations of innocent Jews
have been burdened unfairly with blame for Jesus' death, which
has been heaped upon them for centuries.

Historically speaking, the cry of the Jewish assembly as
reported in Matthew 27:25 has been the source of much terrible treatment of the Jewish people. Nonetheless, neither this
passage nor any other justifies unrighteous, inhuman treatment
of any member of our Heavenly Father's family. It was not the
Jewish people who crucified the Savior but individual evil men.
Jesus was a Jew, and so were the apostles and almost every other
member of the early Church up to the time of the first mission
to the Gentiles during the ministry of Paul of Tarsus. As one
Book of Mormon prophet declared, we ought to thank the Jews:
"Do [the Gentiles] remember the travails, and the labors, and

the pains of the Jews, and their diligence unto me, in bringing forth salvation unto the Gentiles?" (2 Nephi 29:4).

Of course, it is true that many bore responsibility for the Crucifixion, as the scriptures teach, including Herod, Pontius Pilate, and certain other Gentiles, members of the Jerusalem community, and, above all, the Jewish rulers and chief priests of the people. As the early apostles Peter and John said: "The kings of the earth stood up, and the rulers were gathered together against the Lord, and against his Christ. For of a truth against thy holy child Jesus, whom thou hast anointed, both Herod, and Pontius Pilate, with the Gentiles, and the people of Israel, were gathered together" (Acts 4:26–27).

No amount of hand washing could absolve Pilate of responsibility for Jesus' execution; he had the power and the opportunity to stop the illegal and immoral proceedings, but he did not—even though, as I believe, he knew Jesus was the Christ. Elder Neal A. Maxwell declared: "Pilate sought to refuse responsibility for deciding about Christ, but Pilate's hands were never dirtier than just after he had washed them" ("Why Not Now?" 13). In a perceptive comment about Pilate that teaches us the most important lesson of this episode for our own lives, President Spencer W. Kimball asked: "Could the Lord forgive Pilate? Certainly he could not without Pilate's repentance. Did Pilate repent? We do not know what Pilate did after the scripture drops him. He had a desire to favor the Savior. He did not display full courage in resisting the pressures of the people. . . . We leave Pilate to the Lord as we do all other sinners, but remember that 'to know and not to do' is sin" (*Miracle of Forgiveness*, 167).

In another significant irony of history, a few months after the Crucifixion, the same Jewish leaders who had deliberately provoked the early-morning mob to cry for the Savior's blood to be upon them became indignant over the apostles' eyewitness testimony and powerful preaching. They forgot the facts surrounding Jesus' condemnation and accused the apostles, saying, "Ye have filled Jerusalem with your doctrine, and intend to bring this man's blood upon us" (Acts 5:28). Indeed!

## SCOURGING

After Pilate's ceremony of self-absolution, Jesus was turned over to the torture of scourging, followed by mocking and more abuse inflicted by soldiers of the governor. Though Luke omits these horrors from his record, and John presents a slightly different chronology, there can be no doubt that these tortures exacted a terrible physical toll from the Savior. Scourging was a legal preliminary to every Roman execution, and prisoners sometimes died from it alone.

The usual instrument delivering the punishment was a short whip (*flagrum,* or *flagellum*) having a wooden handle with several single strands or braided leather thongs that had a lead ball attached to each end. Sometimes pieces of glass or chunks of bone were woven into the thongs. The victim was stripped of all clothing and tied by his wrists to an upright post or pillar. The feet would be dangling and the skin on the back and buttocks stretched tight. The back, buttocks, and back of the legs were flogged with extreme force either by two soldiers (*lictors*) taking turns or by one scourger who alternated positions to get at both halves of the victim's back. The first blows of the thongs cut through the skin only. But subsequent blows cut deeper and deeper into the subcutaneous tissue. The lead balls at the ends of the thongs first produced deep bruises, and then open wounds as the blows were repeated (Davis, "Physician Testifies about Crucifixion," 37).

When the Roman soldiers repeatedly struck the victim's back with full force, the flesh would be torn away in chunks. As the flogging continued, the lacerations would "tear into the underlying skeletal muscles and produce quivering ribbons of bleeding flesh" (Edwards et al., "Physical Death of Jesus Christ," 1457). The number of lashes was supposed to be limited to thirty-nine, according to Jewish law. Deuteronomy 25:3 states that if a guilty man deserves to be beaten, he must not be given more than forty lashes. Later rabbinic law prescribed thirty-nine—"forty stripes save one," as the apostle Paul writes in 2 Corinthians 11:24. This regulation "set a fence around the Torah," as the rabbis said, or, in other words, officially prevented zealous administrators from overstepping the bounds of the Mosaic law. Whether the Roman soldiers exceeded the prescribed number of lashes is unknown, but after his flogging the half-fainting Jesus was untied, slumping to the stone pavement made slippery with his own blood (Davis, "Physician Testifies about Crucifixion," 37).

It was not uncommon for scourging victims to die from lacerated arteries or from extreme shock as a result of trauma to the kidneys or other organs. The severity of the scourging depended on the disposition of the lictors, but the practice was intended to bring the victim to a condition just short of death. The extent of shock and blood loss undoubtedly determined the length of time the victim could survive on the cross. The severity of the scourging Jesus received is not discussed in the four Gospel accounts, but some scholars are convinced that it was particularly harsh in his case (Edwards et al., "Physical Death of Jesus Christ," 1457–58).

Scourging was a brutal, bloody business. But, then again, so was the whole atoning act of our Lord—from Gethsemane through Golgotha. He endured it for the whole human family collectively, as well as for each human being individually and personally. In this regard, the words of President James E. Faust remain forever etched in my mind: "In the words of the hymn, 'Let me not forget, O Savior, / Thou didst bleed and die for me.' I wonder how many drops were shed for me" ("Atonement: Our Greatest Hope," 3).

It has been said that Pilate was trying to create compassion for Jesus as a result of the terrible scourging. But if he was, it did not work. In fact, it may have had the opposite effect on the minds of bloodthirsty leaders who would have revelled in the increasing intensity of the Savior's physical suffering. Certainly, the scene of the Savior's scourging points out another great irony of this situation, as Elder James E. Talmage notes: "Pilate seems to have counted on the pitiful sight of the scourged and bleeding Christ to soften the hearts of the maddened Jews. But the effect failed. Think of the awful fact—a heathen, a pagan, who knew not God, pleading with the priests and people of Israel for the life of their Lord and King!" (*Jesus the Christ*, 598).

The scourging was undoubtedly accomplished at the Praetorium, but Matthew and Mark describe the ensuing mocking by the soldiers as a separate action within the judgment hall.

> Then the soldiers of the governor took Jesus into the common hall, and gathered unto him the whole band of soldiers.
>
> And they stripped him, and put on him a scarlet robe.
>
> And when they had platted a crown of thorns, they put it upon his head, and a reed in his right hand: and they bowed the knee before him, and mocked him, saying, Hail, King of the Jews!

And they spit upon him, and took the reed, and smote him on the head. (Matthew 27:27–30)

The cohort of Roman soldiers in the Praetorium was a large one, perhaps as many as six hundred men—the whole Jerusalem garrison. They were an elite military unit serving under the command of the Roman governor, commissioned to keep the peace in one of the most volatile regions of the empire. Because Jews were exempted from military service in Palestine, all the soldiers must have been Gentiles. At least some of these soldiers were likely part of the arresting party who had seized Jesus the night before in Gethsemane. Many in the cohort had undoubtedly gathered to watch the mocking and abuse, which their comrades knew how to dish out so effectively. One author has written that "Pilate's orders were to scourge and crucify Jesus, but the cruel mockery they heaped upon Him reveals their own wickedness" (MacArthur, *Murder of Jesus*, 190). If not outright wickedness, certainly the soldiers' actions highlight the harshness or brutality of Roman military life.

The mockery continued as the soldiers made a great spectacle of clothing their Prisoner in a robe whose color signified royalty. The "scarlet robe" of the King James Version (Matthew 27:28) is changed in the Joseph Smith Translation to "purple robe" (Matthew 27:30), thus matching Mark's and John's descriptions (Mark 15:17; John 19:5). Purple was the color of royalty, but its use in this case was no compliment. The Roman soldiers must have seen a great joke in a lowly provincial Jew from Galilee, beaten within an inch of his life, who claimed to be the King of the Jewish nation. In fact, the soldiers' humiliating actions mocked both Jesus' true royalty and his true divinity. And still his suffering was far from over. "It seemed as if the whole world was against Jesus. Jews and Gentiles alike were now willfully, even gleefully, participating in His murder, determined to see Him die in the most agonizing way possible. A catalogue of the pains of crucifixion would fill an entire volume" (MacArthur, *Murder of Jesus*, 190).

The apostle John records that after Jesus was scourged and mocked, Pilate made one more attempt to secure Jesus' release. But when he heard the Jews cry out that if he let Jesus go, he was no friend of Caesar, Pilate could no longer resist their incessant demands. He had to issue his final order.

> Pilate therefore went forth again, and saith unto them, Behold, I bring him forth to you, that ye may know that I find no fault in him.
>
> Then came Jesus forth, wearing the crown of thorns, and the purple robe. And Pilate saith unto them, Behold the man! . . .
>
> And from thenceforth Pilate sought to release him: but the Jews cried out, saying, If thou let this man go, thou art not Caesar's friend: whosoever maketh himself a king speaketh against Caesar.
>
> When Pilate therefore heard that saying, he brought Jesus forth, and sat down in the judgment seat in a place that is called the Pavement, but in the Hebrew, Gabbatha. . . .
>
> But they cried out, Away with him, away with him, crucify him. Pilate saith unto them, Shall I crucify your King? The chief priests answered, We have no king but Caesar.
>
> Then delivered he him therefore unto them to be crucified. (John 19:4–5, 12–13, 15–16)

Amazingly, not only were the Jewish leaders guilty of murdering their true God and King, they were now guilty of abandoning their own traditional statements about God actually being their King, for the sake of their premeditated scheme. But even more stunning than Jewish antagonism toward Jesus is the way the Savior faced up to all that befell him. To think of the God of the universe battered, bruised, dehydrated, exhausted, stripped, and bleeding in front of a taunting crowd is almost more than we can allow ourselves to ponder. His physical suffering is incomprehensible. Not only was he flogged to the point of collapse but he was stripped again, dressed in a robe of mock royalty, spat upon, made to hold a wooden stick in his right hand as a scepter, and beaten on the head after the crown of thorns had been placed on top, thus driving the thorns deeper into his scalp.

The Roman emperor, Caesar, wore a crown made from a laurel wreath; the crown of thorns was undoubtedly a sadistic play on that practice. Many varieties of thorns grow in the Holy Land in modern times, which help us visualize the scene involving the Savior. It is possible his cruel crown that fateful Friday morning was made out of the gruesome inch-long thorns seen occasionally in religious souvenir shops in the Holy Land. In addition, the purple robe being torn from his back would have caused Jesus more pain and fresh bleeding because clots of blood from the scourging would have begun to adhere to the robe (Davis, "Physician Testifies about Crucifixion," 37). How could any human being fail to be moved by such a scene?

One suspects that Jesus was able to endure all of this patiently because his mind and heart were focused on his Father and his Father's will. He knew his Father loved him and that this was what his Father wanted him to do in order to ransom all of his Father's family. Like the firstborn in Israelite society, who was given a double portion of the inheritance to rescue the family and help family members out of their difficulties, Jesus, the firstborn of all our Heavenly Father's spirit children, used all of his strength, all of his physical, emotional, mental, and spiritual reserves, to rescue his Father's family. He was draining the dregs of the bitter cup once again so that none of his brothers and sisters would have to. And even though he had life in himself—that is, he had the power to give up his life of his own accord, to determine the time of his own decease, or to continue to live (John 10:18)—he was quickly reaching his extremity as he stood before his mockers and abusers after his scourging. Only his great reservoirs of strength and superior endowments of power were seeing him through.

There are lessons in this for all of us. First, we are asked by the same Savior who suffered his own tribulations patiently to "be patient in tribulation until I come" (D&C 54:10) and to "continue in patience until ye are perfected" (D&C 67:13). Patience is the pattern of Christlike behavior. It is the highest standard. He showed us the way. He really is the way, the truth, and the life. Given what the Savior endured in patience, we cannot say anything to him about life's unfairness or frustrations that he does not already know by his own experience. Patience is required of all, even the greatest of all. Elder Bruce R. McConkie taught: "To fill the full measure and purpose of our mortal probation, *we must have patience*. This mortal existence is the Lord's sifting sphere, the time when we are subject to trials, testing, and tribulations. Future rewards will be based on our *patient* endurance of all things" (*Mormon Doctrine*, 557; emphasis added).

President John Taylor taught a profound lesson about the importance of submitting patiently to whatever God sees fit to inflict upon us in this schooling process we call mortality. "I have seen men tempted so sorely that finally they would say, 'I'll be damned if I'll stand it any longer,' Well, you will be damned if you do not" (*Journal of Discourses*, 22:318). On the other hand, we may take great comfort in the words of Elder James E. Talmage: "No pang that is suffered by man or woman upon the earth will be without its compensating effect . . . if it be met with patience" (quoted in Kimball, *Faith Precedes the Miracle*, 98).

Second, in order for us to be able to endure all things patiently, we must build up reservoirs of strength and seek endowments of power just as the Savior did in order to get us through the wrenching circumstances of life. An important source of strength and power comes to us from the endowment, or rich gift, given in our temples. Elder Robert D. Hales said:

> In our day, the steadying arm of the Lord reaches us through the ordinances of His holy temples. Said the Prophet Joseph to the early Saints in Nauvoo, "You need an endowment, brethren, in order that you may be prepared and able to overcome all things." How right he was! Being blessed with the temple covenants and endowed with power made it possible for the Latter-day Saints to endure tribulation with faith. At the end of her own pioneer journey, Sarah Rich recorded, "If it had not been for the faith and knowledge that was bestowed upon us in that temple . . . our journey would have been like . . . taking a leap in the dark." ("Faith through Tribulation Brings Peace and Joy," 17)

All of us will have challenging circumstances to pass through in life. The Lord himself will reach out and tug at our very heart-strings, and if we cannot submit patiently to his molding and shaping, we will not be fit for his kingdom. Sometimes we may think that his molding and shaping are more than we can handle or that they are not worth the pain. Nevertheless, we may take comfort in knowing that even for God, the greatest of all, a crown of thorns had to precede his crown of glory. And it is precisely because Jesus experienced the crown of thorns that he has the knowledge and power to wipe away all our tears. Of those who are exalted in God's kingdom, John the Revelator wrote:

> And I said unto him, Sir, thou knowest. And he said to me, These are they which came out of great tribulation, and have washed their robes, and made them white in the blood of the Lamb.
>
> Therefore are they before the throne of God, and serve him day and night in his temple: and he that sitteth on the throne shall dwell among them.
>
> They shall hunger no more, neither thirst any more; neither shall the sun light on them, nor any heat.
>
> For the Lamb which is in the midst of the throne shall feed them, and shall lead them unto living fountains of waters: and God shall wipe away all tears from their eyes. (Revelation 7:14–17)

The image of someone wiping away the tears of another connotes profound tenderness. For me, it conjures up images of a loving parent easing the pains of an injured child. Perhaps the Lord intended to evoke such thoughts when he inspired his apostle John to use the language found in Revelation. All of us are children of God, and all of us are injured in many ways as a result of mortality. The Lord's concern for each of us is individual and personal: His ministrations are intimate, he always takes into consideration our needs and desires, and he knows us by name, as the scriptures demonstrate. It is no small thing for the Lord to promise that he will dry *all* our tears. The price for that power was Gethsemane and Golgotha.

And when they had mocked him, they took off the purple from him, and put his own clothes on him, and led him out to crucify him.

And they compel one Simon a Cyrenian, who passed by, coming out of the country, the father of Alexander and Rufus, to bear his cross.

And they bring him unto the place Golgotha, which is, being interpreted, The place of a skull.

MARK 15:20–22

And there followed him a great company of people, and of women, which also bewailed and lamented him.

But Jesus turning unto them said, Daughters of Jerusalem, weep not for me, but weep for yourselves, and for your children.

For, behold, the days are coming, in the which they shall say, Blessed are the barren, and the wombs that never bare, and the paps which never gave suck.

Then shall they begin to say to the mountains, Fall on us; and to the hills, Cover us.

For if they do these things in a green tree, what shall be done in the dry?

And there were also two other, malefactors, led with him to be put to death.

And when they were come to the place, which is called Calvary, there they crucified him, and the malefactors, one on the right hand, and the other on the left.

LUKE 23:27–33

# CHAPTER 8

# The Way of the Cross

After Jesus had been made sufficient sport of, to the enjoyment of the taunting and jeering crowd, the Roman soldiers took from him their mock royal robe and, in deference to Jewish custom, put his own clothes back on him (Matthew 27:31). In other cultures the victim was usually left naked. Jesus was then forced to carry his own cross and was led away from the judgment hall with two thieves to the place where the crucifixions were to be carried out (Luke 23:32).

It has been argued, and probably rightly, that the cross Jesus carried (Matthew 27:32; Mark 15:21; Luke 23:26) was not the entire Latin cross as traditionally portrayed. Rather, it was likely only the crossbar, or *patibulum,* which would have been a heavy piece of wood (probably olive) weighing about 75 to 125 pounds and capable of being fastened to a vertical pole or beam. An important ancient source for crucifixion practices refers to the crossbar being carried by the victim through the city beyond the gate (Plautus, *Braggart Warrior,* 161). The Savior's patibulum would have been placed across the nape of his neck, balanced along his shoulders, and tied to both arms (Edwards et al., "Physical Death," 1459). Because crucifixion practices in the ancient world varied according to region and time, it has also been argued that Jesus could have carried the whole cross, either a T-shaped cross or the more familiar Latin cross (✝). The writers of the Gospels use the term *stauros* (Greek, "cross"), which does not clarify the picture very much. Whatever Jesus carried, he bore a tremendous physical load, in addition to the mental, emotional, and spiritual burdens of the whole experience.

No executions were performed within the city walls (Numbers 15:35; 1 Kings 21:13; Acts 7:58). The procession to the site of crucifixion outside the city was led by a centurion and at least a quaternion (four soldiers), according to John 19:23. One of the soldiers carried a sign (*titulus*), on which the condemned man's name and crime were written. The titulus would later be fastened to the top of the cross.

Beyond Jerusalem's walls would have been upright wooden posts, or poles (Latin, *stipes*), upon which a victim's patibulum would be fastened. The practice of crucifixion probably began in Persia, where the victim was tied to or impaled upon a tree or upright post to keep his feet from touching the ground so that the torturous process of crucifixion could do its ghastly work of slow death by asphyxiation. It is likely that the upright post, or stipes, to which the Savior's patibulum was fastened was a tree whose branches had been cut off.

The apostle Paul seems to refer to this in his discussion of Christ's many-faceted redemptive act: "Christ hath redeemed us from the curse of the law, being made a curse for us: for it is written, Cursed is every one that hangeth on a tree" (Galatians 3:13). Paul was quoting Deuteronomy 21:23, which may be viewed as a prophetic reference made by Moses to the future crucifixion of the Savior (the book of Deuteronomy consists of Moses' final three sermons). This Deuteronomic passage was used by later Jews to emphasize the abhorrent nature of crucifixion as a way to die—"cursed is every one that hangeth on a tree." Thus, Paul was saying that Jesus redeemed us from the impossibility of being perfected through the Mosaic law by being crucified on a tree, an abhorrent form of death.

The apostle Peter also refers to the tree as the method of Jesus' crucifixion. He speaks of our Savior as the One "who his own self bare our sins in his own body on the tree, that we, being dead to sins, should live unto righteousness: by whose stripes ye were healed" (1 Peter 2:24).

As Jesus made his way from the Praetorium to the place of crucifixion, it appears that the cumulative effects of the events of the previous twenty-four hours had so weakened the Savior that he stumbled or collapsed. Clearly he needed help carrying his cross. The soldiers compelled one Simon of Cyrene, "who passed by, coming out of the country, the father of Alexander and Rufus, to bear his cross" (Mark 15:21). Luke tells us that Simon followed behind the Savior, now carrying the burden that had caused the Savior to stumble (Luke 23:26).

The Savior's collapse is understandable. His redemptive suffering and agony of atonement had caused him to sweat blood in Gethsemane. He was arrested, treated like a criminal, and marched up to the palace of the high priests, then to Pilate, then to Herod, and then back to Pilate. He had been beaten, held without sleep all night, beaten again, stripped, scourged, beaten once more, stripped again, and mocked. Is it any wonder he stumbled under the weight of the cross?

Also understandable is the impatience of the Roman

soldiers who, responding to Jewish impetus, wanted to get this crucifixion over with. Jesus was slowing things down, and the law outlined in Deuteronomy 21:22–23 was undoubtedly on everyone's mind: "And if a man have committed a sin worthy of death, and he be to be put to death, and thou hang him on a tree: His body shall not remain all night upon the tree, but thou shalt in any wise bury him that day." John also indicates that the Jews were anxious that the body of Jesus "not remain on the cross" (John 19:31). The sooner the crucifixion could be accomplished, the better—from their perspective.

## THE LESSON OF SIMON OF CYRENE

We know little about the man whom the Roman soldiers picked out of the crowd and "compelled" to carry the Savior's cross (Matthew 27:32). He is one of nine characters in the New Testament named Simon. The Gospel of Mark says he was a passerby, on his way into Jerusalem from the country (Mark 15:21), undoubtedly to participate in the Passover feast. The Mosaic law required all males of the covenant to appear before the Lord three times a year in the place that He chose. The three occasions were the Feast of Unleavened Bread (or Passover), the Feast of Weeks (or Pentecost), and the Feast of Tabernacles (Deuteronomy 16:16; Exodus 23:14–17). By this time in Israel's history, the place chosen was understood to be the Temple in Jerusalem.

Simon seems to have had no previous association with Jesus. His meeting with the Savior was a seeming chance encounter, not planned by Simon, at any rate. But he was not an idle rabble-rouser and not part of the crowd in attendance at the Savior's trial for the purpose of mocking him. Simon was from Cyrene, a leading town of Libya in North Africa, west of

Egypt, with a large Jewish population. That Jews from Cyrene went to Jerusalem regularly to keep the law of pilgrimage festivals as prescribed in the Torah may be inferred from a later New Testament account that indicates representatives from Cyrene were present in the capital city on the day of Pentecost, fifty days after Passover (Acts 2:10). We can imagine Simon standing in the Jerusalem thoroughfare simply out of curiosity about the spectacle taking place that Friday morning as Passover approached.

Mark adds a further detail, unrelated to anything immediately connected with Jesus' trial but which seems to indicate that Simon's service proved to be of eternal consequence for Simon himself. Mark says, without explanation, that Simon was "the father of Alexander and Rufus" (Mark 15:21). Was this information mentioned at this point because an important connection would be understood by Mark's readers in the early Church? Apparently so.

In Romans 16:13 the apostle Paul mentions Rufus, "chosen in the Lord," as well as Rufus's mother, who was also a mother (nurturer) to Paul himself. As has been suggested by others, it is quite possible that the gospel came into Simon's life as well as to his family as a result of his seemingly chance encounter with the Savior of the world at the very moment He was on His way to Golgotha to complete the atoning event that is at the core of our Father's plan for all creation. The power of the event in which Simon had a role, and which he later came to comprehend, ultimately resulted in his own conversion as well as that of his wife, his sons, and possibly future generations. Mark, who mentioned Simon's sons, was a companion and scribe to Peter, the chief apostle, when Peter was in the twilight of his ministry in Rome. There he recounted details that

Mark used to write his Gospel. Rufus and Alexander would have been known to the early Church, and Mark was providing details about their family association. Thus, Simon may not have been happy at first about having to carry the cross of a convicted enemy of Rome and the Jewish people, but the path to Golgotha seems to have become the path to eternal life for him and his family.

Archaeologists working in Jerusalem believe that a group of ossuaries (stone boxes for the burial of human bones) discovered in 1941 belonged to the family of Simon of Cyrene. Ossuaries were widely used in Jerusalem in the first century after Christ. The Simon family ossuaries were found in a Kidron Valley tomb and bear names pointing "to a family that originated in Cyrenaica [Cyrene]; one inscription bears the name Alexander, a name rare among Jews at the time; he is identified as the Son of Simon" (Powers, "Treasures in the Storeroom," 51). What better location for Simon and his family to be buried than in the place where they found salvation.

The story of Simon of Cyrene has an important application to our lives. Like Simon, we never know when some act of service, even some unintended act of consideration, will return to us many fold. The scriptures teach this lesson profoundly: "Cast thy bread upon the waters: for thou shalt find it after many days" (Ecclesiastes 11:1). This verse urges us to do good to those around us, to give help to those who need it, and it promises that rewards will come back to bless us. One small real-life example will suffice.

Years ago I was serving as a bishop in a city where a Latter-day Saint temple was nearing completion. Simply because I was the current bishop, I received two admission passes to the celestial room to witness the dedicatory service. My wife suggested that the passes really ought to go to a couple who had worked hard throughout the previous several years to ensure the timely opening of the temple rather than me, since I had only been called as bishop after the planning and construction of the new edifice were well along. Having been raised in the city where a temple was finally becoming a reality after long years of waiting, I really wanted to be in the celestial room for the dedication. In the end I decided my wife was right (as she usually is), and besides, two passes would not allow us to have our two eligible children with us to witness the dedication in the celestial room. We desired above all else to participate in the proceedings together as a family, and so I gave the two passes to the eminently deserving couple.

On the day of the dedication, our family entered the temple with great anticipation. We sat together in one of the rooms of the temple, ready to participate via closed circuit television with those in the celestial room. Then one of the stake presidents in the region who was acting as an usher, but whom I had never met, came into our room. He looked around, walked directly up to me, and asked how many members of my family were there. I answered "Four," and he responded, "Please come with me." He led our little family to the celestial room to enjoy the dedicatory service in the presence of the Brethren and our stake choir as well. There were exactly four vacant seats in the celestial room that morning. With overflowing hearts my wife and I turned to each other and said, almost in unison, "Cast your bread upon the waters, and it will come back many fold." What added to our joy was seeing in the celestial room the couple to whom we had given the original tickets. Everyone was blessed that day but no one more than I for the opportunity of witnessing a demonstration of the principle that also seems to have blessed Simon of Cyrene.

## A FINAL WARNING

The Gospel of Luke alone records that after Simon was forced to carry the cross, Jesus turned to the "great company of people" that had been following him and pointedly delivered his last public message on the road to Golgotha (Luke 23:27). Luke is careful to tell us that the group was composed of women who had been mourning and wailing for Him in their traditional manner. In fact, Luke seems to have had a greater interest in the women who had associated themselves with Jesus from the beginning of his ministry than the other Gospel writers. He alone points out that as the Savior traveled from one town and village to another, many women traveled with him and the Twelve and "ministered unto him [Jesus] of their substance" (Luke 8:3; see also vv. 1–2). Luke's witness helps us to see that faithful women have always played an important role in the Lord's Church. From the earliest period onward, they have ministered to those who needed support, even out of their own means.

Now approaching Golgotha, Jesus, ever the Master Teacher, turned to some of these same women, as we suppose, and spoke this warning: "Daughters of Jerusalem, weep not for me, but weep for yourselves, and for your children. For, behold, the days are coming, in the which they shall say, Blessed are the barren, and the wombs that never bare, and the paps which never gave suck. Then shall they begin to say to the mountains, Fall on us; and to the hills, Cover us. For if they do these things in a green tree, what shall be done in the dry?" (Luke 23:28–31).

This warning was of impending disaster of the greatest

proportions. In Jewish society the birth of a child was understood to be among the highest blessings that God could bestow upon a woman and a people. It was a tangible symbol of hope in the future. On the other hand, the greatest curse for women in Old Testament times was barrenness and miscarriage (Hosea 9:14). By quoting Hosea 10:8 ("they shall say to the mountains, Cover us; and to the hills, Fall on us") to those who were following him, the Savior was prophesying that things in the future would get so ugly, so terrible, for the Jewish nation and the people in Jerusalem that women would not want to bring children into the world to experience such horrors. Rather, they would wish for themselves to be annihilated without the blessing of motherhood. They would gladly accept escape through natural calamity rather than have to endure the kind of suffering that was to come. The Joseph Smith Translation of Luke 23:32 tells us that this prophecy of future devastation was also meant to include the desolation of the Gentiles as well as the scattering of Israel.

In the last part of his warning, Jesus explicitly tied the disasters of the future to the leaders' treatment of himself. He himself is the Green Tree referred to in the warning; he is the Life and the Light, the giver of enlightenment and all good things, the provider of the very environment in which righteousness could most easily flourish. Jesus was saying, in effect, that if the Jewish nation could carry out such wickedness (as the Crucifixion) when the very Son of God was among them *and* at a time when they could have flourished religiously, what would happen to them after the Green Tree was killed and gone and only "the withered branches and dried trunk of apostate Judaism" remained? (Talmage, *Jesus the Christ*, 654). What would happen to Judaism after disaster overtook the Jews?

Virtually the same image was invoked when the martyrdoms of the Prophet Joseph Smith and his brother, the Patriarch Hyrum Smith, were announced: "If the fire can scathe a green tree for the glory of God, how easy it will burn up the dry trees to purify the vineyard of corruption" (D&C 135:6).

Little did the Jewish people of the Savior's day realize that in only forty short years their world would be devastated—changed forever. By A.D. 70 the Romans would lay siege to Jerusalem and ultimately obliterate the Temple. Things would indeed get so bad, as the Jewish historian Josephus would later report, that the besieged inhabitants of Jerusalem, even the women, would one day resort to cannibalism. "Mothers snatched food from their children's mouths and one mother roasted her own son to survive. The time foreseen by Jesus when she who had no child or babe at the breast would bless herself, or when one might call upon mountains to fall and bring merciful release, was at hand. Women of Jerusalem were bitterly weeping for themselves" (Peterson and Tate, *Pearl of Great Price*, 190; see Josephus, *Wars of the Jews*, 6.3.4).

The Temple itself was destroyed on the ninth of Av (August 28), A.D. 70. "As the Temple burned, frenzy gripped both attackers and defenders. Roman shock troops burst through, and Titus was able to dash into the Temple just long enough for a brief look; then heat forced him out. His soldiers continued burning whatever could be kindled, and killing all they could reach, whether combatants, women, or children. Many Jews flung themselves into the fire and perished with their Temple. Others, hiding in corners, were burned to death as Roman torches set new fires" (Klein and Klein, *Temple beyond Time*, 112).

The final scenes of Jerusalem's total devastation a month

later, on a September day in A.D. 70, are reported with equal vividness: "Pouring into the alleys, sword in hand, [the soldiers] massacred indiscriminately all whom they met, *and burnt the houses with all who had taken refuge within*. Often in the course of their raids, on entering the houses for loot, they would find whole families dead and the rooms filled with victims of the famine. . . . Running everyone through who fell in their way, they choked the alleys with corpses and deluged the whole city with blood, insomuch that many of the fires were extinguished by the gory stream. Towards the evening they ceased slaughtering, but when night fell the fire gained the mastery" (Josephus, *Wars of the Jews*, 6.8–10, quoted in Avigad, *Discovering Jerusalem*, 137).

Such are the scenes the Savior foresaw when he prophesied to the people of their impending doom even as he himself approached his own death at Golgotha. Ironically, the Jewish inhabitants of Jerusalem that Friday morning had as much regard for the possibility that their great city could be destroyed as had Laman and Lemuel six hundred years before (1 Nephi 2:13). To them it was impossible. But obliviousness did not forestall the destruction, either in Lehi's time or a few decades after the Savior's. Of the fulfillment of the Savior's prophecy, Elder Bruce R. McConkie wrote:

> And now the ax was laid at the root of the rotted tree. Jerusalem was to pay the price. Daniel had foretold this hour when desolation, born of abomination and wickedness, would sweep the city. . . . Moses had said the siege would be so severe women would eat their own children. (Deut. 28.) Jesus specified the destruction would come in the days of the disciples.
>
> And come it did, in vengeance, without restraint.

Hunger exceeded human endurance; blood flowed in the streets; destruction made desolate the temple; 1,100,000 Jews were slaughtered; Jerusalem was ploughed as a field; and a remnant of a once mighty nation scattered to the ends of the earth. The Jewish nation died, impaled on Roman spears, at the hands of Gentile overlords. (*Doctrinal New Testament Commentary*, 1:644)

What caused such devastation? Some would argue that the root cause was wickedness of this kind or that—godlessness, conspiracy, murder, brigandage, secret combinations, or the like. It is true that Book of Mormon prophets attributed the fall of their own civilizations to such activity; however, I believe that ultimately Jerusalem and her inhabitants were destroyed because they rejected their true King. Their supreme act of disloyalty was dismissing Jesus' claims to be the long-awaited Messiah, who came to earth to fulfill millennia-old prophecies. The rabbis taught that "all the prophets prophesied only concerning the days of the Messiah" (*Tractate Sanhedrin*, 141), and yet the Fulfillment of those prophecies was put to death in the most ignominious way, crucified between two thieves.

The events of A.D. 70 should have been no surprise to the inhabitants of the Holy City. Jesus had said near the end of his ministry, "Except ye repent, ye shall all likewise perish" (Luke 13:5), and he gave the parable of the fig tree as an illustration: "If it bear fruit, well: and if not, then after that thou shalt cut it down" (Luke 13:9). The image of the fig tree was familiar to the Savior's listeners, for Israel was described as a fig tree in Jewish teachings. And yet, after the Crucifixion, after so many witnesses, Jerusalem's leaders sank deeper into the mire of hatred for Jesus, though they knew the truth, as the book of Acts confirms (Acts 4:1–30; 5:17–33).

The Gospels of Matthew and John report in more or less the same language as the Gospel of Mark that, having delivered his final public warning, Jesus was brought "unto the place Golgotha, which is, being interpreted, The place of a skull" (Mark 15:22; Matthew 27:33; John 19:17). Interestingly, the Joseph Smith Translation changes "skull" to "burial" (JST Mark 15:25). Only the Gospel of Luke calls the site Calvary (Luke 23:33), the Latin equivalent (*calvaria*) of the Aramaic name, *Golgotha*. The four Gospel writers record that at Golgotha the sinless Son of God was crucified between two other men. Luke refers to them as malefactors (criminals), Matthew and Mark call them thieves, and John does not label them. But all the Gospels state explicitly that at Golgotha the Savior of the world was subjected to the slow, agonizing torture of crucifixion, a form of execution that modern, civilized readers can only begin to comprehend.

And when they were come to the place, which is called Calvary, there they crucified him, and the malefactors, one on the right hand, and the other on the left.

Then said Jesus, Father, forgive them; for they know not what they do. And they parted his raiment, and cast lots.

And the people stood beholding. And the rulers also with them derided him, saying, He saved others; let him save himself, if he be Christ, the chosen of God. And the soldiers also mocked him, coming to him, and offering him vinegar, and saying, If thou be the king of the Jews, save thyself.

And a superscription also was written over him in letters of Greek, and Latin, and Hebrew, THIS IS THE KING OF THE JEWS.

And one of the malefactors which were hanged railed on him, saying, If thou be Christ, save thyself and us. But the other answering rebuked him, saying, Dost not thou fear God, seeing thou art in the same condemnation? And we indeed justly; for we receive the due reward of our deeds: but this man hath done nothing amiss.

And he said unto Jesus, Lord, remember me when thou comest into thy kingdom. And Jesus said unto him, Verily I say unto thee, To day shalt thou be with me in paradise.

LUKE 23:33–43

Now there stood by the cross of Jesus his mother, and his mother's sister, Mary the wife of Cleophas, and Mary Magdalene.

When Jesus therefore saw his mother, and the disciple standing by, whom he loved, he saith unto his mother, Woman, behold thy son!

Then saith he to the disciple, Behold thy mother! And from that hour that disciple took her unto his own home.

JOHN 19:25–27

# CHAPTER 9

# The Character of Christ

When Jesus, his captors, and the crowd following them reached the area called "The Skull," the actual crucifixion took place. So continued the fulfillment of prophecies long foretold by Israel's ancient prophets. That all of the Lord's prophets spoke of such things is attested by Abinadi:

> For behold, did not Moses prophesy unto them concerning the coming of the Messiah, and that God should redeem his people? Yea, and even all the prophets who have prophesied ever since the world began—have they not spoken more or less concerning these things?
>
> Have they not said that God himself should come down among the children of men, and take upon him the form of man, and go forth in mighty power upon the face of the earth?
>
> Yea, and have they not said also that he should bring to pass the resurrection of the dead, and that he, himself, should be oppressed and afflicted? (Mosiah 13:33–35)

We do not know precisely where Golgotha was located. Despite many paintings over the centuries showing Jesus being crucified on a hill and despite some of our hymns referring to the "hill" of Calvary, nothing in scripture indicates that his crucifixion occurred on a hill. It could have taken place alongside the main road just outside Jerusalem's walls, to show everyone who passed by that the Romans were in charge and that anyone who defied their authority could meet a similar ignominious death and themselves be thus reviled by future onlookers. The Roman writer Quintilian (ca. A.D. 35–95) recorded: "Whenever we crucify the guilty, the most crowded roads are chosen, where the most people can see and be moved by this fear. For penalties relate not so much to retribution as to their exemplary effect" (*Decl.* 274, as cited in *Anchor Bible Dictionary*, 1:1208).

Two principal sites have been considered as possibilities for the exact spot where the Savior's crucifixion occurred: the Church of the Holy Sepulchre, now located inside the old city of Jerusalem, and Gordon's Calvary, commonly known as the Garden Tomb, north of Damascus Gate. Both sites have pros and cons, but as I view the evidence, I am inclined to regard as a primary factor the important geographical symbolism behind the ancient Mosaic requirement that all animal sacrifices and offerings of the Tabernacle and Temple be killed "on the side of the altar northward before the Lord" (Leviticus 1:11). In other words, from Mosaic times onward, the animal sacrifices that constituted the most important element of the various sanctuary offerings (burnt, peace, sin, etc.), and which symbolized the great and last sacrifice of the Son of God (Alma 34:13–14), were always slaughtered north of the altars of both the Tabernacle in the wilderness and, later, the Temple. Therefore, wherever we look for the precise location of Golgotha, symbolic necessity dictates that we look north of the great altar of the Temple at Jerusalem. This geographic symbolism is simply one of the many foreshadowings of the Lord's crucifixion found in ancient Israelite religion.

## THE CRUELTIES OF CRUCIFIXION

Crucifixion was one of the most brutal forms of execution ever invented. "No word can be found adequate to describe so monstrous a proceeding," wrote the Roman statesman Cicero (quoted in McConkie, *Doctrinal New Testament Commentary*, 1:814). It is instructive to note that our English word *excruciating* ("unbearably intense pain, agony, torture") derives from the same Latin root as does *crucifixion* (*crucis*). Though the practice of crucifixion was not original to the Romans, they adopted and perfected it into a form of capital punishment that brought about an agonizingly slow death with the greatest possible pain and suffering. Sometimes a victim lived on for days—with ever-increasing torment. The victim was stripped naked, nailed to the cross (not tied, as in some earlier cultures, such as Egypt) by driving spikes through the victim's outstretched hands or wrists as well as through his feet and then into the wooden cross. The nails were expertly pounded in to avoid breaking bones and penetrating major blood vessels so the victim would not bleed to death. But the driven nails would crush or sever important nerves in the wrists, producing "excruciating bolts of fiery pain in both arms . . . [and] paralysis of a portion of the hand, [while] ischemic contractures and impalement of various ligaments by the iron spike might produce a clawlike grasp" (Edwards et al., "Physical Death of Jesus Christ," 1460).

When the victim was thrown to the ground on his back so that the executioner could stretch out the victim's arms against the patibulum, or crossbar, and drive the nails through his hands and wrists and feet, the wounds from the preceding scourging would likely be torn open again and become contaminated from the dirt on the ground. When the victim was lifted into place on the *stipes* (pole), or tree, the victim's arms would bear the full weight of his body. As the victim sagged and more weight was put on the wrists, excruciating pain would shoot along the fingers and up the arms. "To relieve some of the pain in the hands, wrists, and arms, the victim would push down on his feet to raise himself up with the result that searing pain would shoot up the legs from the nail-wounds in the feet. At some point, waves of cramps would sweep over the muscles of the legs and feet, causing throbbing pain as well as the inability to push upward and relieve the pain and pressure in the arms and wrists. Also, with the arms stretched out on the cross, breathing became increasingly difficult. Air could be drawn into the lungs, but not exhaled and asphyxiation eventually resulted" (Davis, "Physician Testifies about Crucifixion," 39). When the legs of the victim were broken, as reported in John 19:31–33, death resulted much more quickly because of the added shock to the body and, especially, the inability of the victim to raise up his body and stave off asphyxiation.

In 1968 the remains of a man crucified in the first century after Christ were discovered in an ossuary (casket for bones) from an ancient burial site located in present-day north Jerusalem (Giv'at ha-Mivtar). The victim's name, Yehohanan ben Hagkol, was engraved on the ossuary. He seems to have been between twenty-four and twenty-eight years of age. This find was of monumental proportions because it constituted the first and greatest archeological evidence of crucifixion, even though thousands of people were known from literary evidence to have been crucified by the Romans, who usually reserved the practice for male slaves, prisoners, and rebels.

In the ossuary of Yehohanan was a heel bone that still had the four-and-one-half-inch-long crucifixion nail embedded in it. Significantly, scholarly analysis indicates that the feet of this condemned man were nailed laterally, and thus separately, to the upright part of the cross, so that he straddled it. Furthermore, when this victim's feet were nailed to the cross, an olive wood plaque had been placed between the head of the spike and the foot to prevent the victim from pulling free of the spike (Zias and Sekeles, "Crucified Man from Giv'at ha-Mivtar," 190). The crucifixion of the Savior may have proceeded in a similar fashion.

Elder Bruce R. McConkie graphically describes some of the physical aspects of crucifixion:

> A death by crucifixion seems to include all that pain and death can have of the horrible and ghastly—dizziness, cramp, thirst, starvation, sleeplessness, traumatic fever, tetanus, publicity of shame, long continuance of torment, horror of anticipation, mortification of untended wounds, all intensified just up to the point at which they can be endured at all, but all stopping just short of the point which would give to the sufferer the relief of unconsciousness. The unnatural position made every movement painful; the lacerated veins and crushed tendons throbbed with incessant anguish; the wounds, inflamed by exposure, gradually gangrened; the arteries, especially of the head and stomach, became swollen and oppressed with surcharged blood; and, while each variety of misery went on gradually

increasing, there was added to them the intolerable pang of a burning and raging thirst. Such was the death to which Christ was doomed. (*Doctrinal New Testament Commentary*, 1:816)

It was not uncommon for the dying and helpless victim on the cross to be plagued by insects that would light upon or burrow into his flesh. After the victim died, his body was often left on the cross to decompose and be eaten by scavenging birds and animals (Edwards et al., "Physical Death of Jesus Christ," 1460).

## JESUS ON THE CROSS: PROPHECIES FULFILLED

The Gospel of Mark tells us that the Savior was crucified at nine o'clock in the morning (Mark 15:25). Both Matthew and Mark report that when Jesus reached Golgotha, before he was placed on the cross, he was offered a drink, which he refused. Matthew 27:34 describes the liquid as wine (the Greek *oinos* here is translated as "vinegar" in the King James Version) mixed with gall, while Mark 15:23 says "wine mingled with myrrh." The precise reason for the drink is not made clear in either Gospel. The Babylonian Talmud indicates that wine mixed with frankincense was given to condemned men as a mild analgesic to diminish pain without loss of consciousness, and the drink offered to Jesus is often regarded as having this purpose (see, for example, Davis, "Physician Testifies about Crucifixion," 37). In Jesus' case, some scholars say, the drink was intended to prolong the agony of crucifixion. Others point out that gall is a poison, and its addition to wine would have produced a mildly poisonous substance. Thus, Jesus could have been refusing something that would have made him sick (*Interpreter's Dictionary of the Bible*, s.v. "Gall," 350).

The scriptures do not describe the scene of Jesus being nailed to the cross, but we know that he was stripped of his clothing, as were other crucifixion victims. All four Gospels report that after the soldiers had crucified Jesus, they took his garments and cast lots for ownership because the clothing was valuable (John 19:23–24). In first-century Palestine, Jewish men traditionally wore five pieces of clothing: shoes or sandals, a headdress, an inner tunic, an outer cloak, and a girdle or wide belt. According to Roman custom, these articles became the property of the soldiers performing the crucifixion.

The unnatural and contorted position of the Savior's body nailed on the cross was foreseen by Israel's ancient psalmist. He expressed his graphic prophecy in poetic form: "I am poured out like water, and all my bones are out of joint: my heart is like wax; it is melted in the midst of my bowels" (Psalm 22:14).

It is well known that spikes were driven through the Savior's wrists in addition to the palms of his hands for fear that the weight of his body would cause it to tear away from the cross. Medical authorities attest that it "has been shown that the ligaments and bones of the wrist can support the weight of a body hanging from them, but the palms cannot" (Edwards et al., "Physical Death of Jesus Christ," 1460). The nails driven into the Savior's wrists fastened him securely to the cross and also fulfilled a messianic prophecy of Isaiah, whose graphic imagery resonates deeply with faithful members of the Church:

> And I will clothe him with thy robe, and strengthen him with thy girdle, and I will commit thy government into his hand: and he shall be a father to the inhabitants of Jerusalem, and to the house of Judah.
>
> And the key of the house of David will I lay upon

his shoulder; so he shall open, and none shall shut; and he shall shut, and none shall open.

And I will fasten him as a nail in a sure place; and he shall be for a glorious throne to his father's house.

And they shall hang upon him all the glory of his father's house, the offspring and the issue, all vessels of small quantity, from the vessels of cups, even to all the vessels of flagons.

In that day, saith the Lord of hosts, shall the nail that is fastened in the sure place be removed, and be cut down, and fall; and the burden that was upon it shall be cut off: for the Lord hath spoken it. (Isaiah 22:21–25)

Here Isaiah, whose entire book constitutes a powerful witness of both the first and the second comings of the Messiah, describes the multifaceted role of our Redeemer in the guise of a servant of God named Eliakim (a name that means "God shall cause to rise" and is itself messianic). In one way or another, all the characteristics Isaiah enumerates describe the Lord, Jesus Christ:

1. He would be given the government, or right to rule (v. 21).

2. He would be a father to the house of Judah (v. 21).

3. He would be given "the key of the house of David" (v. 22).

4. He would be fastened to something as "a nail in a sure place" (v. 23).

5. Upon him would be "hung," or placed, the glory of his father's house (v. 24)

6. He would be involved in the removing of the burden associated with "the nail that is fastened in the sure place" (v. 25).

Indeed, this list describes the mission and ministry of Jesus Christ, for by virtue of his mortal mission and atoning sacrifice, he alone fits the characteristics enumerated by Isaiah:

1. He alone possesses "the government"—the power and authority to rule in heaven and on earth—and he will do so at his second coming (D&C 58:22).

2. He is the father, or king, of the Jews (as the title on his cross rightly declared; Matthew 27:37), and he alone is the spiritual father of Israel and of all who obey him (Mosiah 27:25).

3. He alone possesses the "key of the house of David," the symbol of absolute power and authority (both monarchial and priestly) invested in the true Messiah, who descends literally from Israel's greatest monarch, King David (Revelation 3:7).

4. He was in very deed fastened to the cross both *as* and *with* "a nail in a sure place" (Isaiah 22:23).

5. He alone was given his Father's power and glory through divine investiture of authority: "The Father has honored Christ by placing his name upon him, so that he can minister in and through that name as though he were the Father; and thus, so far as power and authority are concerned, his words and acts become and are those of the Father" (Smith, *Doctrines of Salvation*, 1:29–30).

6. He had the glory of his Father's house placed upon him during the last week of his ministry when he referred to the Jerusalem Temple not as "my Father's house" (which he had done at the beginning of his ministry; John 2:16) but rather as "my house" (after his triumphal entry; Matthew 21:13).

7. Last, but not least, he alone is the One who took upon himself the great "burden" referred to by Isaiah, and who

removed that burden from the world when "the nail that was fastened in the sure place was removed" (Isaiah 22:25). In other words, Jesus the Messiah removed from us the burden of physical and spiritual death when he completed the Atonement (that is, after he was removed from the cross, buried, and resurrected).

There is hardly a more powerful image in scripture than the image Isaiah uses of the nail in the sure place. It links the physical act of Christ's crucifixion with the profoundest rituals and remembrances of that act in Latter-day Saint theology and practice.

## THE TITLE ON THE CROSS

All four Gospels mention the titulus, or inscription, that was affixed to the cross above Jesus' head. John's account of it is the fullest, attributing the inscription to Pilate, the Roman governor:

> And Pilate wrote a title, and put it on the cross. And the writing was, Jesus of Nazareth the King of the Jews.
>
> This title then read many of the Jews: for the place where Jesus was crucified was nigh to the city: and it was written in Hebrew, and Greek, and Latin.
>
> Then said the chief priests of the Jews to Pilate, Write not, The King of the Jews; but that he said, I am King of the Jews.
>
> Pilate answered, What I have written I have written. (John 19:19–22)

Other ancient texts describe the use of such inscriptions, which announced the official crimes of the condemned and which the convicted was sometimes obliged to wear around his neck until he reached the place of execution. Its use here was clearly intended by Pilate to chide the Jews, for when the chief priests, those most responsible for the Savior's crucifixion, wanted the titulus changed to reflect their charge of blasphemy, Pilate finally showed some backbone and ordered that the inscription stand as originally composed: "What I have written I have written" (John 19:22). Pilate knew not only that Jesus was innocent of any real crime but also that Jesus was who he said he was. Pilate knew the truth. He really knew! (Talmage, *Jesus the Christ*, 657).

Though such inscriptions as the one placed over Jesus' head were intended as a declaration of the condemned man's crimes, ironically Jesus' titulus declared the absolute truth. Jesus was the king of the Jews by lineage and birthright. The Jewish leaders were engulfed in such apostasy that they refused to recognize in Jesus of Nazareth the fulfillment of their own prophecies and traditions. Pilate was engulfed in such concerns about his position that he did not act on the knowledge he possessed.

That the message of the titulus was composed in Hebrew, Greek, and Latin (Luke 23:38) points out the complicated cultural and linguistic situation in Roman Palestine. Latin was the language of the Roman overloads, Greek the lingua franca of the hellenistic world of which Palestine was part, and Hebrew—probably meaning Aramaic—was the common language of the Jews in Jesus' day. Individuals passing the site of crucifixion on that day would have been able to read Jesus' titulus for themselves, no matter what Mediterranean culture they belonged to. In fact, a large proportion of Jews in Jesus' day could read.

John's Gospel contains the fullest account of the scene

at the foot of the cross involving soldiers casting lots for the Savior's clothing as he hung above them (John 19:23–24). John helps us to see how Israel's ancient psalms presented prophecies of the Savior's atoning act. After reporting the actual words of the soldiers, who said, in effect, "Let's not tear the seamless coat; let's decide by lot who will get it," John provides indispensable interpretive commentary that links this event with Psalm 22:18. John declares that the soldiers did what they did "that the scripture might be fulfilled, which saith, They parted my raiment among them, and for my vesture they did cast lots" (John 19:24), an exact quotation of Psalm 22:18.

## STATEMENTS FROM THE CROSS

It is at this point in the story that Luke's Gospel places the first of the Savior's seven recorded utterances from the cross, that is, immediately after Luke's brief description of the titulus and right before his mention of the soldiers casting lots for Jesus' raiment. It is instructive to view these statements together, for they teach us much about the Master's last thoughts and feelings. Even today we tend to regard a person's dying declarations with utmost credibility and significance.

1. "Father, forgive them; for they know not what they do" (Luke 23:34).

2. "Verily I say unto thee, To day shalt thou be with me in paradise" (Luke 23:43).

3. "Woman, behold thy son! . . . Behold thy mother!" (John 19:26–27).

4. "My God, my God, why hast thou forsaken me?" (Matthew 27:46; Psalm 22:1).

5. "I thirst" (John 19:28).

6. "It is finished" (John 19:30).

7. "Father, into thy hands I commend my spirit" (Luke 23:46; Psalm 31:5).

Perhaps it was the sight of the soldiers' activity at the crucifixion site that prompted the Savior to make his first and probably best known plea: "Father, forgive them; for they know not what they do" (Luke 23:34). No explicit motivation behind the statement is recorded other than the comment about the soldiers casting lots, which Luke describes taking place while Jesus asks for forgiveness for his executioners. Because of its position in the narrative, some confusion has arisen over just who the Savior was asking forgiveness for. The Joseph Smith Translation clarifies this, adding the phrase, "Meaning the soldiers who crucified him" (JST Luke 23:35). Elder Spencer W. Kimball makes this point clearly and teaches us a valuable lesson at the same time:

> When the Lord, in his dying moments, turned to the Father and requested, "Father, forgive them; for they know not what they do" (Luke 23:34), he was referring to the soldiers who crucified him. They acted under the mandate of a sovereign nation. It was the Jews who were guilty of the Lord's death. Again how could he forgive them, or how could his Father forgive them, when they were not repentant. These vicious people who cried, " . . . His blood be on us, and on our children" (Matt. 27:25) had not repented. Those who "reviled him" on Calvary (Matt. 27:39) had not repented. The Jewish leaders who tried Jesus illegally, demanded his crucifixion

from Pilate, and incited the mob to their vilest actions had not repented. Nor had the Roman soldiers who, though no doubt obligated under their military law to crucify Jesus as instructed, were under no compulsion to add the insults and cruelties to which they subjected the Savior prior to his crucifixion. (*Miracle of Forgiveness*, 167)

As Jesus hung on the cross, the synoptic Gospels report, passersby as well as the members of the gathered crowd mocked and ridiculed him. These included the same ones who engineered the whole conspiracy (the chief priests, scribes, and elders). They not only railed at him and reviled him, wagging their heads as one might do to a fool who had been told better, but also twisted his own words to make those words appear to be the height of foolishness and arrogance. "Thou that destroyest the temple, and buildest it in three days, save thyself" (Matthew 27:40). "He trusted in God; let him deliver him now . . . for he said, I am the Son of God" (Matthew 27:43). "Save thyself, and come down from the cross" (Mark 15:30). "Let Christ the King of Israel descend now from the cross, that we may see and believe" (Mark 15:32). "He saved others; let him save himself, if he be Christ, the chosen of God" (Luke 23:35).

All of these statements, as well as the general scene at the cross that they depict, hark back to Psalm 22:7–8, a poetic messianic prophecy of incredible prescience found in ancient Israel's hymnbook (the book of Psalms): "All they that see me laugh me to scorn: they shoot out the lip, they shake the head, saying, He trusted on the Lord that he would deliver him: let him deliver him, seeing he delighted in him."

To all of these taunts and verbal barbs the Savior answered

nothing. He was the personification of meekness. His goodness showed through his adversity. His character towered over his trauma. Again, we are reminded of Peter's comment: "When he was reviled, [he] reviled not again" (1 Peter 2:23). Even one of the two criminals between whom Jesus was hanging began to goad him. "And one of the malefactors which were hanged railed on him, saying, If thou be Christ, save thyself and us" (Luke 23:39). Still, the Son of God responded to insults with quiet dignity.

Soon, however, the Savior did speak to the second thief because he had rebuked his counterpart for his insolence and also asked for the Savior's mercy. As with the first of the Savior's utterances from the cross (his plea for forgiveness for the soldiers), Luke alone records the Savior's second statement: "But the other answering rebuked him, saying, Dost not thou fear God, seeing thou art in the same condemnation? And we indeed justly; for we receive the due reward of our deeds: but this man hath done nothing amiss. And he said unto Jesus, Lord, remember me when thou comest into thy kingdom. And Jesus said unto him, Verily I say unto thee, To day shalt thou be with me in paradise" (Luke 23:40–43).

Some confusion has arisen through the years regarding the doctrinal implications of Jesus' comment. The crux of the matter seems to lie with the word "paradise," which ultimately derives from a Persian loanword meaning "garden" and could have meant in Jesus' day "the place of the departed." The Prophet Joseph Smith taught that Jesus was saying, "This day thou shalt be with me in the world of spirits" (*Teachings of the Prophet Joseph Smith*, 309). Thus, the fixed principles of repentance were not being altered by Jesus. President Spencer W. Kimball provides powerful doctrinal clarification:

Another mistaken idea is that the thief on the cross was forgiven of his sins when the dying Christ answered: "Today shalt thou be with me in paradise." (Luke 23:43.) These men on the cross were thieves. How could the Lord forgive a malefactor? They had broken laws. There was no doubt of the guilt of the two men, for the one voluntarily confessed their guilt.

The Lord cannot save men *in* their sins but only *from* their sins, and that only when they have shown true repentance. The one thief did show some compassion, whether selfishly with hope we are not sure. He was confessing, but how could he abandon his evil practices when dungeon walls made evil deeds impossible? How could he restore the stolen goods when hanging on the cross? How could he, as John the Baptist required, "bring forth fruits meet for repentance?" How could he live the Lord's commands, attend his meetings, pay his tithing, serve his fellowmen? All these take time. Time was the one thing he was running out of very rapidly. "No unclean thing can enter the kingdom of heaven." This thought has been repeated throughout the scriptures numerous times and is a basic truth. We may be sure that the Savior's instructions to the thief on the cross were comparable to his instructions to the woman caught in adultery: "Go your way and transform yourself and repent."

As the hours passed, the thief's life would ebb out and his spirit would abandon the lifeless body and go into the spirit world, where Christ was going to organize his missionary program. (See 1 Pet. 3:18–20; 4–6.) There he would live along with the antediluvians and

136

all others who had died in their sins. All the Lord's statement promised the thief was that both of them would soon be in the spirit world. The thief's show of repentance on the cross was all to his advantage, but his few words did not nullify a life of sin. The world should know that since the Lord himself cannot save men *in* their sins, no man on earth can administer any sacrament which will do that impossible thing. Hence the mere display of death-bed faith or repentance is not sufficient. (*Miracle of Forgiveness*, 166–67)

Ultimately, we must concede that we do not know the mind of the mercy-seeking thief nor the final disposition of his case. It seems quite possible, however, that he truly was on the road to repentance. We must keep in mind that repentance after this life is a doctrinal reality—else why preach to those spirits in prison who have never heard of Christ nor been converted to him? (1 Peter 3:18–19; 4:6; D&C 138:30–37). Furthermore, we believe that repentance in the spirit world is possible for those of us who knew the truth while in mortality but were not always valiant. We also believe, however, that such repentance is not without additional challenges, as Elder Melvin J. Ballard of the Quorum of the Twelve Apostles declared:

It is my judgment that any man or woman can do more to conform to the laws of God in one year in this life than they could in ten years when they are dead. The spirit only can repent and change, and then the battle has to go forward with the flesh afterwards. It is much easier to overcome and serve the Lord when both flesh and spirit are combined as one. This is the time when men are more pliable and susceptible. When clay is pliable, it is much easier to change than when it gets hard and sets.

This life is the time to repent. That is why I presume it will take a thousand years after the first resurrection until the last group will be prepared to come forth. It will take them a thousand years to do what it would have taken but three score years and ten to accomplish in this life. (Hinckley, *Sermons and Missionary Services of Melvin Joseph Ballard*, 241)

## DISCIPLES AT THE CROSS

Just as one would have hoped, not all of the Savior's followers left him alone to face the agonies and humiliations of his crucifixion. Matthew tells us that many women watched the proceedings of the execution from a distance. These women had "followed Jesus from Galilee, ministering unto him" (Matthew 27:55) and were likely among that great company who wept and lamented the Savior's plight as he walked from the place of judgment, the Praetorium, to Golgotha (Luke 23:27). John, writing about the Savior's last moments on the cross, tells us that he, John, was also there with the women at Golgotha, although he never calls himself by name. He refers to himself in his Gospel as the disciple whom Jesus loved (John 13:23; 19:26; 20:2; 21:7, 20).

Close to the end, as his life ebbed away, Jesus looked down from the cross and, seeing his mother as well as the disciple whom he loved, made his third utterance: "Woman, behold thy son! Then saith he to the disciple, Behold thy mother! And from that hour that disciple took her unto his own home" (John 19:26–27).

Though "Woman," the form of address used by Jesus to

speak to his mother, may sound harsh to modern ears, it was, in the culture of that day, a term of endearment and respect. Jesus seems to be saying something like, "Dear Woman, you see the circumstances your Son is in. I won't be around much longer, but John will care for you as though you were his own mother."

No doubt a special bond existed between the Savior and John the Beloved, but that does not diminish Jesus' love for the other disciples. He cared for each one individually. Jesus may have singled out John to care for His mother because John had the desire and the means to do so and because he was there at Golgotha with his own mother. John's mother, who would have heard her son's special commission from the Savior, would also have been able to help care for Mary. Matthew's Gospel mentions the mother of the sons of Zebedee (of whom John was one) being in attendance at the cross (Matthew 27:56), and Mark apparently gives her name: Salome (Matthew 4:21; Mark 15:40).

It is also possible that John's relationship with the Savior was familial—that is, John the Beloved may have been a cousin of Jesus. Both Matthew and Mark name three women at Golgotha: Mary Magdalene; Mary, the mother of James (the Less) and Joses; and the mother of Zebedee's sons, or Salome. John appears to name four women: Mary Magdalene; Mary, the mother of Jesus; "his mother's sister"; and Mary, the wife of Cleophas (John 19:25). Could Salome, the mother of Zebedee's sons, be the same person as the sister of Mary, the mother of Jesus? Though we cannot know with certainty, other students of the New Testament have considered it. Elder James E. Talmage wrote: "From the fact that John mentions the mother of Jesus and 'his mother's sister' (19:25) and omits mention of Salome by name, some expositors hold that Salome was the sister of Mary the mother of Jesus; and therefore the Savior's aunt. This relationship would make James and John cousins to Jesus" (*Jesus the Christ*, 521).

It makes perfect sense that John the Beloved would possess a special relationship with Jesus, being his "beloved disciple" on the basis of family connection and not on the basis of arbitrary favoritism. Also, Jesus' saying to John, "Behold thy mother," reflects a genuine family relationship, and John is being asked to care for his aunt, his "other mother," as she would have been regarded in that culture. Furthermore, it seems likely that although many women would have been near the crucifixion site, Jesus would have specifically spoken to members of his biological family—his mother, cousin, and aunt—as he neared the end of his life. The early Church of Jesus Christ was a family affair in many ways. John the Baptist was a cousin of the Savior, and the original Quorum of the Twelve included at least two sets of brothers and probably three: Peter and Andrew (John 1:40), James and John (Matthew 4:21), and probably Matthew and James, who was nicknamed the Less to distinguish him from James the son of Zebedee (Mark 2:14; Matthew 10:3). That the mother of James the Less was also waiting by the cross may hint at a strong relationship between her and Mary, the mother of Jesus.

## THE CHARACTER OF CHRIST

The few recorded statements made by the Savior on the cross teach us much about him. "It might well be stated as a rule of human nature that when a man reaches his greatest extremity, a moment of extreme danger, pain, emotion, or critical need, a point in life which is marked by imminent destruction or death, the true nature of his soul becomes evident." Is he basically thoughtful or selfish, courageous or cowardly, self-absorbed or concerned with others? During the most trying and difficult circumstances of life, an individual's "words mirror his innermost soul. His speech betrays what his character is really like—the quality of his concerns, his compassion, his love—the whole focus or thrust of his life, whether noble or mean, depraved or exalted" (*Life and Teachings of Jesus and His Apostles*, 185).

The greatest example of this principle is found in Jesus of Nazareth. While he hung and suffered on the cross, his petition for forgiveness on behalf of the Roman soldiers who carried out the order of execution demonstrates his basic nature. His mercy and compassion, which constitute the very essence of who and what he is, were demonstrated many times during his life—to the leper (Mark 1:41), to the man possessed (Mark 5:19), to the whole multitude during a moment of personal sadness (Matthew 14:14), and on, and on, and on. His acts of forgiveness grow out of his pure love, or perfect charity (Moroni 7:47).

The Savior's mercy, compassion, forgiveness, and pure love will be extended to all, even at the time of judgment. President J. Reuben Clark Jr. said: "I feel that [the Lord] will give that punishment which is the very least that our transgression will justify. . . . I believe that when it comes to making the rewards for our good conduct, he will give the maximum that is possible to give" (*As Ye Sow*, 7–8).

It is likewise apparent from President Clark's comments that mercy does not rob justice. Jesus was loving, kind, fair, and compassionate. But he was not indulgent. Elder McConkie wrote that on the cross "Jesus did not, it should be noted, pray for Judas who betrayed him; for Caiaphas and the chief priests who conspired against him; for the false witnesses who perjured their souls before the Sanhedrin and in the judgment halls of Rome; for Pilate and Herod, either of whom could have freed him; nor for Lucifer whose power and persuasive ability underlay the whole wicked procedure. All these are left in the hands of Eternal Justice to be dealt with according to their works. Mercy cannot rob justice; the guilty do not go free simply because the righteous bring no railing accusation against them" (*Doctrinal New Testament Commentary*, 1:819).

The Savior thought of others to the very end of his life. To the mercy-seeking thief on the cross, Jesus extended a merciful response. To his mother, Jesus demonstrated love and concern for her welfare in the midst of his own terrible suffering. He knew what his mother was going through as she saw the unspeakable horrors of crucifixion snuffing out the life of her precious Son. She was now witnessing the fulfillment of a prophecy made thirty-three years before in the Temple in Jerusalem when she had officially presented her infant Son to the righteous witnesses in the house of the Lord. At that time Simeon foretold the future to Mary, as Luke records: "And Simeon blessed them, and said unto Mary his mother, Behold, this child is set for the fall and rising again of many in Israel; and for a sign which shall be spoken against; (Yea, a sword shall pierce through thy own soul also,) that the thoughts of many hearts may be revealed" (Luke 2:34–35).

Now, thirty-three years later, Mary was witnessing the death throes of her Son on the cross and experiencing the fulfillment of Simeon's prophecy. As Simeon indicated, Mary would be pierced emotionally when her Son was pierced physically. Jesus knew of this circumstance, and of course he wanted to ease his mother's pain. Therefore, "with supreme solicitude, and though he himself was in agony on the cross, Jesus [placed] his mother in the care and keeping of John" (McConkie, *Doctrinal New Testament Commentary*, 1:826).

The Savior was continually, inevitably, thinking of the welfare of others to the very end. From his comments on the cross we learn of the essence of the Savior's personality: his merciful and forgiving nature, his concern for others, his endurance in patience, and his character and supreme goodness. How grateful we should be that we can call him our Master.

*Now from the sixth hour there was darkness over all the land unto the ninth hour.*

*And about the ninth hour Jesus cried with a loud voice, saying, Eli, Eli, lama sabachthani? that is to say, My God, my God, why hast thou forsaken me?*

*Some of them that stood there, when they heard that, said, This man calleth for Elias.*

MATTHEW 27:45–47

# CHAPTER 10

# Darkness and Abandonment

T he synoptic Gospels all report that about the sixth hour of the day (noon), darkness gathered over the whole land and remained until the ninth hour, or 3 P.M. (Matthew 27:45; Mark 15:33; Luke 23:44). We can imagine that as the life of the Savior waned under the horrible effects of crucifixion, the darkness in the world grew thicker. Just as it was light for a day and a night and a day when Jesus, the Light of the World, came into the world (3 Nephi 1:15), so now nature was beginning to dim, preparing to reel and convulse, as the death of Jesus approached and the Light of the World would make his exit from the world. All this was in accord with prophecy uttered years before by Samuel the Lamanite (Helaman 14:20).

Certainly, there is much we do not know about the physics of the universe and much to be explored regarding the physical connection between the Lord of Light and the light we discern every day. Yet, the crucifixion helps us to see that the Prophet Joseph Smith's cosmological revelation on the nature of light, life, and our Redeemer is far more than just metaphor.

That single revelation tells us why darkness gathered on the earth from the sixth to the ninth hour, until the sun itself was eclipsed (the Greek word in Luke 23:45 is *eklipontos*).

> This is the light of Christ. As also he is in the sun, and the light of the sun, and the power thereof by which it was made.
>
> As also he is in the moon, and is the light of the moon, and the power thereof by which it was made;
>
> As also the light of the stars, and the power thereof by which they were made;
>
> And the earth also, and the power thereof, even the earth upon which you stand. . . .
>
> Which light proceedeth forth from the presence of God to fill the immensity of space—
>
> The light which is in all things, which giveth life to all things, which is the law by which all things are governed, even the power of God who sitteth upon his throne, who is in the bosom of eternity, who is in the midst of all things. (D&C 88:7–10, 12–13)

## THE SAVIOR ABANDONED BY HIS FATHER: PROPHECY FULFILLED

As the ninth hour arrived, according to Matthew and Mark, Jesus cried out with a loud and startling (as the text implies) voice. It must have been a great surprise to those who were not expecting such volume from one so weakened from the tortures he had endured and who appeared to be teetering on the brink of death. "*Eli, Eli, lama sabachthani?*" "My God, my God, why hast thou forsaken me?" (Matthew 27:46; Mark 15:34). The Aramaic verb here, *shabaq*, means to "leave alone," "to abandon." This fourth statement from the cross is a direct quotation, uttered in Aramaic, from the opening verse of Psalm 22, that unparalleled poetic prophecy of the Atonement. This profoundly agonized query from the Savior was a fulfillment of the inspired prediction by Israel's psalmist almost a thousand years before and which had been chanted by Israel for centuries as one of their hymns.

We cannot fully appreciate nor comprehend the terror and spiritual pain so great as to produce in that moment so anguished a cry from God himself. Perhaps only those who have experienced the torment of real abandonment, the abject misery of true loneliness, can begin to appreciate the feelings the Savior was enduring. Personally, I can only begin to relate to his feelings when I contemplate my emotions at three different times in my life: the panic I felt as a child the first time I was lost in a huge crowd far from home; the horrors my mind conjured up when I was unable to find one of my own small children in a potentially dangerous situation; and the profound sense of loss I experienced when my father died. I was a young teenager and those were difficult days—a time of great aloneness. But I suspect that these three episodes do not begin to approach the Savior's experience.

President Brigham Young taught that Jesus was left completely alone by his Father once before—in the Garden of Gethsemane—and that experience was so traumatic, so devastating, so utterly horrible for the sinless Son of God that it alone caused him to sweat blood. Said President Young, "If he [Jesus] had had the power of God upon him, he would not have sweat blood; but all was withdrawn from him, and a veil was cast over him" (*Journal of Discourses*, 3:206). I take "all" to mean "everything."

Now, upon the cross of Golgotha, the horror he knew in Gethsemane returned. These were the only two times in his life when he was truly alone. Friends and family could abandon him, and he could take that kind of forsakenness. The one thing he could not take, the one thing far worse for him than everything else, was abandonment by his Father, the total loss of his Father's sustaining influence. To this one Being who was perfect, without sin, who had always enjoyed his Father's closeness and unrestrained Spirit, abandonment by his Father was more than he could bear. Because Jesus was perfect, he was perfectly sensitized to the Spirit. He possessed the Spirit in its fulness, whereas each of us possesses only a measure of it and to a greater or lesser degree (JST John 3:34). Total absence of his Father's influence was spiritual death, the very atmosphere of hell itself, the deepest pit of despair, the darkest depression. To go from possessing the fulness of the Father's Spirit to having it completely withdrawn, totally absent, produced in Jesus an intensity of agony such as no other being will experience or endure. He descended below *all* things (D&C 88:6; 122:8).

We might be tempted to argue that others, including sons of perdition, have known or will know this kind of hell, but that would not be true. No one started out from the same point as the Savior did, and thus no one ever has or ever will go as low—no one! Even for the Savior, greater pain or anguish was not possible. One simply cannot go lower than below *all* things.

## LESSONS FOR HIS DISCIPLES

All of this discussion of the extremity that the Savior had to endure is not to discount the pain or the loneliness or the anguish of abandonment that the rest of Heavenly Father's children experience in their mortal lives. Rather, it serves to emphasize, in a monumental way, three uplifting and comforting truths.

First, Jesus can succor us and nurture us precisely because he has perfect empathy. To provide succor implies something more than nurturing. It connotes someone running to another to provide aid or help. It aptly depicts the Savior's inherent essence and personality. That is the reason that he, being God, came to earth as a mortal.

> And he shall go forth, suffering pains and afflictions and temptations of every kind; and this that the word might be fulfilled which saith he will take upon him the pains and the sicknesses of his people.
>
> And he will take upon him death, that he may loose the bands of death which bind his people; and he will take upon him their infirmities, that his bowels may be filled with mercy, according to the flesh, that *he may know according to the flesh how to succor his people* according to their infirmities. (Alma 7:11–12; emphasis added)

Notice the phrase "according to the flesh." Jesus knows from his own mortal experience *what* to do to assist us and *how* best to do it. "For in that he himself hath suffered being tempted, he is able to succor them that are tempted"—or sick, or in pain, or lonely or abandoned, or afflicted with a thousand other maladies or challenges or handicaps (Hebrews 2:18). President John Taylor testified:

> It was necessary, when the Savior was upon the earth, that he should be tempted in all points, like unto us, and "be touched with the feeling of our infirmities," [Hebrews 4:15] to comprehend the weaknesses

and strength, the perfections and imperfections of poor fallen human nature. And having accomplished the thing he came into the world to do: having had to grapple with the hypocrisy, corruption, weakness, and imbecility of man; having met with temptation and trial in all its various forms, and overcome; he has become a "faithful high priest" [Hebrews 2:17] to intercede for us in the everlasting kingdom of his Father.

He knows how to estimate and put a proper value upon human nature, for he, having been placed in the same position as we are, knows how to bear with our weaknesses and infirmities, and can fully comprehend the depth, power, and strength of the afflictions and trials that men have to cope with in this world. And thus understandingly and by experience, he can bear with them. (*John Taylor, 53*)

Jesus is perfectly sensitized to each of our trials, our circumstances of loneliness, because he alone experienced all of them—absorbed to himself our pain and abject misery. The bad things in life cannot magically be made to disappear, but Jesus can help us through them, can take the burdens that come from them, until they trouble us no more.

Second, as a result of the Savior's anguished cry at Golgotha, we come to understand that no one in mortality is exempt from suffering of the highest order, not even God. We also better understand *why* we are going through tough times—especially tough times all alone. It is all part of the grand design to help us grow, as Elder Neal A. Maxwell taught:

There is, in the suffering of the highest order, a point that is reached—a point of aloneness—when the individual (as did the Savior on a much grander scale) must bear it, as it were, alone. Even the faithful may wonder if they can take any more or if they are in some way forsaken.

Those who, as it were, stand on the foot of the cross often can do so little to help absorb the pain and the anguish. It is something we must bear ourselves in order that our triumph can be complete. Elder James E. Talmage said of the Savior at the point of greatest suffering on the cross, "that the supreme sacrifice of the Son might be consummated in all its fulness, the Father seems to have withdrawn the support of His immediate Presence, leaving to the Savior of men the glory of complete victory over the forces of sin and death." (*Jesus the Christ*, p. 661.)

Thus there ought to be expectations that in this laboratory of life we will actually see each other in the process of being remodeled, sometimes succeeding and sometimes failing. We will obviously be aware of others who are also in the "furnace of affliction." However, we will not always have a smooth, ready answer to the question, "Why me?" "Why now?" "Why this?"—for as Moroni observed, "Ye receive no witness until *after* the trial of your faith." (Ether 12:6. Italics added.) (*All These Things Shall Give Thee Experience*, 43–44)

Third, a reciprocal truth operates. Because Jesus' disciples will pass through something of his experiences, including loneliness and abandonment in its many forms, we are privileged to understand to a degree what he went through and cultivate empathy for him—even coming to know what he knows and receiving what he has received as a result of our own faithful suffering and trials. "If we suffer, we shall also reign with him: if we deny him, he also will deny us" (2 Timothy 2:12).

Faithful endurance and loyalty to God in the face of feeling abandoned, feeling loneliness of every kind, is one of the key ways God has of sifting and sorting as well as of teaching. God's prophets, too, have been tried in the furnace of abandonment. Elijah, the powerful guardian of priesthood keys, at one point complained to the Lord because he felt abandoned to carry the weight of the world on his shoulders: "And he said, I have been very jealous for the Lord God of hosts: because the children of Israel have forsaken thy covenant, thrown down thine altars, and slain thy prophets with the sword; and I, even I only, am left; and they seek my life, to take it away" (1 Kings 19:14). Ultimately, the Lord helped Elijah to see that he was not alone and that all things supported divine purposes. Because of Elijah's faithfulness in the face of life-threatening circum-stances, he was blessed and taken into heaven (2 Kings 2:11).

On the other hand, there have been prophets and oth-ers whose lives did not have a happy ending in mortal-ity even though they remained faithful and true during long periods of feeling abandoned. Perhaps the most notable and heart-wrenching example is that of the Prophet Joseph Smith. We cannot read the opening lines to Doctrine and Covenants 121 without noticing the obvious parallels to the Savior's expe-rience at Golgotha. "O God, where art thou? And where is the pavilion that covereth thy hiding place?" (D&C 121:1). Perhaps Joseph's cry, like the Savior's, is the elemental expres-sion of all those who, at some point, have experienced tragedy or feelings of unrelenting loneliness or feelings of abandon-ment. And like Joseph, we will come to know we have not, nor ever will be, abandoned like the Savior was. We may ask for, and receive, assurances of our Father's watchful care. The act of asking is important. And if we are patient, we will see just how much both Jesus and Joseph can teach us about the hows and whys of pain, sorrow, suffering, and tribulations.

> My son, peace be unto thy soul; thine adversity and thine afflictions shall be but a small moment;
>
> And then, if thou endure it well, God shall exalt thee on high; thou shalt triumph over all thy foes. (D&C 121:7–8)
>
> If thou art called to pass through tribulation; if thou art in perils among false brethren; if thou art in perils among robbers; if thou art in perils by land or by sea. . . .
>
> And if thou shouldst be cast into the pit, or into the hands of murderers, and the sentence of death passed upon thee; if thou be cast into the deep; if the billowing surge conspire against thee; if fierce winds become thine enemy; if the heavens gather blackness, and all the elements combine to hedge up the way; and above all, if the very jaws of hell shall gape open the mouth wide after thee, know thou, my son, that all these things shall give thee experience, and shall be for thy good.
>
> The Son of Man hath descended below them all. Art thou greater than he? (D&C 122:5, 7–8)

Joseph Smith remained faithful and had his exaltation sealed upon him (D&C 132:49). But we also note that Joseph's life did not turn out as Elijah's did, nor did it end up the way Joseph may have thought it would at the time he was sealed up, owing to the unusual wording of the last part of God's promise to him: "I have seen your sacrifices in obedience to that which I have told you. Go, therefore, and I make a way for your escape, as I accepted the offering of Abraham of his son Isaac" (D&C 132:50). Abraham, of course, was not required to offer up the life of Isaac. God made a way for Isaac's escape by providing a ram in the thicket (Genesis 22:12–13). In the end, however, there was no ram in the thicket for Joseph Smith, and he was required to give his life.

The point here is that God's ways are different from man's ways. He "seeth not as man seeth" (1 Samuel 16:7). He regards a happy ending in eternity of infinitely greater worth than a so-called happy ending in mortality, especially considering the way some men and women understand happiness. We have been promised by the Lord that he will make a way for our escape in our lives (1 Corinthians 10:13). But we must remember that our ways are not God's ways, and sometimes life's episodes do not conform to storybook endings. Mortal life is not fair. The lives of both Jesus Christ and Joseph Smith demonstrate that. But because of the life and death of Jesus Christ, because of his willing submissiveness in the face of total abandonment on the cross, he has the right, and the power, and the unwavering desire to make up to us all of the unfairness of life. Even though we may not be able to understand why things happen the way they do (and it is usually pointless to think about that question very much), we know that our Heavenly Father and Jesus Christ love us perfectly. And we know with perfect surety that we will be compensated for every trial, tragedy, and sorrow, every episode of loneliness, abandonment, and undeserved suffering. Christian theologian Richard Mouw said it well:

> We admit that we can't understand the mysteries
> of God's purposes. But we can go to the cross of Jesus

Christ. We can see that, at the cross, God took upon himself that abandonment, that abuse, that forlornness, that depth of suffering, Christ himself cried out from the depths of his being, "My God, why hast thou forsaken me?" When we see what God did, through Jesus Christ, we can say, "Yes, there is a safe place in the universe, in the shelter of the Almighty, in the shadow of the Most High." That place we know to be *Calvary*. ("Christian Responses to a World in Crisis," 11)

What was said long ago by chief apostle Peter bears repeating. Fiery trials work a great work in us. They are more precious than gold, for if faithfully endured, they bring us eternal glory (1 Peter 1:7). One of the truly great doctrines is this: Adversity and suffering make the veil very thin. President Harold B. Lee indicated that because of his struggles and trials the veil had become thin and that perhaps the veil would even have disappeared had the trials been greater:

"I thank the Lord that I may have passed some of the tests, but maybe there will have to be more before I shall have been polished to do all that the Lord would have me do.

"Sometimes when the veil has been very thin, I have thought that if the struggle had been still greater that maybe then there would have been no veil. I stand by, not asking for anything more than the Lord wants to give me, but I know that he is up there and he is guiding and directing" (Conference Report, October 1973, 170).

What Isaiah said more than twenty-seven hundred years ago ought to have great meaning to us today: "But now, O Lord, thou art our father; we are the clay, and thou our potter; and we all are the work of thy hand" (Isaiah 64:8). Raw clay usually does not possess immediate beauty or usefulness. Similarly, most of us human beings, if not all, are not the best, most valuable vessels we can be without significant shaping. But if we allow the Master Potter, the Lord, to put his hand to our lives and mold us, he can and will make us into enduring vessels of beauty and strength. The tools he uses to do the shaping are those kind of painful moments the Savior himself experienced in his mortal life, right up to the end.

Make no mistake about it. Our Heavenly Father and his divine Son are not interested in merely saving us. They want to change us, reshape us, transform us. In truth, full and complete salvation, what we know to be exaltation, cannot occur unless we are transformed. But the reshaping, the changing, and the transforming are painful. A parable from the writer George MacDonald, made famous by English churchman and theologian C. S. Lewis, is wonderfully illustrative:

> Imagine yourself as a living house. God comes in to rebuild that house. At first, perhaps, you can understand what He is doing. He is getting the drains right and stopping the leaks in the roof and so on: you knew that those jobs needed doing and so you are not surprised. But presently he starts knocking the house about in a way that hurts abominably and does not seem to make sense. What on earth is He up to? The explanation is that He is building quite a different house from the one you thought of—throwing out a new wing here, putting on an extra floor there, running up towers, making courtyards. You thought you were going to be made into a decent little cottage: but He is building a palace.

He intends to come and live in it Himself. (*Mere Christianity*, 176)

The tools God uses to shape and transform us are trials, tribulations, and suffering. Suffering of the highest order—the kind that comes not as a natural result of mortality or our own transgressions but as a result of what God himself gives to us— is customized to our spiritual needs. Our trials are tailor-made for each one of us, uniquely crafted for our individual circumstances and personalities. But I have noticed that often in these customized trials and suffering there is a common element: the feeling at some point of somehow being abandoned or betrayed or left alone by God at a time when he is desperately needed.

C. S. Lewis indicates that he experienced this feeling of abandonment when, after years of writing and speaking about God's personal interest in our suffering, he had to endure the pain and sorrow of losing his wife, Joy, to cancer. That was the greatest trial of his life. He felt that God had left him on his own to flounder, that God was not attuning His ear, that the portals of heaven were shut tight and locked. Lewis records his initial feelings in the face of his great trial: "Where is God? . . . Go to Him when your need is desperate, when all other help is vain, and what do you find? A door slammed in your face, and a sound of bolting and double bolting on the inside. After that, silence" (*Grief Observed*, 21–22).

Lewis is honest enough to let us see that he asked the same questions other noble and great disciples have asked: "Where are you, God? Why are you abandoning me?" It seems to me that such an experience is very much like the Savior's own experience at Golgotha. Jesus did not doubt the existence of his Father. He knew he was there. It was just that he felt his Father had left him alone at his time of greatest need. The lesson we learn is that all of us are given a glimpse, a taste, of Jesus' very experience during the Atonement: "My God, my God, why hast thou forsaken me?" (Matthew 27:46).

Lewis observes that God does not abandon us but allows us to learn crucial lessons we can learn *only* by experience, and He monitors our growth. Lewis gives us a window of insight into his own growth when he recorded: "I have gradually been coming to feel that the door is no longer shut and bolted. Was it my own frantic need that slammed it in my face? The time when there is nothing at all in your soul except a cry for help may be just the time when God can't give it: you are like the drowning man who can't be helped because he clutches and grabs. Perhaps your own reiterated cries deafen you to the voice you hoped to hear.

"On the other hand, 'Knock and it shall be opened.' But does knocking mean hammering and kicking the door like a maniac?" (*Grief Observed*, 63–64).

Elder Neal A. Maxwell, a man well acquainted with C. S. Lewis and a man whose own trials have qualified him to teach with authenticity, has said:

> To those of you who so suffer and who, nevertheless, so endure and so testify by the eloquence of your examples, we salute you in Christ! Please forgive those of us who clumsily try to comfort you. We know from whence your true comfort comes. God's "bosom" is there to be leaned upon. . . .
>
> We can confidently cast our cares upon the Lord because, through the agonizing events of Gethsemane and Calvary, atoning Jesus is already familiar with our

sins, sicknesses, and sorrows (see 1 Pet. 5:7; 2 Ne. 9:21; Alma 7:11–12). He can carry them now because He has successfully carried them before (see 2 Ne. 9:8). ("Yet Thou Art There," 32–33).

The scriptures teach us that God has not forsaken us nor will he ever forsake us. He is waiting and able to help us in our extremity. No less powerful to help is his divine Son, who has perfect empathy for us and can carry us through those times when we cannot go on, precisely because of his own experience. In fact, one reason Jesus was abandoned by his Father in Gethsemane and on the cross of Golgotha was so he could descend below all things to know every human circumstance and thus emerge victor over all things, with the knowledge and power to help us. By his confirming witness, I know that Jesus suffered on the cross the fierceness of the wrath of Almighty God, and because Jesus suffered that wrath on the cross, I do not have to. Even more important, I know that because Jesus was lifted up on the cross, I can be lifted up also—to eternal life. Furthermore, I know that because God forsook his Son on the cross, he will never have to forsake me.

And straightway one of them ran, and took a spunge, and filled it with vinegar, and put it on a reed, and gave him to drink.

The rest said, Let be, let us see whether Elias will come to save him.

Jesus, when he had cried again with a loud voice, yielded up the ghost.

And, behold, the veil of the temple was rent in twain from the top to the bottom; and the earth did quake, and the rocks rent. . . .

Now when the centurion, and they that were with him, watching Jesus, saw the earthquake, and those things that were done, they feared greatly, saying, Truly this was the Son of God. . . .

When the even was come, there came a rich man of Arimathaea, named Joseph, who also himself was Jesus' disciple:

He went to Pilate, and begged the body of Jesus. . . . And when Joseph had taken the body, he wrapped it in a clean linen cloth,

And laid it in his own new tomb, which he had hewn out in the rock: and he rolled a great stone to the door of the sepulchre, and departed.

And there was Mary Magdalene, and the other Mary, sitting over against the sepulchre.

MATTHEW 27:48–51, 54, 57–61

And there came also Nicodemus, which at the first came to Jesus by night, and brought a mixture of myrrh and aloes, about an hundred pound weight. Then took they the body of Jesus, and wound it in linen clothes with the spices, as the manner of the Jews is to bury.

Now in the place where he was crucified there was a garden; and in the garden a new sepulchre, wherein was never man yet laid.

There laid they Jesus therefore because of the Jews' preparation day; for the sepulchre was nigh at hand.

JOHN 19:39–42

# CHAPTER 11

# Death and Burial

The Savior's tortured cry of abandonment that awful Friday afternoon was misunderstood by some of the crowd gathered at the cross. They apparently thought it was a plea for help from the ancient prophet Elijah. Perhaps this misunderstanding was influenced by a Jewish tradition that Elijah often came to the aid of those in distress. But Jesus received no help, no angelic intervention, as he had in Gethsemane. He had to face the terrible consequences of Golgotha alone in order to come off conqueror over death and hell and to satisfy the demands of justice. "In that bitterest hour the dying Christ was alone, alone in most terrible reality. That the supreme sacrifice of the Son might be consummated in all its fulness, the Father seems to have withdrawn the support of His immediate Presence, leaving to the Savior of men *the glory of complete victory* over the forces of sin and death" (Talmage, *Jesus the Christ*, 661; emphasis added).

## THE END APPROACHES: PROPHECY FULFILLED

After Jesus had endured hours of unlimited pain and partial asphyxiation, the pericardium (the sack around the heart) would have begun to fill up with serum and compress the heart. As Jesus tried to move his body up and down to facilitate breathing, his already lacerated back would have been torn open again by the rough wood of the cross. His lungs would have made a frantic effort to gulp even small amounts of air. Loss of body fluid would have created heavy, thick, sluggish blood and made it increasingly difficult for the heart to pump. Dehydration would have been at a critical level (Davis, "Physician Testifies about Crucifixion," 39). At this point, Jesus uttered his fifth statement from the cross: "I thirst" (John 19:28). Here, the poetic prophecy of Psalm 22 is again recalled: "My strength is dried up like a potsherd; and my tongue cleaveth to my jaws; and thou hast brought me into the dust of death" (v. 15).

Because the Romans knew what developments to expect from their crucified victims, a small vessel of vinegar had been set near the cross of Jesus, and one of the crowd ran and "filled a spunge with vinegar, and put it upon hyssop, and put it to [Jesus'] mouth" (John 19:29). This action fulfilled another of the poetic messianic prophecies of the Psalmist: "And in my thirst they gave me vinegar to drink" (Psalm 69:21). But the event also harked back to the inauguration of the ancient Passover ordinance when the use of hyssop was instituted as a type or symbol of the atoning sacrifice of Jesus Christ: "Then Moses called for all the elders of Israel, and said unto them, Draw out and take you a lamb according to your families, and kill the passover. And ye shall take a bunch of hyssop, and dip it in the blood that is in the bason, and strike the lintel and the two side posts with the blood that is in the bason; and none of you shall go out at the door of his house until the morning" (Exodus 12:21–22). Again, we are made to appreciate the principle taught by ancient prophets: "All things which have been given of God from the beginning of the world, unto man, are the typifying of him" (2 Nephi 11:4).

Once all things had been accomplished that were intended by God and comprehended in his sweeping plan of salvation, Jesus cried out in a loud voice, bowed his head, and gave up the ghost. "Sweet and welcome as would have been the relief of death in any of the earlier stages of His suffering from Gethsemane to the cross, He lived until all things were accomplished as had been appointed" (Talmage, *Jesus the Christ*, 662). John 19:30 records: "When Jesus therefore had received the vinegar, he said, It is finished: and he bowed his head, and gave up the ghost."

Joseph Smith's translation of Matthew 27:54, provided in the LDS edition of the Bible (footnote 50a), gives us the full account of the Savior's sixth statement from the cross: "Jesus, when he had cried again with a loud voice, saying, Father it is finished, *thy will is done*" (emphasis added). This utterance is tremendously significant. It encapsulates the whole plan of salvation; it sums up the whole reason Jesus was sent to earth: to do his Father's will, as he himself had indicated on other occasions (John 6:38; 3 Nephi 27:13–14). The Prophet's translation of Matthew 27:54 brings us full circle to the time in premortality when the Savior volunteered to be our Redeemer, to do the will of the Father, and to let all the honor be his—"Father, thy will be done, and the glory be thine forever" (Moses 4:2).

The will of the Son was fully swallowed up in the will of the Father. The unparalleled prayer and desire of the Savior articulated in Gethsemane—"thy will be done"—was now fulfilled in every way, completely satisfying every aim, goal, purpose, and requirement of the plan of salvation. That is, in actuality, the sense of the Greek verb used in John's account of Jesus' sixth statement: "It is *finished*" (John 19:30; emphasis added). The verb translated into English as "finished" is *tetelestai* (from *teleo*), which means "to fulfill something, to make something complete." That is what Golgotha did. That which was started in Gethsemane was completed at Golgotha. How grateful we ought to be for the Prophet Joseph Smith's illuminating efforts to help us appreciate more completely the Savior's work and words.

Immediately after making this significant sixth declaration, Jesus uttered his final statement in mortality, as only Luke tells us: "Father, into thy hands I commend my spirit: and having said thus, he gave up the ghost" (Luke 23:46).

## THE MORTAL DEATH OF GOD

The very Son of God had died. The God who created the universe had experienced mortal death and passed through the veil to the spirit world, just as each of us will do. His physical body ceased to function. He now knew from his own experience what death was like—and the most horrible, torturous form of death that can be imagined. It should not be thought, however, that his decease was due merely to the natural processes of organ failure. Jesus died because he voluntarily gave up his life. Perhaps it might be said that the enervating effects of crucifixion brought him to the point where he could choose to give up his mortal life. But it was ultimately his choice—the only Being we know of with the power to determine the moment of his own decease. Death did not have power over him, did not control him. He controlled it. He decided to submit to it.

The Savior taught this doctrine when he said, "For as the Father hath life in himself; so hath he given to the Son to have life in himself" (John 5:26). "Therefore doth my Father love me, because I lay down my life, that I might take it again. No man taketh it from me, but I lay it down of myself. I have power to lay it down, and I have power to take it again. This commandment have I received of my Father" (John 10:17–18). In other words, our Father in Heaven passed on genetically to his literal, biological Son the power of life. That is why it is so crucial to possess a correct understanding of Jesus' literal, divine Sonship. The nature of his birth determined the nature of his death. Thus, possessing the genetic makeup of his Father—life—Jesus had power over death, could determine the time of his death, and had the power to take up his mortal body again, which he would do after three days.

Jesus possessed the powers and attributes of eternal life independently, "on the same principle that His Father who gave Him these divine powers and attributes possesses them," and this gave Jesus the ability to choose to die only after all things necessary to the plan had been accomplished (Andrus, *God, Man, and the Universe*, 417). But another factor also influenced the Savior's death: the withdrawal of the Father's Spirit and power. The Father's Spirit is pure life and light, especially the intensity or extent to which Jesus enjoyed it. As the Joseph Smith Translation says in John 3:34, "For God giveth him [Jesus] not the Spirit by measure, *for he dwelleth in him, even the fulness*" (emphasis added). In short, Jesus was able to die because the Father completely withdrew his life-giving, life-sustaining influence and powers.

Thus, here is another reason for the Father's withdrawal from his Son. Besides the need for the Son to descend below all things, besides the requirement that Jesus suffer spiritual death and hell, besides the need for him to know all our circumstances in order to be able to succor us according to the flesh, the Father withdrew from Jesus so that he, the Son, could have the sole power to determine his own death. "The Savior of the world was left alone by His Father to experience, of His own free will and choice, an act of agency which allowed Him to complete His mission of the Atonement" (Hales, "Behold, We Count Them Happy Which Endure," 75).

If the Father had not withdrawn from the Son again on the cross as he did in Gethsemane, Jesus would have been sustained and nourished by the life and light of his Father's Spirit. Total degeneration of the body could not have occurred, and thus he could not have died by an act of will so readily. One gospel scholar has approached the idea from a slightly different angle but with the same basic principle in mind: "The withdrawal of the Spirit from Jesus, with the influence which the powers of spiritual death and darkness then had upon Him, apparently caused a critical breakdown to occur in His bodily organs and tissues so that, when He willed that He should die, His spirit could readily depart into the spirit world" (Andrus, *God, Man, and the Universe*, 425).

## THE TESTIMONY OF NATURE: PROPHECY FULFILLED

At the moment Jesus died, the synoptic Gospels record, "the veil of the temple was rent in twain from the top to the bottom" (Matthew 27:51; Mark 15:38; Luke 23:45). Matthew adds, "And the earth did quake, and the rocks rent." It is to be expected that all nature would convulse and the earth would mourn while darkness covered the land because the Light and Life of the World had departed the world. As Nephi had said six hundred years earlier, "The rocks of the earth must rend" because "the God of nature suffers" (1 Nephi 19:12). This earthquake was also a graphic fulfillment of the ancient prophecy given by Enoch when he had his vision of the crucifixion. "And the Lord said unto Enoch: Look, and he looked and beheld the Son of Man lifted up on the cross, after the manner of men; and he heard a loud voice; and the heavens were veiled; and all the creations of God mourned; and the earth groaned; and the rocks were rent" (Moses 7:55–56).

This upheaval in the Holy Land paralleled events occurring on the American continent at the death of the Savior. The geologic destruction had been prophesied by Samuel the Lamanite more than thirty years before:

> Yea, at the time that he shall yield up the ghost there shall be thunderings and lightnings for the space of many hours, and the earth shall shake and tremble; and the rocks which are upon the face of this earth, which are both above the earth and beneath, which ye know at this time are solid, or the more part of it is one solid mass, shall be broken up;
>
> Yea, they shall be rent in twain, and shall ever after be found in seams and in cracks, and in broken fragments upon the face of the whole earth, yea, both above the earth and beneath.
>
> And behold, there shall be great tempests, and there shall be many mountains laid low, like unto a valley, and there shall be many places which are now called valleys which shall become mountains, whose height is great.
>
> And many highways shall be broken up, and many cities shall become desolate. (Helaman 14:21–24)

## TESTIMONY OF THE TEMPLE VEIL

Even more startling and horrifying, at least to the Jewish leaders, was that at the time of the Savior's death the veil of the Temple, the great curtain that had separated the Holy Place from the Most Holy Place, or Holy of Holies, was torn asunder. The most sacred room in the Temple was now exposed. The priests and other Jewish leaders would have looked upon this scene with horror. The holiest place on earth was desecrated. God's sanctity was violated. Such a devastating occurrence symbolized the end of the Mosaic dispensation, the fulfillment of the law of Moses, and the opening of a new dispensation with the restoration of the higher law and the greater availability of the Melchizedek Priesthood. It was a dramatic announcement of the fulness of the Gospel as the new and only acceptable covenant. It was also a signal sent by God himself, as Elder McConkie described:

> The veil itself . . . is said to have been sixty feet long, thirty feet wide, "of the thickness of the palm of the hand, and wrought in 72 squares, which were joined together." It was so heavy that it took hundreds of priests to manipulate it. "If the Veil was at all such as is described in the Talmud, it could not have been rent in twain by a mere earthquake or the fall of the lintel, although its composition in squares fastened together might explain, how the rent might be as described in the Gospel.
>
> Indeed, everything seems to indicate that, although the earthquake might furnish the physical basis, the rent of the Temple-Veil was—with reverence be it said— really made by the Hand of God. As we compute, it may

just have been the time when, at the Evening-Sacrifice, the officiating Priesthood entered the Holy Place, either to burn the incense or to do other sacred service there. To see before them . . . the Veil of the Holy Place rent from top to bottom . . . and hanging in two parts from its fastenings above and at the side, was, indeed, a terrible portent, which would soon become generally known, and must, in some form or other, have been preserved in tradition. And they all must have understood, that it meant that God's Own Hand had rent the Veil, and for ever deserted and thrown open that Most Holy Place. (*Mortal Messiah*, 4:229–30)

The apostle Paul called attention to another powerful meaning of the tearing of the veil of the Temple on that Friday afternoon two thousand years ago. According to Mosaic ritual established long before the Savior was born, once a year the Aaronic high priest passed through the veil of the Temple into the Holy of Holies on the Day of Atonement (*Yom Kippur*) to perform the Mosaic rituals associated with the Atonement. Only the high priest was allowed to enter, for the Holy of Holies represented God's presence. In Paul's symbolic interpretation of the tearing of the veil, the veil represented the physical body, the flesh, of Jesus Christ. The tearing of the veil from top to bottom (Mark 15:38) represented the physical suffering, the atoning sacrifice, the tearing of the Savior's flesh to open the way for all to enter God's presence, to be justified or approved of God, without the yearly mediation of the Aaronic high priest. Christ was the great and last mediator, the great and last sacrifice (D&C 76:69; Alma 34:10). His spilt blood was the fulfillment of the blood of animal sacrifices that the high priest sprinkled in the Holy of Holies. All of this is explained in chapters 9 and 10 of the book of Hebrews, especially the following verses:

> For when Moses had spoken every precept to all the people according to the law, he took the blood of calves and of goats, with water, and scarlet wool, and hyssop, and sprinkled both the book, and all the people,
>
> Saying, This is the blood of the testament which God hath enjoined unto you.
>
> Moreover he sprinkled with blood both the tabernacle, and all the vessels of the ministry.
>
> And almost all things are by the law purged with blood; and without shedding of blood is no remission.
>
> It was therefore necessary that the patterns of things in the heavens should be purified with these; but the heavenly things themselves with better sacrifices than these.
>
> For Christ is not entered into the holy places made with hands, which are the figures of the true; but into heaven itself, now to appear in the presence of God for us. (Hebrews 9:19–24)

> Having therefore, brethren, boldness to enter into the holiest by the blood of Jesus,
>
> By a new and living way, which he hath consecrated for us, through the veil, that is to say, his flesh. (Hebrews 10:19–20)

In our own day, the torn flesh of the Savior is symbolized in the torn bread of the sacrament. By means of this tangible emblem, we remember the Savior's physical, redemptive suffering in Gethsemane and on the cross at Golgotha.

## TESTIMONY OF OTHER WITNESSES

Following the testimony of the earth itself, along with the various elements of nature that also cried out and affirmed that this crucified Jesus was indeed the God of the universe, certain members of the party gathered at Golgotha were also deeply affected. Matthew reports that the Roman centurion who supervised the execution and some of those who were with him were impelled to exclaim, "Truly this was the Son of God" (Matthew 27:54). In addition, many women were there, those who had come up with Jesus to Jerusalem from Galilee (Luke 23:49). These were "great and faithful women who followed our Lord and who, for their faith and righteousness, shall be exalted to thrones of glory" (McConkie, *Doctrinal New Testament Commentary*, 1:833). Jesus' other friends ("all his acquaintance"; Luke 23:49) were at Golgotha as well.

No mention is made of any of the apostles being there, except for John. There is no doubt that the original members of the Quorum of the Twelve came to know exactly what happened at Golgotha and also came to know for themselves that Jesus was truly the Son of God. Jesus himself declared to the eleven apostles gathered at the Mount of Ascension after his resurrection that they were witnesses of him (Acts 1:8). Afterward, the apostles bore powerful testimony of their Savior (Acts 4:33). Peter, on the occasion of Cornelius's conversion, declared that the apostles were "witnesses of all things which [Jesus] did both in the land of the Jews, and in Jerusalem; whom they slew and hanged on a tree" (Acts 10:39).

In our own day, the same kind of witness as that possessed by the original apostles regarding the crucifixion has also been affirmed by living apostles and prophets. Elder Harold B. Lee bore his personal witness of the concluding events of the Atonement: "It was a week following the conference, when I was preparing myself for a radio talk on the life of the Savior when I read again the story of the life, the crucifixion and, the resurrection of the Master—there came to me as I read that, a reality of that story, more than just what was on the written page. For in truth, I found myself viewing the scenes with a certainty as though I had been there in person. I know that these things come by the revelations of the living God" (*Divine Revelation*, 12).

Another powerful illustration comes from the 1989 October general conference, when Elder David B. Haight of the Quorum of the Twelve recounted an experience he had had during a recent life-threatening episode. After becoming unconscious, he said, the terrible pain and commotion ceased. He was in a calm and peaceful place. He heard no voices but was conscious of being in a holy presence and atmosphere.

> During the hours and days that followed, there was impressed again and again upon my mind the eternal mission and exalted position of the Son of Man. . . .
>
> I was shown a panoramic view of His earthly ministry. . . .
>
> During those days of unconsciousness I was given, by the gift and power of the Holy Ghost, a more perfect knowledge of His mission. . . . My soul was taught over and over again the events of the betrayal, the mock trial, the scourging of the flesh of even one of the Godhead. I witnessed . . . His being stretched upon [the cross] as it lay on the ground, that the crude spikes could be driven with a mallet into His hands and wrists

and feet to secure His body as it hung on the cross for public display.

Crucifixion—the horrible and painful death which He suffered—was chosen from the beginning. By that excruciating death, He descended below all things, as is recorded, that through His resurrection He would ascend above all things (see D&C 88:6). . . .

I cannot begin to convey to you the deep impact that these scenes have confirmed upon my soul. ("The Sacrament—and the Sacrifice," 59–60)

## TYPES, SHADOWS, AND SYMBOLS OF HIS DEATH

Normally the Romans left the bodies of their crucified victims on their crosses to decompose. But Jewish law required the same-day burial of victims so that the land "be not defiled" (Deuteronomy 21:22–23). In the case of Jesus and the two thieves, therefore, Jewish leaders requested of Pilate that the legs of the crucified men be broken to hasten their deaths. They could thus be taken down off the crosses so as not to defile the coming Sabbath, which was also a high holy day (John 19:31). But when the soldiers came to Jesus to break his legs and they saw that he was already dead, "they brake not his legs" and so fulfilled the ancient typology and prophetic symbolism associated with the Paschal lamb (Exodus 12:46). Just as no bone of the Passover lamb was to be broken before it was slaughtered, so no bone of Jesus was broken, as the Psalmist had foreseen (Psalm 34:20). Jesus remained without blemish, as the lamb set aside for the Passover sacrifice was required to be (Exodus 12:5).

Then one of the Roman soldiers who was tending the victims thrust his spear into the side of Jesus, probably to reassure himself that He really was dead. In so doing, the soldier also fulfilled more ancient prophecy and symbolism. Out of the Savior's side wound flowed blood and water, indicative of a ruptured heart. Elder James E. Talmage declares his conviction that the Lord Jesus died of a "physical rupture of the heart" and provides ample evidence of this rare but recognized medical condition. He concludes: "Great mental stress, poignant emotion either of grief or joy, and intense spiritual struggle are among the recognized causes of heart rupture. The present writer believes that the Lord Jesus died of a broken heart" (*Jesus the Christ,* 669). More important, Jesus' death from a broken heart was also foreseen by the Psalmist: "Reproach hath broken my heart; and I am full of heaviness: and I looked for some to take pity, but there was none" (Psalm 69:20).

Indeed, Jewish and Roman leaders who contributed to Jesus' death offered neither help nor pity and thus fulfilled the prophecy of Psalm 69. But the symbolism of the blood and water resulting from the Savior's broken heart connects his atoning death with the specific elements and requirements of spiritual rebirth: "Inasmuch as ye were born into the world by water, and blood, and the spirit, which I have made, and so became of dust a living soul, even so ye must be born again into the kingdom of heaven, of water, and of the Spirit, and be cleansed by blood, even the blood of mine Only Begotten" (Moses 6:59). When Jesus completed the Atonement, he died of a broken heart, which involved blood and water. If we are to be born again, we must offer a broken heart, accept the cleansing blood of Jesus Christ, and come up out of the water of baptism (3 Nephi 9:20; Romans 6:3–6).

The blood and the water from the wound in Jesus' side is also linked to the ancient Jewish tradition of mixing water with wine for the third cup that was to be drunk during the Passover, or Seder, dinner. This third cup, the "cup after supper" or "cup of blessing," is explicitly associated with the inauguration of the sacrament of the Lord's Supper, which was instituted specifically for participants in the sacrament to remember the blood sacrifice of the Son of God on their behalf (Luke 22:20). Thus, the mixing of water with wine for the third cup of the Passover supper is symbolic of the Messiah's death by a broken heart.

As the Roman soldiers stood at the foot of the cross, no doubt gaping at the wounded side of their victim, a wound made notable by the blood *and* water issuing forth, the prophet Zechariah's ancient prophecy, spoken as though he were the Lord, reached fulfillment: "They shall look upon me whom they have pierced" (Zechariah 12:10). And like other prophetic statements about the Messiah, this declaration will likely see fulfillment again at the Second Coming when the Jewish people will also gape at the same side wound, as well as the wounds in the hands and feet of the Savior, and ask what they mean. And Jesus will reply: "These wounds are the wounds with which I was wounded in the house of my friends. I am he who was lifted up. I am Jesus that was crucified. I am the Son of God" (D&C 45:51–52; Zechariah 13:6).

## JOSEPH OF ARIMATHAEA AND JESUS' BURIAL

One of the unsung heroes in the tragic drama of the Savior's death was Joseph of Arimathaea, a member of the Sanhedrin, "an honourable counsellor," and a disciple of the Master who "waited for the kingdom of God" (Mark 15:43; Luke 23:51; Matthew 27:57; John 19:38). Some New Testament students have pointed to a nonscriptural tradition that identifies

Joseph of Arimathaea as Jesus' great-uncle, that is, uncle to Jesus' mother, Mary, and brother to Anna, Mary's mother. He is also described as a rich and powerful man, which is in harmony with the scriptures. We cannot prove the family connection described by this tradition, but we are sure that Joseph boldly, even courageously, lobbied Pilate for the Savior's body and then "bought fine linen, and took him down, and wrapped him in the linen" (Mark 15:46). John adds that Nicodemus assisted by purchasing an expensive mixture of myrrh and aloes and helped Joseph prepare the body of Jesus for burial after the manner of the Jews by wrapping his body in the linen cloth with the spices (John 19:39–40).

It took great courage for Joseph to appear before Pilate to procure the Savior's body (Mark 15:43). He was taking a risk to act so boldly before Roman authority, and he was certainly in peril from Jewish leaders and fellow members of the Sanhedrin eager to stamp out the new Jesus movement (Acts 9:2). There was much reason to fear the Jews, as all the disciples knew (John 19:38; 20:19).

That Pilate gave to Joseph the body of Jesus, considering the risks that he in turn was taking in surrendering the corpse of a troublemaker to Jesus' family or close friends, is indicative of at least two things. First, Pilate wanted to avoid further conflict with the Jews by making sure that Jewish concerns over the approaching Sabbath were honored. Second, Pilate really did understand that Jesus was innocent and was willing to allow him a proper, or honorable, burial.

Dishonorable persons, those convicted of the kind of crimes for which Jesus was crucified received tough treatment after death, as Josephus described: "He that blasphemeth God let him be stoned, and let him hang upon a tree all that day, and then let him be buried in an ignominious and obscure manner" (*Antiquities of the Jews*, 4.8.96). On the other hand, an honorable burial is believed to have consisted of washing and anointing the corpse, laying out the body, wrapping it in new cloth and spices, and interring it in a known, high-quality, family tomb (Brown, *Death of the Messiah*, 2:1261). In large measure the body of Jesus was treated this way, and, thus, his innocence and honor were affirmed even in the manner of his burial.

No mention is made in the Gospels of Jesus' body being anointed. Time did not permit the family or the disciples to give Jesus' body the type of anointing appropriate for an honorable man, let alone true royalty. "The preparations had to be hurried, because when the sun had set the Sabbath would have begun. All that they could do, therefore, was to wash the corpse, to lay it amid the spices, to wrap the head in a white napkin, to roll the fine linen round and round the wounded limbs, and to lay the body reverently in the rocky niche" (McConkie, *Mortal Messiah*, 4:239). Five days earlier, however, Mary, sister of Martha, had anointed Jesus at her home, "in token of [his] burial" (JST John 12:7). This action seems most appropriate because the home of the righteous is next to the house of the Lord in sanctity. Additionally, Mark and Luke tell us that certain women did plan to anoint the body of Jesus to insure a proper and honorable burial. "And when the sabbath was past, Mary Magdalene, and Mary the mother of James, and Salome, had bought sweet spices, that they might come and anoint him" (Mark 16:1; Luke 23:55–24:1).

Joseph offered his new, rock-cut tomb located in a garden and laid the lifeless corpse of the Son of God in the never-before-used burial chamber (John 19:41–42). We have the sense that this was also symbolic of royalty. One scholar has pointed out the parallel between Luke's description of the tomb, "wherein never man before was laid" (Luke 23:53), and the phrase he used earlier in his text to describe Jesus' triumphal entry into Jerusalem on a colt, "whereon yet never man sat" (Luke 19:30). "Luke may have favored this particular expression, 'where no one was yet laid,' as an echo of the clause he had used to describe the entry of Jesus as king into Jerusalem on a colt 'on which no person has ever sat' (19:30, 28). . . . there was a regal character to the burial in [the Gospel of] John" (Brown, *Death of the Messiah*, 2:1255).

Just as the new colt was symbolic of royalty, so too was the new tomb symbolic of royalty. Jesus was the Great King. He was also literally King of the Jews. The fulness of the earth was his; the interment of a Jewish monarch was his due. And yet he had been treated and executed as if he were a criminal. Again, we note the irony here as well. Jesus was condemned to die by the vehemence of the Jewish council, and yet he was laid to rest in the tomb of one of the most honorable members of that council (Mark 15:43). Matthew and Mark report that as a final act Joseph rolled a great stone to the door of the sepulchre and departed (Matthew 27:60; Mark 15:46).

All of this was pure, unadulterated, selfless service. Preparing another person's lifeless body for burial is a true act of kindness and charity, because it is one thing that can never be repaid by the individual being served. It can be done without expectation of recompense. Such was the largeness of soul possessed by Joseph of Arimathaea.

Another "ruler of the Jews" (John 3:1) also volunteered his time and substantial means to help bury the lifeless body of the Messiah. He was Nicodemus, the same man who was a member of the Sanhedrin, who had earlier gone to Jesus by night

(John 3:2), who revered him as a rabbinic master (John 3:2), and who had defended the Savior against the illegal machinations of the chief priests and Pharisees (John 7:45–52). It is not hard to envision the initially reticent Nicodemus experiencing the transforming power of Christ to the extent that he felt moved upon to participate in the burial of his Lord. The Gospel of John alone tells us that Nicodemus not only accompanied his colleague Joseph of Arimathaea but also purchased a sizable quantity of myrrh and aloes to prepare Jesus' body for burial (John 19:39). This was a very large, costly amount, representative of what was used in royal burials, and is another indication that Jesus' kingly status was acknowledged symbolically (2 Chronicles 16:14).

Both Joseph of Arimathea and Nicodemus were righteous leaders of the Jews who recognized the special nature of the Savior's life and teachings. They remained loyal to him and performed a special act of love and respect. The actions they took in association with the Savior's burial, once again, fulfilled prophecy. Isaiah had said the Messiah would be "with the rich in his death" (Isaiah 53:9), and so he was.

The final act in the drama of Golgotha culminated in the placement of guards at the Garden Tomb. This was done to satisfy the concerns of the chief priests and Pharisees that the disciples of Jesus be prevented from stealing his body and making it look like Jesus had come alive again, as he had prophesied. Several ironies emerge in this scene. First, the Jewish leaders had no qualms about going to the Gentile leader, Pilate, on the day after the crucifixion, a special and most sacred Sabbath day (John 19:31). They wanted to ensure the ultimate success of their conspiracy, even though it brought upon them ritual defilement, and they had gone to great lengths to remain ritually pure in other matters of Jewish life. "By personally arranging for the watch and sealing the tomb, the chief priests and Pharisees, according to their own tradition, suffered defilement" (McConkie, *Doctrinal New Testament Commentary*, 1:838). Second, in speaking to Pilate, they referred to Jesus as "that deceiver," when they themselves were guilty of the ultimate deceptions (Matthew 27:63). And third, the Jewish leaders—the inveterate enemies of Christ, as Elder Talmage calls them—had paid close attention to the words of the Savior about his resurrection, but those words had no spiritual effect on them, even though they were charged to be the spiritual guardians of their people (*Jesus the Christ*, 665–66).

Following Pilate's terse retort to Jewish leaders that they could make the tomb of Jesus as secure as they pleased, the leaders of the Jews placed an armed guard at the sepulchre and affixed some kind of a seal between the great stone and the portal of the tomb. Undoubtedly, both the Roman and Jewish leaders hoped that this would be the end of their problems.

To the apostles, disciples, and friends of Jesus who had been watching and waiting for the end to come, who were still at Golgotha when the Savior expired, and who were wrung out physically, emotionally, and spiritually by the events of that terrible Friday, the next day must have been the darkest of days. Their own sorrow and anguish must have been beyond words; their grief and uncertainty over the future, overwhelming. The crucifixion and suffering of one so compassionate and pure as Jesus of Nazareth was a horrible sight. It was compounded by Jesus' claim to be the Messiah, the Son of God, and the Redeemer of the children of men. And yet he seemed to die the ignominious death of a common criminal and an enemy of

Rome. The apostles, disciples, family members, and friends of Jesus had invested their whole lives in him. Now he was gone.

But Friday and Saturday were not the end of the story for the disciples then nor for disciples now. From the long hours of gloom, depression, and despondency came a morning of brilliant hope and complete triumph for the Savior's associates, a joy and gladness more glorious than was their deepest despair. How grateful we ought to be that there is a grand sequel in the story of God's infinite love for humankind and mercy toward each one. Truly, the story and the effects of the Atonement never end.

*Behold I have given unto you my gospel, and this is the gospel which I have given unto you—that I came into the world to do the will of my Father, because my Father sent me.*

*And my Father sent me that I might be lifted up upon the cross; and after that I had been lifted up upon the cross, that I might draw all men unto me, that as I have been lifted up by men even so should men be lifted up by the Father, to stand before me, to be judged of their works, whether they be good or whether they be evil.*

3 Nephi 27:13–14

# CHAPTER 12

# The Doctrine of the Cross

What was begun in the Garden of Gethsemane was consummated on the cross of Golgotha. Two times the Savior shed his blood for you and for me. In two places he endured this ghastly physical suffering to pay for our sins as well as our sorrows, sufferings, sicknesses, and fallen condition, even our mortality. The Savior himself acknowledged both Gethsemane and Golgotha, the bleeding from every pore (D&C 19:18; Luke 22:44) and the crucifixion (D&C 35:2; 138:35). Both the garden and the cross are integral parts of his atoning sacrifice.

## THE CROSS

For Latter-day Saints the symbol of the cross of Christ is as important, is as much a part of our theology, as it is for other Christians. Though latter-day prophets, under divine inspiration, have chosen not to display or portray material representations of the cross (icons) in our buildings of worship, the symbol of the cross of Christ still bids us to do as Christ did:

1. To forgive all men (D&C 64:10)

2. To extend mercy to others—that we may obtain mercy (3 Nephi 12:7; D&C 88:40)

3. To put others before ourselves and serve one another (Mosiah 2:17)

4. To take up our crosses and follow him (Matthew 10:38; Luke 9:23)

5. To endure all things with patience and dignity (D&C 67:13; 1 Peter 2:23)

The image of the cross of Christ lies at the heart of the foundational document of our religion—the Book of Mormon. In describing his early visions, the prophet Nephi testified that he "saw that [the Lamb of God] was lifted up upon the cross and slain for the sins of the world" (1 Nephi 11:33). But the capstone testimony regarding the cross came approximately six hundred years later when another Nephi reported the New World visitation of the very God of whom Lehi's son Nephi had prophesied. The resurrected Lord Jesus Christ affirmed to his American Israelites that he had come into the world to do his Father's will: "My Father sent me that I might be lifted up upon the cross; and after that I had been lifted up upon the cross, that I might draw all men unto me, that as I have been lifted up by men even so should men be lifted up by the Father, to stand before me, to be judged of their works, whether they be good or whether they be evil" (3 Nephi 27:14).

The cross was an important image and symbol to many prophets in different dispensations across time. The earliest mention of the cross was made by the prophet Enoch, sixth from Adam, who saw in vision "the Son of Man lifted up on the cross, after the manner of men" (Moses 7:55). Enoch also saw all the creations of God mourn at the crucifixion (Moses 7:56).

It is difficult to imagine that Adam, the first man, did not also have some knowledge of the crucifixion. He was taught about altar offerings and their similitude of the sacrifice of the Only Begotten (Moses 5:5–7). And he prophesied what would happen to his posterity unto the latest generation (D&C 107:56).

To the brother of Jared great things were revealed, including a knowledge of the cross, as Moroni recorded: "And the Lord commanded the brother of Jared to go down out of the mount from the presence of the Lord, and write the things which he had seen; and they were forbidden to come unto the children of men until after that he should be lifted up upon the cross; and for this cause did king Mosiah keep them, that they should not come unto the world until after Christ should show himself unto his people" (Ether 4:1).

In the meridian dispensation, just a few years after the Savior's death, the cross of Jesus Christ became for Christian disciples one of the most profound symbols of his suffering and atoning sacrifice. That was particularly true for the apostle Paul, who would not "glory [boast], save in the cross of our Lord Jesus Christ" (Galatians 6:14), for it was by the cross that God and man were reconciled (Ephesians 2:16). In a powerful image presented to the Corinthian Saints, Paul declared that "the preaching of the cross" was the very "power of God" unto those of us who are saved (1 Corinthians 1:18).

In the dispensation of the fulness of times, President Joseph F. Smith received a panoramic vision of the spirit world and the Savior's ministry to it. The Savior did not go in person to preach the everlasting gospel unto the wicked and rebellious (D&C 138:20–21). Messengers from among the righteous in the spirit world went instead (D&C 138:30–31). "It was made known among the dead, both small and great, the unrighteous as well as the faithful, that redemption had been wrought through the sacrifice of the Son of God upon the cross" (D&C 138:35). Thus we see that the cross was preached beyond the veil.

## TAKING UP OUR CROSSES

One of the most powerful uses of the image of the cross in Restoration scripture concerns the invitation, even command, to take up one's cross and follow the Savior. To the Nephite multitude assembled at the temple in the land Bountiful, the Savior described some of the wicked ideas and attitudes his people should never allow to enter their hearts, and then he said: "For it is better that ye should deny yourselves of these things, wherein ye will take up your cross, than that ye should be cast into hell" (3 Nephi 12:30).

In his mortal ministry, the Savior had explained to his disciples in the Old World that for one to take up his cross meant "to deny himself all ungodliness, and every worldly lust, and keep my commandments" (JST Matthew 16:26). The Savior added another significant qualifier and definition to the phrase "take up your cross" when he spoke to Joseph Knight in April 1830: "Behold, I manifest unto you, Joseph Knight, by these words, that you must take up your cross, in the which you must pray vocally before the world as well as in secret, and in your family, and among your friends, and in all places" (D&C 23:6).

To take up one's cross is to adopt the Savior's pattern of living, to think as he thinks, to eschew unworthy thoughts, to pray as he prays, to testify as he testifies, to proclaim truth boldly to the world as he proclaims truth boldly without concern for what the world will think of him. And if we do these things, the consequences of our actions will turn out to be beyond our fondest hopes and dreams—the joy and glory of eternal life. The Book of Mormon prophet Jacob emphasized the need for us to pay no heed to what the world may say or think of us as we press forward in Christ, living lives of quiet dignity in the face of sufferings, tribulations, and persecutions—even being chided for our very convictions and way of life because, after all, "we aren't really Christian," according to some. Said Jacob: "But, behold, the righteous, the saints of the Holy One of Israel, they who have believed in the Holy One of Israel, they who have endured the crosses of the world, and despised the shame of it, they shall inherit the kingdom of God, which was prepared for them from the foundation of the world, and their joy shall be full forever" (2 Nephi 9:18).

Jacob's language immediately recalls the image of the Savior on the cross, enduring unimaginable pain, suffering, and hardship, being the object of ridicule and shame, and yet accepting all of it with quiet dignity. The phrase used by Jacob, "despised the shame of it," is intriguing. I take him to be saying that one of the profound ways we endure our own crosses is by regarding the ridicule or views of the world as "negligible, worthless, or distasteful," which is one of the definitions of the word *despise*. We will treat the shame or ridicule of the world as being of no account. In fact, if we are truly imitating the Savior on the cross, we will not just accept what is dished out but will do as he did: "Not rendering evil for evil, or railing for railing: but contrariwise blessing; knowing that ye are thereunto called, that ye should inherit a blessing" (1 Peter 3:9).

The apostle Paul is a powerful example of one who took up his cross and despised the shame of it, rendering blessing for railing. He testified:

We are fools for Christ's sake, but ye are wise in Christ; we are weak, but ye are strong; ye are honourable, but we are despised.

Even unto this present hour we both hunger, and thirst, and are naked, and are buffeted, and have no certain dwelling place;

And labour, working with our own hands: being reviled, we bless; being persecuted, we suffer it:

Being defamed, we intreat: we are made as the filth of the world, and are the offscouring of all things unto this day. (1 Corinthians 4:10–13)

Shame and ridicule come in subtle forms these days. They can become a part of our own attitudes without our even realizing it. Sometimes they take the form of pity for others because of their weaknesses, handicaps, or misfortunes, real or perceived. Sometimes they come in the form of looking down on individuals because their economic circumstances have taken a turn for the worse. Sometimes they come in the form of intrusive attempts to "help" bring people up to "our level" socially and culturally or educate them or disabuse them of their naive ways. I am persuaded that just as we hope that the ridicule of the world towards us will be tempered, so we must examine our attitudes to make sure that pride, egocentrism, and self-importance do not put us into the category of those who ridicule—even subtly. We never know when life will turn the tables on us, when our lives will take a downturn, and we will be facing other burdens of the cross.

## REVERENCE FOR THE CROSS

The cross of Christ is a powerful symbol and image for us as Latter-day Saints. Through the image of the cross, the Savior himself bids us to follow him in every way and in every thing. The image of the cross ought to evoke in us the deepest feelings of gratitude for what the Savior did—and did for all of us— individually as well as collectively.

Several years ago, President Gordon B. Hinckley told a story that helps us understand and appreciate just what the Savior did for all of us. That story was retold by President James E. Faust in a magnificent address entitled "The Atonement: Our Greatest Hope." The setting for the story was a one-room schoolhouse in the mountains of Virginia where the boys were so rough no teacher had been able to handle them.

> Then one day an inexperienced young teacher applied. He was told that every teacher had received an awful beating, but the teacher accepted the risk. The first day of school the teacher asked the boys to estab- lish their own rules and the penalty for breaking the rules. The class came up with 10 rules, which were writ- ten on the blackboard. Then the teacher asked, "What shall we do with one who breaks the rules?"
>
> "Beat him across the back ten times without his coat on," came the response.
>
> A day or so later, . . . the lunch of a big student, named Tom, was stolen. The thief was located—a little hungry fellow, about ten years old.
>
> As Little Jim came up to take his licking, he pleaded to keep his coat on. "Take your coat off," the teacher said. "You helped make the rules!"
>
> The boy took off the coat. He had no shirt and revealed a bony little crippled body. As the teacher

hesitated with the rod, Big Tom jumped to his feet and volunteered to take the boy's licking.

"Very well, there is a certain law that one can become a substitute for another. Are you all agreed?" the teacher asked.

After five strokes across Tom's back, the rod broke. The class was sobbing. Little Jim had reached up and caught Tom with both arms around his neck. "Tom, I'm sorry that I stole your lunch, but I was awful hungry. Tom, I will love you till I die for taking my licking for me! Yes, I will love you forever!"

President Faust then said that after telling the story, President Hinckley quoted Isaiah: "Surely he hath borne our griefs, and carried our sorrows. . . . He was wounded for our transgressions, he was bruised for our iniquities: the chastisement of our peace was upon him; and with his stripes we are healed" (Isaiah 53:4–5).

Continuing, President Faust declared:

No man knows the full weight of what our Savior bore, but by the power of the Holy Ghost we can know something of the supernal gift He gave us. In the words of our sacrament hymn:

*We may not know, we cannot tell,*
*What pains he had to bear,*
*But we believe it was for us*
*He hung and suffered there.*
[*Hymns, no. 194, "There Is a Green Hill*
*Far Away"*] (*Ensign, November 2001, 18–19*)

Our freedom, our relief, our redemption from the crushing

pain we deserve on account of our sins came at a dear price, not to us but to the One Perfect Being who ever walked the earth. Because of him, we don't get what we deserve! He alone took our punishment. Like Big Tom in our story, he took what would have come to us without his intervention.

Jesus said that he trod the winepress alone. None were with him when he "took our licking," not even his own Father, who withdrew his Spirit from his Son while the Son was on the cross. There, on the cross, the Savior of his own free will took to himself our stains and our sins, as well as the blood and sins of all generations (Jacob 1:19; 2 Nephi 9:44). Alma reminds us that without the Atonement operating in our lives, we would have to "stand before the bar of God, having [our] garments stained with blood and all manner of filthiness" (Alma 5:22). In the garden and on the cross Jesus initiated the great exchange: He cleansed our garments and imputed our stains and blood to his garments. That is why when he comes again, at the great and terrible second coming, he will be wearing red garments:

> And it shall be said: Who is this that cometh down from God in heaven with dyed garments; yea, from the regions which are not known, clothed in his glorious apparel, traveling in the greatness of his strength?
>
> And he shall say: I am he who spake in righteousness, mighty to save.
>
> And the Lord shall be red in his apparel, and his garments like him that treadeth in the wine-vat. (D&C 133:46–48)

Red is the color of stains that accrue to a person's garments when working in a winepress. Red is also symbolic of the

Savior's spilled blood in Gethsemane and on the cross. Red becomes symbolic of victory—victory over the devil, hell, and endless torment. At the Second Coming, Jesus Christ will be recognized as the ultimate victor by his wearing red garments. Also at the Second Coming, all shall recognize the Savior by the wounds he has chosen to retain in his hands and feet, which wounds he received on the cross. Even those who have been unable to know the Lord because of what certain leaders of their people did long ago will receive the blessing of knowing their Redeemer:

> And then shall the Jews look upon me and say: What are these wounds in thine hands and in thy feet?
>
> Then shall they know that I am the Lord; for I will say unto them: These wounds are the wounds with which I was wounded in the house of my friends. I am he who was lifted up. I am Jesus that was crucified. I am the Son of God.
>
> And then shall they weep because of their iniquities; then shall they lament because they persecuted their king.
>
> And then shall the heathen nations be redeemed, and they that knew no law shall have part in the first resurrection; and it shall be tolerable for them. (D&C 45:51–54)

Truly, the cross is a powerful and lasting symbol of the Savior's all-encompassing atonement.

Last but not least, the marks of the cross are at the center of the most profound expressions of our worship of the Savior. These expressions are reserved for our most sacred places of worship. We renew our commitment to remember the cross of

Christ, and, in a sense, we renew our commitment to take up our crosses when we worship in the house of the Lord. Temples are one more evidence of how serious Latter-day Saints are about remembering the cross. Almost twenty-eight centuries ago, Jehovah promised Israel that he would never forget his people: "Behold, I have graven thee upon the palms of my hands" (Isaiah 49:16; 1 Nephi 21:16). In turn, this prophetic reference to the marks of the crucifixion bids us, the Lord's people—latter-day Israel—never to forget him.

## THE LIVING CHRIST

Some have asked, "If the cross is such an important image and symbol, why don't the Latter-day Saints honor it more, wear it, or display it in their homes and churches?" There may be several parts to the answer.

First, there is the danger that any symbol of the Savior, whom we worship, may itself become the thing venerated when it is made into a tangible artifact, as ancient Israel demonstrated. Moses set up the brass serpent in the wilderness as a type and symbol of the Messiah (1 Nephi 17:41; 2 Nephi 25:20; Alma 33:18–22; Helaman 8:13–15; John 3:14–15). But after many hundreds of years, the symbol had become the thing being worshiped and had to be destroyed by righteous King Hezekiah (2 Kings 18:4).

Second, even though the cross was a powerful theological symbol and image to the earliest Christians, the idea of wearing a replica of the tool of crucifixion probably would have seemed abhorrent.

Third, modern prophets have encouraged us to keep images of the living Christ uppermost in our minds and to live lives worthy of his presence. In this connection Elder Gordon B. Hinckley related the following story many years ago:

> We recently held an open house in the Arizona Temple. Following a complete renovation of that building, nearly a quarter of a million people saw its beautiful interior. On the first day of the opening, clergymen of other religions were invited as special guests, and hundreds responded. It was my privilege to speak to them and to answer their questions at the conclusion of their tours. I told them that we would be pleased to answer any queries they might have. Many were asked. Among these was one which came from a Protestant minister.
>
> Said he: "I've been all through this building, this temple which carries on its face the name of Jesus Christ, but nowhere have I seen any representation of the cross, the symbol of Christianity. I have noted your buildings elsewhere and likewise find an absence of the cross. Why is this when you say you believe in Jesus Christ?"
>
> I responded: "I do not wish to give offense to any of my Christian brethren who use the cross on the steeples of their cathedrals and at the altars of their chapels, who wear it on their vestments and imprint in on their books and other literature. But for us, the cross is the symbol of the dying Christ, while our message is a declaration of the living Christ."
>
> He then asked: "If you do not use the cross, what is the symbol of your religion?"
>
> I replied that the lives of our people must become

the only meaningful expression of our faith and, in fact, therefore, the symbol of our worship. ("Symbol of Christ," 92)

President Harold B. Lee taught the same principle through an experience he related:

> At the World's Fair in New York, President G. Stanley McAllister, of the New York Stake, told us of an experience that he had that probably defines the distinction that I am trying to make. He was on a plane returning from a business assignment in St. Louis and his seatmate was a Catholic priest. As they flew toward New York and became acquainted with each other, each discovered the other's identity as to church relationships. As they talked about various things, the Catholic priest said, "Have you been to the World's Fair?" "Yes," Brother McAllister said, "I am on the committee that helped to plan our pavilion." "Well, have you visited our Catholic exhibit?" And again Brother McAllister said yes. The priest said, "Well, I have been to the fair and I have visited your exhibit. At the Catholic exhibit we have the dead Christ—the *Pieta*. But the Mormon Pavilion has the live Christ, or the living Christ." And in that I think there is a distinguishing difference. (*Stand Ye in Holy Places*, 149–50)

Living prophets have asked that we emphasize, think of, and live our lives bathed in the light of the living Christ. The living Christ signals that the heavens are not sealed. They are open, and revelation continues daily. That revelation continues to reveal the mind of Christ to each one of us.

## SOME FINAL THOUGHTS

Long after money, power, and prestige—the fleeting trinkets and treasures of the world—have slipped away and mean nothing, the actions of our Lord in Gethsemane and on the cross will grow in stature and mean everything to us. The image of Jesus, bloody, bruised and humiliated, stumbling along while attempting to bear the weight of the cross, finally reaching Golgotha and being nailed to the cruel cross of crucifixion, in many ways symbolizes and encapsulates the profound lessons we need to learn in this mortal existence. Under the most adverse circumstances, the Savior moved along the course that would take him to the completion of his mission. What happened to him did not come because Pilate or the Jewish leaders had the power to impose it but because he was willing to accept it (Packer, Conference Report, April 1988, 80). Through it all he was loyal to the Father.

Faithfully bearing up under our loads and facing our trials and tribulations while at the same time resolving to serve God at all hazards and accept his will moulds us and makes us fit for the kingdom of God. When we submit to that which God sees fit to inflict, we become like the Savior. In fact, we cannot enjoy the association of the Savior without offering sacrifice in the similitude of the Savior, suffering tribulation in his name (D&C 138:12–13). The *Lectures on Faith* tell us that "the faith necessary unto life and salvation never could be obtained without the sacrifice of all earthly things," for "it is in vain for persons to fancy to themselves that they are heirs with those, or can be heirs with them, who have offered their all in sacrifice, and by this means obtained faith in God and favor with him so as to obtain eternal life, unless they, in like manner, offer unto him the same sacrifice, and through that offering obtain the knowledge that they are accepted of him" (6:7–8).

When we have determined that we are willing to sacrifice all we possess, we are actually living lives in the similitude of Jesus of Nazareth: We are living lives of consecration. Taking up our crosses and living lives of consecration are really synonymous. We need only look around us (and not very long at that) to find individuals whose lives are reflections of the Savior's premier sacrifice. They make us want to do our very best out of appreciation for their personal examples as well as the Lord's.

A couple my wife and I know put the Lord first and accepted a call to preside over a Latter-day Saint mission in a faraway country. Within the first weeks of their service, they encountered serious challenges that had to be dealt with. And within the first year, the husband's father died, the wife's father died, and their first child was married—all back in the United States. Of course, the husband, who was the mission president, could not leave the mission. He did not flounder or complain. He did what the Lord asked because he had consecrated his life to the Master. When I think of him, I think of the Savior, and I want to be better and to do better. In this man I see glimpses of the kind of "character and capacity and the purity to endure what the Atonement required of Him," to use Elder Neal A. Maxwell's phrase (quoted in Weaver, "God Will Protect Us," 3).

How profoundly grateful I am for a Savior who shows us the way in so many ways. In the Sermon on the Mount, he tells us that we are to be the salt and the light of the world (Matthew 5:13–14). As Robert Sloan, president of Baylor University, points out, "Salt and light extend their influences to their environment" ("Character of Leadership," 29). Like-wise, character influences its environment. As the Savior is the Salt and the Light of the World, so we as his disciples are called upon to possess the character he possesses and then to influence the world—as do salt and light. In other words, we are to take up our crosses and follow him. After all is said and done, we must follow the Savior at all hazards, for he is not just our best hope, he is our only hope.

# The Garden Tomb

# Introduction

My father was a powerful influence on me. I suppose a realist would say that I was overly protected, sheltered, perhaps even coddled, by my father. Maybe so. My father was an affectionate and very patient man. I know he loved my mother, my sister, and me. Perhaps his own formative years without a mother or father, as well as several years in the United States Marine Corps, made him a more sensitive soul, more nurturing with my sister and me. I came to love what he loved—God, Church, country, family, the underdog, and trout fishing. I idolized him. I knew I could trust him.

My father was a convert to The Church of Jesus Christ of Latter-day Saints, and he knew a great deal about correct principles and important doctrine. I remember significant, substantive discussions with him, just the two of us, about such things as the life of Jesus and what it meant to be a bearer of the priesthood. He said to me on more than one occasion that he would rather be a deacon in the Aaronic Priesthood than president of the United States. A priesthood holder, he told me, has more of the kind of power that really counts than do kings or presidents. I liked that kind of inspiring encouragement. I never wanted to be president of the United States, but I always wanted to hold the priesthood. My father held the priesthood. The gospel of Jesus Christ was very important to him.

A significant childhood memory is of my father, sitting on the edge of his bed reading from the standard works every night. Quite probably that example is where I began to gain my own passionate interest in the scriptures. Of course, I now realize that in this, as well as in other matters, my father possessed flaws. He read the scriptures by himself. It would have been better had he read them with the family. But his unflagging, consistent practice of reading from the standard works before he went to bed (he retired early and arose early) left a powerful impression on me.

It came as a monumental blow when my father died suddenly right after Christmas the year I was fourteen. I was left nearly devastated. I did not know what to do. I could not understand why God would take him away. I was empty and lonely and cast adrift. All activities, all things, were empty and hollow. For a time I could not see how I would ever be happy again. Good men and women came to our home to comfort my mother, my sister, and me. They spoke of eternal family bonds and bore testimony of the certainty of the resurrection—that my father would live again. But I was not comforted. I was consumed with grief. I was not paying attention. I *could not* hear because I thought my world was gone.

Enter Jesus and his ancient disciples, the principal characters who are the subject of the story discussed in this present book. Jesus was a powerful influence on his disciples. Jesus was the foundation on which the disciples had built the last few years of their lives. He loved them, and they loved him.

But at 3 o'clock one Friday afternoon, Jesus died by

crucifixion. Though his death and burial inaugurated the final act in the grand drama that was the Atonement, his disciples did not know that they were witnessing the Atonement. They saw only cruelty, humiliation, suffering, and dissolution. Jesus did not look like the Messiah, let alone the Son of God, as he hung on the cross, died the ignominious death of a condemned criminal, and was buried in a tomb not his own.

Of course, the disciples did not comprehend the kind of messiah Jesus was, nor the meaning of his resurrection. When they laid Jesus to rest, they did not anticipate the glorious morning of his rising from death to immortality and eternal life. Death seemed like the end. "For as yet they knew not the scripture, that he must rise again from the dead" (John 20:9). Surely they felt a grief beyond belief—that is, if they felt anything at all through their numbness. In those first hours following Jesus' burial, death itself may well have looked like the ultimate victorious enemy.

Jesus' death left the disciples' world in a shambles. It left a hole in their lives just as the death of my father had left a hole in mine. It left them hurting and doubting. Even after Mary Magdalene and the other women had seen the risen Lord and reported it, most of the other disciples did not believe he had taken up his body again. It took several visits by the resurrected Savior to convince all of them. At first they *could not* hear, just as I could not hear, because they were consumed with grief and thought their world was gone, just as I had.

Many of us modern disciples, I think, have felt some sympathy for our counterparts in the early Church as we ourselves have tried to work through the death of a loved one. I think of what the ancients faced. For three intense years they followed their Master, the "prophet from Galilee," putting their trust in him as the Anointed One. They had given up much, in some cases everything, to embrace Jesus' superlative teachings, his exemplary life, and his promise of an eternal kingdom of glory beyond this fallen, mortal realm. Then their hopes were dashed on a Roman cross and in an unfinished, borrowed tomb. I can well imagine that for those uncertain, miserable hours of Friday evening through Sunday morning, the disciples felt devastated. They may well have thought that the enemy had won, once and for all.

The truth is that without the Savior's victory over death on that incomparable Sunday morning, death would have been the ultimate enemy. Death would have won. Without the resurrection there would have been no redemption. Resurrection is redemption! Even laying aside for a moment the miraculous and infinite sacrifice of Jesus for our sins and sufferings, resurrection itself redeems each one of us from the grasp of death and the ultimate subjugation to the devil. For without the resurrection, the spirits of all humankind *would* have become just like the devil. Listen to Nephi's sure witness:

> Wherefore, it must needs be an infinite atonement— save it should be an infinite atonement this corruption could not put on incorruption. Wherefore, the first judgment which came upon man must needs have remained to an endless duration. And if so, this flesh must have laid down to rot and to crumble to its mother earth, to rise no more.
>
> O the wisdom of God, his mercy and grace! For behold, if the flesh should rise no more our spirits must become subject to that angel who fell from before the

presence of the Eternal God, and became the devil, to rise no more.

And our spirits must have become like unto him, and we become devils, angels to a devil, to be shut out from the presence of our God, and to remain with the father of lies, in misery, like unto himself; yea, to that being who beguiled our first parents, who transformeth himself nigh unto an angel of light, and stirreth up the children of men unto secret combinations of murder and all manner of secret works of darkness. (2 Nephi 9:7–9)

I have great empathy for the Savior's ancient disciples as they witnessed the death and burial of their Master. For just those few hours before the resurrection, they were, of all human beings, most miserable (1 Corinthians 15:19). Without faith in, or any understanding of, the literal resurrection, they were without hope and spiritual stability, at least to some extent. Thankfully, they did not have to endure that trauma for very long. But even that short period was long enough.

Some may say that the early disciples brought it on themselves—that they should have had greater faith; that they should have paid more attention to their Master's promises and declarations about rising from the dead after three days; that they should have believed. But sometimes the death of someone we love so much can overwhelm us, even if only momentarily, and skew our perception of gospel concepts gained through years of instruction. Sometimes such an event can even cause some to question their beliefs and can be the ultimate test of faith. Certainly it causes many of us to reflect on our most cherished and deeply held convictions. As I reflect on my own experience with the death of my father, I now marvel at the strength of the ancient disciples. When I consider what they had to contend with and the brutality they witnessed, I frankly appreciate their endurance all the more.

Ultimately, the disciples were able to emerge from their darkness and misery into the brilliant light of truth. They came to *know* that Jesus was who he said he was. He had shed his blood and redeemed all humankind, just as he said he would. He went to the world of spirits and fulfilled Isaiah's prophecy of preaching deliverance to the captives, opening the doors of the prison, and ransoming the prisoners so that they could go free, just as he said he would. He reentered his sealed tomb, took up his physical body again, and appeared to many who thought their world and their hope had vanished forever, just as he said he would. Truly, he healed the brokenhearted, just as he said he would. He ascended to heaven to watch over his Church and reveal his will as well as himself to mortals on this earth until the time of his glorious second coming.

This, then, is the story that is told in the present volume. *The Garden Tomb* recounts the singular and sacred events that transformed the place of ultimate sadness into the place of ultimate triumph. It is the last in a three-volume series describing our Lord's infinite atonement, which began in the garden of Gethsemane, continued at Golgotha, and culminated in the Garden Tomb with the wondrous resurrection. Truly, the atonement of Jesus Christ, which of course includes his resurrection, is the single most powerful and important event that ever has occurred or ever will occur in time or all eternity. From Creation's dawn through all the ages of a never-ending eternity, nothing will equal in significance the sacred events that transpired from Thursday through Sunday of the most pivotal week in the history of our universe.

Having said that, I return briefly to the days of my own misery. Gradually, my family, my friends, and my Scoutmaster helped me out of my black hole. They would not leave me alone (no insignificant modeling of the Savior's message and example in this case). They engulfed me in affection and activity. But, as much as anything, I really believe the Atonement operated on my behalf in those days. The Spirit of the Lord lifted the fog, so to speak, and the Savior lifted my suffering. Now, many years later, the story discussed in the following pages—the story of the Garden Tomb and the first resurrection—means more to me than words can express. I am convinced of the truth of the Lord's promises of redemption and resurrection, and I cherish my associations with those, past and present, who have helped strengthen my conviction of those promises. It is my hope that those who read what follows will also have their own convictions of Christ's infinite mercy and saving power strengthened.

---

And after this Joseph of Arimathaea, being a disciple of Jesus, but secretly for fear of the Jews, besought Pilate that he might take away the body of Jesus: and Pilate gave him leave. He came therefore, and took the body of Jesus.

And there came also Nicodemus, which at the first came to Jesus by night, and brought a mixture of myrrh and aloes, about an hundred pound weight.

Then took they the body of Jesus, and wound it in linen clothes with the spices, as the manner of the Jews is to bury.

Now in the place where he was crucified there was a garden; and in the garden a new sepulchre, wherein was never man yet laid.

There laid they Jesus therefore because of the Jews' preparation day; for the sepulchre was nigh at hand.

---

# CHAPTER 1

# A Garden Tomb

At 3 o'clock in the afternoon of the final Friday of his life (the eve of Passover), Jesus of Nazareth breathed his last breath (Luke 23:46). He had been hanging, impaled, on a Roman cross for six hours, since 9 A.M., just outside Jerusalem's city wall (Mark 15:25; Luke 23:44). The place-name for the grisly death scene was *Golgotha* (Aramaic) or *Calvary* (Latin), meaning "a skull." Perhaps the name denoted topographical features (tradition identifies the site as an old stone quarry), or maybe it was a symbolic name representing death much the same way the image of a skull and crossbones connotes death. It has even been suggested that Golgotha may have been so named because executed criminals were buried nearby, and the skulls or bones from interred bodies became exposed, on rare occasions, due to the ravages of animals or the elements—though leaving any portion of a corpse unburied was contrary to Jewish law and would have been rectified immediately (Talmage, *Jesus the Christ*, 667).

Death by crucifixion was the most drawn out and painful of all forms of execution in the ancient world. Its horrors were known to all. It was looked upon by many as inhumane and revolting, and its practice was finally abolished by the Roman emperor Constantine the Great (d. 337). The welcome relief of death came to the victim of crucifixion as a result of complete exhaustion due to unrelenting, excruciating pain and congestive organ failure from the unnatural position of the body nailed to the cross (Talmage, *Jesus the Christ*, 655). The word *excruciating*, in fact, comes from the same root as does *crucifixion*.

Jesus suffered all of the pain and physical breakdown that every other victim of crucifixion suffered. But Jesus was no ordinary human being. He could not die until he *decided* to die and that required the spirit, power, life, and influence of his actual Father, our Heavenly Father—the Mighty Elohim—to be completely withdrawn from him so that he could determine the actual moment of his death. This total abandonment by his Father caused Jesus to cry out, in Aramaic, the opening words of Psalm 22: "Eli, Eli, lama sabachthani?—My God, my God, why hast thou forsaken me?" (Matthew 27:46) and then caused the "critical breakdown to occur in His bodily organs and tissues so that, when He willed that He should die, His spirit could readily depart into the spirit world" (Andrus, *God, Man, and the Universe*, 425).

## MOURNING

All of the bystanders and onlookers who had gathered at Golgotha for the sole purpose of watching the spectacle of crucifixion that afternoon left the scene smiting their breasts (Luke 23:48), a sign of anguish or contrition (Luke 18:13). But those who were personal friends of Jesus, including the women who had followed him from Galilee, stood as witnesses of the Savior's crucifixion to the very end of the ordeal, first beholding events from a distance (Luke 23:49) and then near the cross (John 19:25–27).

To the faithful followers of Jesus who had been involved in one way or another in the wrenching and tragic drama of the previous twenty-four hours—and it was truly a tragic drama of unduplicated intensity—the Crucifixion must have seemed a heart-sickening end to all their messianic hopes. After all, "a dead Messiah was no Messiah at all," in the contemporary Jewish view of things (Walker, *Weekend That Changed the World*, 38). The atmosphere of gloom and doom at the site of the Crucifixion was undoubtedly magnified by the darkness that had gathered in the skies three hours earlier (Matthew 27:45).

The women who had ministered to Jesus so caringly, all of them nurturers and spiritual giants themselves, surely must have been wounded emotionally and spiritually beyond our comprehension. Though others may have been present, we know of four women who were at the cross along with John the Beloved: Jesus' mother; His mother's sister (Salome, the mother of the evangelist John and his brother James); Mary, the wife of Cleophas; and Mary Magdalene (Talmage, *Jesus the Christ*, 668). Death is challenging to deal with no matter what the circumstances. But when there has been great love, death brings great sorrow. This I know from personal experience and believe it was true for those closest to Jesus. In addition, their grief was intensified because they had not yet comprehended the glorious promise of resurrection: "For as yet they knew not the scripture, that he must rise again from the dead" (John 20:9). A modern revelation provides not only counsel but also insight into those natural, divinely understood and approved emotions that so easily come to the surface when we mourn. "Thou shalt live together in love, insomuch that thou shalt weep for the loss of them that die, and more especially for those that have not hope of a glorious resurrection" (D&C 42:45).

Sorrow, mourning, and tears have their place in God's plan. We humans are creations who are supposed to weep and mourn. In fact, we are commanded to love and to mourn! These feelings are what make us like our Creator. They are part of godhood. The realization that this is true seems to have greatly surprised the great seer Enoch when he witnessed the God of heaven crying. "And it came to pass that the God of heaven looked upon the residue of the people, and he wept; and Enoch bore record of it, saying: How is it that the heavens weep, and shed forth their tears as the rain upon the mountains? And Enoch said unto the Lord: How is it that thou canst weep, seeing thou art holy, and from all eternity to all eternity?" (Moses 7:28–29).

Enoch learned that God, the greatest of all, weeps and mourns. Apparently, he thought that because of God's infinite goodness, power, and knowledge, he was impervious to sorrow and emotion, or at least demonstrable emotion. It seems that he believed tears and outward displays of sorrow were not part of God's demeanor or his character: "And thou hast taken Zion to thine own bosom, from all thy creations, from all eternity to all eternity; and naught but peace, justice, and truth is the habitation of thy throne; and mercy shall go before thy face and have no end; how is it thou canst weep?" (Moses 7:31).

What Enoch learned, and what we learn, is that stoicism is for the birds—literally. Lesser creatures may not weep and mourn, but God surely does, and so must we.

I do not think it possible to overemphasize the sorrow Jesus' family and friends must have experienced. At that moment they did not possess the hope that only a knowledge of resurrection can bring. Even for those with a firm belief in the resurrection and the eternal nature of the soul, grief resulting from the death of one so dear can seem overpowering. How much more so is the case if that death is brought about by the brutality of others. As we contemplate what happened to Jesus, the unfairness and violence that engulfed him, and the sorrow that surely overwhelmed his mother and family members, no other circumstance can fully compare. Perhaps, however, there is something of a parallel in our own latter-day history—the martyrdom of the Prophet Joseph Smith. From the autobiography of Wandle Mace, we learn of reactions in Nauvoo to the death of Joseph Smith and his brother Hyrum. It takes little imagination to apply these same feelings to the family and friends of Jesus as they witnessed their beloved Master's crucifixion:

> Who can depict the scene? What pen describe the sorrow and mourning manifested by all? Strong men wept like children; women moaned as they gathered their little children around them and told them of the fearful crime that had taken place at Carthage, where the Governor had promised protection to those two innocent men, they had been left by him to be murdered.
>
> Who could describe the anguish of the families of those Martyrs? Their aged Mother who had already passed through so many trying scenes, she had seen her son dragged before the courts and discharged honorably because they could find no guilt attached to him, near fifty times—now he and her oldest son, two of earth's noblest sons, are shot down in cold blood by a mob, in the prime of life; their wives and innocent babes, left widowed and fatherless to face a relentless foe without the encouragement and assistance of those they dearly loved. ("Journal of Wandle Mace," 149)

To me, the words of Lucy Mack Smith, mother of the

Prophet Joseph Smith, when she described her feelings at the martyrdom of Joseph and Hyrum, convey more powerfully than most other writings the likely feelings of Mary and others at the foot of the cross.

On the morning of the twenty-fifth, Joseph and Hyrum were arrested for treason. . . .

I will not dwell upon the awful scene which succeeded. My heart is filled with grief and indignation, and my blood curdles in my veins whenever I speak of it.

My sons were thrown into jail, where they remained three days in company with Brothers Richards, Taylor and Markham. . . . Soon after this two hundred of those discharged in the morning rushed into Carthage, armed and painted black, red and yellow, and in ten minutes fled again, leaving my sons murdered and mangled corpses! . . .

Their bodies were attended home by only two persons. . . .

After the corpses were washed and dressed in their burial clothes, we were allowed to see them. I had for a long time braced every nerve, roused every energy of my soul and called upon God to strengthen me, but when I entered the room and saw my murdered sons extended both at once before my eyes and heard the sobs and groans of my family and the cries of "Father! Husband! Brothers!" from the lips of their wives, children, brothers and sisters, it was too much; I sank back, crying to the Lord in the agony of my soul, "My God, my God, why hast thou forsaken this family!" A voice replied, "I have taken them to myself, that they might have rest." Emma was carried back to her room almost in a state of insensibility.

Her oldest son approached the corpse and dropped upon his knees, and laying his cheek against his father's, and kissing him, exclaimed, "Oh, my father! my father!" As for myself, I was swallowed up in the depths of my afflictions, and though my soul was filled with horror past imagination, yet I was dumb until I arose again to contemplate the spectacle before me. Oh! at that moment how my mind flew through every scene of sorrow and distress which we had passed, together, in which they had shown the innocence and sympathy which filled their guileless hearts. As I looked upon their peaceful, smiling countenances, I seemed almost to hear them say, "Mother, weep not for us, we have overcome the world by love; we carried to them the gospel, that their souls might be saved; they slew us for our testimony, and thus placed us beyond their power. (*History of Joseph Smith by His Mother*, 323–25)

Perhaps the great difference between Lucy Mack Smith and those at the cross of Jesus is precisely the difference John seems to emphasize: The early disciples did not comprehend the promise of a glorious resurrection (John 20:9). Their grief was not so easily assuaged. What was said by William Clayton of Joseph and Hyrum's mother surely must apply to Mary of Nazareth: "[She] is distracted with grief & it will be almost more than she can bear" (Allen, *Trials of Discipleship*, 142). It would be a wonderful thing indeed to learn someday that our Father in Heaven did give to Mary, the mother of his Divine Son, some measure of hope in the form of personal revelation, some little insight like that given to Lucy Mack Smith, so that Mary could know her Divine Son was at peace, that he was beyond the power of anyone to harm him anymore.

## FULFILLING THE BURIAL CUSTOM

At some point Jesus' disciples must have realized that when the end finally came, if someone did not intervene, Jesus' body would simply be thrown into a common grave along with the bodies of other criminals crucified that day. A secret disciple of Jesus who had previously "feared" the Jews, perhaps because of his position in the Sanhedrin, did intercede, ultimately declaring himself to be a follower of Jesus by his bold action. This disciple was Joseph of Arimathea.

Joseph of Arimathea is a true hero. He is named in all four Gospels. He was a respected member of the great Sanhedrin, "an honourable counselor, which also waited for the kingdom of God" (Mark 15:43), "a rich man" (Matthew 27:57), and "a good man, and a just: [who] had not consented to the counsel and deed of them" (Luke 23:50–51). He bravely went to Pontius Pilate to acquire the body of Jesus and bury the lifeless remains of his Master in his own family tomb. If Jesus' body had been thrown into a common grave, it would have become the property of the Roman government. Joseph's action not only salved a bit of the anguish felt by Jesus' family and friends but also kept Jesus' physical remains a Jewish issue. "No doubt the religious authorities would not have been best pleased with this—not least because it meant that responsibility for Jesus' body was now once again within Jewish, rather than Roman, jurisdiction. But by this stage in the afternoon many of them were involved in the ceremonial 'waving of the first-fruits,' and so would only hear about Joseph's maneuver some hours later" (Walker, *Weekend That Changed the World*, 39).

The written testimony of John the apostle—the very same who was at Golgotha's cross with the women and who was commissioned to look after Jesus' mother—reports that Joseph was assisted by another member of the Sanhedrin, Nicodemus, in the burial detail (John 19:39–42). Their first task was to take down the body of Jesus from the cross. Although the Romans had no legal requirement that a victim's body must be removed from the cross (they often left corpses on their crosses to be scavenged by birds or wild animals), they allowed the Jews to follow their own law (Deuteronomy 21:23), which required "burial of a criminal the same day as his execution" (Maier, *In the Fullness of Time*, 176).

It is profoundly sobering to think of Joseph of Arimathea and Nicodemus, "two of Jerusalem's most distinguished leaders laboring in the darkening twilight to loosen the shattered remains of their Master from the horrible spikes" (Keller, *Rabboni*, 280). That had to have been a ghastly job, considering Jesus' physical appearance, but with love and care these loyal followers prepared his body for burial. Perhaps they shed many tears. Who could have performed such labor and not wept? I well remember grown men weeping on the day my father died and later as they helped with the burial arrangements. Their love and concern were moving. Their sensitive and thoughtful help was truly comforting. They showed my family that compassionate discipleship is not related to time, place, position, or convenience. They, like the disciples of old, reflected the image of the Master in their countenances.

Nicodemus didn't bring just a huge amount of embalming spices to prepare the corpse of Jesus—"about an hundred pound weight" (John 19:39)—but in fact a regal amount, representative of what was used in Israelite royal burials (2 Chronicles 16:14). Interestingly, Josephus mentioned huge quantities of spices in connection with the burial of King Herod the Great (*Wars*, 1.33.9; *Antiquities*, 17.8.3). This use of a large quantity of spices to prepare the Savior's body was another symbolic acknowledgment of his kingly status and the honorable burial he deserved.

Joseph and Nicodemus wrapped the Savior's body in layers of linen cloth, interspersed with Nicodemus's spices, myrrh, and aloes, according to the custom of the Jews (John 19:40). A smaller separate cloth, a *tallit*, or Jewish prayer shawl, according to tradition, was wrapped around the Savior's head. The corpse was then carried to the new, rock-hewn family tomb owned by Joseph. Some of the devoted women of the group, especially Mary Magdalene and the other Mary, observed the sepulchre and watched Jesus' body being laid to rest, but they did not enter the tomb. They intended to return to the sepulchre after they had observed the Sabbath day and then anoint the corpse with spices and ointments they had prepared (Luke 23:55–56; Mark 15:47; Matthew 27:61). But that was for another day. On Friday night everyone left the tomb. Because of the nearness of the Sabbath, Jesus' interment had to be accomplished hastily. At least his tomb was not too far away; neither was it unworthy of its occupant. Joseph was a rich man, and his new, unused sepulchre was located in a lovely spot—in a recognized garden, and the garden was "in the place where [Jesus] was crucified" (John 19:41).

John's Gospel mentions, almost in passing, the burial custom of the Jews (John 19:40). These customs are largely to be gleaned from passages of scripture:

> After death the body was washed, its eyes were closed and its mouth and other orifices were bound shut (Jn 11:44). A mixture of spices was applied to the body, perhaps as a preservation or perhaps to ward off the smell of decomposition for those who visited the tomb later (Jn 11:39; 19:39–40). It was then dressed in its own

clothes or placed in a linen shroud (Mt 27:59). Next, a procession, including musicians, family, and (if the family could afford it) professional mourners followed the corpse to the tomb (Mt 9:23). It was customary for mourners to continue to visit the tomb for 30 days, to reanoint the body (Mk 16:1) or to check to be sure the person had not been buried prematurely (Jn 11:31). (Matthews, *Manners and Customs of the Bible*, 239)

No procession is explicitly mentioned in scripture regarding the burial of Jesus, but surely one took place, even though it almost certainly omitted professional mourners and musicians because Jesus was regarded as a convicted criminal and because it was done in haste owing to the quickly approaching Sabbath. That the outcasts of society, including the poor, the strangers, social pariahs, and the criminally convicted, were buried in common unmarked, shallow graves (Luke 11:44) or in a "potter's field" (Matthew 27:1–10) makes us appreciate the service and sacrifice of Nicodemus and Joseph of Arimathea all the more. Because of them, the mortal body of the true King was allowed a clean and private resting place.

## THE SAVIOR'S GARDEN TOMB

No site mentioned in scripture has received more attention in Christendom than the Savior's Garden Tomb, even though its exact geographical location is not certain. Doctrinally, when we speak of the Savior's Garden Tomb, we come full circle to the inauguration of the plan of salvation on this earth, to another garden at the beginning of time, a garden called Eden. Major events of our Heavenly Father's plan of salvation, or great plan of happiness, have occurred in sacred gardens: the garden of

Eden, the garden of Gethsemane, and the garden of the Empty Tomb. The Creation, the Fall, and the Atonement thus become inextricably linked by gardens. The garden of the burial tomb, the site of Jesus' burial, resurrection, and completed atonement, is tied to the garden of Eden, the place where the Creation was completed and the Fall took place. Those gardens, in turn, are linked with the garden of Gethsemane, where Christ suffered for all the sin, sorrow, and pain resulting from the Fall and where he experienced his greatest suffering. Elder Bruce R. McConkie articulates this significant concept with apostolic power:

> As we read, ponder, and pray, there will come into our minds a view of the three gardens of God—the Garden of Eden, the Garden of Gethsemane, and the Garden of the Empty Tomb where Jesus appeared to Mary Magdalene.
>
> In Eden we will see all things created in a paradisiacal state—without death, without procreation, without probationary experiences.
>
> We will come to know that such a creation, now unknown to man, was the only way to provide for the Fall.
>
> We will then see Adam and Eve, the first man and the first woman, step down from their state of immortal and paradisiacal glory to become the first mortal flesh on earth.
>
> Mortality, including as it does procreation and death, will enter the world. And because of transgression a probationary estate of trial and testing will begin.
>
> Then in Gethsemane we will see the Son of God

ransom man from the temporal and spiritual death that came to us because of the Fall.

And finally, before an empty tomb, we will come to know that Christ our Lord has burst the bands of death and stands forever triumphant over the grave. ("Purifying Power of Gethsemane," 9–11).

For more than a century, two separate sites, each with its advocates, have been regarded as the possible location of Golgotha and the nearby Garden Tomb. One site, the earliest recognized location, is inside the Church of the Holy Sepulchre, west of the Temple Mount and within the present-day Old City walls. The other site is Gordon's Calvary, north of the Temple Mount and outside the present-day Old City walls.

Historians and archaeologists have generally favored the site inside the Church of the Holy Sepulchre. Traditions regarding its authenticity reach back to the second century after Christ when the Roman emperor Hadrian (A.D. 117–38) tried to remake Jerusalem into a thoroughly Roman town by obliterating the sites sacred to Jews and Christians. Over the place thought to have been Jesus' tomb, Hadrian erected a temple to Aphrodite (Venus).

In A.D. 325, during the council of Nicaea, Bishop Makarios of Jerusalem requested help from the emperor Constantine in restoring sacred sites. He immediately obtained permission to remove the Roman Temple of Aphrodite. The following year Constantine's mother, the intrepid seventy-nine-year-old Helena, made a pilgrimage to Jerusalem and directly contributed to the work of Christian restoration, which eventually resulted in the construction of the Church of the Holy Sepulchre.

The significance of the spot on which the Church of the

Holy Sepulchre was built, at least for Roman Catholic and Greek Orthodox Christians, lies in their belief that the church was constructed over both the Rock of Crucifixion (Golgotha) and the very tomb where Jesus was laid to rest before his resurrection. An eyewitness to the building excavations, Eusebius, the fourth-century historian and bishop of Caesarea, records: "At once the work was carried out, and, as layer after layer of the subsoil came into our view, the venerable and most holy memorial of the Savior's resurrection, beyond all our hopes, came into view" (Eusebius, *Life of Constantine*, 3.28, as quoted in Murphy-O'Connor, *Holy Land*, 50). That memorial was the empty tomb of Jesus.

In addition, according to a tradition dating from 351, Helena found fragments of the actual cross of crucifixion in a cave or cistern adjacent to the Rock of Crucifixion (also believed to be preserved inside the church) during her tour of Jerusalem in 326. The later provenance of this tradition makes it problematic, however.

At least two issues make the Church of the Holy Sepulchre unlikely as the site of Jesus' tomb. The first is a prohibition, extant in first-century Palestine, against placing burial sites to the west of Jerusalem. This prohibition is reflected in both the Talmud and the archaeological record. Reasons for its existence center on the requirements of ritual purity and the fact that prevailing winds in the Holy Land are from the west. As one scholar explained:

> Jews did not embalm dead bodies prior to burial; and corpses were left exposed in the tomb to desiccate, which could take over a year. Tombs to the west of the city presented two problems: (1) the scent of decomposing corpses would be carried over the city by breezes

> from the west, and (2) Jews believed ritual impurity rising from interred corpses could be carried over the city by those breezes, causing the living inhabitants of the city to become "defiled" or unclean. (Chadwick, "Revisiting Golgotha and the Garden Tomb," 16)

Thus, Jerusalemites would have placed their tombs to the east, north, or south of the city but not to the west.

The prohibition against tombs to the west of Jerusalem also involved the Temple. From about 20 B.C. onward, Herod the Great and his successors supervised the expansion of the Temple and Temple Mount, making it the architectural jewel of the Mediterranean world. Modern scholars working in the Holy Land have shown that the beliefs and practices of the Pharisees were the basis for most Jewish practices, including those involving the Temple, during the Herodian period. The Pharisees predominated in the Sanhedrin during this time. Pharisaic tradition "would not have permitted tomb construction anywhere directly west of the expanded Temple Mount because wind passing over western tombs would also have passed over the sacred temple enclosure, thus defiling it and anyone in it" (Chadwick, "Revisiting Golgotha and the Garden Tomb," 17). Scholars thus conclude that since "burial customs in the first half of the first century C.E. [A.D.] preclude burials and their attendant impurities west (windward) of the Temple, then the crucifixion and burial of Jesus could not have taken place at the site of the Church of the Holy Sepulchre, which is almost exactly due west of the Holy of Holies" (Rousseau and Arav, *Jesus and His World*, 169).

The second issue bearing on the location of Golgotha and the Garden Tomb has to do with symbolism and typology. We know that all animal sacrifices in ancient Israel were a similitude and foreshadowing of the great and last sacrifice that would be made by Jesus Christ (Moses 5:4–8). The most important geographical symbolism associated with animal sacrifices and offerings of the Tabernacle and the Temple from Mosaic times onward required that the sacrifice of a lamb be made "on the side of the altar northward before the Lord" (Leviticus 1:11). In other words, the animal sacrifices—which constituted the most important elements of the various sanctuary offerings (burnt, peace, sin, etc.) and which symbolized the great and last sacrifice of the Son of God (Alma 34:13–14)—were slaughtered north of the altars of both the wilderness Tabernacle and the Jerusalem Temple. Therefore, wherever we look for the location of Golgotha and the nearby Garden Tomb, symbolic necessity dictates that we look north of the great altar of the Jerusalem Temple. This geographic symbolism is an important one of the many foreshadowings of the Lord's death and burial.

The other site that some believe to be the location of the Savior's death and resurrection, Gordon's Calvary, is often referred to simply as the Garden Tomb. It is an enclosed tomb and garden located near a skull-shaped hill overlooking the Old City of Jerusalem just north of Damascus Gate. It was identified only in 1883 as the crucifixion and burial site of Jesus by British General Charles ("Chinese") Gordon, just two years before he was killed at Khartoum. Some archaeologists and historians discount this site because there are no early historical traditions to authenticate it and because the tomb itself has been dated six centuries too early (from about the seventh century before Christ) by archaeologists. It must be noted, however, that latter-day prophets who have visited sites in the Holy Land have voiced some strong and impressive feelings about Gordon's

Calvary, or the Garden Tomb. Of this site President Harold B. Lee said in 1970:

> My wife and I were in the Holy Land. We have spent some glorious days visiting those places. . . .
>
> But a strange thing happened after we had gone to the garden tomb, and there we felt it was definitely the place. It was in the hill, it was a garden, and here was a tomb. . . . But the strange thing was that when we moved it seemed as though we had seen all this before. We had seen it before somewhere. ("Qualities of Leadership," 7)

Two years later President Lee reiterated his view of the Garden Tomb:

> We followed the way of the cross supposedly to the place of crucifixion and the place of the holy sepulchre. But all of this, according to tradition, we felt, was in the wrong place. We felt none of the spiritual significance which we had felt at other places. . . .
>
> There was yet another place we had to visit, the garden tomb. . . . Here our guide took us as though it were an afterthought, and as the woman guide with her little son led us through the garden, we saw a hill outside the gate of the walled city of Jerusalem, just a short way from where the hall of judgment had been inside the city walls. The garden was right close by, or "in the hill," as John had said, and in it was a sepulchre hewn out of a rock, evidently done by someone who could afford the expense of excellent workmanship.
>
> Something seemed to impress us as we stood there that this was the holiest place of all, and we fancied we

could have witnessed the dramatic scene that took place there. ("I Walked Today Where Jesus Walked," 6)

In 1979 President Spencer W. Kimball said of his visit to the Garden Tomb: "We accept this as the burial place of the Savior. We realize people have different ideas about these places, but this seems to be the logical place. I feel quite sure that this is the place where His body was laid. It gives me such a sacred feeling just to be here. I've preached quite a few sermons about this spot" (*Church News*, 3 November 1979, 5).

Just a few years ago, in a video presentation entitled *Special Witnesses of Christ*, President Gordon B. Hinckley said the following as he stood at the Garden Tomb: "Just outside the walls of Jerusalem, in this place or somewhere nearby was the tomb of Joseph of Arimathea, where the body of the Lord was interred."

## CRITICAL ISSUES

As most authorities acknowledge, ultimately it does not matter very much *where* Jesus was buried; rather, it does matter a great deal *why* and for *how long* he was buried and *what* happened in the tomb. A venerable instructor said to me once, when teaching with great power, "Suppose someone very dear to you died and was buried, but you did not know the location of the gravesite. And then suppose that after a few days, in the midst of your sadness, you saw this person walking toward you—fully alive. It is unlikely your first impulse would be to run about checking for the location of the grave to make sure it was really empty! Without a doubt your first impulse would be to run and embrace your loved one and revel in a joy as great as, or even greater than, was your sadness. If, therefore, you do not find the exact location of the Garden Tomb, revel in the joy of having found him who originally occupied the grave but now has left the tomb forevermore."

This does not mean that modern disciples should not be interested at all in the exact location of Golgotha and the Garden Tomb, places of such monumental import for the history of the world. But we ought to prayerfully consider the sacred texts describing the final moments of the Master's ministry, as well as the statements of the living witnesses, as our foundation, and then review the best analysis scholarship has to offer.

Another point of discussion that has arisen in the last few years centers on the nature of Jesus' sepulchre, particularly its size but also the type of stone used to seal it. Some authorities assert that because 98 percent of the Jewish tombs discovered by archaeologists in and around Jerusalem dating to the Second Temple period were sealed with square stones or plugs, and because the Greek verb *kulio,* translated in Matthew and Mark as "rolled," can also mean "moved," it is likely that the tomb of Jesus was sealed with a square stone and not a round, or a rolling, stone. Thus, these authorities argue, passages in the Gospels in the King James Version stating that the stone used to seal the tomb was "rolled" into place should be retranslated as "moved" into place. Furthermore, they assert, Jesus' tomb was of the standard small variety with a small entrance or opening (Kloner, "Did a Rolling Stone Close Jesus' Tomb?" 23–27).

In my view, the latest theories of archaeologists should not automatically be preferred over the actual wording of the King James New Testament. First, even though the actual number is very small, there are examples of tombs from the period in question that used round or disk-shaped stones to seal the entrance. These blocking stones are large, at least four feet in diameter, and the tombs that they sealed housed the wealthy and influential members of society (Herod's family tomb and the tombs of the kings are examples). In fact, round blocking stones "appeared only in the tombs of the wealthiest Jews" (Kloner, "Did a Rolling Stone Close Jesus' Tomb?" 28).

Second, both Matthew 27:60 and Mark 15:46 use the verb *kulindo*, which does not denote in its primary or secondary definitions the meaning "to move." It means "to roll." If Matthew and Mark didn't mean that the stone was rolled into place, why didn't they use a verb that did not carry so strongly the connotation of rolling or circular movement? (Remember, the Joseph Smith Translation does *not* change the text when it says the stone was "rolled" into place—though it does change other small points.) Isn't it possible that Matthew and Mark are actually saying what they really mean? Given that Joseph of Arimathea was a rich as well as an influential man and that the few rolling-stone tombs unearthed by archaeologists were *only* for the wealthy and influential, isn't it possible that the Garden Tomb of Jesus—Joseph's own intended tomb—was sealed with a rolling stone and that Jesus really was buried as a king in every way, including even the type and size of his sepulchre?

In the end, the New Testament leaves us with the most important information and lasting impressions about the site of our Savior's burial:

1. In the place where Jesus was crucified was a garden (John 19:41).

2. In the garden was a sepulchre (John 19:41). That the Savior's tomb was located in a real garden and not in an overgrown weed patch, as some have argued, is confirmed by Mary Magdalene on the first Easter morning when she initially supposed she was talking to the "gardener" (John

20:15). She was, of course, talking to *the* gardener—the Gardener of the Father's vineyard. But John's report was not metaphoric.

3. The tomb was new; no corpse had ever been placed there before (John 19:41; Luke 23:53).

4. The site of the tomb, and hence of the Crucifixion, was very close to the city (John 19:20).

5. The place of crucifixion (and of the tomb) was within moderate calling distance of the road. People passing by the site derided the Savior on the cross (Matthew 27:39; Mark 15:29). Bystanders misunderstood the Savior and thought he was calling to Elijah. In fact, what he said was, "Eli, Eli . . . My God, my God" (Matthew 27:46–47; Mark 15:34–35).

6. The tomb was hewn out of the rock; it was not a natural cave, and it cost its owner a fair amount (Matthew 27:60; Mark 15:46; Luke 23:53).

7. The tomb was closed up by rolling a *great* stone in front of the door (Matthew 27:60; Mark 15:46; 16:4), implying that the tomb was a rolling-stone tomb, the kind used by the wealthy and influential members of society, and that the stone was large.

8. The tomb was opened when the great stone was rolled back from the door by an earthquake and two angels (JST Matthew 28:2), also indicating that the stone was very large (Mark 16:4) and could keep the tomb secure.

9. The entrance of the tomb was low-cut; one had to stoop to look in (Luke 24:4; John 20:5).

10. The interior of the tomb, however, was large enough that

people could stand inside (Mark 16:5; Luke 24:3–4; John 20:6, 8). It was the family tomb of a wealthy man (Matthew 27:57).

As anyone knows who has ever laid a loved one to rest, it is comforting to have a befitting gravesite available for the deceased. All disciples of the Savior, ancient and modern, may be grateful that a man of the stature of Joseph of Arimathea was raised up to provide, at great personal sacrifice, a tomb fit for the King of heaven and earth. Isaiah had prophesied that the Messiah would be "with the rich in his death" (Isaiah 53:9), and so he was. Once Jesus' body had been laid to rest, Joseph "rolled a great stone to the door of the sepulchre, and departed" (Matthew 27:60).

## On the Sabbath After the Crucifixion

Of all the Lord's disciples, the women (including those from Galilee) bore the brunt of the Lord's death. Most of the other disciples were not at the cross; they had fled. In addition, Luke's Gospel indicates that after Jesus' interment, the women returned to their places of abode to prepare additional burial spices and ointments because they had agreed to meet again at the tomb after the Sabbath and administer final burial preparations to the Savior's body in anticipation of a long entombment. And yet, though they may have been anxious to complete the burial procedures, they kept the Sabbath! Their reason for observing the day of rest was that it was the commandment of the Mosaic law, and they were obedient (Luke 23:56). They obeyed with exactness even when circumstances were at their worst.

Such faithfulness in the face of such a monumental loss is humbling, especially when we consider that their supposed "day of rest" could have been anything but restful for these sisters. The anguish of the previous day would have remained constant in their minds and hearts. They would have remembered every gory detail. We turn to an account from one who was at Nauvoo when Joseph and Hyrum Smith were murdered in order to understand more fully how overpoweringly vivid the Savior's death scene became for those early disciples who were at the cross. From Lyman Omer Littlefield we learn:

> The bodies of Joseph and Hyrum were brought to Nauvoo, dressed and laid in state at the Mansion House, where thousands of people, bathed in tears, passed in procession, two abreast, to view their mangled remains. The writer of this, with his wife, thus had the mournful privilege of looking one sad and brief adieu upon the noble forms of those men of God.
>
> That was an hour marked in the history of this people, and although forty-four years have since passed away, the powers of memory seldom go back and review the scene—though in gleams of momentary fleetness—without sensations of pain. (*Reminiscences of Latter-day Saints*, 162–63)

The Lord's disciples would never forget the events of what the world now calls Good Friday. It seems unlikely, however, that any of the disciples the following Saturday would have found anything good about it. Yet, as Joseph of Egypt had testified more than a thousand years earlier, God turns bad things into good. "But as for you, ye thought evil against me; but God meant it unto good, to bring to pass, as it is this day, to save much people alive" (Genesis 50:20). Isn't this the essence of the Atonement, a capsulized summary of the Savior's suffering? Though some thought evil against Jesus' life and ministry, God meant it unto good, to save much people alive! Truly, the life of Joseph of Egypt was itself a foreshadowing of the life and mission of the Messiah.

In stark contrast to the strict obedience manifested by Jesus' disciples on the day after His crucifixion, Matthew describes the continuing evil activity of the self-same religious leaders who were charged with ensuring that the Sabbath, as well as all other requirements of the Law, were complied with. They themselves violated the Sabbath by going to Pilate to request that a guard be placed at the tomb. At least two reasons made this extraordinary action necessary, although the Jewish leaders mentioned only one.

First, as they indicated, they were concerned that the disciples of Jesus might steal his body to make it appear as though he had risen from the dead. "Now the next day, that followed the day of the preparation, the chief priests and Pharisees came together unto Pilate, saying, Sir, we remember that that deceiver said, while he was yet alive, After three days I will rise again. Command therefore that the sepulchre be made sure until the third day, lest his disciples come by night, and steal him away, and say unto the people, He is risen from the dead: so the last error shall be worse than the first" (Matthew 27:62–64). In other words, from their point of view, any attempts by the disciples to validate Jesus' predictions about his own resurrection three days after his death would be worse than the predictions themselves. It is noteworthy that the Jewish leaders were quite conscious of Jesus' predictions about his own resurrection (Matthew 27:63).

A second reason why religious leaders wanted a guard posted went unspoken. Jesus had been an extremely popular figure with certain segments of the populace. Some of these segments resided in Galilee—Jesus' home district—and Galilee was already known as a hotbed of messianic expectation and zealot unrest! "When the news of his death became known and the Sabbath came to an end, would there be a popular outpouring of grief—or worse, of anger? A few days earlier those same religious authorities had been fearful of how the crowds would react if Jesus were arrested (Mark 14:2; Luke 22:2). We can imagine they might now have been even more fearful, when it became public knowledge that he had been arrested *and* put to death" (Walker, *Weekend That Changed the World*, 43–44).

Thus, Jewish leaders had no qualms about going to Pilate, a Gentile leader, on the day after the Crucifixion, a special and most sacred Sabbath day (John 19:31). Ultimately, they wanted to guarantee the secrecy of their conspiracy to have Jesus murdered and ensure the success of showing him to be a false messiah, even though it brought upon them ritual defilement according to their own tradition (McConkie, *Doctrinal New Testament Commentary*, 1:838).

The stage was now set for the earthshaking events of the next day. As Sunday approached, the women disciples were preparing to return to the tomb. The Jewish religious leaders had extracted permission from the Roman authorities to have guards keep the tomb rock-solid secure. "Two groups of guards (no doubt tired after the demanding activities of this Passover weekend) [were] beginning their night watch and waiting eagerly for daylight when their shift would be complete" and the world could begin to forget about the prophet from Galilee (Walker, *Weekend That Changed the World*, 45).

Little did anyone realize what lay ahead.

---

*Now, concerning the state of the soul between death and the resurrection—Behold, it has been made known unto me by an angel, that the spirits of all men, as soon as they are departed from this mortal body, yea, the spirits of all men, whether they be good or evil, are taken home to that God who gave them life.*

ALMA 40:11

---

# CHAPTER 2

# While His Body Lay in the Tomb

The moment after Jesus took his final breath, his immortal spirit left his physical body and entered a different dimension of eternal existence—the spirit world. Like every other person who has ever died, Jesus did not cease to exist when his physical body stopped functioning. The real Jesus continued to live. As with each one of us, the real Jesus had been a spirit being before he came to this earth, clothed with a spirit body that will never cease to exist—never cease to function. In fact, Joseph Smith consistently taught that our spirits are eternal. In 1833 the Lord revealed to the Prophet that "man was also in the beginning with God. Intelligence, or the light of truth, was not created or made, neither indeed can be. . . . For man is spirit. The elements are eternal" (D&C 93:29–30, 33). In 1839 Joseph taught that "the Spirit of Man is not a created being; it existed from Eternity & will exist to eternity. . . . earth, water, &c.—all these had their existence in an elementary State from Eternity" (Ehat and Cook, *Words of Joseph Smith,* 9).

By 1844, the Prophet's understanding of man's nature had been refined to the point where he could deliver his magnificent

King Follett Discourse, in which he spoke at length about the eternal existence of spirits:

> We say that God himself is a self-existent being. Who told you so? It is correct enough; but how did it get into your heads? Who told you that man did not exist in like manner upon the same principles? Man does exist upon the same principles. God made a tabernacle and put a spirit into it, and it became a living soul. . . . How does it read in the Hebrew? It does not say in the Hebrew that God created the spirit of man. It says "God made man out of the earth and put into him Adam's spirit, and so became a living body."
>
> The mind or the intelligence which man possesses is co-equal [co-eternal] with God himself. I know that my testimony is true; hence, when I talk to these mourners, what have they lost? Their relatives and friends are only separated from their bodies for a short season: their spirits which existed with God have left the tabernacle of clay only for a little moment, as it were; and they now exist in a place where they converse together the same as we do on the earth.
>
> I am dwelling on the immortality of the spirit of man. Is it logical to say that the intelligence of spirits is immortal, and yet that it had a beginning? The intelligence of spirits had no beginning, neither will it have an end. That is good logic. That which has a beginning may have an end. There never was a time when there were not spirits; for they are co-equal [co-eternal] with our Father in heaven. (*Teachings of the Prophet Joseph Smith*, 352–53)

Not only is Jesus' spirit eternal, as is each of ours, but it is composed of actual matter; it is elemental. It has size, shape, and occupies space. Again, the Prophet Joseph Smith revealed: "There is no such thing as immaterial matter. All spirit is matter, but it is more fine or pure, and can only be discerned by purer eyes; we cannot see it; but when our bodies are purified we shall see that it is all matter" (D&C 131:7–8). Elder Parley P. Pratt taught, "The spirit of man consists of an organization of the elements of spiritual matter in the likeness and after the pattern of the fleshly tabernacle." In fact, he expressed his conviction that the spirit body possesses "all the organs and parts exactly corresponding to the outward tabernacle" (*Key to the Science of Theology,* 79).

Elder Pratt's conviction is in perfect harmony with the revealed word of God as found in restoration scripture. Our physical bodies are created in the exact image of the bodies of our heavenly parents—male and female (Moses 6:8–9; Abraham 4:27). And our spirit bodies are in the likeness of our physical bodies, each possessing the corresponding features, organs, and parts of the other. This was true for Jesus, and it is true for us (Ether 3:15–16).

Thus, in the world of spirits after his mortal death, Jesus possessed form and substance, consciousness and sentience (ability to think and feel), volition (ability to choose and act), and accountability (obligation to face the consequences of his thoughts and actions), just as each of us will. We will find that after this life there is more life and more insight about life. Jesus' spirit body had the same form and features as his physical body, and so does each of ours. President Joseph Fielding Smith declared: "When the Lord appeared to the brother of Jared, he showed him his body. It was the body of his

Spirit, and it was in the exact form of his tabernacle when he walked the streets and highways of Palestine" (*Answers to Gospel Questions*, 1:8).

## TAKEN HOME TO GOD

When human beings die and their physical bodies cease to function, their spirits go to the world of spirits to await the time of reuniting with their physical bodies. This was true for Jesus. The Book of Mormon prophet Alma taught this doctrine in these words: "Now, concerning the state of the soul between death and the resurrection—Behold, it has been made known unto me by an angel, that the spirits of all men, as soon as they are departed from this mortal body, yea, the spirits of all men, whether they be good or evil, are taken home to that God who gave them life" (Alma 40:11).

Some misunderstandings have arisen over Alma's phrase "taken home to that God who gave them life" and require a little explanation. Several of the earlier apostles and prophets of this present dispensation have helped clarify the picture. To be taken home to God does not mean that each spirit will be immediately ushered into God's physical presence but rather that it will go into the spirit world, which is under His ultimate direction and control. Elder Orson Pratt indicated that the phrase "presence of God" does not necessarily require a close spatial relationship: "What are we to understand by being in the presence of God? Is it necessary to . . . be in the same vicinity or within a few yards or feet of him? I think not" (*Journal of Discourses*, 16:364–65).

Perhaps the clearest interpretation of Alma's use of the phrase "taken home to that God who gave them life" has been proffered by President George Q. Cannon, counselor in the First Presidency for many years:

> Alma, when he says that "the spirits of all men, as soon as they are departed from this mortal body, . . . are taken home to that God who gave them life," has the idea, doubtless, in his mind that our God is omnipresent—not in His own personality but through His minister, the Holy Spirit.
>
> He does not intend to convey the idea that they are immediately ushered into the personal presence of God. He evidently uses that phrase in a qualified sense. Solomon . . . makes a similar statement: "Then shall the dust return to the earth as it was: and the spirit shall return unto God who gave it." (Ecclesiastes 12:7.) The same idea is frequently expressed by the Latter-day Saints. In referring to a departed one it is often said that he has gone back to God, or he has gone "home to that God who gave him life." Yet it would not be contended that the person who said this meant that the departed one had gone where God, the Father Himself is, in the sense in which the Savior meant when He spake to Mary. (*Gospel Truth*, 58).

President Heber C. Kimball, also a counselor in the First Presidency in the nineteenth century, added the important insight that to enjoy the literal, physical presence of God the Father on a continuing basis, one must be a resurrected being, having one's spirit and body eternally reunited. Said he:

> As for my going into the immediate presence of God when I die, I do not expect it, but I expect to go into the world of spirits and associate with my brethren, and

preach the Gospel in the spiritual world, and prepare myself in every necessary way to receive my body again, and then enter through the wall [veil] into the celestial world. I never shall come into the presence of my Father and God until I have received my resurrected body, neither will any other person. (*Journal of Discourses,* 3:112–13)

What Heber C. Kimball taught is that in order to enter and stay in the literal, physical presence of God the Father, each of us *must* be a resurrected personage with a celestial body capable of enduring the Father's environment. President Kimball probably learned this doctrine from the Prophet of the Restoration, who taught that we prepare for God's presence "by going from one small degree to another, and from a small capacity to a great one; from grace to grace, from exaltation to exaltation, until [we] attain to the resurrection of the dead, and are able to dwell in everlasting burnings, and to sit in glory, as do those who sit enthroned in everlasting power" (*Teachings of the Prophet Joseph Smith,* 346–47).

This does not mean that God the Father cannot and does not visit nonresurrected beings for brief periods from time to time. Joseph Smith is a case in point. But in order for us to come into the Father's presence and live with him, we must be resurrected beings able to live in "everlasting burnings."

That brings us back to another part of Heber C. Kimball's statement, namely, that the spirit world is a place where we continue to associate with each other and prepare to receive again our physical bodies. The kind of body with which we are resurrected (celestial, terrestrial, or telestial) depends on the kind of spirit son or daughter we have developed into. A telestial spirit cannot be resurrected with a celestial body.

This statement of President Heber C. Kimball is in perfect harmony with Jesus' own experience and helps to explain the Savior's statement to Mary Magdalene on the morning of his resurrection. As she came forward to embrace him as a newly resurrected Being, he said to her, "Touch me not; for I am not yet ascended to my Father: but go to my brethren, and say unto them, I ascend unto my Father, and your Father; and to my God, and your God" (John 20:17). To be sure, there was now a special divine dignity attached to the Savior that discouraged too much familiarity. But more important, "no human hand was to be permitted to touch the Lord's resurrected and immortalized body until after He had presented Himself to the Father" (Talmage, *Jesus the Christ*, 682). Jesus had entered the spirit world as the disembodied Son of God, but he did not then enjoy the personal company and physical presence of his Father, our Father in Heaven. That came after he was resurrected.

## NEARNESS OF THE SPIRIT WORLD

From several sources, then, we learn that the spirits of those who have passed through the veil at the time of death (Jesus included) go to the spirit world but not immediately into the physical presence of God. The patriarch Abraham beheld our physical universe and saw that the throne of God is an actual place in the universe, near a celestial orb named Kolob. More than that, other prophets have seen that the spirit world itself is also an actual location in the universe, but that it is right here on this earth! President Brigham Young taught this doctrine straightforwardly: "When you lay down this tabernacle, where are you going? Into the spiritual world. . . . Where is the spirit world? It is right here. Do the good and evil spirits go together? Yes they do. Do they go beyond the boundaries of this organized earth? No they do not" (*Journal of Discourses*, 3:368).

Jesus never left this earth when he entered the spirit world. While his body was laid to rest *in* the earth, Jesus' spirit entered a different realm of existence *on* the earth. By the time of his resurrection, Jesus had not yet been with his Father physically because his Father resided in a different locale as a glorified, divine Man with a body of flesh and bone (D&C 130:2–22). Certainly Jesus felt the influence of his Father as he resided in the spirit world.

Elder Parley P. Pratt taught that the spirit world for the inhabitants of this earth is located on this earth. But he also implied that the spirit worlds for the other planets like our own are located on those other planets. Said he:

> As to its location [the spirit world], it is here on the very planet where we were born; or, in other words, the earth and other planets of a like sphere, have their inward or spiritual spheres, as well as their outward, or temporal. The one is peopled by temporal tabernacles, and the other by spirits. A veil is drawn between the one sphere and the other, whereby all the objects in the spiritual sphere are rendered invisible to those in the temporal. (*Key to the Science of Theology*, 80)

We do not know when Jesus visited the spirit worlds of all his creations, but I am inclined to view the report of his visit to the spirits in prison recorded in Doctrine and Covenants 138 as referring to this earth only. Nonetheless, just as we know he visits each of his kingdoms in due season, we also believe he did or will visit each spirit world in its appropriate season. The parable of the lord of the fields, which describes the owner or lord of many fields visiting each and every field, "beginning at the first, and so on unto the last," is recorded in Doctrine and Covenants 88:51–61. In my view, it may be applied to the spirit worlds of every earth. Regarding the meaning of this parable, Elder Orson Pratt said that the Lord "has other worlds or creations and other sons and daughters, perhaps just as good as those dwelling on this planet, and they, as well as we, will be visited, and they will be made glad with the countenance of their Lord" (*Journal of Discourses*, 17:332). More important, the Lord not only visits all of the worlds he created but he redeems each and every one through the infinite power of his atonement (D&C 76:22–24, 41–42).

The Prophet Joseph Smith knew that the spirit world was very close. In fact, regarding the spirits of the righteous, he said not only are they "not far from us" but they "know and understand our thoughts, feelings, and motions, and are often pained therewith" (*Teachings of the Prophet Joseph Smith*, 326). Because of the nearness of the world of spirits, and their cognizance of and sensitivity to our circumstances in mortality, mortals are sometimes accorded the privilege of receiving visitations from those beings of the unseen world of spirits, if such visits are in harmony with the mind and will of the Lord.

During the Lord's earthly ministry, his apostles manifested their belief in visitations from disembodied spirits (Matthew 14:26; Luke 24:37). After his resurrection, when they began to lead the Church and leave written testimonies for the Saints, the apostles came to know the living reality of beings from the unseen world. They understood the nature of visitations by spirits to Mary, Joseph, and others (Luke 1:19). They themselves communed with angels and spirit beings as a natural course of events. They were saved from harm by them and testified of their reality (Acts 1:11; 5:19; Jude 1:6). New Testament records leave no doubt that spirits and angels worked with mortals in the meridian dispensation.

In our present dispensation, the dispensation of the fulness of times, apostles and prophets have also testified of the reality of visitations by spirits from the world beyond. Some examples may be instructive as well as fortifying, serving to strengthen our testimonies of the reality of life beyond the grave.

The Prophet Joseph Smith was visited by both resurrected beings and the spirits of just men made perfect, and he knew others were and would be visited as well. He said: "There are two kinds of beings in heaven, namely: Angels, who are resurrected personages, having bodies of flesh and bones—For instance, Jesus said: Handle me and see, for a spirit hath not flesh and bones, as ye see me have. Secondly: the spirits of just men made perfect, they who are not resurrected, but inherit the same glory" (D&C 129:1–3). Therefore, the Prophet presented significant instructions on how to discern the type of messenger with whom one was communicating—angels, the spirits of just men made perfect, or the devil (D&C 129:4–9). In 1843 he commented that "the spirits of just men are made ministering servants to those who are sealed unto life eternal. . . . Patriarch [James] Adams is now one of the spirits of the just men made perfect. . . . Angels [resurrected beings] have advanced higher in knowledge and power than spirits" (*Teachings of the Prophet Joseph Smith*, 325).

Elder Parley P. Pratt, a spiritual giant himself, knew a great deal about the spirit world. He taught:

Persons who have departed this life and have not yet been raised from the dead are spirits. These are of two kinds: good and evil.

These two kinds also include many grades of good and evil.

The good spirits, in the superlative sense of the word, are they who, in this life, partook of the Holy Priesthood and of the fulness of the gospel. This class of spirits minister to the heirs of salvation, both in this world and in the world of spirits. They can appear unto men when permitted. (*Key to the Science of Theology*, 71–72)

President Wilford Woodruff, fourth president of the Church, bore a powerful witness of ministrations from those who had passed on:

Joseph Smith visited me a great deal after his death, and taught me many important principles. On one occasion he and his brother Hyrum visited me while I was in a storm at sea. . . . The night following [the storm at sea] Joseph and Hyrum visited me, and the Prophet laid before me a great many things. Among other things he told me to get the Spirit of God; that all of us needed it. . . .

Joseph Smith continued visiting myself and others up to a certain time, and then it stopped. The last time I saw him . . . [he] came to me and spoke to me. He said he could not stop to talk with me because he was in a hurry. . . . I met half a dozen brethren who had held high positions on earth, and none of them could stop to talk with me because they were in a hurry. I was much astonished. (*Discourses of Wilford Woodruff*, 288–89).

On another occasion President Woodruff commented about visitations from the spirit world:

> I believe the eyes of the heavenly hosts are over this people; I believe they are watching the elders of Israel, the prophets and apostles and men who are called to bear off this kingdom. I believe they watch over us all with great interest. . . .
>
> I have had many interviews with Brother Joseph until the last 15 or 20 years of my life; I have not seen him for that length of time. But during my travels in the southern country last winter I had many interviews with President Young, and with Heber C. Kimball, and Geo. A. Smith, and Jedediah M. Grant, and many others who are dead. They attended our conference, they attended our meetings.
>
> And on one occasion, I saw Brother Brigham and Brother Heber ride in [a] carriage ahead of the carriage in which I rode when I was on my way to attend conference; and they were dressed in the most priestly robes. When we arrived at our destination I asked Prest. Young if he would preach to us. He said, "No, I have finished my testimony in the flesh. I shall not talk to this people any more. But (said he) I have come to see you; I have come to watch over you, and to see what the people are doing. Then, said he, I want you to teach the people—and I want you to follow this counsel yourself—that they must labor and so live as to obtain the Holy Spirit, for without this you cannot build up the kingdom; without the spirit

of God you are in danger of walking in the dark, and in danger of failing to accomplish your calling as apostles and as elders in the church and kingdom of God. And, said he, Brother Joseph taught me this principle. And I will here say, I have heard him refer to that while he was living. . . .

The thought came to me that Brother Joseph had left the work of watching over this church and kingdom to others, and that he had gone ahead, and that he had left this work to men who have lived and labored with us since he left us. This idea manifested itself to me, that such men advance in the spirit world. And I believe myself that these men who have died and gone into the spirit world had this mission left with them, that is, a certain portion of them, to watch over the Latter-day Saints. (*Journal of Discourses*, 21:317–18; paragraphing altered)

Closer to our day, we have the testimony of apostles and prophets who have certified to us that beings from the spirit world do return to offer instruction and encouragement. At the funeral of President Ezra Taft Benson, President Boyd K. Packer spoke of the spirit world:

Now this dear, venerable prophet has entered in, there to rejoice with his beloved Flora and to speak of their wonderful family, there to rejoice with Joseph and Brigham and John and Wilford and the others.

The prophets who preceded him, ancient and modern, have on occasion communed with the servants of the Lord on this earth. So it well may be that we have not seen the last of this great prophet of God.

I testify that the veil between this mortal realm and the spirit world opens to such revelation and visitation as the needs of the church and kingdom of God on earth may require. ("We Honor Now His Journey," 34).

In addition to apostles and prophets, other righteous men, women, and children have been privileged to enjoy visitations from those residing temporarily in the spirit world. Andrew C. Nelson, a stalwart member of the Church living at the close of the nineteenth century, recorded such an experience in his journal. He was visited by his father shortly after his father's death:

> On the night of April 6th, 1891, I had a strange dream or vision in which I saw and conversed with my father who died January 27th, 1891. . . .
>
> Though some may scorn and laugh at the idea of such a visitation, yet I feel assured that it was real, and it has been and I hope always will be a source of much pleasure and satisfaction to me. To corroborate my testimony of the possibility of such a visitation I quote the following: "Spirits can appear to men when permitted; but not having a fleshy tabernacle can not hide their glory." [*Key to Theology*, p. 120.] I was in bed when father came in or entered the room; he came and sat on the side of the bed. . . .
>
> When father came to the bed, he first said: "Well, my son, being you were not there (at Redmond) when I died, so that I did not get to see you, and as I had a few spare minutes, I received permission to come and see you a few minutes." "I am very glad to see you father.

How do you do?" "I am feeling well my son, and have had very much to do since I died."

"What have you been doing since you died father? . . ."

. . . "My son, I have been travelling together with Apostle Erastus Snow ever since I died; that is, since three days after I died; then I received my commission to preach the Gospel. You can not imagine, my son, how many spirits there are in the Spirit world that have not yet received the Gospel; but many are receiving it, and a great work is being accomplished. Many are anxiously looking forth to their friends, who are still living, to administer for them in the Temples. I have been very busy in preaching the Gospel of Jesus Christ."

"Will all the spirits believe you, father, when you teach them the Gospel?" "No, they will not." . . .

"Father, can you see us at all times, and do you know what we are doing?" "No, my son, I can not. I have something else to do. I can not go when and where I please. There is just as much, and much more, order here in the Spirit world than in the other world. I have been assigned work and that must be performed." . . .

"How do you feel at all times, father?" "O, I feel splendid, and enjoy my labors, still, I must admit that at times I get a little lonesome to see my family; but it is only a short time till we will again see each other." . . .

"Father, is it natural to die? or does it seem natural? Was there not a time when your spirit was in such a pain that it could not realize what was going on or taking place?" "No, my son, there was not such a time. It is just as natural to die, as it is to be born, or for you to pass out of that door (here he pointed at the door). When I had told the folks that I could not last long, it turned dark and I could not see anything for a few minutes. Then, the first thing I could see was a number of spirits in the Spirit world. Then, I told the folks that I must go. . . ."

"Father, is the principle and doctrine of the Resurrection as taught us true?" "True. Yes, my son, as true as can be. You can not avoid being Resurrected. It is just as natural for all to be Resurrected as it is to be born and die again. No one can avoid being Resurrected. There are many spirits in the Spirit world who would to God that there would be no Resurrection."

"Father, is the Gospel as taught by this Church true?" "My son, do you see that picture?" (pointing to a picture of the First Presidency of the Church hanging on the wall) "Yes, I see it." "Well, just as sure as you see that picture, just so sure is the Gospel true. The Gospel of Jesus Christ has within it the power of saving every man and woman that will obey it, and in no other way can they ever obtain a salvation in the Kingdom of God." (Nelson, *From Heart to Heart*, 16–17)

## INTEREST IN US

There is no doubt that beings from the unseen world of spirits can and do visit righteous mortals from all walks of life and stations in the Church, from prophets to Primary children. The spirits who return are part of that category of beings we call angels (both resurrected and not yet resurrected) who are promised to all the Saints, especially missionaries, as they go forth to do the Lord's work. Often the term *angels* is used to refer to resurrected beings, but sometimes it includes spirits not yet resurrected: "Behold, I [the Lord] send you out to reprove the world of all their unrighteous deeds. . . . And whoso receiveth you, there I will be also. . . . I will be on your right hand and on your left, . . . *and mine angels* round about you, to bear you up" (D&C 84:87–88; emphasis added). Most often these angels (resurrected beings and righteous spirits) from beyond the veil do not make dramatic appearances to us but are there helping us along, as President George Q. Cannon testified: "But there are also angels around us. Though invisible to us they are continually inviting us and pleading with us to do that which is right. The Spirit of God, too, rests upon us, and it prompts us to keep the commandments of God. By means of these influences, therefore, we are receiving experience and we are growing in knowledge" (*Gospel Truth*, 66).

From a great many witnesses we learn that the spirits of the righteous have a genuine interest in the progress and welfare of those in mortality. It seems to me that these ministering angels and spirits are as likely as not to be members of one's own family or one's circle of friends in mortality. They aid us in our missionary work as well as our family history research and temple work. They know us and know best how to help us. Their experiences and activities are very much like our own activities on this side of the veil. They yearn to be reunited with their family and friends. The same sociality which exists among us here on this side of the veil exists among them on that side of the veil (D&C 130:2). Beings in the spirit world may even pray for the health and happiness of us mortals.

The experience of one of my own family members taught her that those on the other side of the veil can and do pray for us on this side and that she herself was prayed for at a difficult time in her life by family members who had gone before her. She learned this by personal revelation. In her history she tells of the death of her nineteen-year-old daughter and of being "frantic with grief." She was nearly devastated. She had already lost another child years earlier. In that moment of her extremity, a vision opened to her. She saw departed loved ones on the other side of the veil praying for her. Just as important, her personal record of this and other experiences has taught her descendants valuable lessons about life beyond the veil. As the Prophet Joseph Smith said, the spirit world is very near.

It is also true that inhabitants of the spirit world are themselves, in turn, ministered to by servants of God. "Angels [meaning resurrected beings in this case] are ministers both to men upon the earth and to the world of spirits. They pass from one world to another with more ease and in less time than we pass from one city to another" (Pratt, *Key to the Science of Theology*, 69). All of this is according to our Heavenly Father's watchful care over his children on both sides of the veil and is made possible by the very atoning act that had brought Jesus to the spirit world.

Therefore, when Jesus entered the spirit world and began the next phase of his foreordained mission and ministry, he did so as the great Liberator—the Bearer of light, life, and release to those who had been held captive by the bands of death since the time they themselves had passed through the veil. It is not hard to imagine that as he entered the world of spirits he was welcomed and hailed as the true King and God he really is by those righteous Saints whom he has known for eons. "While the corpse lay in Joseph's rock-hewn tomb, the living Christ existed as a disembodied Spirit. . . . He went where the spirits of the dead ordinarily go; and . . . in the sense in which while in the flesh He had been a Man among men, He was, in the disembodied state a Spirit among spirits" (Talmage, *Jesus the Christ*, 670).

And there were gathered together in one place an innumerable company of the spirits of the just, who had been faithful in the testimony of Jesus while they lived in mortality.

And there he preached to them the everlasting gospel, the doctrine of the resurrection and the redemption of mankind from the fall, and from individual sins on conditions of repentance.

And as I wondered, my eyes were opened, and my understanding quickened, and I perceived that the Lord went not in person among the wicked and the disobedient who had rejected the truth, to teach them;

But behold, from among the righteous, he organized his forces and appointed messengers, clothed with power and authority, and commissioned them to go forth and carry the light of the gospel to them that were in darkness, even to all the spirits of men; and thus was the gospel preached to the dead.

DOCTRINE AND COVENANTS 138:12, 19, 29–30

# CHAPTER 3

# His Ministry in the Spirit World

J ust as death came to the Savior as a natural consequence of
mortality, so it comes to all people—not to punish but rather
"to fulfil the *merciful* plan of the great Creator" (2 Nephi 9:6;
emphasis added). Just as the transition from this world to the
next was immediate for the Savior, so it is for all people. Just as
the Savior did not leave this earth when he entered the spirit
world, so each one of us will go to that very same spirit world
that exists on this earth, whether we are male or female, good
or bad, old or young. We will not immediately all go to the same
part of the spirit world, however. When Jesus passed through
the veil, he entered a world of great division where the righteous
were *separated* from the wicked by a vast, unbridged gulf that had
been in place since the time of Adam.

## A GREAT DIVISION

During his mortal ministry, Jesus had spoken of the great
division in the world of spirits. His best-known illustration of
that doctrine and reality came in the parable of the rich man
and Lazarus. A certain rich man, who lived in opulence, and

a beggar named Lazarus, who lived in abject poverty and misery, both died. The former looked up from hell (spirit prison) and saw Lazarus in Abraham's bosom (paradise). The rich man cried out to Father Abraham to send Lazarus to bring him some relief. Abraham responded by explaining that in the spirit world the law of complete justice holds sway (including equity, fairness, recompense for thoughts and deeds, and recompense for mortality's *injustices*). "Son, remember that thou in thy lifetime receivedst thy good things, and likewise Lazarus evil things: but now he is comforted, and thou art tormented" (Luke 16:25).

This part of the story simply reinforces what we already know about the lasting effects of the Savior's atonement: As a result of Gethsemane and Golgotha, justice becomes the friend of the righteous! All the injustices and unfairnesses of mortality are made up to the humble followers of Jesus—all of this world's inequities are made right and whole and fair for eternity. This is one of the most magnificent and gratitude-inspiring aspects of Jesus' unmatched act of love. If we honestly commit to follow him, he promises that the stain of our sins will be removed, and every pain, every sorrow, every sickness, every heartache not of our own making will be soothed and salved and healed. Every unfair circumstance of life will be made up to us. Our condition in eternity will not be determined by what happened *to* us but rather what will happen *in* us as a result of the Savior's atonement.

The other great lesson about life beyond our mortal probation comes in the next verse of the parable and illustrates the environment of the spirit world into which Jesus entered. "And beside all this," says Abraham to the rich man, "between us and you there is a *great gulf fixed:* so that they which would pass from hence to you cannot: neither can they pass to us, that would come from thence" (Luke 16:26; emphasis added). Of course, Lazarus and the rich man represent the two basic categories of people found in mortality (righteous and unrighteous), and the profound lesson of the parable focuses on their separation in the eternities, beginning in the spirit world. In the spirit world of Jesus' day, the great gulf prevented any social interchange between the righteous and the unrighteous. Elder Bruce R. McConkie further taught that the two groups of people, represented by the rich man and Lazarus "knew each other in mortality, so they remember their former acquaintanceship. But no longer are they accessible to each other so that one might minister to the needs of the other. Christ [had] not yet bridged the gulf between the prison and palace, and there [was] as yet no communion between the righteous in paradise and the wicked in hell" (*Mortal Messiah*, 3:263). Thus, the parable of the rich man and Lazarus not only illustrates the existence of a great division, including the idea that justice operates in the next life and that there is torment awaiting the wicked, but also the fact that each individual will remember the associations and experiences of this mortal life.

Long before the Savior taught and ministered personally on the earth as the mortal Messiah, Book of Mormon prophets spoke of the great division in the spirit world. Nephi, speaking almost six hundred years before the birth of Jesus, said of the fountain of filthy waters in his father's dream: "It was an awful gulf, which separated the wicked from the tree of life, and also from the saints of God" (1 Nephi 15:28). In this verse Nephi told his audience that the awful gulf not only separated the unrighteous from the righteous or "saints of God" but also that it separated the unrighteous from the tree of life, which is a symbol for Jesus Christ himself as Nephi learned earlier (1 Nephi

11:4–7, 9–22). Twenty-five hundred years later, another prophet, Joseph F. Smith, would receive a vision of the spirit world and see that Nephi was exactly right—the wicked in the world of spirits were never privileged to enjoy the physical presence of the Savior, nor hear his voice in person, when he entered the spirit world (D&C 138:20–21). The unrighteous were indeed separated from the tree of life by an awful gulf.

Centuries after Nephi, another Book of Mormon prophet, Alma, uttered what is arguably the classic statement on the great unbridged division that existed in the spirit world before the coming of Christ to the ranks of the disembodied spirits:

> And then shall it come to pass, that the spirits of those who are righteous are received into a state of happiness, which is called paradise, a state of rest, a state of peace, where they shall rest from all their troubles and from all care, and sorrow.
>
> And then shall it come to pass, that the spirits of the wicked, yea, who are evil—for behold, they have no part nor portion of the Spirit of the Lord; for behold, they chose evil works rather than good; therefore the spirit of the devil did enter into them, and take possession of their house—and these shall be cast out into outer darkness; there shall be weeping, and wailing, and gnashing of teeth, and this because of their own iniquity, being led captive by the will of the devil.
>
> Now this is the state of the souls of the wicked, yea, in darkness, and a state of awful, fearful looking for the fiery indignation of the wrath of God upon them; thus they remain in this state, as well as the righteous

in paradise, until the time of their resurrection. (Alma 40:12–14)

## CONDITIONS IN THE TWO REALMS

Alma's discourse on the world of spirits is very helpful for its description of the spirit world when Jesus went there. The righteous lived in paradise—a state of happiness and peace, a place where, according to President Joseph F. Smith, they could "expand in wisdom, where they have respite from all their troubles, and where care and sorrow [did] not annoy" (*Gospel Doctrine*, 448). It truly was an environment where the hardships, struggles, and pains of mortality, especially those associated with the physical body, were left behind.

> Paradise is a place where the spirit is free to think and act with a renewed capacity and with the vigor and enthusiasm which characterized one in his prime. Though a person does not rest per se from the work associated with the plan of salvation (for . . . that labor goes forward with at least an equal intensity in the spirit world), at the same time he is delivered from those cares and worries associated with a fallen world and a corrupt body. (Millet and McConkie, *Life Beyond*, 18)

On the other hand, that part of the spirit world called hell or spirit prison was a place where there was weeping, hardship, and misery. Hell was and is both a place and a condition or state of mind. As the Prophet Joseph Smith explained, it is hell because of mental torment and anguish owing to disobedience and lack of repentance in mortality. "The great misery of departed spirits in the world of spirits, where they go after death, is to know that they come short of the glory that others enjoy and that they

might have enjoyed themselves, and they are their own accusers" (*Teachings of the Prophet Joseph Smith*, 310–11). On another
occasion the Prophet reinforced this doctrine by stating that "a
man is his own tormentor and condemner. Hence the saying,
They shall go in the lake that burns with fire and brimstone.
The torment of disappointment in the mind of man is as exquisite as a lake burning with fire and brimstone" (*Teachings of the
Prophet Joseph Smith*, 357).

Thus, those who were confined to that part of the spirit
world known as spirit prison or hell, from Adam's day to the time
when the Savior himself entered the spirit world, were awakened
to a lively sense of their own guilt and shrank from the Spirit
and presence of the Lord (Mosiah 2:38; Mormon 9:3–4). They
themselves did not want, of their own free will and choice, to
be in the presence of the temporarily disembodied Messiah, the
Jehovah of earlier days, the man known as Jesus of Nazareth in
the meridian dispensation. Hence, Jesus did not move among
the wicked, did not have any interaction with them—both on
account of *their* own desires as well as *his* own inability to look
upon, to tolerate, to be in the presence of unrepented sin (D&C
1:31). The "damnation of hell," said Joseph Smith, is "to go with
that society who have not obeyed His commands" (*Teachings of
the Prophet Joseph Smith*, 198). The distasteful environment of
hell is intensified precisely because a person is forced to dwell
with other wicked and depraved individuals. Jesus had already
experienced the environment of hell once before, during his time
in Gethsemane. He would not go back.

## DEATH—A PARTIAL JUDGMENT

At least three other significant implications of the doctrine
of the great gulf or division in the spirit world are important to

mention. First, the existence of the two separate places of abode for the spirits of the departed implies at least a partial judgment at the time of death. The disembodied spirits of all who have ever lived on the earth will receive a temporary inheritance in either paradise or spirit prison based on their actions in mortality. At the time of death each individual will be judged according to several factors. These include the following:

1.  A person's accountability and age (Mosiah 3:16; Moroni 8:8–19); little children who die before they arrive at the years of accountability are saved automatically in the celestial kingdom of heaven (D&C 137:10)

2.  The degree of knowledge individuals possessed, and their opportunity for righteous living during their mortal probation (Moroni 8:22; 2 Nephi 9:25–26)

3.  A person's deeds, desires, and intents or motives (Mosiah 4:6; 1 Nephi 15:33; D&C 33:1; Alma 41:3; D&C 137:9)

4.  Individuals' own acknowledgment of their true standing before the Lord—a self-judgment, if you will (2 Nephi 9:46; Mosiah 16:1; 27:31; 29:12)

Elder Bruce R. McConkie teaches an important concept when he speaks of death as a day of judgment:

> Death itself is an initial *day of judgment* for all persons, both the righteous and the wicked. When the spirit leaves the body at death, it is taken home to that God who gave it life, meaning that it returns to live in the realm of spiritual existence (Eccles. 17:7). At that time the spirit undergoes a partial judgment and is assigned

an inheritance in paradise or in hell to await the day of the first or second resurrection. (*Mormon Doctrine*, 402)

The second implication of the doctrine of a great gulf in the spirit world is the question of who is deemed righteous and who is not, and what the ultimate criteria are for determining who receives paradise and who does not. President Joseph Fielding Smith provides clear, invaluable commentary on this question:

> It is the righteous who go to paradise. It is the righteous who cease from those things that trouble. Not so with the wicked. They remain in torment. . . . They are aware of their neglected opportunities, privileges in which they might have served the Lord and received a reward of restfulness. . . .
>
> The righteous, *those who have kept the commandments* of the Lord, are not shut up in any such place, but are in happiness in paradise. . . .
>
> All spirits of men after death return to the spirit world. There, as I understand it, *the righteous—meaning those who have been baptized and who have been faithful*—are gathered in one part and all the others in another part of the spirit world. (*Doctrines of Salvation*, 2:229–30; emphasis added)

Thus, President Smith cites two criteria which are the final or ultimate determiners of the destiny of the spirits of all men and women: keeping the commandments *and* participating in the ordinance of baptism. In other words, the righteous are those who had "been faithful in the testimony of Jesus while they lived in mortality; and who had offered sacrifice in the similitude of the great sacrifice of the Son of God, and suffered tribulation in their Redeemer's name" (D&C 138:12–13). The righteous in the spirit world are also referred to as "the spirits of the just" (D&C 138:12). They are those who lived the celestial law while in mortality. The ranks of the wicked on the other hand—those in spirit prison—are composed of men and women who lived a terrestrial or a telestial law in mortality. This includes those who died without knowing the law of the gospel or the truths of salvation; those who received not the testimony of Jesus in the flesh, but afterward received it; those who received not the gospel of Christ nor the testimony of Jesus at all; those thrust down to hell (D&C 76:72–84).

Even though there were good people living on the earth before the birth of Jesus, those who did not have the opportunity of hearing about the Messiah or accepting the gospel message had to wait in that part of the spirit world called spirit prison, or hell, until the arrival of the Savior in the spirit world made it possible for them to hear the gospel preached. Again, Elder McConkie corroborates that the circumstances or environment existing in the spirit world prior to the Savior's visit affected every person who had ever lived and died upon the earth:

> There was no intermingling by the spirits in paradise and hell until after Christ bridged the "great gulf" between these two spirit abodes (Alma 40:11–14). This he did while his body lay in the tomb of Joseph of Arimathea and his own disembodied spirit continued to minister to men in their spirit prison (1 Peter 3:18–21; 4:6; Joseph F. Smith, *Gospel Doctrine*, 5th ed., pp. 472–476). "Until that day" the prisoners remained bound and the gospel was not preached to them (Moses 7:37–39).

The hope of salvation for the dead was yet future. (*Doctrinal New Testament Commentary,* 1:521–22)

In truth, the term *prison,* though used to distinguish one part of the spirit world from the other part, called paradise, also applies to the whole of the spirit world. All of the spirit world is, in a sense, a prison. This is true because the spirits of *both* the righteous and the wicked are separated from their physical bodies, and to be without one's physical body is an intensely undesirable state of bondage. In the words of the revelation to President Joseph F. Smith: "For the dead [the righteous dead] had looked upon the long absence of their spirits from their bodies as a bondage" (D&C 138:50). So, even though the spirits of the righteous will be happy in paradise, they will not be, cannot be, perfectly happy while a part of them is lying in the grave. In the language of the revelations of the Restoration, the spirit and the body are the soul of man. When inseparably connected, the spirit and the physical body can receive a fulness of joy. When separated they cannot receive a fulness of joy (D&C 88:15; 93:33; 138:17). Without their physical bodies, the spirits of all men and women "are in prison," said President Brigham Young (*Journal of Discourses,* 3:95).

Elder Melvin J. Ballard gave this explanation:

> I grant you that the righteous dead will be at peace, but I tell you that when we go out of this life, leave this body, we will desire to do many things that we cannot do at all without the body. We will be seriously handicapped, and we will long for the body; we will pray for the early reunion with our bodies. . . .
>
> . . . we are sentencing ourselves to long periods of bondage, separating our spirits from our bodies, or we

are shortening that period, according to the way in which we overcome and master ourselves [in mortality]. (Quoted in Hinckley, *Sermons and Missionary Services of Melvin Joseph Ballard*, 240–42)

This leads us to a third implication of the doctrine of the great gulf in the spirit world. It is significant that modern prophets and inspired teachers who have spoken about conditions extant in the spirit world not only talk about the great gulf or division of spirits *before* the Savior's visit but also speak of that division in the present tense. This is so because the great gulf, though bridged by the Savior for the first time when he visited the spirit world, still exists. The spirits of the wicked are still separated from the spirits of the righteous in our day, and that gulf is removed only by the preaching of the gospel and its acceptance by the spirits in spirit prison, or hell.

Concerning the environment that has existed in the spirit world since the Savior's liberating visit two thousand years ago, Elder Heber C. Kimball said: "Can those persons who pursue a course of carelessness, neglect of duty, and disobedience, when they depart from this life, expect that their spirits will associate with the spirits of the righteous in the spirit world? I do not expect it, and when you depart from this state of existence, you will find out for yourselves" (*Journal of Discourses*, 2:150).

Elder Parley P. Pratt likewise described the conditions of the spirit world all of us will encounter when we die:

> The spirit world is not the heaven where Jesus Christ, his Father, and other beings dwell who have, by resurrection or translation, ascended to eternal mansions and been crowned and seated on thrones of power; but it is an intermediate state, a probation, a place of

preparation, improvement, instruction, or education, where spirits are chastened and improved and where, if found worthy, they may be taught a knowledge of the gospel. In short, it is a place where the gospel is preached and where faith, repentance, hope, and charity may be exercised; a place of waiting for the resurrection or redemption of the body; while to those who deserve it, it is a place of punishment, a purgatory or hell, where spirits are buffeted till the day of redemption. (*Key to the Science of Theology*, 80)

## No Need for the Righteous to Fear Death

Therefore, death holds no terror for those trying to keep God's commandments while living in mortality, trying to do as the Lord wants them to do. None of us need fear death. In making this point, President George Q. Cannon presented an extremely comforting picture of death for the righteous:

How delightful it is to contemplate the departure of those who have been faithful, as far as their knowledge permitted, to the truth which God has revealed! There is no sting nor gloom nor inconsolable sorrow about the departure of such persons. Holy angels are around their bedside to administer unto them. The Spirit of God rests down upon them, and His messengers are near them to introduce them to those who are on the other side of the veil. (*Gospel Truth*, 61)

President Cannon went on to state that Satan has no power

over the righteous dead—that is, those who have been baptized and have tried to live good lives in mortality:

> Satan is bound as soon as the faithful spirit leaves this tabernacle of clay and goes to the other side of the veil. That spirit is emancipated from the power and thraldom and attacks of Satan. Satan can only afflict such in this life. He can only afflict those in that life which is to come who have listened to his persuasions, who have listed to obey him. These are the only ones over whom he has power after this life. . . .
>
> They are his servants; they are under his influence. He takes possession of them when they pass from this mortal existence, and they experience the torments of hell. (*Gospel Truth*, 61)

In addition, for the righteous who pass through death, the spirit world will be a place of reunion, just as it surely was for Jesus when he entered the spirit world. Though we will undoubtedly miss our loved ones who are still living in mortality, paradise will be a time of happiness and excitement as we meet those who have gone before. The Prophet Joseph Smith taught this concept with assurance: "I have a father, brothers, children and friends who have gone to a world of spirits. They are only absent for a moment. They are in the spirit, and we shall soon meet again" (*Teachings of the Prophet Joseph Smith*, 359).

President Joseph F. Smith added this thought: "What is more desirable than that we should meet with our fathers and our mothers, with our brethren and our sisters, with our wives and our children, with our beloved associates and kindred in the spirit world, knowing each other, identifying each other . . . by the associations that familiarize each to the other in mortal life? What do you want better than that?" ("The Resurrection," 178)

Armed with this information, we find that death takes on a different perspective for all of us who are trying to be faithful, just as it did for those ancient righteous Saints in the spirit world two thousand years ago, awaiting the arrival of the Messiah. Because of the gospel of Jesus Christ, death loses its fearfulness.

It seems to me that this glorious truth cannot be emphasized enough. I wish I had understood it better at the time my own father died. I think my grieving would have been different. If we rely on the Savior and try to live good and decent lives in mortality, death actually becomes a blessing, a time of peace and rest, a time when physical pain and mortal cares cease, a time of reunion with those who have gone before us, a time of continuing intellectual and spiritual increase and development, a time when Satan is bound and can never again afflict or torment us, a time of great security. In fact, Elder Bruce R. McConkie spoke of life after death as a time when righteous individuals could no longer fall off the straight and narrow path. He said, in effect, there is no apostasy from paradise:

> In order to be saved in the Kingdom of God and in order to pass the test of mortality, what you have to do is get on the straight and narrow path—thus charging a course leading to eternal life—and then, being on that path, pass out of this life in full fellowship. . . . If you're on that path and pressing forward, and you die, you'll never get off the path. There is no such thing as falling off the straight and narrow path in the life to come, and the reason is that this life is the time that is given to men to prepare for eternity. . . . You don't have to live a life

that's truer than true. You don't have to have excessive zeal that becomes fanatical and becomes unbalancing. What you have to do is stay in the mainstream of the Church and live as upright and decent people live in the Church—keeping the commandments, paying your tithing, serving in the organizations of the Church, loving the Lord, staying on the straight and narrow path. If you're on that path when death comes—because this is the time and the day appointed, this the probationary estate—you'll never fall off from it, and, for all practical purposes, your calling and election is made sure. ("Probationary Test of Mortality," 219)

Not only is the spirit world a place of security for the righteous but it also is a place of great learning. Elder Orson Pratt of the Quorum of the Twelve (1811–81) spoke powerfully of the increased capacities of spirits in paradise to learn, grow intellectually, and increase in knowledge exponentially:

When I speak of the future state of man, and the situation of our spirits between death and the resurrection, I long for the experience and knowledge to be gained in that state, as well as this. We shall learn many more things there; we need not suppose our five senses connect us with all the things of heaven, and earth, and eternity, and space; we need not think that we are conversant with all the elements of nature, through the medium of the senses God has given us here. Suppose He should give us a sixth sense, a seventh, an eighth, a ninth, or a fiftieth. All these different senses would convey to us new ideas, as much so as the senses of tasting, smelling, or seeing communicate different ideas from that of hearing. (*Journal of Discourses*, 2:247)

The spirit is inherently capable of experiencing the sensations of light; if it were not so, we could not see. You might form as fine an eye as ever was made, but if the spirit, in and of itself, were not capable of being acted upon by the rays of light, an eye would be of no benefit. Then unclothe the spirit; and instead of exposing a small portion of it about the size of a pea to the action of the rays of light, the whole of it would be exposed. I think we could then see in different directions at once, instead of looking in one particular direction, we could then look all around us at the same instant. (*Journal of Discourses*, 2:243)

This statement seems to me to be an extension of the doctrine taught in Doctrine and Covenants 88:67: "And if your eye be single to my glory, your whole bodies shall be filled with light, and there shall be no darkness in you; and that body which is filled with light comprehendeth all things."

Elder Pratt believed that the Spirit of God operating in the next life will have a more powerful and direct effect on the disembodied spirit of a person than it had upon the joined spirit and mortal body of that individual while in mortality:

But when this Spirit of God, this great telescope that is used in the celestial heavens, is given to man, and he, through the aid of it, gazes upon eternal things, what does he behold? Not one object at a time, but a vast multitude of objects rush before his vision, and are present before his mind, filling him in a moment with the

knowledge of worlds more numerous than the sands of
the sea shore. Will he be able to bear it? Yes, his mind
is strengthened in proportion to the amount of information imparted. It is this tabernacle, in its present
condition, that prevents us from a more enlarged understanding. . . . I believe we shall be freed, in the next
world, in a great measure, from these narrow, contracted
methods of thinking. Instead of thinking in one channel,
and following up one certain course of reasoning to find
a certain truth, knowledge will rush in from all quarters;
it will come in like the light which flows from the sun,
penetrating every part, informing the spirit, and giving
understanding concerning ten thousand things at the
same time; and the mind will be capable of receiving and
retaining all. (*Journal of Discourses*, 2:246)

For Elder Pratt, as well as for many others possessing the
gift of seership, the spirit world is a wonderful place. There we
will be more awake, more alive, more sensitive to the powers of
godliness than we ever were in this mortal sphere.

Thus, the great message of the death and resurrection of
Jesus is twofold: first, the object of this life is more life; second,
for those who try their best to keep the commandments, death
is not a fearful event. We will still long to be reunited with our
physical bodies, but the sting of death is eradicated through the
incomprehensible power of the Lord Jesus Christ.

## TEACHING THE SPIRITS

What joy, rejoicing, gladness, and gratitude greeted Jesus as
he passed through the veil into paradise, there to extend his
powers of mercy, redemption, and liberation to all who would

receive them (D&C 138:15). When Jesus arrived in the spirit world, he commenced a unique work, something that had never been done before. President Brigham Young declared: "Jesus was the first man that ever went to preach to the spirits in prison, holding the keys of the Gospel of salvation to them. Those keys were delivered to him in the day and hour that he went into the spirit world, and with them he opened the door of salvation to the spirits in prison" (*Discourses of Brigham Young,* 378). Jesus is *the* Being in the universe who holds the keys of unlimited power over sin, death, hell, sorrow, suffering, the bottomless pit, the devil, and captivity (Revelation 1:18; 3:7; 9:1; 21:1–4).

This aspect of his ministry had long been foretold by Israel's ancient prophets. Isaiah spoke of it more than seven hundred years before it occurred: "The Spirit of the Lord God is upon me; because the Lord hath anointed me to preach good tidings unto the meek; he hath sent me to bind up the brokenhearted, to proclaim liberty to the captives, and the opening of the prison to them that are bound; to proclaim the acceptable year of the Lord, and the day of vengeance of our God; to comfort all that mourn" (Isaiah 61:1–2).

Jesus himself quoted this same prophecy at the beginning of his public ministry when he boldly proclaimed his messiahship in the little synagogue in his hometown of Nazareth. There he announced that the time had finally come for the preaching of the gospel to the living *and* the dead, that the spirits of the departed who had been confined in darkness in spirit prison would also be redeemed. They would go free from bondage upon accepting the Savior's gospel.

The Savior's visit to the spirit world and the commencement of his unique work among the dead involved as much delegation of authority as did his ministry in mortality. In one of the greatest revelations of this dispensation, President Joseph F. Smith saw for himself that Jesus Christ confined his visit to paradise and that, as holder of the keys of the work for the dead, he commissioned and organized the faithful spirits in paradise to visit the other spirits of the unbaptized, unrighteous, ungodly, unrepentant, disobedient, rebellious, and ignorant in order to proclaim liberty to them by teaching the gospel of Jesus Christ. Wrote President Smith:

> And as I wondered, my eyes were opened, and my understanding quickened, and I perceived that the Lord went not in person among the wicked and the disobedient who had rejected the truth, to teach them;
>
> But behold, from among the righteous, he organized his forces and appointed messengers, clothed with power and authority, and commissioned them to go forth and carry the light of the gospel to them that were in darkness, even to all the spirits of men; and thus was the gospel preached to the dead.
>
> And the chosen messengers went forth to declare the acceptable day of the Lord and proclaim liberty to the captives who were bound, even unto all who would repent of their sins and receive the gospel.
>
> Thus was the gospel preached to those who had died in their sins, without a knowledge of the truth, or in transgression, having rejected the prophets.
>
> These were taught faith in God, repentance from sin, vicarious baptism for the remission of sins, the gift of the Holy Ghost by the laying on of hands,
>
> And all other principles of the gospel that were necessary for them to know in order to qualify themselves that

they might be judged according to men in the flesh, but live according to God in the spirit. (D&C 138:29–34)

## PRIESTHOOD IN THE SPIRIT WORLD

As the Savior passed through the veil, he was met by such noble and great leaders in mortality as Adam and Eve—the parents of all mortals—and Abel, Seth, Noah, Shem, Abraham, Isaac, Jacob, Moses, Isaiah, Ezekiel, Daniel, Elias, Malachi, all the prophets who dwelt among the Nephites, and many, many more (D&C 138:38–49). These formed part of the missionary force organized to teach the gospel to those in spirit prison. They were delegated keys of power and authority to do so by the Savior. Just as none in mortality are sanctioned to go forth to preach the gospel or build up the Church without authorization (D&C 42:11), so none in the spirit world were sent forth without being given authority. Note again the language of President Smith's vision: "But behold, from among the righteous, he organized his forces and appointed messengers, clothed with power and authority, and commissioned them to go forth and carry the light of the gospel to them that were in darkness, even to all the spirits of men; and thus was the gospel preached to the dead" (D&C 138:30).

Such delegation by the Lord Jesus Christ implies the continuing operation of the priesthood in the world of spirits. "As in earth, so in the spirit world," declared Elder Parley P. Pratt. "No person can enter into the privileges of the Gospel, until the keys are turned, and the Gospel opened by those in authority" (*Journal of Discourses*, 1:11). Of the authorized ministers in the spirit world, President Joseph F. Smith further said, "They are there, having carried with them from here the holy

Priesthood that they received under authority, and which was conferred upon them in the flesh" (*Gospel Doctrine*, 471–72). President Brigham Young observed that "when a person passes behind the vail, he can only officiate in the spirit world; but when he is resurrected he officiates as a resurrected being, and not as a mortal being" (*Journal of Discourses*, 9:89).

The Savior's work among the righteous dead in the spirit world, and his act of delegating authority to them so they could help others there, enlarges our picture of the operation of the priesthood in time and eternity. Truly, the priesthood is eternal. Its existence spans premortality, mortality, and the postmortal world. The Prophet Joseph Smith declared, "The Priesthood is an everlasting principle, and existed with God from eternity, and will to eternity, without beginning of days or end of years" (*Teachings of the Prophet Joseph Smith*, 157). Moreover, modern prophets have declared that righteous men did indeed hold the priesthood in our premortal existence. President Joseph Fielding Smith presents us with this insightful declaration: "With regard to the holding of the priesthood in the preexistence, I will say that there was an organization there just as well as an organization here, and men there held authority. Men chosen to positions of trust in the spirit world held the priesthood" (Conference Report, October 1966, 84).

The foregoing is consistent with President Joseph F. Smith's panoramic vision and perspective, which also spanned pre-mortality and the postmortal spirit world. Speaking of the missionaries and ministers of the gospel in the spirit world, he said: "I observed that they were also among the noble and great ones who were chosen in the beginning to be rulers in the Church of God. Even before they were born, they, with many others, received their first lessons in the world of spirits and were prepared to come forth in the due time of the Lord to labor in his vineyard for the salvation of the souls of men" (D&C 138:55–56). President Joseph F. Smith also saw that the missionary work begun in the spirit world at the time Jesus inaugurated the spirit-prison mission continues in our own day by "the faithful elders of this dispensation" who have passed on (D&C 138:57).

Memories of my own father come flooding back to my mind when I read this portion of President Smith's vision. My father was a seventy and a stake missionary at the time he passed away, a real force for missionary work in the area where we lived. Even at a young age I could tell he felt genuine passion for the work and for his quorum. Members of that quorum helped bury my father. Members of that quorum helped comfort my family. Members of that quorum helped send me on a full-time mission, and I love them as my father did. My father's regular Sunday assignment was teaching a special Gospel Doctrine class to inmates at the nearby federal prison. I know he cherished that opportunity. I have thought since, and I believe it is so, that he is now teaching prisoners of a different kind.

Priesthood holders are not the only ones involved in this work among the dead. President Smith offered this truly profound and important insight about sisters involved in the work of salvation in the spirit world:

> Now, among all these millions of spirits that have lived on the earth and have passed away, from generation to generation, since the beginning of the world, without the knowledge of the gospel—among them you may count that at least one-half are women. Who is going to preach the gospel to the women? Who is going

to carry the testimony of Jesus Christ to the hearts of the
women who have passed away without a knowledge of
the gospel? Well, to my mind, it is a simple thing. These
good sisters who have been set apart, ordained to the
work, called to it, authorized by the authority of the holy
Priesthood to minister for their sex, in the House of God
for the living and for the dead, will be fully authorized
and empowered to preach the gospel and minister to the
women while the elders and prophets are preaching it
to the men. The things we experience here are typical
of the things of God and the life beyond us. There is a
great similarity between God's purposes as manifested
here and his purposes as carried out in his presence and
kingdom. Those who are authorized to preach the gospel
here and are appointed here to do that work will not
be idle after they have passed away, but will continue
to exercise the rights that they obtained here under the
Priesthood of the Son of God to minister for the salvation of those who have died without a knowledge of the
truth. (*Gospel Doctrine*, 461)

Just as sisters in this life are called and authorized to preach
the gospel in the earth, often working among other women, so
sisters in the next life are called and authorized to be messengers of the Lord's gospel, ministering specifically among women.
It will be remembered that President Smith made it a point of
stating explicitly in his vision of the spirit world that he saw
"our glorious Mother Eve, with many of her faithful daughters
who had lived through the ages and worshiped the true and living God" (D&C 138:39). It is to be assumed that these were
part of the Savior's "forces and appointed messengers, clothed

with power and authority, and commissioned . . . to go forth and carry the light of the gospel to them that were in darkness" (D&C 138:30). In addition, it should be remembered that sisters are delegated specific authority, under priesthood direction, to minister to women who enter the Lord's house to receive temple ordinances.

## ANOTHER PHASE
## OF THE ATONEMENT COMPLETED

Truly, the gospel is for all of our Heavenly Father's children—"black and white, bond and free, male and female; and he remembereth the heathen; and all are alike unto God" (2 Nephi 26:33). In no place or way do we see with greater clarity the fulfillment of this scripture than in the Savior's continuing ministry to the spirit world. The chief apostle in the meridian dispensation, Peter, confirmed Nephi's statement about God's all-inclusive love and fairness when he explained how the Atonement applies to both the living and the dead and why Jesus went to the spirit world after his mortal mission was finished: "For Christ also hath once suffered for sins, the just for the unjust, that he might bring us to God, being put to death in the flesh, but quickened by the Spirit: by which also he went and preached unto the spirits in prison. . . . For for this cause was the gospel preached also to them that are dead, that they might be judged according to men in the flesh, but live according to God in the spirit" (1 Peter 3:18–19; 4:6).

These verses are quite remarkable. Many in the Christian community cannot fully explain them. But as Latter-day Saints, we can imagine quite easily what powerful visions of the spirit world Peter was privileged to see that enabled him to teach this doctrine so succinctly and with such power. His experience must have been akin to Joseph F. Smith's manifestation as recorded in Doctrine and Covenants 138. Though no canonical record of Peter's own manifestations have survived, the distillations and conclusions of such manifestations have been preserved, both in the writings of Peter as well as Paul.

Before the coming of Jesus to the world of spirits, those spirits could not be judged according to men in the flesh while living according to God in the Spirit because the gospel had not ever been preached to the dead. The great gulf had not been bridged. Baptisms for the dead had not been performed. "Not until Christ had organized his missionary forces in the world of spirits do we find references to the Saints practicing the ordinance of baptism for the dead (1 Corinthians 15:29)" (Millet and McConkie, *Life Beyond*, 51). Jesus' visit to the spirit world changed the universe forever. Those "dead who had been confined in darkness *not knowing their fate*" could be set free (Smith, *Answers to Gospel Questions*, 2:81; emphasis added).

With the great gulf in the spirit world finally bridged after thousands of years of waiting on the part of all those who had died from Adam to Christ, Jesus was prepared to fulfill the next phase of the glorious and infinite atonement. President Howard W. Hunter called this phase "the single most fundamental and crucial doctrine in the Christian religion," the one thing that "cannot be overemphasized, nor . . . disregarded," and "the ultimate triumph" as well as "the ultimate miracle" (Conference Report, April 1986, 18). This, of course, is the literal, physical, bodily, resurrection of Jesus of Nazareth.

*But now is Christ risen from the dead, and become the firstfruits of them that slept.*

*For since by man came death, by man came also the resurrection of the dead.*

*For as in Adam all die, even so in Christ shall all be made alive.*

*But every man in his own order: Christ the firstfruits; afterward they that are Christ's at his coming.*

1 CORINTHIANS 15:20–23

# CHAPTER 4

# Firstfruits of the Resurrection

To bring to pass the resurrection, Jesus left the spirit world and went back to the dark, sealed tomb where his lifeless physical body had been interred since Friday. It was very early Sunday morning, at sunrise (Mark 16:2).

The scriptural record is silent regarding the moments just before and just after the Savior reentered his physical body to become an incorruptible, living "soul" (the spirit *and* the body compose the soul; D&C 88:15). We possess accounts of what death is like from those who have actually passed through the veil, but we have no reliable records of what it is like for a spirit to reenter his or her physical body and become a resurrected being. Yet, from the truth that to be without one's physical body is a bondage and a period of anxious waiting for the resurrection, we deduce that the time of the reuniting of spirit and body is a moment of great joy, exultation, and wonderment. We also believe that when the Savior of all humankind left the spirit world to take up his physical body, every spirit in paradise and many in spirit prison felt the same joy, gladness, and rejoicing as when he first arrived in the spirit world (D&C 138:15) and that they bowed the knee in acknowledgment and appreciation of Jesus' absolute power over death (D&C 138:23).

Jesus' departure from the world of spirits signaled the long-awaited actual opening of the prison doors. The righteous spirits knew that after the Savior's resurrection they too would be able to leave the spirit world and take up their own physical bodies forever. They would go free! It must have been a moment of jubilation in the spirit world as well as in the heavenly courts when the Savior's spirit departed for his body in the Garden Tomb.

Jesus himself had many ancestors and family members in the spirit world when he went there. His illustrious mortal genealogy is listed in the Gospels of Matthew (chapter 1) and Luke (chapter 3). Included are the names of kings and prophets in ancient Israel whom Jesus undoubtedly visited personally during his sojourn in the spirit world—Adam, Abraham, Jacob, Jesse, Hezekiah, Josiah, and many, many more. While Matthew's genealogy is generally regarded as the kingly list (the list of legitimate successors to the Davidic throne), Luke's is regarded as the father-to-son genealogy and hence the Savior's ancestry on Mary's side. It is particularly illuminating and satisfying to note that of the four women named in Matthew's genealogical list, three are gentile converts to the covenant (Tamar, Rahab, and Ruth), thus teaching us in subtle ways that there are *no* second-class citizens in the kingdom of God and that the Son of God himself descended from "converts."

All these were in the world of spirits. They were there when the greatest of all their descendants prepared to leave the realm of spirits and take up his physical body again. And among them there was great joy and exultation over the Savior's ultimate victory over sin and death, members of his own extended mortal family praising the name of him who was their actual great- . . . grandson, as well as the literal son of Elohim. (God and mortal man were thus linked through the birth of Jesus.)

Watershed events in our eternal journey, events marking the passage from one phase of our eternal existence to the next, are sacred moments. The birth of a child and the death of a loved one are such events, and many of us have felt the sanctity of these occasions. A close friend related to me how he was with his mother when she passed through the veil. With profound emotion he said that even though it was hard to see her go, it was a sacred experience. Surely, the passage from the spirit world to the resurrected state is such an occasion, and this was no less true for Jesus than for any of us. It also seems true that while the actual moments of these sacred occurrences (birth and death specifically) are private, the commemorations surrounding them often involve many people. Perhaps some living in our day were privileged to participate in the celebration of the Savior's resurrection, even though they would have been unembodied premortal spirits at the time, not disembodied postmortal spirits. After all, the hosts of heaven, some of which are undoubtedly living today, were privileged to participate in the heavenly celebration of the Savior's birth into mortality, which the Gospel of Luke chronicles (Luke 2:13–14).

The scriptures impress us with the thought that there are no mortal words sufficient to express what the Savior's resurrection meant to those in the spirit world, as well as countless unborn spirits. In fact, when we contemplate the magnitude of what the Savior accomplished as he left the spirit world and reentered his physical body, which had been lying in the Garden Tomb since his crucifixion, we marvel at the awesome power held uniquely by Jesus of Nazareth. Of all who have lived or will live on the earth, Jesus stands alone in his genetic makeup and powers. He is "the only one who possessed life in himself and power over death inherently. Christ was never subject unto death, even on the cross, but death was ever subject unto him" (Smith, *Doctrines of Salvation,* 1:31).

We do not know what it was like for the Savior, who in one moment had been a conscious, thinking entity in the spirit world and in the next moment was opening his eyes, clothed again in a physical body. Would it have been similar to awakening from sleep? We do not know. What we do know is that Jesus had that experience and, because of him, so will every other person who has ever lived on the earth (Alma 11:41). But the scriptures do not record the details of the resurrection itself.

It is significant that the most dramatic and remarkable moment in the history of Creation—the resurrection of Jesus Christ—is not described by any authoritative sacred text. This is perhaps witness enough that the actual moment of resurrection is intensely sacred and private. "This is one of the most remarkable things about the Gospel accounts of those strange early morning events. Not one of them actually describes Jesus' resurrection! This is the great event which the women (and eventually others) concluded must have taken place before their arrival at the tomb. This is the great event on which the rest of the New Testament entirely depends. It can be deduced by reflecting on the subsequent appearances of Jesus to his disciples (how could he be seen, if he had not first been raised?), but in itself it is never described" (Walker, *Weekend That Changed the World,* 46).

The reluctance of the Gospel writers to describe the details of the resurrection adds to their credibility rather than detracts from it. They wrote what they knew and what they were inspired to communicate. They were not in the spirit world when the Savior departed to go back to the sepulchre, nor were they in the tomb at the moment of resurrection. Either Jesus did not tell them what had happened or they were constrained by the Spirit not to write what they had learned. Some details of sacred events are not for public knowledge, as the Savior's prayers and interactions with his American Israelites show us (3 Nephi 17:15; 19:32). More than a hundred years after the Gospels were written an apocryphal work entitled the Gospel of Peter attempted to fill in the gaps and satisfy the readers' "need to know." But in the end, reading such things turns out to be a spiritually unfulfilling and unsatisfying experience, whereas the power of the canonical Gospels continues to draw us back to the Lord's atonement.

## FIRSTFRUITS

Jesus was the firstfruits of the resurrection, meaning he was the first living thing of all Creation to be resurrected. He was the "firstfruits of them that slept" (1 Corinthians 15:20). When Jesus' spirit reentered his physical body in the Garden Tomb that first resurrection morning, he became the first person on this earth to take up again an immortal physical body, nevermore to die. Our English word *resurrection* derives from two Latin terms, *re* ("again") and *surgere* ("to rise"), and literally means "to rise again." Furthermore, the Latin *surgere* is the basis of our English word *surge* and conveys a sense of power. Jesus' rising again was accomplished with power.

Jesus inherited the power to choose when to lay down his life and the power to take it up again from his literal Father, Elohim. He testified of this fact on at least two occasions during his mortal ministry (John 5:26; 10:17–18). Genetically, he had life in himself. In this regard, as well as in other significant aspects, he was different from all human beings who ever have or ever will live on this earth or the millions like it in the universe. And this godly power, in association with his sinless life and substitutionary payment for our sins by the shedding of his blood, is the power by which all others will be resurrected. President Joseph Fielding Smith affirmed this doctrine:

> Now, we have not power to lay down our lives and take them again. But Jesus had power to lay down his life, and he had power to take it up again, and when he was put to death on the cross, he yielded to those wicked Jews. When he was nailed to the cross, he meekly submitted, but he had power within himself, and he could have resisted. He came into the world to die that we might live, and *his atonement for sin and death is the force by which we are raised to immortality and eternal life.* (*Doctrines of Salvation,* 1:128; emphasis added)

Elder Bruce R. McConkie also taught that "because of his [Jesus'] resurrection, 'by the power of God,' all men shall come forth from the grave. (Morm. 9:13.)" (*Mormon Doctrine,* 639).

The power of Christ's atonement and resurrection is so great, so profound, that all people will be resurrected. Whether or not they have been righteous makes no difference. Whether or not they want to be resurrected makes no difference. The resurrection is inevitable—all who have lived in mortality will be resurrected. The apostle Paul's sure witness is still one of the clearest: "For since by man came death, by man came also the resurrection of the dead. For as in Adam all die, even so in Christ shall all be made alive. But every man in his own order:

Christ the firstfruits; afterward they that are Christ's at his coming" (1 Corinthians 15:21–23).

While the certainty of a universal resurrection for human beings may be well known, the applicability of the universal resurrection to all created things possessing a spirit may not be so well known. But so far-reaching is the power of the Savior's Atonement that it extends to this earth as well as to the creatures living on it. President Joseph Fielding Smith taught that "the Lord intends to save not only the earth and the heavens, not only man who dwells upon the earth, but all things which he has created. The animals, the fishes of the sea, the fowls of the air, as well as man, are to be recreated, or renewed, through the resurrection, for they too are living souls. The earth, as a living body, will have to die and be resurrected, for it, too, has been redeemed by the blood of Jesus Christ" (*Doctrines of Salvation*, 1:74).

This teaching is in precise harmony with the revelations of the Restoration. The Doctrine and Covenants provides a poignant example:

> And again, verily, verily, I say unto you that when the thousand years are ended, and men again begin to deny their God, then will I spare the earth but for a little season;
>
> And the end shall come, and the heaven and the earth shall be consumed and pass away, and there shall be a new heaven and a new earth.
>
> For all old things shall pass away, and all things shall become new, even the heaven and the earth, and all the fulness thereof, both men and beasts, the fowls of the air, and the fishes of the sea;

And not one hair, neither mote, shall be lost, for it is the workmanship of mine hand. (D&C 29:22–25)

The passing away of the earth and its becoming new are simply another way of saying that the earth will be resurrected to a celestial condition and become the abode of celestial beings. "This earth is living and must die, but since it keeps the law it shall be restored through the resurrection by which it shall become celestialized and the abode of celestial beings" (Smith, *Doctrines of Salvation*, 1:73; see also D&C 130:9). The reference to neither hair nor mote being lost is precise language used by the Lord in this revelation to convey the idea of the infinite restorative power of the resurrection (see also Alma 40:19–23).

Still more stunning is the truth that not only this earth but also the millions of earths like this one will be resurrected by the infinite power of Jesus Christ. In explaining this doctrine, President Joseph Fielding Smith acknowledged that this earth, on which we now dwell, is destined for a celestial resurrection. Then he said:

> Other earths, no doubt, are being prepared as habitations for terrestrial and telestial beings, for there must be places prepared for those who fail to obtain celestial glory, who receive immortality but not eternal life. Moreover, since the Lord has never created anything to be destroyed, every earth, whether created for celestial glory, or for terrestrial or telestial, will have to pass through the condition of death and the resurrection, just the same as our earth will have to do. The "passing away," therefore, means that after they have finished their "probationary state" in mortality, they will die and be raised again to receive the "glory" for which

they were designed, and to become the eternal abodes of man. (*Doctrines of Salvation,* 1:72–73)

The ramifications of Jesus' resurrection are not just staggering but truly incomprehensible to our finite minds. His greatness is towering, his power is limitless, and yet his love for each individual, for you and for me, is private and personal. On the one hand, he can send a planet hurtling through space, and yet, on the other hand, know the name and innermost thoughts of every one of his followers. No wonder we ought to remember him always (D&C 20:77, 79); we ought to worship him and our Father from the depths of our soul every day; we ought to have a prayer in our hearts continually (Alma 34:18–27). Even then we can scarcely begin to comprehend him, or his power, or the magnitude of what happened in the Garden Tomb that first Easter Sunday morning.

## KEYS OF RESURRECTION

Those who have spoken authoritatively about the resurrection have sometimes spoken of it as an ordinance involving keys, the same way other priesthood ordinances require the operation of priesthood power and priesthood keys. President Brigham Young has given us profound and insightful commentary on the core doctrine of the Christian faith:

All who have lived on the earth according to the best light they had, and would have received the fulness of the Gospel had it been preached to them, are worthy of a glorious resurrection, and will attain to this by being administered for, in the flesh, by those who have the authority. All others will have a resurrection, and receive a glory, except those who have sinned against the Holy Ghost. It is supposed by this people that we have all the ordinances in our possession for life and salvation, and exaltation, and that we are administering in these ordinances. This is not the case. We are in possession of all the ordinances that can be administered in the flesh; but there are other ordinances and administrations that must be administered beyond this world. I know you would ask what they are. I will mention one. We have not, neither can we receive here, the ordinance and the keys of the resurrection. They will be given to those who have passed off this stage of action and have received their bodies again, as many have already done and many more will. They will be ordained by those who hold the keys of the resurrection, to go forth and resurrect the Saints, just as we receive the ordinance of baptism, then the keys of authority to baptize others for the remission of their sins. This is one of the ordinances we cannot receive here, and there are many more. We hold the authority to dispose of, alter and change the elements; but we have not received authority to organize native element, to even make a spear of grass grow. (*Discourses of Brigham Young,* 397–98)

Closer to our day, President Spencer W. Kimball, in a general conference address in April 1977, confirmed that no one now living holds the keys of resurrection. And that is *not* because we lack the desire to possess them. President Kimball said: "Do we have the keys of resurrection? . . . I buried my mother when I was eleven, my father when I was in my early twenties. I have missed my parents much. If I had the power of resurrection as did the Savior of the world, I would have been tempted to try to have kept them longer. . . . We do not know of anyone who can resurrect the dead as did Jesus the Christ when he came back to mortality" (Conference Report, April 1977, 69).

Nevertheless, President Kimball promised, the faithful will receive not only the keys of resurrection but also the power of godhood in the resurrection: "We talk about the gospel in its fulness; yet we realize that a large part is still available to us as we prepare, as we perfect, and as we become more like our God. In the Doctrine and Covenants we read of Abraham, who has already attained godhood. He has received many powers, undoubtedly, that we would like to have and will eventually get if we continue faithful and perfect our lives" (Conference Report, April 1977, 71).

When Jesus' spirit reentered his physical body in the Garden Tomb that first Easter morning, he became the first person on this earth to receive the keys of resurrection. It is true that he inherited *the power* to take up his body again from his Father (Elohim) at the time of his mortal birth. But he received *the keys* of resurrection only after his own resurrection. President Joseph Fielding Smith explained the sequence this way: "Jesus Christ did for us something that we could not do for ourselves, through his infinite atonement. On the third day after the crucifixion he took up his body and *gained the keys of the resurrection,* and thus has power to open the graves for all men, but this he could not do until he had first passed through death himself and conquered" (*Doctrines of Salvation,* 1:128; emphasis added).

This is important doctrine, for it means that the keys of resurrection are conferred *after* one has been resurrected and those keys are then used to resurrect others. Jesus was the prototype. Having obtained the keys of resurrection himself (after his own experience with resurrection), he then possessed power to resurrect all others. According to President Brigham Young, those keys of resurrection first acquired by the Savior are then further given, extended, or delegated to others who have died and been resurrected. "They will be ordained, by those who hold the keys of the resurrection, to go forth and resurrect the Saints, just as we receive the ordinance of baptism, then the keys of authority to baptize others" (*Discourses of Brigham Young*, 398).

Thus, in one respect we might think of the ordinance of resurrection as being like other ordinances which we see performed on this earth. It involves those who possess the authority and keys of resurrection. As President Brigham Young and Elder Erastus Snow also taught, the resurrection will be conducted much as other things are done in the kingdom, by delegation (*Journal of Discourses*, 6:275; 15:136–39; 25:34). Just as we cannot bless or baptize ourselves, so we cannot resurrect ourselves. Ordinances are performed on our behalf by those who are authorized to perform the ordinances.

Knowing what we do about the importance of worthy fathers guiding and blessing their families in righteousness, it does not seem out of order to believe that worthy fathers and priesthood holders will have the privilege of calling forth their wives, or their children, or even other members of their family from the grave. Is it not the order of heaven for righteous patriarchs (fathers, grandfathers, and others) to bless, baptize, and perform other ordinances for their loved ones?

Before Jesus was resurrected, only his Father, our Father in Heaven, possessed the keys of resurrection (even though as the Son of God he possessed the power of life in himself—independently). After he was resurrected, Jesus acquired the keys of resurrection which could then be given to others.

The illuminating statements of President Young, President

Kimball, and President Smith, taken together, help us to see once again that God's house is a house of order. As a result of his own resurrection, Jesus now controls all power and all keys, under the direction of his Father, which he delegates to others as they are worthy and become prepared to possess the various powers of godliness. These powers are then used to bless the human family. This is true for the keys of resurrection as well as all other power and authority.

## LEAVING THE TOMB BEHIND

Early in the morning on that first Easter Sunday, when Jesus took up his physical body again in the Garden Tomb, where it had been placed the previous Friday, the entire universe, all of creation, every earth in the cosmos, every living thing, were changed for eternity. We do not know the details of the actual resurrection process or what went on inside the Garden Tomb immediately after the resurrection. We do not know how long Jesus was there. We *do* know that Jesus passed through his burial clothes, leaving them lying in place, in the outline and form of the body around which they had been wrapped. Resurrected bodies have the power to move through solid objects. John records in his own Gospel that when he came to the tomb and looked inside and when Peter entered it shortly thereafter, they both saw the strips of burial linen lying in place in the burial chamber as well as the burial cloth that had been wrapped around Jesus' head (John 20:4–7). The strips of cloth "were left in such a way as to show that his resurrected body had passed through their folds and strands without the need of unwinding the strips or untying the napkin" (McConkie, *Mortal Messiah*, 4:268).

This was explicit evidence of Jesus' resurrection. No mortal man had disturbed his body. The cloth that had been wrapped about Jesus' head ("napkin" in the King James Version) was still by itself, separate from the linen, just as it had been before the resurrection. The Greek word used in John 20:7, *entetuligme-non* (literally, "having been wrapped up"), has sometimes been translated as "folded," presumably because translators have not understood the power a resurrected body has over the elements and solid objects.

Jesus, then, left his burial clothing in place as one more wit-ness of the greatest of the miraculous acts that compose the Atonement. The scriptures make no mention of Jesus donning postresurrection robes or clothing, but such was surely the case.

Thus, we know very little of the details regarding what happened inside the Garden Tomb on resurrection morning. Outside the tomb, however, momentous events were unfolding. These events are described in varying degrees of completeness by the four Gospels. At some point early in the morning there was a violent earthquake. Two angels of the Lord descended from heaven and rolled back the great stone from the door of the tomb (JST Matthew 28:2). The guards on watch were so afraid at the sight of the angels that they shook uncontrollably and became like dead men—meaning that they collapsed on the ground (Matthew 28:2–4; Mark 16:3–4; Luke 24:2; John 20:1). One scholar has pointed out an early Christian tradition that identified the angels as Michael and Gabriel (Matthews, "Resurrection," 317). Perhaps this is true. Surely, the angelic messengers were not chosen randomly. Michael is Adam, the Father of the human family that included Jesus. Adam intro-duced mortality through the Fall, which condition Jesus atoned for. Gabriel is Noah. He stands next in authority to Adam and announced the births of Jesus and John the Baptist (Luke 1:11–37; Smith, *Teachings of the Prophet Joseph Smith,* 157).

The guards, who had been commissioned to keep watch at Jesus' tomb and who thought they acted in the strength of Roman and Jewish support, were now helpless. All their military might was powerless. Days earlier, Jesus had declined the assistance of angels when he was arrested by a lynch mob at the entrance to the garden of Gethsemane (Matthew 26:53–54). Now, he did not mind at all their presence at the Garden Tomb (Keller, *Rabboni,* 289). Their presence was incontrovertible evidence that God was in charge there.

Once the guards had sufficiently recovered from their fright, they fled from the place in terror, even though Roman military law decreed death as the penalty for soldiers deserting their posts (Talmage, *Jesus the Christ,* 678). Matthew is ambiguous concerning when the tomb was opened, but the other Gospels make it clear that this happened before the women arrived at the tomb to complete their preparations of Jesus' body in anticipation of a long interment.

Jesus did not need angels to roll away the great stone from the door of the sepulchre so that he could leave. Resurrected beings have power to pass through the elements and objects of the earth, as we have seen with Jesus' burial clothing. In the resurrection we shall become acquainted with a whole other dimension of the laws of physics. President Joseph Fielding Smith taught:

> Resurrected bodies pass through solid objects. Resurrected bodies have control over the elements. How do you think the bodies will get out of the graves at the resurrection? When the Angel Moroni appeared to the

Prophet Joseph Smith, the Prophet saw him apparently come down and ascend through the solid walls, or ceiling of the building. If the Prophet's account had been a fraud, he never would have stated such a story . . . but would have had the angel come in through the door. Why should it appear any more impossible for a resurrected being to pass through solid objects than for a spirit, for a spirit is also matter?

It was just as easy for the Angel Moroni to come to the Prophet Joseph Smith down through the building as it was for our Savior to appear to his disciples after his resurrection in the room where they were assembled when the door was closed. . . .

How could he do it? He had power over the elements. (*Doctrines of Salvation*, 2:288)

Why, then, did the angels roll the stone away and open the tomb? First, there was undoubtedly important symbolic meaning in this act. Just as the door of the Garden Tomb was now open, signaling its Occupant was no longer there, so too the door of spirit prison was now open, signaling that its righteous inhabitants were free and would no longer be confined there. This is not unlike the tearing of the veil of the Jerusalem Temple at the moment of the Crucifixion. The exposed Holy of Holies symbolized, among other things, a new order or dispensation that allowed, through the atonement of Christ, all the righteous to enter the presence of God—which the Holy of Holies represented (Hebrews 9:19–24; 10:19–20).

Second, with the opening of the tomb, the disciples could look inside as well as enter the sepulchre and know for themselves that the tomb was empty, that Jesus had come back to life, that he really was the Messiah! And that is exactly the effect the empty tomb and the discarded burial clothes had on the disciples when they had the opportunity to peer inside, as John poignantly describes: "Then went in [to the Garden Tomb] also that other disciple [in addition to Peter], which came first to the sepulchre, and he saw, *and believed*" (John 20:8; emphasis added). We know from internal evidence in the Gospel of John that "the other disciple" was John himself. Sometimes he also referred to himself in his Gospel account as the "disciple whom Jesus loved" (John 13:23; 19:26; 20:2; 21:7, 20).

Others would likewise come to the tomb, and out of their initial experience with its emptiness would eventually blossom the witness that Jesus was who he said he was, that he had told the truth, that he was the Savior, Messiah, and Son of God alive again!

---

But Mary stood *without at the sepulchre weeping: and as she wept, she stooped down, and looked into the sepulchre,*

*And seeth two angels in white sitting, the one at the head, and the other at the feet, where the body of Jesus had lain.*

*And they say unto her, Woman, why weepest thou? She saith unto them, Because they have taken away my Lord, and I know not where they have laid him.*

*And when she had thus said, she turned herself back, and saw Jesus standing, and knew not that it was Jesus.*

*Jesus saith unto her, Woman, why weepest thou? whom seekest thou? She, supposing him to be the gardener, saith unto him, Sir, if thou have borne him hence, tell me where thou hast laid him, and I will take him away.*

*Jesus saith unto her, Mary. She turned herself, and saith unto him, Rabboni; which is to say, Master.*

JOHN 20:11–16

---

# CHAPTER 5

# First Witnesses of His Resurrection

There is general agreement among the synoptic Gospels that it was very early on Sunday morning, at dawn, the first day of the week, when Mary Magdalene and the other women (including Mary, mother of James, and Salome) went back to the Garden Tomb (Matthew 28:1; Mark 16:2; Luke 24:1). John adds the detail that it was still dark (John 20:1). Their main purpose in going to the tomb so early was to anoint the body of Jesus, to complete the unfinished business of final burial preparations of the corpse (Mark 16:1; Luke 24:1). There may also have been another reason for the visit as well, which is hinted at by Matthew when he states that they came "to see the sepulchre" (Matthew 28:1).

According to Jewish custom, a visit to the tomb of a deceased person within three days after interment was required in order to check the condition of the corpse. This obligation is outlined in the Mishnah, *Tractate Semahot* 8:1: "One should go to the cemetery to check the dead within three days, and not fear that such [an action] smacks of pagan practices. There was actually one buried man who was visited after three days

99

and lived for twenty-five more years and had sons, and died afterward" (quoted in Kloner, "Did a Rolling Stone Close Jesus' Tomb?" 76).

Presumably, Jesus' disciples did not go to the tomb expecting to find the Master revived, for they had witnessed for themselves the horrible effects of the crucifixion process. It is possible, however, and perhaps even probable, that they also visited the tomb within three days to fulfill the custom of the Jews—the oral tradition. (We know these disciples were exacting in keeping other parts of the Law.) Also important to note is that their counting of burial days followed Jewish custom, which included both the day of burial and the next two days (any portion of the third day) in the count (Kloner, "Did a Rolling Stone Close Jesus' Tomb?" 29). Thus, the resurrection of Jesus of Nazareth, King of the Jews, on "the third day" (Matthew 16:21) accorded with Jewish custom and practice.

## WOMEN FIND THE TOMB OPEN

As the women entered the garden area and approached the tomb in the early-dawn darkness, surely there must have been a somber, even grief-stricken, mood among them. As they carried their spices and preparations, they naturally wondered out loud how they would get the heavy, cumbersome stone rolled away from the entrance of the sepulchre (Mark 16:3). So preoccupied with grief and plans for final burial preparations had they been that they had not thought of this little detail.

Much to their surprise, and perhaps apprehension, when they arrived at the tomb they found the "very great" stone already rolled away. From John's comment we realize that Mary Magdalene certainly was not thinking in terms of resurrection, though resurrection was part of the Jewish belief system of that time. Rather, upon seeing the opened tomb Mary Magdalene immediately left the other women and ran to find Peter and John, two of the three chief apostles of the Church, to alert them that mischief was afoot: "They have taken away the Lord out of the sepulchre, and *we* know not where they have laid him" (John 20:2; emphasis added). Her worst fears were now realized. Even in death her Master, their Master, could not be allowed to rest in peace. John does not tell us who Mary suspected of tampering with Jesus' body, but both the Jewish conspirators and the Roman crucifiers would have been possibilities.

Because John's account of Sunday morning does not mention the other women named in the synoptic Gospels, some have reasoned that Mary Magdalene was alone and not in the company of these other women when she first went to the tomb. Yet, we note her use of the pronoun *we* in her description of surprise at discovering the tomb already open. Perhaps she was the one who ran back to find Peter and John because hers was a more immediate sense of loss at seeing no corpse in the tomb.

## ANGELS AT THE TOMB

Though it is not made explicitly clear how the exact sequence of events unfolded next, especially when we read the four Gospel accounts together, it is more than likely that Matthew, Mark, and Luke describe details of the story involving the rest of the women left back at the tomb, while John recounts the details of Mary Magdalene's departure to notify Peter and John.

As the other women drew near to the opened sepulchre for the first time that morning, they saw two angels, not one as reported in the King James Version of Matthew and Mark. The angels were dressed in long, white, shining (glorious) garments

(JST Matthew 28:2; JST Mark 16:3; JST Luke 24:2). Matthew adds that their countenance was like lightning and their raiment was as white as snow (JST Matthew 28:3). The Joseph Smith Translation is a tremendous gift in helping to clarify our understanding of events that first resurrection morning. Even that inspired document, however, preserves some of the disagreements between the individual Gospel accounts regarding details. For example, Mark and Luke do not agree about whether the angels were sitting on or standing by the great stone. But such things are of lesser importance.

Mark next reports that to assuage the fear of the women upon seeing two heavenly beings (and certainly also to build their faith in the resurrection), the angels declared the monumental, universal, culminating message of the Atonement: "Be not affrighted; ye seek Jesus of Nazareth, who was crucified; he is risen; he is not here; behold the place where they laid him; and go your way, tell his disciples and Peter, that he goeth before you into Galilee; there shall ye see him as he said unto you. And they, entering into the sepulcher, saw the place where they laid Jesus" (JST Mark 16:4–6). It is striking that Peter is mentioned separate and apart from the other disciples. There is no question that the Gospel authors regard him as the leader of the group. In fact, he is usually singled out in texts that discuss the disciples.

Luke describes a slightly different order in the sequence of events when the women encountered the angels. He notes that they experienced both perplexity and fear but that those feelings surfaced *after* they entered the tomb and saw there was no body: "And they found the stone rolled away from the sepulcher, and two angels standing by it in shining garments. And they entered into the sepulcher, and not finding the body of the Lord Jesus, they were much perplexed thereabout; and were affrighted, and bowed down their faces to the earth. But behold the angels said unto them, Why seek ye the living among the dead?" (JST Luke 24:2–4).

Though real, the differences in the testimonies of the synoptic Gospels regarding details of the women's experience at the tomb are understandable. The authors were different individuals, writing from their own perspectives based on personal knowledge or remembrances of the events, or, in the case of Luke and perhaps Mark, reflecting what eyewitnesses had told them. The fact that not even the Joseph Smith Translation attempts to harmonize the accounts indicates to me that the authors were not in collusion, not making up a story, nor repeating a popular legend. I am persuaded that the Prophet Joseph Smith was inspired to simply restore what each of the authors had originally written. The Joseph Smith Translation is preserving original text here because that is what the Lord wanted us to have. The Gospel writers were not infallible nor flawless. They may have seen things differently or understood things differently. But they were authentic witnesses. What is impressive in the Joseph Smith Translation is the emphasis in all three synoptic Gospels on the appearance of two angels, not one, and, thus, the fulfillment of the ancient law of witnesses to establish the certainty of the event (Deuteronomy 19:15; 2 Corinthians 13:1). The angels constituted a powerful and sure witness that the resurrection of Jesus Christ really did happen.

All of us have had great teachers. The greatest teachers help us to know what teachings are most important; they help us to order our thoughts by emphasizing what is critical and turning our minds to significant connections with past information. The two angelic witnesses did this very thing for the women at the tomb by recalling the Savior's own testimony of his inevitable resurrection given on an earlier occasion. After asking the women why they were seeking the living among the dead, the angels then declared: "He is not here, but is risen: remember how he spake unto you when he was yet in Galilee, saying, The Son of man must be delivered into the hands of sinful men, and be crucified, and the third day rise again. And they remembered his words" (Luke 24:6–8).

As a result of this divine instruction, the women began to understand. They began to gain a testimony of the Savior's resurrection. That testimony would become complete and made sure a little while later when the living Lord himself appeared to them personally. In the meantime, the women had also been instructed to go quickly and tell the other disciples what they had just learned—that Jesus "is risen from the dead; and, behold, he goeth before you into Galilee: there shall ye see him" (Matthew 28:7; Mark 16:7). A testimony is strengthened in the bearing of it.

In a wonderfully poignant description of their reaction to all that they had just experienced in the last several minutes at the tomb, Matthew says of the women, "And they departed quickly from the sepulchre with *fear* and *great joy;* and did run to bring his disciples word" (Matthew 28:8; emphasis added). There was no dallying. They had been told the Master was alive, and their errand was pressing. They did depart quickly, so much so that they *ran* to tell the others what they had just seen and heard. They were filled with both joy and fear.

Though there are many ways to interpret the word "fear," its use here in tandem with the phrase "great joy" seems to intend something like excitement mingled with a feeling of anxiety. Mark's Gospel says of the women, "They trembled and were amazed" (Mark 16:8). In moments such as the one just described, single words or phrases are often inadequate to convey the range of emotions that we feel. "Anyone in similar circumstances would have been startled out of their minds—and these were aging women after an emotionally draining weekend, now caught unawares in a dim, damp tomb at dawn" (Walker, *Weekend That Changed the World*, 48). Sometimes we experience fear over things we do not understand. Sometimes we become anxious over our own worthiness or status before the Lord. Doubtless the women did not comprehend all that was happening, but they knew they had experienced something colossal.

## APOSTLES RECEIVE THE NEWS

Luke reports that the women who had been instructed by the angels returned from the tomb, located the eleven living members of the Quorum of the Twelve, and rehearsed their experience to them as well as "to all the rest," meaning the other disciples who were staying in close contact with the apostles (Luke 24:9). Luke also reveals the identity of the women who were now in the presence of the apostles explaining their encounter with the empty tomb and the angels. They were Mary Magdalene, Joanna, Mary the mother of James, and the other women who were with them (Luke 24:10). We do not know how many of these "other women" there were, but it may have been several, and we know of their long-time devotion to Jesus (Luke 8:2–3).

That Luke includes Mary Magdalene in his list is puzzling at first glance when, as we have seen, John implies that Mary left the group of women upon first seeing the stone rolled away from the tomb. If we regard Mary Magdalene as having been with the rest of the women the whole time—that is, from the beginning of their experience with the two angels—then we face the challenge of explaining the language and tone of Mary's speech reported in John 20:2: "They have taken away the Lord . . . and we know not where they have *laid* him" (emphasis added). These words imply that Mary had not heard the testimony of the angels, that she did not know about Jesus' coming back to life, and that she believed the corpse had simply been laid somewhere else by someone of unknown identity.

It seems to me that Mary Magdalene was included in Luke's list for two reasons. First, she was originally with the women who approached the tomb during the early hours of that Sunday morning, and Luke was aware of who was in the group of women that first went to the tomb. Second, Mary Magdalene was reunited with the rest of the women when they also arrived to talk to Peter, John, and the others to report their experience with the angels. By that time Mary Magdalene had already spoken with the apostles and explained her fear and consternation over the disappearance of Jesus' body. So all the women who started out together for the Garden Tomb ended up together at the abode of the apostles. Luke may not have known about Mary's separate appeal to the apostles, or knowing about it, he may not have written down the details exactly as we would have wished.

I do not believe that Mary Magdalene would have maintained a posture or tone of disbelief over the idea of Jesus' resurrection (as is portrayed in John 20:2) if she had been privileged to hear the powerful testimony of the two angelic sentinels at the tomb. We must remember that when the other women heard the angels recount Jesus' own words about his eventual resurrection, "they remembered his words" (Luke 24:8). Mary's speech as reported by John does not sound like she yet remembered anything about the Savior's predictions of his resurrection. Furthermore, if Mary Magdalene had been privy to the powerful witness of the angels at the tomb, along with the other women, we would expect her to have more readily recognized the identity of the Savior when he appeared to her in the garden. But instead, she seems to possess no sense of forewarning that her Master could have been resurrected; there is no hint of anticipation when it comes to the declaration of the angels, "He is risen."

Not only did Mary Magdalene not yet believe in the resurrection of Jesus but the apostles also dismissed the report of the other women regarding Jesus' resurrection. The words of the women "seemed to them as idle tales, and they [the apostles] believed them not" (Luke 24:11). In fact, we are inclined to think that Mary's previous comments about the body of Jesus being stolen away had prejudiced the apostles against the idea of Jesus being resurrected.

It was because of the reports by Mary and the other women that "Peter, therefore, went forth, and that other disciple, and came to the sepulchre" (John 20:3). As leaders of the band of Jesus' disciples, they undoubtedly felt the need to investigate the happenings at the tomb, if for no other reason than the fact that Mary's report conflicted with the report of the other women. Though they ran together, John was faster afoot and arrived at the sepulchre first, but did not enter. He reserved that honor for the senior and chief apostle, Peter. Elder Russell M. Nelson provided an important insight into this episode as it relates to the principle of seniority in the Quorum of the Twelve Apostles:

> Seniority is honored among ordained Apostles—even when entering or leaving a room. . . .
>
> Some [years] ago Elder Haight extended a special

courtesy to President Romney while they were in the upper room in the temple. President Romney was lingering behind for some reason, and [Elder Haight] did not want to precede him out the door. When President Romney signaled [for him] to go first, Elder Haight replied, "No, President, you go first."

President Romney replied with his humor, "What's the matter, David? Are you afraid I'm going to steal something?"

Such deference from a junior to a senior apostle is recorded in the New Testament. When Simon Peter and John the Beloved ran to investigate the report that the body of their crucified Lord had been taken from the sepulcher, John, being younger and swifter, arrived first, yet he did not enter. He deferred to the senior apostle, who entered the sepulcher first. (See John 20:2–6.) Seniority in the apostleship has long been a means by which the Lord selects His presiding high priest. (Conference Report, April 1993, 52)

Apparently, the angels had departed from the garden by the time Peter and John arrived, leaving the special witnesses alone to contemplate the meaning of the empty tomb and the burial clothing that had been left behind. In those sacred moments of reflection and inspiration, these amazing men gained a conviction of the reality of the resurrection of Jesus. "Upon John, reflective and mystic by nature, the reality dawns first. It is true! They had not known before; now they do" (McConkie, *Doctrinal New Testament Commentary*, 1:842).

They saw and felt and believed! Up to that point, they had not comprehended the meaning or import of the scripture "that he must rise again from the dead" (John 20:9; see also vv. 4–8). Now, possessing new light and fresh understanding, the chief apostle and his counselor "went away again unto their own home" as believers (John 20:10).

Some students of the New Testament have pointed out that Luke seems to contradict John's account by describing only Peter's visit to the empty tomb and omitting any mention of John's participation (Luke 24:12). Yet John was there, and Luke was not. John knew that both he and Peter had participated together in an extraordinary experience. In fact, Luke 24:12 is missing from some ancient manuscripts of the New Testament and may well be a later addition.

The two chief apostles did not need to see Jesus to believe in the resurrection, but they did need the Holy Spirit. The power of the Holy Ghost to reorder men's thinking, to change their beliefs, is limited only by the receptivity and spirituality of the individuals themselves. The power that the Holy Ghost has to change men and the universe is incomprehensible to our finite minds. This power includes the varied forces of nature—gravitation, sound, heat, light, electricity, nuclear forces—and other forces so far beyond our comprehension as to make what we know and understand, compared to what the Holy Ghost knows and understands, look like a packhorse compared to a locomotive (Talmage, *Articles of Faith,* 160–61).

The witness of the Holy Ghost is even greater and more important than a witness gained by experiencing visitations or seeing miracles. President Harold B. Lee said that he knew "that Jesus is the Christ, the Son of the Living God" by "a witness more powerful than sight" (*Ensign,* November 1971, 17). That witness came from the Holy Ghost, as President Joseph Fielding Smith declared: "The Lord has taught that there is a stronger witness than seeing a personage, even of seeing the Son of God in a vision. Impressions on the soul that come from the Holy Ghost are far more significant than a vision. When Spirit speaks to spirit, the imprint upon the soul is far more difficult to erase. Every member of the Church should have impressions that Jesus is the Son of God indelibly pictured on his soul through the witness of the Holy Ghost" ("First Presidency and the Council of the Twelve," November 1966, 979).

## MARY MAGDALENE

During all that had transpired up to this point Sunday morning, no one had yet seen the risen Lord. That changed with Mary Magdalene, as Mark's terse comment proclaims: "Now when Jesus was risen early the first day of the week, he appeared *first* to Mary Magdalene" (Mark 16:9; emphasis added). Mary was the first mortal to whom Jesus showed himself as the resurrected Lord.

We do not know a great deal about Mary Magdalene from scriptural sources. More was written about her in postapostolic writings purporting to be scripture but which are part of the Apocrypha and Pseudepigrapha. And much more can be found in modern culture—both in print (fiction and nonfiction) as well as in movies. But none of these are canonical or even authoritative. We should not trust very much of what we hear or see written about Mary Magdalene outside of scripture. For example, there is a false tradition that equates Mary Magdalene with the unnamed sinner who washed the feet of Jesus with her tears and then anointed and wiped them with her hair (Luke 7:37–38). Perhaps the false identification arose, in part, because of the close proximity of this story in the last half of Luke 7 to the initial introduction of the name of Mary Magdalene in the first verses of Luke 8. But though the identification is wrong, it still continues to circulate (Talmage, *Jesus the Christ*, 263–64).

Mary (Hebrew, *Miriam*) was a very common name in first-century Judaism, and each was differentiated by some notable distinction. Mary Magdalene, or, better, Mary of Magdala, was denominated by her association with the small town of Magdala on the western shore of the Sea of Galilee. Many scholars identify it with the village known in the Talmud as Magdala Nunayya, or Magdala of the Fishes. The Aramaic name *Magdala* derives from the Hebrew *migdal*, meaning a "tower." The tower which gave this village its distinctive quality "was probably used to hang fish to dry in the sun and wind" (Murphy-O'Connor, "Fishers," 27). It would have been a place well known to Jesus and his apostles, who were fishermen on the Sea of Galilee.

Mary Magdalene was a woman of tremendous faith, charity, and action, as described in the Gospels. She was part of the group of women who traveled with Jesus and the Twelve from one town and village to another in the Galilee and who helped to support these brethren out of her own means (Luke 8:2–3). She had been healed by Jesus of demonic possession; out of her went seven devils, or evil spirits (Mark 16:9; Luke 8:2). It is likely that she, having remained with the Master throughout his ministry, was part of the group of women who watched and mourned as Jesus carried his cross to Golgotha and whom he specifically addressed when he turned and said, "Daughters of Jerusalem, weep not for me, but weep for yourselves, and for your children" (Luke 23:27–28). Mary Magdalene was at the cross during Jesus' crucifixion (Matthew 27:55–56; Mark 15:40–41; John 19:25). She was at the Garden Tomb during Jesus' burial (Matthew 27:61; Mark 15:47). And she was back at the

Garden Tomb early that Sunday morning with the other women (Matthew 28:1; Mark 16:1; Luke 24:10; John 20:1).

One other thing is certain. Like the other women from Galilee, Mary Magdalene was devoted to Jesus and the early Church of Jesus Christ. Elder James E. Talmage of the Quorum of the Twelve called Mary Magdalene a "noble woman" and "a devoted soul." She "became one of the closest friends Christ had among women; her devotion to Him as her Healer and as the One whom she adored as the Christ was unswerving; she stood close by the cross while other women tarried afar off in the time of His mortal agony; she was among the first at the sepulchre on the resurrection morning" (*Jesus the Christ*, 264–65). Therefore, it is not surprising to find Mary Magdalene back at the empty tomb, lingering for a while after Peter and John had seen the burial clothing and returned to their own homes as believers in the resurrection. "The sorrowful Magdalene had followed the two apostles back to the garden of the burial. No thought of the Lord's restoration to life appears to have found place in her grief-stricken heart; she knew only that the body of her beloved Master had disappeared" (*Jesus the Christ*, 680). She stayed, looking for answers, "because she had not seen the angels or heard their message . . . [She was] still uncertain and wondering at what [had] happened" (Mumford, *Harmony of the Gospels*, 163).

## FIRST RESURRECTION APPEARANCE

John alone reports the powerful and touching scene that occurred as Mary, lingering alone with her thoughts, weeping from grief made doubly intense over the unknown whereabouts of the corpse of the Master she loved, full of tears at this final indignity and injustice, stooped down and looked into the tomb. There she saw two angels in white, sitting where the body of

Jesus had lain (John 20:12). From John's brief report, it appears that she did not recognize them as heavenly messengers, bearers of good tidings, perhaps because of her consuming grief. Her response to their tender inquiry about her tears was essentially the same she had given to Peter and John earlier that morning, "Because they have taken away my Lord, and I know not where they have laid him" (John 20:13).

Earlier, when Mary Magdalene talked with Peter and John, her statement was in the plural: "*We* know not where they have laid him." Now her response was in the singular. Before, she spoke for the whole group of women, expressing a sentiment whose essence was one of exasperation more than grief over the fulfillment of their suspicions that the body would not be left alone. Now Mary's expression was intensely personal and sorrowful. "The absence of the body, which she thought to be all that was left on earth of Him whom she loved so deeply, was a personal bereavement" (Talmage, *Jesus the Christ*, 680). As Elder Talmage further intimates, there is a volume of pathos, affliction, and affection in her words "They have taken away my Lord."

John makes no further mention of the angels, whose presence presaged the appearance of One greater. Turning away from the entrance to the empty tomb, Mary actually saw Jesus standing close by, but she did not know that it was he. It is not hard to understand why she would have mindlessly supposed that Jesus was the caretaker of the garden in which the tomb was located. It wasn't just that she was consumed by sorrow, although that was certainly overwhelming. It was also a matter of being desperate to find the body of her Master in order to spare him further indignities and prevent further disruptions of the Jewish customs for honorable burials, which, not inconsequentially, were regarded as carrying the force of Jewish law.

I have seen how important it is for faithful Orthodox Jews to observe their burial customs and how distraught they can become when those customs are in danger of being disrupted. On an airplane flight from the United States to the Holy Land, a group of Jews became panicky when the plane landed late and sundown was rapidly approaching, preventing them from properly observing burial customs for one of their great rab-binic leaders. The members of the traveling group were out of their seats and racing to the front of the plane as the aircraft was only beginning to taxi to the gate. As the flight attendants were trying to push them back to their seats and issuing stern commands over the intercom, one man kept saying, "You don't understand! You don't understand!" Similarly, perhaps, Mary's own grief and frustration prevented her from really "seeing" and comprehending reality.

When Jesus spoke to Mary, his was the first utterance of a resurrected being ever in history. He asked her the same thoughtful, sympathetic question that the angels had just put forward moments before: "Woman, why weepest thou? whom seekest thou?" Mary responded in a tone that indicates she pre-sumed the gardener already knew something about the tomb's occupant because she did not mention Jesus' name. She referred to him only by the pronoun *him*. "Sir, if thou have borne *him* hence, tell me where thou hast laid *him*, and I will take *him* away" (John 20:15; emphasis added).

What happened next surely must rank among the most dra-matic moments in human history. Uttering Mary's name as only he could, in an intonation that only she would recognize imme-diately, Jesus identified himself to the woman from Magdala. "Jesus saith unto her, Mary. She turned herself, and saith unto him, Rabboni; which is to say, Master" (John 20:16). We can only imagine the leap of Mary's heart as instantaneously the feelings of bewilderment and then recognition swept over her. "Who is this? Could it actually be—? Is he really alive after all I have seen happen? Yes, it really is Jesus—the Lord of life!"

Though scripture is silent regarding the exact thoughts and feelings of Mary at this moment of transcendent realization, Elder Talmage provides inspired commentary:

> One word from His living lips changed her agonized grief into ecstatic joy. . . . The voice, the tone, the tender accent she had heard and loved in the earlier days lifted her from the despairing depths into which she had sunk. She turned, and saw the Lord. In a transport of joy she reached our her arms to embrace Him, uttering only the endearing and worshipful word, "Rabboni," meaning My beloved Master. Jesus restrained her impulsive manifestation of reverent love, saying, "Touch me not; for I am not yet ascended to my father," and adding, "but go to my brethren, and say unto them, I ascend unto my Father, and your Father; and to my God, and your God." To a woman, to Mary of Magdala, was given the honor of being the first among mortals to behold a resurrected Soul, and that Soul, the Lord Jesus (Mark 16:9). (*Jesus the Christ*, 681)

As to why Mary was privileged to be the first mortal to see the risen Lord, the first Being ever to be resurrected, we are not told. For that matter, we are not told why all the women to whom the resurrected Savior first appeared were so blessed, but surely it had something to do with the way they cared for the Savior, giving all they had (economically, emotionally, materially, mentally) for him, in life and in death. There is no doubt that a special relationship existed between Jesus and Mary. But this part of the story of Christ's redeeming mission is noteworthy because of the way it highlights the relationship between the Savior and several women of the early Church. The women were the first to *see* the Lord—the first eyewitnesses of the resurrection. Elder Bruce R. McConkie wrote:

> How much there is incident to the death, burial, and resurrection of our Lord which ennobles and exalts faithful women. They wept at the cross, sought to care for his wounded and lifeless body, and came to his tomb to weep and worship for their friend and Master. And so it is not strange that we find a woman, Mary of Magdala, chosen and singled out from all the disciples, even including the apostles, to be the first mortal to see and bow in the presence of a resurrected being. Mary, who had been healed of much and who loved much, saw the risen Christ! (*Doctrinal New Testament Commentary,* 1:843)

It is interesting to me that Jesus does not, at this juncture, stop to give a discourse on the doctrine of resurrection. He does not stop to answer questions about the nature of his own experience. He does not stop to note the fulfillment of prophecies about this moment—either his own prophecies or those of other prophets. He does not ask that Mary or the others worship him. What he does do is refocus Mary's attention on God the Father. And he bids Mary do the same for others through her testimony. "Jesus saith unto her, Touch me not; for I am not yet ascended to my Father: but go to my brethren, and say unto them, I ascend unto my Father, and your Father; and to my God, and your God" (John 20:17).

The Savior's whole orientation, his life, his teaching focus, was always fixed on his Father, our Father in Heaven. It was *never* about himself, except as his role and position as the Only Begotten Son and Messiah related to his Father's plan, purposes, and desires. But here again we're back to the Father. This is an important model for us to follow. The best teacher, the best leader, the best parent, will always step out of the limelight and focus the attention of his or her students and family on the Father and the Son. In the most triumphant moment of his life, when Jesus had every right to proclaim his monumental victory over the great enemies of humankind—physical and spiritual death—the Redeemer of the universe quietly pointed Mary and the rest of us to his Father and his God, who is also our Father and our God.

John reports simply that Mary did as she had been instructed: "Mary Magdalene came and told the disciples that she had seen the Lord, and that he had spoken these things unto her" (John 20:18).

Entrenched ideas die hard. New notions are not easily accepted when they contradict previous experience. Such seems to have been the case with those disciples of the Lord whom Mary now tried to persuade that Jesus really had come back to life, that he was now a resurrected Personage. As Mark implies, their great grief seems to have kept them from believing Mary's eyewitness account: "And she went and told them that had been with him, as they mourned and wept. And they, when they had heard that he was alive, and had been seen of her, believed not" (Mark 16:10–11). It would take nothing less than the literal appearance of the Lord himself to change their sorrow into joy.

## THE OTHER WOMEN

Absent from the group of unbelieving disciples at this juncture were the other women who had accompanied Mary

Magdalene to the Garden Tomb that early Sunday morning, and who had first heard the good news of Jesus' resurrection from angelic witnesses. To these women, the Lord appeared personally and confirmed their hopes and bolstered their believing hearts: "And as they went to tell his disciples, behold, Jesus met them, saying, All hail. And they came and held him by the feet, and worshipped him" (Matthew 28:9). They were given a personal audience with the Lord and felt the overwhelming desire to worship him. In this regard, Elder McConkie presents an interesting perspective:

> In his own infinite wisdom, Jesus chose to appear to and be handled by a group of other women—all before he came even to Peter and the rest of the Twelve. . . .
>
> These other women included Mary the mother of Joses; Joanna, evidently the wife of Chuza, Herod's steward (Luke 8:3); and Salome, the mother of James and John. Among them were women who had been with Jesus in Galilee. Certainly the beloved sisters from Bethany were there; and, in general, the group would have been made up of the same ones who have hovered in sorrow around the cross. Their total number may well have been in the dozens or scores. We know that women in general are more spiritual than men. . . .
>
> . . . But whoever they were, Jesus is using them and the fact of his resurrection to show the unity and oneness and equality of the man and the woman. (*Mortal Messiah*, 4:265–67)

To Mary Magdalene, Jesus forbade too-close physical contact, yet to these women he permitted their embrace of his feet. Why?

I believe four things are true. First, this was now a different Jesus, a different kind of Being from the one the disciples were used to associating with in mortality. He was now God resurrected. "There was about Him a divine dignity that forbade close personal familiarity" (Talmage, *Jesus the Christ*, 682).

Second, in John 20:17 Jesus was not actually forbidding Mary to "touch" him but rather forbidding her to hold on to or embrace him. In the Greek text of the English phrase, "Touch me not" (*me mou aptou*), the verb *aptou* means "to hold, to cling, or to fasten to." Jesus was saying, "Hold me not. Do not cling to me." Some translators even render this passage as, "Stop touching me." It seems only natural to me that Mary would be touching the Savior to confirm that she was not just seeing a mirage, but that he was a physical reality.

Third, as God resurrected, Jesus was now to be recognized as the successful agent of his Father's will, the One who had now fulfilled the Father's plan of salvation and had done *all* that the Father had asked of him. It was only fitting and proper that the Savior's first lengthy embrace be reserved for his literal Father, the God who loved him, empowered him, and sent him to earth (and whom the Savior loved in return with equal intensity). Thus, no one was permitted to cling to the Savior "until after He had presented Himself to the Father," who was deserving and desirous of that first postresurrection embrace (Talmage, *Jesus the Christ*, 682).

Fourth, when Mary spoke with her Lord, he had not yet been with his Father. She was the first to see him as a resurrected Being. Later, when he appeared to the other women, the Savior had already ascended to his Father and received his love and approbation. It is not difficult to imagine that Mary Magdalene would yet receive an embrace from her Lord.

The image presented by Matthew of the Savior greeting the women who had so affectionately cared for him in life and in death (Luke 8:2; 23:55–56; 24:1), and their response—embracing his feet and, no doubt, wetting those feet with their tears—is a particularly joyous and vibrant one. We do not know what words of comfort the Master spoke; however, the Greek word used by Matthew to indicate Jesus' greeting to the women (*chairete*) is translated as "All hail" in the King James Version. It derives from the Greek root *chairo,* meaning "to rejoice, be glad, be delighted." In other words, Matthew depicts a scene in which the risen Lord was as joyful at meeting and greeting the women as they were at meeting him. This is a profound moment captured in scripture.

The Book of Mormon preserves a similarly profound moment when disciples of the Savior worshiped at his feet at the time he first appeared to them on the American continent after his resurrection. Their response was the same as that of the women in the Old World: "And when they had all gone forth and witnessed for themselves, they did cry out with one accord, saying: Hosanna! Blessed be the name of the Most High God! And they did fall down at the feet of Jesus, and did worship him" (3 Nephi 11:16–17). Even though both groups of disciples knew that the Savior's love was personal and undemanding, their every instinct, impulse, and desire were to fall at his feet and worship the great God of the universe, so powerful was the force of his presence and personality.

The Sunday morning following Friday's crucifixion was the most important Sunday in history and a day of many firsts. It was the first time mortals had seen a resurrected being. It was the first time a resurrected being had spoken or been spoken to. It was the first time a resurrected body had been touched by mortal hands. It was the first time a Jewish Sabbath or holy day had been overshadowed by a regular week day. And now it was no longer a "regular" weekday. It would be memorialized forever as the day when the Lord God of Israel arose from the dead to bring life to all Creation for eternity. It was the first day that the first witnesses began to spread the news of the first resurrection—the ultimate act in the drama that is the Atonement.

---

*For I delivered unto you first of all that which I also received, how that Christ died for our sins according to the scriptures;*

*And that he was buried, and that he rose again the third day according to the scriptures:*

*And that he was seen of Cephas, then of the twelve:*

*After that, he was seen of above five hundred brethren at once; of whom the greater part remain unto this present, but some are fallen asleep.*

*After that, he was seen of James; then of all the apostles.*

*And last of all he was seen of me also, as of one born out of due time.*

1 CORINTHIANS 15:3–8

---

# CHAPTER 6

# Other Sunday Witnesses

Though the first Easter morning had already been filled with momentous events, many more would occur before the day ended. We can hardly imagine a more stunning twenty-four hours. After the Savior's resurrection and his appearance to the group of first witnesses—the devoted women of the early Church—many ancient Saints were resurrected, and several more people saw the living Lord for themselves, including all but one of the members of the Quorum of the Twelve. These gained a personal assurance of the Savior's triumph over death.

## THE FIRST RESURRECTION AFTER CHRIST'S

In Matthew's record of the Crucifixion, which took place from 9 o'clock Friday morning to 3 o'clock Friday afternoon, is a brief notice telling us of others who were resurrected:

Jesus, when he had cried again with a loud voice, yielded up the ghost.

And, behold, the veil of the temple was rent in twain

from the top to the bottom; and the earth did quake, and the rocks rent;

And the graves were opened; and many bodies of the saints which slept arose,

And came out of the graves after his resurrection, and went into the holy city, and appeared unto many. (Matthew 27:50–53)

Though this report of additional resurrected beings is placed right after Jesus' death on the cross, it is unquestionably out of order chronologically from the sequence of events as they actually occurred on those fateful days—Friday through Sunday. We know with certainty that no living thing was resurrected before Jesus Christ, for he was "the firstfruits of them that slept" (1 Corinthians 15:20). Many individuals were resurrected after him, perhaps immediately after him on Sunday morning. But no person's resurrection preceded the Savior's.

Those who came forth from the grave and began appearing in Jerusalem's streets and byways after the Savior's resurrection were part of that group promised to come forth in the first resurrection. That this is actually the first resurrection spoken of in the scriptures is confirmed by Elder Bruce R. McConkie:

> To us the first resurrection shall commence when Christ comes again, and the second resurrection shall start at the end of the millennium. But for those who lived prior to the time of the resurrection of Christ, the first resurrection, itself a resurrection of the just, was the one which accompanied the coming forth of the Son of God from the grave. (*Doctrinal New Testament Commentary*, 1:847)

Several antemeridian prophets foretold this first resurrection years and even centuries before the birth of Jesus in Bethlehem. Enoch, Isaiah, and Samuel the Lamanite all spoke of others who would be resurrected when the Messiah took up his physical body again (Moses 7:55–56; Isaiah 26:19; Helaman 14:25; 3 Nephi 23:7–13). The clearest articulation of the doctrine of the first resurrection that would occur at the time of Christ's rising from the dead was given by the prophet Abinadi in the American hemisphere 148 years before the birth of Christ. Abinadi declared:

> And there cometh a resurrection, even a first resurrection; yea, even a resurrection of those that have been, and who are, and who shall be, even until the resurrection of Christ—for so shall he be called.
>
> And now, the resurrection of all the prophets, and all those that have believed in their words, or all those that have kept the commandments of God, shall come forth in the first resurrection; therefore, they are the first resurrection.
>
> They are raised to dwell with God who has redeemed them; thus they have eternal life through Christ, who has broken the bands of death.
>
> And these are those who have part in the first resurrection; and these are they that have died before Christ came, in their ignorance, not having salvation declared unto them. And thus the Lord bringeth about the restoration of these; and they have a part in the first resurrection, or have eternal life, being redeemed by the Lord. (Mosiah 15:21–24)

That which Abinadi prophesied came to pass, as Matthew's

record certifies. At least two other things about Abinadi's prophecy are also impressive. First, he spoke as one who had already witnessed Christ's resurrection (in the past tense), even though he was living some seventeen decades *before* it actually happened. As he said, eternal life comes "through Christ, who *has broken* the bands of death" (Mosiah 15:23; emphasis added). Abinadi operated in the "prophetic future"—his witness was sure and certain. True prophecy is history in reverse.

Second, Abinadi delineated who it was that would be privileged to participate in the first resurrection. He mentioned specifically the prophets, the followers of the prophets, and those who kept the commandments—in short, the righteous, the Saints in ancient times who lived in the Old and in the New World. He also briefly mentioned a curious category of individuals who "died before Christ came" but who died "in their ignorance, not having salvation declared unto them" (Mosiah 15:24).

Upon reflection we realize that Abinadi's description is in harmony with a revelation received by the Prophet Joseph Smith wherein he saw the celestial kingdom of God and the inhabitants of that kingdom, including his father, mother, and brother Alvin. The Prophet marveled over how Alvin had obtained such an inheritance when he had died before the restoration of the gospel occurred and therefore had not been baptized for the remission of sins, which is the entryway to the celestial kingdom. The Lord's response to Joseph's wonderment applies not only to those who have died in this dispensation without hearing the fulness of the gospel of Jesus Christ preached, but also to those who died prior to the first coming of Christ without having been able to hear the gospel of Jesus Christ preached. The Prophet recorded:

> Thus came the voice of the Lord unto me, saying: All who have died without a knowledge of this gospel, who would have received it if they had been permitted to tarry, shall be heirs of the celestial kingdom of God;
>
> Also all that shall die henceforth without a knowledge of it, who would have received it with all their hearts, shall be heirs of that kingdom;
>
> For I, the Lord, will judge all men according to their works, according to the desire of their hearts. (D&C 137:7–9)

This is one of the most heartening scriptural texts ever recorded in regard to the infinite mercy and fairness of God. As Alvin Smith's circumstances testify, only a relatively small percentage of our Heavenly Father's children will have the opportunity to hear and understand the fulness of the gospel of Jesus Christ while living in mortality. But each and every individual will be given a fair and equal chance at some point to hear, understand, and embrace the great plan of happiness, according to the word of the Lord revealed through the Prophet Joseph Smith. How different this message is from the false or uninformed beliefs of some others, who either do not know what will become of those who died before hearing the saving truths of Christ's eternal gospel, or who believe that those who died before hearing the message of salvation through Jesus Christ are lost forever.

Doctrine and Covenants 137 is also one of the most important scriptural passages ever revealed in helping us to understand the unique and incomparable competence of Jesus Christ to preside as the ultimate Judge. Only he and the Father know the desires and intents of our individual hearts (D&C 6:16).

Thus, only he and the Father were in a position to determine who could participate in that first resurrection spoken of by Abinadi and reported by Matthew the apostle.

In the end, all judgment has been delegated to Jesus by the Father (John 5:22). For this we can be eternally grateful. After all, Jesus is not a leader who is immune to, or cannot be moved by, our infirmities. Neither is he partial or unfair in his judgment. Rather, he is perfectly empathetic and perfectly fair. He was tempted and tried and made to suffer like us. And because he experienced personally the greatest injustice ever perpetrated on any being in mortality, he desires (and knows how to bring about) perfect justice, fairness, and equity for each of us. Therefore, we may come boldly to him in time of need and find mercy and help sufficient for any problem or challenge we face (Hebrews 4:15–16).

Because only Jesus and his Father can know every extenuating circumstance of our individual lives and therefore render perfectly fair judgment, we mortals *must* refrain from judging unrighteously. I am reminded of my obligation and opportunity to cultivate a charitable attitude toward others when I think of the Lord's carefully orchestrated plan for all of his children, as described by Elder Ezra Taft Benson:

> God, the Father of us all, uses the men of the earth, especially good men, to accomplish his purposes. It has been true in the past, it is true today, it will be true in the future.
>
> "Perhaps the Lord needs such men on the outside of His Church to help it along," said the late Elder Orson F. Whitney of the Quorum of the Twelve. "They are among its auxiliaries, and can do more good for

the cause where the Lord has placed them, than any-where else. . . . Hence, some are drawn into the fold and receive a testimony of the truth; while others remain unconverted . . . the beauties and glories of the gospel being veiled temporarily from their view, for a wise purpose. The Lord will open their eyes in His own due time. God is using more than one people for the accomplishment of His great and marvelous work. The Latter-day Saints cannot do it all. It is too vast, too arduous for any one people. . . . We have no quarrel with the Gentiles. They are our partners in a certain sense" (*Conference Report*, April 1928, p. 59). ("Civic Standards," 59)

Practically speaking, this means that I must not become depressed or irritated if others, especially friends or loved ones, do not join the Church or do not always see things the way I do. There may be a wise purpose in it, and a higher power may be operating. Heavenly Father is in charge, and he will care for his children. He loved them long before I did. My obligation and opportunity is to be tolerant and kind to everyone and to show gratitude for the talents and contributions of others.

## RESURRECTED WITNESSES

The resurrected persons who came forth from their graves after Jesus' resurrection and appeared unto many living in the city of Jerusalem constituted another mighty and unimpeachable assembly of witnesses testifying to the reality of the resurrection of Jesus Christ, as well as to the certainty of a universal resurrection for all humankind. They had just come from the same spirit world where Jesus had sojourned. They had seen him there and witnessed his ministry to the hosts of disembodied spirits. They exulted in his power to open the doors of their prison. They undoubtedly rejoiced when he left the spirit world to take up his physical body again, and they were still rejoicing at the time of their own resurrection and rescue from the bondage of death and the chains of hell. They knew that all they had experienced in terms of redemption was made possible by the resurrection of the Redeemer, the Son of God, the Prince of Life.

To whom these resurrected Saints appeared, and for how long, we do not know. Matthew does not expound upon his brief description, but knowing what we do about the significance of families in the Father's plan, we should not be surprised if we were to learn that these newly resurrected prophets and righteous Saints of ancient Israel appeared to their descendants as well as to those needing a boost to their faith in those troubled times. We can only imagine the shock or even consternation that the "many" people in Jerusalem must have experienced on that day of resurrection as they saw those who had been dead come back to life.

Whether or not these resurrected persons were able to influence others to believe in Jesus as the Messiah, the scriptures do not say. Perhaps. But sacred history teaches us that even the appearance of angels does not always have a lasting effect on people either to convert them or to motivate them to change their ways. It did not do much for two of father Lehi's sons, Laman and Lemuel (1 Nephi 3:29; 17:45).

After these newly resurrected beings finished their visit among Jerusalem's inhabitants, we assume they left this earth and took up residence in the presence of God as described by the Prophet Joseph Smith: "The angels do not reside on a planet like this earth; but they reside in the presence of God, on a globe like a sea of glass and fire, where all things for their glory are manifest, past, present, and future, and are continually before the Lord. The place where God resides is a great Urim and Thummim" (D&C 130:6–8).

Here the term *angel* is to be understood as meaning a resurrected being (Smith, *Teachings of the Prophet Joseph Smith*, 191). These resurrected personages not only had the privilege of dwelling in the Father's presence, but also of being further taught and ministered to by Jesus Christ himself. The Prophet Joseph taught that "Jesus Christ went in body after His resurrection, to minister to resurrected bodies" (*Teachings of the Prophet Joseph Smith*, 191). The only resurrected bodies to minister to were those who had arisen from the grave after the resurrection of the Lord Jesus Christ.

Of these souls who were resurrected after the Lord, Elder Parley P. Pratt wrote: "When Jesus Christ had returned from his mission in the spirit world, had triumphed over the grave, and had reentered his fleshly tabernacle, then the Saints who had obeyed the gospel while in the flesh and had slept in death or finished their sojourn in the spirit world were called forth to reenter their bodies and *to ascend with him to mansions and thrones of eternal power*, while the residue of the spirits remained in the world of spirits to await another call" (*Key to the Science of Theology*, 82; emphasis added).

Nevertheless, the resurrected righteous will not always dwell on a planet apart from this earth. In a future day this earth itself will be sanctified and transformed into a celestial sphere. It too will be taken "back into the presence of God" as a resurrected entity and be "crowned with celestial glory." It will become the permanent abode of those who once dwelled upon it in mortality, and who were subsequently resurrected and inherited the celestial kingdom (Smith, *Teachings of the Prophet Joseph Smith,* 191; D&C 88:16–20; 130:9). This is the ultimate purpose for which this earth was made. The ultimate destiny of the righteous is to inherit the celestial kingdom and dwell on this earth forever—with our loved ones in a state of glory and true happiness.

Although the scriptures are clear that a universal resurrection is guaranteed and that the ancient Saints mentioned in Matthew's Gospel constituted the vanguard of that all-encompassing resurrection, it is not clear how many have been resurrected since the first century. President Ezra Taft Benson, thirteenth president of The Church of Jesus Christ of Latter-day Saints, taught that the idea of a continuous resurrection since the time of the Savior's resurrection "is not scripturally true." He continued:

> But we do know that it is possible for our Father to call from the graves those whom He needs to perform special missions and special service. For example, we know of at least three who have been called up since the resurrection of the Master and since that first mass resurrection when the graves were opened and many of the Saints arose.
>
> Peter and James who came and laid their hands upon the Prophet Joseph and ordained him to the Melchizedek Priesthood were resurrected beings who lived and ministered after the time that the Master was upon the earth. Moroni, who lived and died many years after the time of the resurrection of the Master, was a resurrected being. So we know that there are some that

have been resurrected, and we know that certain promises are made that if the Lord needs the help of certain special messengers they may be called up. We are trying to live so that we will be worthy to come forth in the morning of this resurrection that will come preceding the great millennial period. The righteous will be caught up to meet the Savior as He comes in glory and makes His second appearance to rule and reign here in the earth when the millennial period will begin. (*Teachings of Ezra Taft Benson*, 18)

From President Benson we learn that though some individuals have been resurrected since the Savior's day, there has not been a constant, on-going resurrection of souls up to the present, involving very many of the Lord's righteous followers. The resurrection of the just is yet future and will take place at the second coming of Christ.

## THE CONSPIRACY CONTINUED

As the ramifications of the empty tomb were becoming increasingly clear, and the number of witnesses to the reality of the resurrection continued to grow, a separate minidrama, of sorts, unfolded inside the city and involved the Roman soldiers who had fled their watch at the Garden Tomb earlier that Sunday morning. Matthew, who reports the event, does not tell us where the scene took place, although we imagine the palace of the high priest as a likely setting. Matthew was the only Gospel writer who told of the initial posting of guards at the tomb (Matthew 27:62–66), and he follows up his earlier account by describing the soldiers' report of their experiences at the tomb (Matthew 28:11–15).

At the same time the women set out on their way to spread the good news of the Savior's resurrection, having been commissioned to do so by the risen Lord moments before, the soldiers were in the city seeking out the chief priests to explain what had happened to them. They were unnerved, unwitting witnesses of God's awesome work. It was now useless for them to return to and stand beside an empty tomb.

The chief priests heard the soldiers and then met with the elders of the people to devise a plan that included bribing the soldiers with a large sum of money in return for their commitment to perpetuate a false report. The chief priests instructed the soldiers: "You are to say, 'His disciples came during the night and stole him away while we were asleep.'" The chief priests guaranteed the soldiers that if their report of this whole business got back to the Roman governor, they (the chief priests and Jewish leaders) would satisfy the governor and keep the soldiers out of trouble (Matthew 28:12–14).

Matthew concludes his account of this great deception by adding poignantly: "So they [the soldiers] took the money, and did as they were taught: and this saying is commonly reported among the Jews until this day" (Matthew 28:15). It must have been a huge sum of money offered to the soldiers, or tremendous pressure put on them, or both. Admitting to falling asleep while on guard duty could have serious consequences for them, even resulting in their execution. Even more amazing is the story the soldiers were supposed to uphold. Upon mature reflection, it becomes downright ridiculous. How could the soldiers know the body of Jesus had been stolen by his disciples if they were asleep?

But the chief priests were desperate to make the whole situation surrounding Jesus go away. They had manipulated his trial, railroaded him into a conviction, and then all but forced the Roman governor to administer the death penalty. Now the hapless soldiers appeared before them, subtly bearing testimony that Jesus really was who he said he was and had indeed risen from the dead. Undoubtedly, this unnerved these Jewish leaders. Therefore, they fell back to that course of action which came so naturally to them in dealing with the case of Jesus of Nazareth—manipulation and deception.

Matthew notes that the false story of the soldiers continued to be perpetuated among the Jewish people up to the time that he was writing his Gospel (he uses the phrase "to this day"). Sadly, the story continued to be promulgated long after Matthew's day. "Justin Martyr's Dialogue with Trypho (ch. 108) shows that the same calumny was current in the middle of the second century" (*Interpreter's Bible*, 7:620). In fact, it continued to circulate among certain groups of Jewish people for centuries. The great and learned biographer of Jesus Christ, Frederic Farrar, notes that the false story "continued to be received among them [certain Jewish groups] for centuries, and is one of the . . . follies repeated and amplified twelve centuries afterwards in the *Toldoth Jeshu*," a book discussing Jesus (*Life of Christ*, 644).

Thus, the legacy of the chief priests' original deception may have been to keep generations of good people from coming to a true understanding and knowledge of their Redeemer. The proclamation of the reality of the resurrection and redemption wrought by Jesus was intended for all humankind. A knowledge of this rescue from sin, death, sorrow, and suffering can lift in times of despair, empower in times of weakness, strengthen in times of sorrow. It is saddening to think that even a few might have been kept from this knowledge because of past leaders. It would seem the chief priests of that period have much to answer for. They hurt their own people—the people of Israel.

## ON THE ROAD TO EMMAUS

After his appearances to Mary Magdalene and the other faithful women of the kingdom, Jesus began confirming his living presence to others, including the chief apostle Peter and two male disciples on the road to Emmaus.

"That Jesus did appear to Peter we know; that this appearance came after that to Mary Magdala, and after that to the other women, we also know—thus making it, as we suppose, his third appearance. But we do not know where or under what circumstances he came, or what words of comfort and counsel and direction he gave. In the upper room, with Peter present, the apostolic witness was borne: 'The Lord is risen indeed, and hath appeared to Simon'; and Paul says, 'he was seen of Cephas, then of the twelve' (1 Cor. 15:5)" (McConkie, *Mortal Messiah,* 4:272).

As Elder McConkie indicates, we know nothing about the setting of Peter's encounter with his risen Master (Luke 24:34), but surely it was a time in which the chief apostle's tears (over his denial of knowing Jesus two days earlier) were dried by the only One who could dry them. Peter was healed emotionally. Perhaps the scriptures are silent about this meeting because "it was an event too sacred and personal to be made a matter for public knowledge" (Walker, *Weekend That Changed the World,* 53).

The next two disciples to know of Jesus' resurrection received their witness in a most dramatic fashion. "It [was] the afternoon of the day of his resurrection" (McConkie, *Mortal Messiah,* 4:275). According to Luke, the two had left Jerusalem that Resurrection Sunday on their way to the village of Emmaus. It was after they had been told by the women who were at the sepulchre early that morning that Jesus was risen from the dead. Piecing things together, we know that this was the report that the women disciples had given to Peter and the others after they encountered the angels at the empty tomb but before they were actually visited by the resurrected Lord himself (Luke 24:9–11, 22–24; Matthew 28:9–10). By their own admission, the report of the women had caused the two travelers to Emmaus some genuine astonishment over, but apparently not acceptance of, the idea that Jesus could possibly be alive again (Luke 24:22).

In fact, the tone of the comments of the disciples on the road to Emmaus betrays their feelings of utter disappointment, sadness, and grief. "We trusted that it *had been* he [note the past tense] which should have redeemed Israel," they said. But, "the chief priests and our rulers delivered him . . . and have crucified him" (Luke 24:20–21; emphasis added). In other words, they were saying they had put their trust in Jesus but that trust was destroyed when he was executed. To them Jesus didn't look very messianic when hanging on the cross. The true Messiah, in their minds, was to be full of power to save, yet Jesus was not, or did not appear to be, empowered to do anything to save himself, let alone others. "And beside all this," they added, "today is the third day since these things were done" (Luke 24:21). This was an obvious reference to Jesus' promises that he would rise again on the third day (Matthew 16:21). They were aware of the promise, but it was the third day and they had not seen any evidence of his resurrection, only heard the wishful comments of emotional women.

As the two brethren walked down the road to the village

of Emmaus, which many scholars believe to have been located at or near the modern village of Moza (three and one-half miles northwest of Jerusalem), naturally they could think and speak about only one matter—"all these things which had happened" in Jerusalem the last three days. A stranger approached. It was Jesus, though they did not recognize him because "their eyes were holden that they should not know him" (Luke 24:16).

Several factors may have contributed to the disciples' lack of recognition. First, Jesus withheld his glory from the two disciples, which is something resurrected beings are capable of doing (Smith, *Teachings of the Prophet Joseph Smith*, 325; Pratt, *Key to the Science of Theology*, 70, 72). Second, the disciples were not expecting Jesus to be resurrected, let alone to appear to them personally on a dusty road outside Jerusalem. Third, as most travelers did, Jesus may have covered his head with a cloak to keep off the sun and the dust as he walked along. This would have partially sheltered his face from the disciples' view. Fourth, the disciples may have been so sad or consumed with grief that they didn't much care about the specific identity of who it was that joined them. He was just another Passover pilgrim as far as they were concerned.

In fact, Jesus spoke to the disciples as though he were just another stranger: "What manner of communications are these that ye have one to another as ye walk, and are sad?" (Luke 24:17). This question is evidence that the disciples' gloom was palpable. Speaking for both of them, Cleopas's response betrayed their incredulity and perhaps even irritation: "Art thou only a stranger in Jerusalem, and hast not known the things which are come to pass there in these days?" Jesus simply asked, "What things?" (Luke 24:18–19).

The disciples went on to explain what had transpired the past three days, including the report of the women that very morning about angels and an empty tomb. Apparently, Cleopas and his unnamed traveling companion had not yet heard of Mary Magdalene's personal experience. They walked along, possessed of that special misery born of lack of hope in the redemption of Christ.

In a remarkable response, Jesus chastised the disciples for their lack of belief as well as limited spiritual understanding. "Then he said unto them, O fools, and slow of heart to believe all that the prophets have spoken: Ought not Christ to have suffered these things, and to enter into his glory? And beginning at Moses and all the prophets, he expounded unto them in all the scriptures the things concerning himself. And they drew nigh unto the village, whither they went: and he made as though he would have gone further" (Luke 24:25–28).

The effect of Jesus' teaching on the disciples was profound and may have taken a rather lengthy period of time, perhaps several hours. For as they approached the village, the disciples asked Jesus to stay with them since it was "toward evening, and the day [was] far spent" (Luke 24:29). He accepted their invitation, and as he sat to eat with them—taking the bread, breaking it and blessing it in familiar fashion—the eyes of the disciples were opened, "and they knew him." The veil that had prevented them from recognizing him vanished. The posture of his body, the way the words of the blessing were pronounced, the expression of the face, and, not inconsequentially, the way the hands moved—the hands that still bore the wounds of crucifixion—all contributed to the disciples' epiphany. I can imagine the shock the two disciples experienced when they saw the hands and wrists of their supposed stranger. This was the

Master! At that moment they too came to know for themselves that all that had been said about Jesus' resurrection was absolutely, unequivocally true. And then he vanished from their sight (Luke 24:29–31).

Many are the lessons to be gleaned from the experience of the disciples on the road to Emmaus. First, sadness, when wallowed in, can sometimes prevent even good people from seeing the obvious. Second, like the ancient disciples, when we modern disciples are "slow of heart to believe all that the prophets have spoken," we are fools. Third, Moses and all the prophets in the Old Testament had the witness of the Messiah as their ultimate message. In fact, as Jesus shows us by his method of scriptural explication to the two disciples, the Old Testament truly was and is the human family's first treatment of Jesus Christ. Fourth, just as the Savior used the scriptures to teach of his divinity, so should all of us. Fifth, Jesus used just the right teaching method that fit the circumstances and created the setting which suited his pedagogical purposes. He did not attempt to deceive the disciples, but he did use their lack of recognition to draw out of them the information he needed to best teach them. This serves as an example for all teachers. Sixth, Jesus also kept his identity hidden from the disciples in order to demonstrate the nature of a resurrected body. "Our Lord had a purpose over and above that of interpreting the Messianic word. . . . His mission was to show them what a resurrected person is like" (McConkie, *Mortal Messiah*, 4:277).

Luke concluded his report of the experience of the two disciples in a most significant way, perhaps because he had experienced personally the same kind of confirming witness of Jesus' divinity and resurrection. He helps us to see that *what* Jesus said to the disciples was important, but how they *felt* when he said it was of greater value in affirming their conviction of his godly stature. After Jesus left, "they said one to another, Did not our heart burn within us, while he talked with us by the way, and while he opened to us the scriptures?" (Luke 24:32).

It is worth repeating that the witness of the Holy Ghost is the greatest conviction we may receive. The Holy Ghost operates under the direction of Jesus Christ (John 16:13–14). The Holy Ghost is commissioned to bear witness of the Father and the Son (2 Nephi 31:18). The Holy Ghost causes our hearts to burn within us (3 Nephi 11:3; D&C 9:8). The Holy Ghost is one of the Lord's greatest gifts to his disciples in any age or dispensation, but it is likely one of the most underused gifts we have ever received.

Now possessing a sure witness of the divinity and resurrection of Christ, the disciples could not wait to return to Jerusalem that very hour and add their testimony to others already born. The group they immediately sought out included the apostles who (except for Thomas) had gathered together with other disciples. Undoubtedly, the women who had already played such a significant role in the day's stunning events were there. The two from Emmaus obviously knew that the disciples would be meeting together that evening and also knew the location of the meeting place. When they arrived they found the group discussing the Resurrection, saying that there was no doubt that Jesus had risen from the dead because he had also appeared unto Peter, their leader (Luke 24:34). Cleopas and his companion then added their witness and "told what things were done in the way, and how he [Jesus] was known of them in breaking of bread" (Luke 24:35).

## SUNDAY EVENING'S PRIVATE MEETING

Back together again after an exhausting day (remember, all that we have described to this point happened on the same day), the disciples had sequestered themselves behind closed doors in a secret meeting Easter Sunday night. They feared what the Jewish leaders might do to followers of Jesus in view of the day's happenings (John 20:19). The meeting place is believed to be an upper room, "perhaps the same room, in the home of John Mark, where Jesus and the Twelve celebrated the Feast of the Passover" just three days before (McConkie, *Mortal Messiah*, 4:278).

As the disciples were sitting around during dinner and talking about Jesus' resurrection (Mark 16:14), they may have even speculated about what all of this meant for the future of the Church, the direction of the kingdom of God which Jesus had often spoken of, and the restoration of Israel (Acts 1:6). While engaged in such sacred and significant conversations, "Jesus himself stood in the midst of them, and saith unto them, Peace be unto you" (Luke 24:36). This greeting, *shalom aleikem,* was the traditional Hebrew exchange between close associates and was reported verbatim by both Luke and John (Luke 24:36; John 20:19). It remains an important expression of comradery and welcome among Jewish people today and was given new significance among Jesus' followers by the reality of the Resurrection.

We can well imagine the consternation this sudden appearance of Jesus caused among those in a room whose doors had remained shut the whole time. Luke indicates that even though the Savior offered the traditional and affectionate greeting, some of the disciples (he does not mention which ones) "were terrified and affrighted, and supposed that they had seen a spirit" (Luke 24:37). It is surprising that there was still such fear and lack of faith among some of the disciples, given all that had been reported that day regarding the Savior's resurrection, and all that had actually been seen by others of the company. But apparently there was, for Jesus "upbraided them with their unbelief and hardness of heart, because they believed not them which had seen him after he was risen" (Mark 16:14). Admittedly, even among those who believed in the Resurrection, such a visitation would have caused most, if not all, to be startled. But Luke and Mark are reporting something deeper—a fundamental lack of faith on the part of some disciples. Hence, the Savior's chastisement.

Ever the exemplar, Jesus rebuked their unbelief with sharpness (clarity), in harmony with the pattern he himself revealed in modern revelation (D&C 121:43). And then he proceeded to manifest his mercy, love, and patience to them so that their faith could increase and their knowledge of his resurrection become certain. He spoke to them as a parent might speak to calm the fear of a child and explain the situation that was causing the fear. It has been well said that usually we fear what we do not understand. I think this was true for the unbelieving disciples in the upper room that first Easter Sunday evening. I think we detect this in the Savior's patient and kind explanation as well as his demonstration to those assembled in the room. "And he said unto them, Why are ye troubled? and why do thoughts arise in your hearts? Behold my hands and my feet, that it is I myself: handle me, and see; for a spirit hath not flesh and bones, as ye see me have. And when he had thus spoken, he shewed them his hands and his feet" (Luke 24:38–40).

The Savior's invitation to handle his hands, feet, and side (John 20:20) was undoubtedly aimed at showing the disciples the very real wounds left in his body by the nails and the spear when he hung on the cross. Such tokens of his suffering would not be tangible if he were merely a spirit or a ghostly apparition.

John adds poignantly that after the Savior showed them his hands, his feet, and his side, "then were the disciples glad, when they saw the Lord" (John 20:20). One suspects that the word "glad" is a monumental understatement, but sometimes human language is simply inadequate to describe emotions and feelings of such overwhelming magnitude.

Luke's more detailed narrative of the Sunday evening meeting indicates that some of the disciples still had difficulty believing that Jesus had returned from the dead with his physical body reinvigorated. Luke's comment indicates that the doubters may not have wanted to let themselves believe in the miraculous event lest their joy be dashed once more if it proved to be false: "They yet believed not for joy, and wondered" (Luke 24:41). After all, they had put their trust in Jesus' messianic claims once before (though they misunderstood the nature of his messiahship) and undoubtedly felt betrayed when their Master was executed.

Jesus patiently continued to work with them in order to dispel their persistent disbelief. He asked for food and demonstrated that he was a genuine physical entity with a body capable of eating a piece of broiled fish and some honeycomb. This is extremely instructive to modern disciples, just as it was to the ancients, for we also now know that resurrected bodies think and speak and act and can perform physical functions, like eating (Luke 24:41–43). As Elder Talmage notes, "These unquestionable evidences of their Visitant's corporeity calmed and made rational the minds of the disciples" (*Jesus the Christ*, 688). They were now composed and receptive and could be taught with a quickened understanding as they stood or sat in their Master's presence. They could now comprehend his divinity as never before.

Having demonstrated physically that he was the resurrected Lord, Jesus next reinforced spiritually that he was the promised Messiah. He opened the scriptures to their understanding as he had done previously and refreshed their memories of past promises and teachings: "Thus it is written, and thus it behoved Christ to suffer, and to rise from the dead the third day" (Luke 24:46). He then reviewed the plan of salvation, emphasizing that his redeeming mission, his atonement, and his resurrection meant "that repentance and remission of sins should be preached in his name among all nations, beginning at Jerusalem" (Luke 24:47). Finally, the Savior reiterated to the disciples, especially the apostles, that they bore a special responsibility: "And ye are witnesses of these things" (Luke 24:48).

Though Jesus himself had said during his mortal ministry that he was not sent to any group except the house of Israel (Matthew 15:24), the risen Lord now foreshadowed a world-wide missionary effort. The twin messages of salvation and resurrection in Christ were to go to "all nations" not just to the Jewish people. They were to be carried forth by the witnesses who were in that upper room that Sunday night. They were to begin in Jerusalem and spread out to the world. The messages were to be sealed by the testimonies of the disciples. No plainer or more exciting directive was ever given by anyone. The missionary thrust of the Lord's Church was affirmed. That same directive has been reconfirmed in our day. For many Latter-day

Saints, missionary labors are among the most rewarding experiences they have ever had.

Surely, there has never been a more patient, kind, consistent, or pedagogically sound teacher than Jesus. He was and is the perfect teacher and modeled the teaching techniques and attributes that all of us should strive to adopt; attributes that, if practiced, would bless our own family and friends immeasurably. In fact, I believe that if each of us were to try to practice the characteristics and techniques of the Master Teacher—cognitive, affective, and motor skill instruction—the progress of our students would be phenomenal. Jesus expanded the mind as well as the heart. He taught by precept as well as by example. He asked his students to think as well as to feel. He required the use of all the five human senses in the learning process.

Once *all* the disciples that Sunday night came to the realization that what they were seeing was real—that Jesus really had overcome death, that he truly was resurrected, that he was Israel's Messiah, who possessed genuine power over life and death—the Savior then repeated again the traditional greeting of welcome and blessing that he had uttered before, as if he were greeting them afresh, welcoming them into an entirely new way of thinking, a new circle of association, and a new realm of discipleship. *Shalom aleikhem*—"Peace be unto you: as my Father hath sent me, even so send I you" (John 20:21). This latter commission applied especially to the apostles in the room.

All of the disciples who had assembled that night in secret, behind closed doors, were now different, changed forevermore. They knew for certain of the fulfillment of promises made in Israel's distant past. They were all eyewitnesses of the resurrection of Jesus the Messiah. Eleven of them, however, would bear an extra burden as "special witnesses of the name of Christ in all the world" (D&C 107:23). A twelfth would soon be named to fill the vacancy left by Judas's betrayal and subsequent death.

The qualifications necessary for Judas's replacement were outlined a short time later by Luke when the eleven apostles met to fill the vacancy. Luke reported these qualifications and requirements in the sequel to his Gospel record, the Acts of the Apostles: "Wherefore of these men which have companied with us all the time that the Lord Jesus went in and out among us, Beginning from the baptism of John, unto that same day that he was taken up from us, must one be ordained to be a witness with us of his resurrection. And they appointed two, Joseph called Barsabas, who was surnamed Justus, and Matthias" (Acts 1:21–23). Luke is telling us that two men were found to possess the necessary basic qualifications and that one of whom would actually be called and ordained. The two men were chosen as candidates because they also had been with the Twelve from the beginning. Thus, I believe both Matthias and Barsabas Justus were in the upper room with the apostles and other disciples on the night of Jesus' resurrection.

## A FITTING END TO RESURRECTION SUNDAY

The last thing Jesus did that Sunday night of which we have record was the bestowing of the gift of the Holy Ghost. Whether he performed the ordinance for all those assembled or just the apostles, we do not know explicitly, though I am inclined to believe it was only the apostles. John's record is ambiguous on this point and, in fact, the language he uses to describe the circumstances could be misunderstood if we did not know he was using a play on words. John records: "And when he had said this, he breathed on them, and saith unto them, Receive ye the Holy Ghost" (John 20:22). In Hebrew and in Aramaic, which

Jesus spoke, the word for "breath" is the same as the word for "spirit," as in the phrase "Holy Spirit." Thus, John was saying that Jesus used his holy breath (spirit) to give the Holy Spirit, or Holy Ghost.

It is clear from Luke's record of the postresurrection Church (the Acts of the Apostles) that the apostles began to possess the actual power of the Holy Ghost only on the day of Pentecost and afterward (Acts 2). What then did Jesus give to the apostles that Sunday evening? Elder Bruce R. McConkie helps us to understand that the realization of blessings or promises associated with an ordinance may not come until an appreciable amount of time has elapsed after the performance of the ordinance:

> From the time of John to this hour when the resurrected Lord stood before his apostolic witnesses, the only legally performed baptisms had been in water, with the promise in each instance of a future baptism of fire. Now the time was at hand to perform the ordinance which would entitle the saints to receive the baptism of fire. And so Jesus "breathed on them," which probably means that he laid his hands upon them as he uttered the decree: "Receive the Holy Ghost."
>
> They thus *received*, but did not at that moment actually *enjoy*, the gift of the Holy Ghost. . . . This gift offers certain blessings provided there is full compliance with the law involved; everyone upon whom the gift is bestowed does not in fact enjoy or possess the offered gift. In the case of the apostles the actual enjoyment of the gift was delayed until the day of Pentecost (Acts 2). . . .

The saints in this day go through the ordinance of the laying on of hands which gives them the gift, which by definition is the right to receive the companionship of the Spirit. *If and when they are worthy,* they are then immersed in the Spirit, as it were, thus actually enjoying the gift. (*Doctrinal New Testament Commentary,* 1:856–57; emphasis added)

The enjoyment of promises and blessings associated with any ordinance are always predicated on worthiness as well as the Lord's timetable. Individuals may participate in an ordinance but not have the terms and conditions of the ordinance become effective until they are worthy.

The ratification of any ordinance, and thus the realization of its associated promises and blessings, comes through the Holy Spirit of Promise (D&C 132:7). He knows when we are worthy and capable of enjoying those blessings and promises. This is for our protection and benefit. It is a great burden to be held accountable for knowledge and power and blessings that we are not ready or able to handle appropriately. The Holy Ghost also knows the Lord's timetable. He helps to implement it. And so even though the disciples participated in the ordinance of the gift of the Holy Ghost that Easter Sunday night, they did not enjoy the full blessings until the day of Pentecost, fifty days after Passover.

To his servants gathered in the upper room the Sunday night of his resurrection, Jesus also promised the power to remit people's sins or to retain them: "Whose soever sins ye remit, they are remitted unto them; and whose soever sins ye retain, they are retained" (John 20:23).

In a sense, that is implicit in the gospel plan. Remission

of sins comes through the principles and ordinances that the apostles, seventies, and elders teach and implement throughout the world. "Thus the legal administrators who preach the gospel have power to remit the sins of men in the waters of baptism, and they have power to retain the sins of those who do not repent and are not baptized for the remission of sins" (McConkie, *Mortal Messiah*, 4:283). There is another sense in which the early Church leaders would possess the power to remit or retain sins. The Twelve, as prophets, seers, and revelators, had the power to direct the Lord's Church. They held the keys of the kingdom of heaven to bind on earth and in heaven and to seal or unseal on earth and in heaven (Matthew 16:19). This is true for our present dispensation as well.

## LEAVING THE DISCIPLES

Having confirmed the reality of his literal resurrection and born witness that he was the fulfilment of the promises in the scriptures, Jesus left the disciples for a time, undoubtedly to ponder what they each had experienced. So very much had happened during that first Easter Sunday, not the least of which was the turning of doubt and fear into certainty and joy. Even those among the disciples who had resisted believing in the literal resurrection were healed of their spiritual malady by the power of pure knowledge and revelation.

Modern disciples must resist the temptation to judge these ancient followers of Christ too harshly. They had to deal with events and circumstances that were completely beyond their (or anyone else's) realm of experience. Jesus' crucifixion was so horrible and these disciples had been hurt so badly (spiritually, emotionally, and psychologically) over Jesus' execution after they had sacrificed so much for his cause that we ought to marvel at the strength and courage they demonstrated. Many of us can scarcely fathom the challenges they faced. Jerusalem was a volatile place, and they were putting themselves at risk by simply continuing to meet together as followers of Jesus. But they came through it all right and in just a few weeks' time became the greatest force for good, as well as for change, the world has ever known.

---

The former treatise have I made, O Theophilus, of all that Jesus began both to do and teach,

Until the day in which he was taken up, after that he through the Holy Ghost had given commandments unto the apostles whom he had chosen:

To whom also he shewed himself alive after his passion by many infallible proofs, being seen of them forty days, and speaking of the things pertaining to the kingdom of God.

ACTS 1:1–3

---

# CHAPTER 7

# Beginning His Forty-Day Ministry

Witnesses of the resurrection of Jesus Christ grew in number and certitude immediately following Resurrection Sunday as Jesus returned on several occasions to instruct his special witnesses and friends whom he had commissioned to lead the Church after his ascension. It is the period known in ecclesiastical history as the forty-day ministry. As Luke testified, Jesus "shewed himself alive [to the apostles] after his passion by many infallible proofs, being seen of them *forty days,* and speaking of the things pertaining to the kingdom of God (Acts 1:3; emphasis added).

## "DOUBTING" THOMAS

Among the first to whom Jesus appeared after his initial visits of Resurrection Sunday was the apostle Thomas. This important leader was completely absent during all of Jesus' appearances to his disciples on that most important Sunday. Scripture does not tell us why or where he was, only that he "was not with them when Jesus came" (John 20:24).

Thomas was one of the original Twelve. His name in

Hebrew and Aramaic means "twin" and thus is translated by the Greek *Didymus* ("twin") in John 11:16. Little is recorded of Thomas in the Gospels, though John's record tells us more about his personality than that of some of the other apostles. One tradition holds that he was the twin brother of Matthew. Another says Thomas was the twin of James. We do not know for sure. Thomas's name appears in all the lists of the Twelve in the synoptic Gospels (Matthew 10:3; Mark 3:18; Luke 6:15; compare Acts 1:13). The episode for which he is best known and the one which has encumbered him with his lasting moniker, "Doubting Thomas," stems from his absence from the Quorum of the Twelve Apostles on Resurrection Sunday and his subsequent attitude toward reports of Jesus' resurrection.

Only John recounts the story of Thomas's revelatory experience. When he got back with his brethren, the other apostles informed Thomas that they had seen the Lord—alive! "But he said unto them, Except I shall see in his hands the print of the nails, and put my finger into the print of the nails, and thrust my hand into his side, I will not believe" (John 20:25).

It is truly unfortunate that the only thing most people associate with Thomas is doubt. Though he was skeptical, it should also be remembered that he was extremely brave and possessed a noble character, if somewhat tinged with pessimism. Earlier, during Jesus' mortal ministry, when the Savior announced his intention of going to Bethany of Judea to visit the home of Lazarus, Thomas brushed aside the protests of the other disciples who warned that Jesus' life was in danger there (though they may have been more worried about their own vulnerability than anything else). Thomas answered his associates, "Let us also go, that we may die with him" (John 11:16). Even if Thomas was looking for the worst in this situation, he had good reason. Jewish leaders in Jerusalem really were plotting to kill Jesus, and Bethany was right next door to the capital city.

It is no wonder that Thomas was pessimistic. He seems to have realized early that Jesus was headed for disaster in Judea when not everyone understood the full gravity of the circumstances. The others might have believed that Jewish leaders would *try* to harm their Master, but it seems unlikely to me that very many actually believed their Messiah could be mortally wounded. In fact, President Wilford Woodruff confirmed this lack of understanding on the part of most of the ancient apostles when he said: "I remember very well the last charge that Joseph [Smith] gave to the Apostles. We had as little idea that he was going from us as the Apostles of the Savior did that He was going to be taken from them. Joseph talked with us as plainly as did the Savior to His Apostles, but we did not understand that he was about to depart from us any more than the Apostles understood the Savior" (*Collected Discourses*, 188).

Thomas's realism, and also his strength of character, showed through during the incident with Lazarus when he stood by the wishes of his Master and told the others they should too, even if it meant dying with Jesus. Of course, it is also fair to say that Thomas himself did not fully understand all that Jesus was really saying when he spoke of his redemptive mission. John records an episode where Jesus used Thomas's lack of understanding to teach a valuable lesson:

> And if I go and prepare a place for you, I will come again, and receive you unto myself; that where I am, there you may be also.
>
> And wither I go ye know, and the way ye know.

Thomas saith unto him, Lord, we know not wither thou goest; and how can we know the way?

Jesus saith unto him, I am the way, the truth, and the life; no man cometh unto the Father, but by me.

If ye had known me, ye should have known my Father also: and from henceforth ye know him, and have seen him. (John 14:3–7)

Therefore, it seems understandable to me that when Jesus' resurrection did occur, Thomas had trouble accepting the word of his colleagues. He himself did not comprehend the true nature and power of Jesus' messiahship. He was also a realist, perhaps a pessimist, but that is what recent experience had taught him. The Savior's crucifixion had confirmed his suspicions and, perhaps more significantly, hurt him deeply. Thomas's bluntly stated personal requirement of needing to feel the nail wounds and the spear wound shows just how well he knew what had happened on the cross and just how painfully and exquisitely the image of his dead Master had been imprinted on his soul. It was not that he mistrusted the testimony of his associates, exactly, but rather that he was dubious about their interpretation of "resurrection" their insistence on "the literal and corporeal nature of it" (McConkie, *Doctrinal New Testament Commentary*, 1:860). After all, he knew without a doubt that Jesus had died a horrible death, and he could see no tangible sign of the establishment of a great and powerful (politically and militarily speaking) messianic kingdom that was to accompany an era of resurrection.

Exactly a week after the Resurrection, the apostles were met together again with Thomas in attendance. It was Sunday, the new Sabbath commemorating the Resurrection, and the doors were again shut. Just as he had done before, Jesus came through solid element, stood in the midst of them, and reiterated the greeting of warmth and affection: *Shalom aleikhem*—"Peace be unto you" (John 20:26).

It is obvious that the Savior knew of the earlier exchange between Thomas and his colleagues in the Quorum of the Twelve Apostles. For after greeting all of them, he immediately singled out Thomas and presented the proof that left no doubt. "Then saith he to Thomas, Reach hither thy finger, and behold my hands; and reach hither thy hand, and thrust it into my side: and be not faithless, but believing" (John 20:27).

Many, if not most, students of the New Testament have pondered the power and profundity of this moment in time. It is, in my view, captured perfectly by John's brief but poignant report: "Thomas answered and said unto him, My Lord and my God" (John 20:28). Thomas now knew for himself that Jesus was the promised Messiah; that Jesus was literally, physically alive again with a body of flesh and bone. All doubt, fear, hurt, and pessimism were swept away. Nonbiblical texts affirm that once Thomas was given the sure witness he said he required, his loyalty and dedication were beyond question. He became a stalwart in the kingdom.

Some may wonder how it is that on the one hand the Lord and his prophets have so often roundly denounced sign-seeking individuals and generations (Matthew 12:39; Jacob 7:13–20; Alma 30:48–60) but on the other have sanctioned the giving of a sign to Thomas when he clearly sought it. Perhaps some resolution of this seeming contradiction is to be found in the word of the Lord as given through the Prophet Joseph Smith. He declared that signs will follow faith: those who possess basic faith, or even a desire to believe, will be rewarded (D&C 63:7–11; Moroni 10:4–5; Alma 32:27). Thomas's faith may have been weakened after Jesus' crucifixion, but he did not lose it. One suspects that he strongly desired to believe in the Resurrection all along, even if he was overcome by skepticism for a time. In the end, he was rewarded for his previous, as well as his continuing, commitment to the Church in the face of great difficulty and grave danger. This, after all, is the essence of faith—doing what we *believe* is right in the face of challenges, walking to the edge of the light and then taking one more step, trusting God that the light will move with us.

How like Thomas are many of us at one time or another in our lives. Overcoming doubt is part of the test of our mortal probation. In fact, I dare say that very few come to the position of authentic assurance without first serving an apprenticeship in uncertainty. God wants to be our mentor and tutor, and he loves to see our change and rebirth. He delights in rewarding our faith. He "delight[s] to honor those who serve [him] in righteousness. . . . Great shall be their reward and eternal shall be their glory" (D&C 76:5–6).

The promised reward for faith is, in fact, the principle underlying Jesus' parting instruction to Thomas and the other apostles that Sunday Sabbath one week after his resurrection. Our faith will be greatly rewarded. In truth, righteous action based on faith is of greater value in the Lord's eyes than righteous action based on knowledge. "Jesus saith unto him, Thomas, because thou hast seen me, thou hast believed: blessed are they that have not seen, and yet have believed" (John 20:29).

## The Law of Restoration

A singular and significant aspect of the doctrine of resurrection concerns the nature of the bodies with which we will all arise. Though Jesus came forth from the grave still possessing the wounds of his crucifixion and showed them to Thomas and the others, he is unique in this regard. All others will come forth having had their wounds, scars, imperfections, and deformities taken away. About one hundred years *before* Jesus arose from the dead, the prophet Alma testified that there would be no physical deformities in the resurrection: "The soul shall be restored to the body, and the body to the soul; yea, and every limb and joint shall be restored to its body; yea, even a hair of the head shall not be lost; but all things shall be restored to their proper and perfect frame" (Alma 40:23).

The perfect nature of our physical bodies in the resurrection is part of the sweeping law of restoration. Yet, the nature of our spirits, the very core of our beings, will not instantly and automatically conform to the nature of our bodies, will not become pure and perfect just because we have passed beyond this mortal sphere. If we have not repented and desired to change while in this life, the "same spirit which doth possess [our] bodies at the time that [we] go out of this life, that same spirit will have power to possess [our] body in that eternal world" (Alma 34:34). This too is part of the grand law of restoration. "When a person rises in the resurrection, his body will be perfect but that does not mean that he will be perfect in faith. There will be different kinds of bodies in the resurrection—celestial, terrestrial, and telestial—and they will not be alike. . . . Every man will receive according to his works" (Smith, *Doctrines of Salvation*, 2:292).

The Book of Mormon is our greatest testament of the doctrine of the resurrection and the restoration that it brings about. The prophets of the Book of Mormon generally speak of three types of restoration that the resurrection is responsible for: the restoration of the spirit to the physical body; the restoration of all people to the presence of God to be judged; and the restoration of our individual memories. Nothing can compare to the power of the resurrection and the changes enacted by it, and nobody summarizes this truth better than Amulek:

> Behold, the day cometh that all shall rise from the dead and stand before God, and be judged according to their works.
>
> Now, there is a death which is called a temporal death; and the death of Christ shall loose the bands of this temporal death, that all shall be raised from this temporal death.
>
> The spirit and the body shall be reunited again in its perfect form; both limb and joint shall be restored to its proper frame, even as we now are at this time; and we shall be brought to stand before God, knowing even as we know now, and have a bright recollection of all our guilt.
>
> Now, this restoration shall come to all, both old and young, both bond and free, both male and female, both the wicked and the righteous; and even there shall not so much as a hair of their heads be lost; but every thing shall be restored to its perfect frame, as it is now, or in the body, and shall be brought and be arraigned before the bar of Christ the Son, and God the Father, and the Holy Spirit, which is one Eternal God, to be judged according to their works, whether they be good or whether they be evil.
>
> Now, behold, I have spoken unto you concerning the death of the mortal body, and also concerning the resurrection of the mortal body. I say unto you that this mortal body is raised to an immortal body, that is from

death, even from the first death unto life, that they can die no more; their spirits uniting with their bodies, never to be divided; thus the whole becoming spiritual and immortal, that they can no more see corruption. (Alma 11:41–45)

Similarly, President Joseph Fielding Smith, a modern prophet, left no doubt that one of the greatest blessings accruing to us as a free gift resulting from the Savior's redemption is a restored body—a body without deformities—in the resurrection: "When we come forth from the dead, our spirits and bodies will be reunited inseparably, never again to be divided, and they will then be assigned to the kingdom to which they belong. All deformities and imperfections will be removed, and the body will conform to the likeness of the spirit" (*Doctrines of Salvation,* 2:289).

Nowhere is the Savior's mercy and grace shown more forcefully than in the doctrine of resurrection. Through the infinite power of Christ's atonement and resurrection, every man, woman, and child will come forth from the grave at the time of their appointed resurrection and be instantly healed of any physical defects they may have struggled with in mortality. President Joseph Fielding Smith also stated:

> Bodies will come up, of course, as they were laid down, but will be restored to their proper, perfect frame immediately. Old people will not look old when they come forth from the grave. Scars will be removed. No one will be bent or wrinkled. . . . Each body will come forth with its perfect frame. If there has been some deformity or physical impairment in this life, it will be removed.

The Lord is not impotent to heal and restore the dead to their perfect frame in the resurrection. If the Savior could restore withered hands, eyes that had never had sight, crooked bodies, in this mortal life, surely the Father will not permit bodies that are not physically perfect to come forth in the resurrection. (*Doctrines of Salvation*, 2:292–93)

Over the years I have had the privilege of teaching a student or two who shared with me their witness of the truth of President Smith's teachings. They have seen, in a dream or vision or by personal revelation, a relative who had lost an arm or leg in mortality or who faced some other physical challenge, stand healed and whole in the resurrection—without any physical deformities. These have been profound tutorials for me, the supposed professor. I quote from an essay written by one of these students:

In or about 1967 my uncle lost his right arm (at the shoulder) in a farming accident. I have no memory of him with his arm. My earliest memory of him was the first time I saw him after the accident.

Years later (1979), one of my aunts died. During her funeral I was sitting in front of my mother, who was seated on my uncle's right side. At some point in the meeting I turned to check on my mother. I could not believe what I saw. At first I wondered what was wrong with what I saw. When I figured it out, I turned again to double-check what I was experiencing. I saw my uncle's right arm around my mother, with his hand wrapped around her right shoulder. This "vision" continued through the entire funeral service. When I told my mother about this experience, she replied that if he had had his arm, that is exactly where it would have been. . . .

Because of this experience I *know* that the body parts will be restored and that deformities will be fixed. I know that our spirits are in perfect form and that is what our bodies will be perfected to when that transition is made.

## THE SAVIOR'S WOUNDS

What is true for all humankind concerning wounds was not true for the Savior, and thus in this respect "we must not judge the resurrection of others by the resurrection of Jesus Christ" (Smith, *Doctrines of Salvation*, 2:290). Jesus retained the wounds of his crucifixion so he could identify himself to others in the meridian dispensation with absolute clarity. Thus, Thomas saw and felt those wounds.

Likewise, at his second coming, when Jesus comes to his own people, the Jews, who are still on the earth at a time of unparalleled distress, he will show to all assembled the wounds in his hands and feet, and they will know that he has always been their Messiah as well as their King. He declared: "And then shall the Jews look upon me and say: What are these wounds in thine hands and in thy feet? Then shall they know that I am the Lord; for I will say unto them: These wounds are the wounds with which I was wounded in the house of my friends. I am he who was lifted up. I am Jesus that was crucified. I am the Son of God. And then shall they weep because of their iniquities; then shall they lament because they persecuted their king" (D&C 45:51–53). This same prophecy was also given to the Old Testament prophet Zechariah (Zechariah 12:9–14; 13:1–9; 14:1–21).

Here again we see that Jesus "doeth not anything save it be for the benefit of the world" (2 Nephi 26:24). Elder Jeffrey R. Holland poignantly reminds us that "Jesus has chosen, even in a resurrected, otherwise perfected body, to retain *for the benefit of His disciples* the wounds in His hands and in His feet and in His side. . . . These wounds are the principal way we are to recognize Him when He comes" ("*Therefore, What?*" 9; emphasis added). Elder Holland reminds us that these wounds are reminders that painful things happen to even the pure and the perfect in mortality. Paradoxically, he who yet bears the scars and lesions of obedience and sacrifice will heal us of our pains and wounds!

## CHILDREN AND THE RESURRECTION

In his writings and teachings, President Joseph Fielding Smith clarified a misunderstanding about the Resurrection that derived from a sermon given by his father, President Joseph F. Smith, sixth president of The Church of Jesus Christ of Latter-day Saints. The latter, when speaking at the funeral sermon of Sister Rachel Grant, said that she would be resurrected in the same form and likeness as she was laid to rest, "even to the wounds in the flesh. Not that a person will always be marred by scars, wounds, deformities, defects or infirmities, for these will be removed in their course, in their proper time, according to the merciful providence of God" (*Gospel Doctrine*, 23).

President Joseph Fielding Smith said of his father's statement:

> While he expresses the thought that *the body will come forth as it was laid down*, he also expresses the thought that it will take time to adjust the body from the condition of imperfections. This, of course, is reasonable,

164

but at the same time the length of time to make these adjustments will not cover an appreciable extent of time.

President Smith never intended to convey the thought that it would require weeks or months of time in order for the defects to be removed. These changes will come naturally, of course, but almost instantly. We cannot look upon it in any other way. For instance, a man who has lost a leg in childhood will have his leg restored. *It does not grow in the grave,* but will be restored naturally, but with the power of the Almighty it will not take extended time for this to be accomplished. (*Doctrines of Salvation,* 2:293–94; emphasis added)

While it is clear that there is no physical growth while our bodies are in the grave, by the same token there is a profound implication of this principle that has to do with children who pass on. Truly, it is one of the most sublime and comforting doctrines ever revealed. Children who have died will be resurrected and come forth as children, without defect or deformity, and their parents will have the privilege of raising them to adulthood. President Joseph F. Smith is one of our most reliable sources on this point. He said:

Joseph Smith taught the doctrine that the infant child that was laid away in death would come up in the resurrection as a child; and, pointing to the mother of a lifeless child, he said to her: "You will have the joy, the pleasure, and satisfaction of nurturing this child, after its resurrection, until it reaches the full stature of its spirit." There is restitution, there is growth, there is development, after the resurrection from death. I love this truth. It speaks volumes of happiness, of joy and gratitude to my soul. Thank the Lord he has revealed these principles to us. . . .

One day I was conversing with a brother-in-law of mine, Lorin Walker, who married my oldest sister. In the course of the conversation he happened to mention that he was present at the funeral of my cousin Sophronia, and that he heard the Prophet Joseph Smith declare the very words that Aunt Agnes had told me.

I said to him, "Lorin, what did the Prophet say?" and he repeated, as nearly as he could remember, what the Prophet Joseph said in relation to little children. The body remains undeveloped in the grave, but the spirit returns to God who gave it. Afterwards, in the resurrection, the spirit and body will be reunited; the body will develop and grow to the full stature of the spirit; and the resurrected soul will go on to perfection. So I had the statement of two witnesses who heard this doctrine announced by the Prophet Joseph Smith, the source of intelligence. (*Gospel Doctrine*, 455–56)

If such a doctrine could be heralded from the rooftops, it would bring amazing relief and soul-satisfying comfort to the many parents who have lost little ones. It is one of the most significant manifestations of God's love, Christ's infinite redeeming power, and the fairness of the law of justice, which guarantees recompense for the unfair circumstances of mortality. In the case of my own family, it serves as a motivation to all of us to live worthy of the company of a little girl, a sister who lived only three days before succumbing to the effects of a congenital heart defect. I am sure it was a source of great sadness to my parents. But by the power of the atonement and resurrection of

Jesus Christ, this little daughter and sister has already received a guarantee of exaltation. She has, in effect, inherited exaltation, though the full realization of all that means lies in the future. She will be resurrected as an infant for my parents to rear to adulthood. No price can be put on that kind of knowledge, which brings such comfort. No price will be able to be put on the feelings of gratitude and fulfillment that will be ours as we enjoy the company of our loved ones in the resurrection.

Years ago, as a full-time missionary, I had the privilege of teaching the doctrines of the Atonement and the exaltation of little children to a young couple who had unexpectedly lost an infant to an unknown cause of death. To this day, I vividly remember watching their great sorrow turn to exquisite joy as they came to know the truth—that their little one did not need baptism before death, did not need last rites, was not lost, but was an exalted being who was waiting for them on the other side of the veil. That was a profound experience for me. I still look back on it with some wonder.

I treasure the words of Elder Bruce R. McConkie, who summarizes the doctrine of salvation for little children and conveys my own deep feelings on this point:

> Among all the glorious gospel verities given of God to his people there is scarcely a doctrine so sweet, so soul satisfying, and so soul sanctifying, as the one which proclaims—Little children shall be saved. They are alive in Christ and shall have eternal life. For them the family unit will continue, and the fulness of exaltation is theirs. No blessing shall be withheld. They shall rise in immortal glory, grow to full maturity, and live forever in the highest heaven of the celestial kingdom—all through

the merits and mercy and grace of the Holy Messiah, all because of the atoning sacrifice of Him who died that we might live. ("Salvation of Little Children," 3)

Little children who die before the age of accountability receive exaltation. They will not be tested in paradise, during the Millennium, or after the Millennium has concluded. They are not subject to any "if" clauses (that is, they will receive exaltation if . . . ) or further probation. Said Elder Bruce R. McConkie:

> Would the Lord test someone who cannot fail the test and whose exaltation is guaranteed? For that matter, all those billions of people who will be born during the millennium, when Satan is bound, "shall grow up without sin unto salvation" (D&C 45:58) and therefore will not be tested.

> Satan cannot tempt little children in this life, nor in the spirit world, nor after their resurrection. Little children who die before reaching the years of accountability will not be tempted (*Doctrines of Salvation*, 2:56–57). Such is the emphatic language of President Joseph Fielding Smith. ("Salvation of Little Children," 6)

In a general conference talk some years ago, President Thomas S. Monson recounted the touching story of Thomas and Sarah Hilton, who went to Samoa in 1892 to preside over the mission there. They took with them a baby daughter and were blessed by the birth of two sons while they served. Then tragedy struck. Within three years' time, all their children died, and in 1895 the Hiltons returned from their mission childless. One can hardly imagine a more sorrowful circumstance. Yet, there was faith in the midst of profound trials.

Elder David O. McKay of the Quorum of the Twelve was a friend of the family and deeply touched by their tragic loss. In 1921, as part of a world tour of the Church, he stopped in Samoa and, owing to a prior promise to the now-widowed Sister Hilton, personally visited the graves of the Hilton children. He wrote home to Sister Hilton:

Dear Sister Hilton:

Just as the descending rays of the late afternoon sun touched the tops of the tall coconut trees, Wednesday, May 18th, 1921, a party of five stood with bowed heads in front of the little Fagali'i Cemetery. . . . We were there, as you will remember, in response to a promise I made you before I left home.

The graves and headstones are in a good state of preservation. . . . I reproduce here a copy I made as I stood . . . outside the stone wall surrounding the spot.

*Janette Hilton*
Bn: Sept. 10, 1891
Died: June 4, 1892
"Rest, darling Jennie"

*George Emmett Hilton*
Bn: Oct. 12, 1894
Died: Oct. 19, 1894
"Peaceful be thy slumber"

*Thomas Harold Hilton*
Bn: Sept. 21, 1892
Died: March 17, 1894
"Rest on the hillside, rest"

As I looked at those three little graves, I tried to imagine the scenes through which you passed during your young motherhood here in old Samoa. As I did so, the little headstones became monuments not only to the little babies sleeping beneath them, but also to a mother's faith and devotion to the eternal principles of truth and life. Your three little ones, Sister Hilton, in silence most eloquent and effective, have continued to carry on your noble missionary work begun nearly 30 years ago, and they will continue as long as there are gentle hands to care for their last earthly resting place.

> *By loving hands their dying eyes were closed;*
> *By loving hands their little limbs composed;*
> *By foreign hands their humble graves adorned;*
> *By strangers honored, and by strangers mourned.*

Tofa Soifua,

David O. McKay

President Thomas S. Monson commented: "This touching account conveys to the grieving heart 'the peace . . . which passeth all understanding'" (*Ensign*, May 1998, 54).

Indeed, tragedy sometimes strikes in the midst of faithful service and sacrifice. But we may rest assured that no pain we are called to pass through will be endured alone. Often family or friends are there to support us, and in truth, the Savior will never forget us. More important, little children who die are not lost. The Savior's atonement guarantees that they will be exalted and so will their parents who endure their temporary loss in patience and faith.

The same principles of resurrection and exaltation that apply to little children who die before the age of accountability also apply to those who are mentally handicapped or developmentally challenged in mortality. They are raised to the status and stature of gods in the eternities. Said Elder Bruce R. McConkie:

> They never arrive at the years of accountability and are considered as though they were little children. If because of some physical deficiency, or for some other reason unknown to us, they never mature in the spiritual and moral sense, then they never become accountable for sins. They need no baptism; they are alive in Christ; and they will receive, inherit, and possess in eternity on the same basis as do all children.
>
> After revealing that little children are redeemed from the foundation of the world through the atoning sacrifice of Him who died to save us all, and after specifying that Satan has no power to tempt little children until they begin to become accountable, the Lord applied the same principles to those who are mentally deficient: "And, again, I say unto you, that whoso having knowledge, have I not commanded to repent? And he that hath no understanding, it remaineth in me to do according as it is written" (D&C 29:49–50). ("Salvation of Little Children," 6–7)

Nowhere is the meaning and message of Easter so clearly evident. Nowhere does it ring so triumphant as when we contemplate the Savior's power to bring about the resurrection and exaltation of little children. I am personally moved to tears when I realize that this aspect of the resurrection is only one dimension of the greatness of Jesus of Nazareth, the Messiah. What a different perspective we are given when we begin to understand more fully the Father's eternal plan, his mercy and goodness, and the incomparable power of the Son's atonement. Indeed, I am persuaded that we may have gotten some things backwards. Instead of feeling sorry for those who struggle with developmental disabilities, maybe we ought to feel bad that we weren't more valiant in our premortal life and thereby worthy of the same immediate guarantee of exaltation that is given to little children and individuals with developmental challenges.

## AT THE SEA OF TIBERIAS

After a time, the apostolic witnesses of Jesus' resurrection left Jerusalem and went back to their homeland, the Galilee region in the north. They returned there because, by prior arrangement, they had an appointment to keep with Jesus, who said he would appear to them in Galilee (Matthew 28:10). Perhaps in waiting for this visit, or feeling frustrated over not knowing exactly what to do next, Peter announced to his associates that he was going fishing (John 21:3).

It is not hard to understand Peter's actions. He probably felt adrift. For three years he had followed Jesus, relied on him for instruction, and depended on him for spiritual nourishment and direction. Now Jesus was gone and with him, so was Peter's personal anchor. He understandably felt he needed further instruction and wasn't getting it. He therefore returned to the one thing he knew to do, the one thing that would at least provide for the temporal and physical needs of the group, the one sure thing in his life after so much of his world had been turned upside down.

With Peter at that time were six of the eleven apostles: James and John (the sons of Zebedee), Thomas and Nathanael, and two unnamed individuals—perhaps Andrew and Philip "since those two had been engaged with Peter and the others in like ventures in earlier days" (McConkie, *Mortal Messiah*, 4:288). These all said to Peter, "We also go with thee," and immediately they entered the ship (John 21:3).

Luke and Mark confirm the basic accuracy of John's account. Fishing on the Sea of Galilee was a well-organized enterprise among the families represented by the apostles who were with Peter. Peter and Andrew, brothers, worked in a partnership with James and John, the sons of Zebedee, and they supervised hired hands (Luke 5:7–10; Mark 1:20). They owned their own boats (Luke 5:11), and thus it wasn't hard for them to find a vessel to go fishing in. Fishing could be a fairly rewarding business. Meat was expensive in antiquity, and fish was an important commodity and major source of protein for most families living around the Sea of Galilee (also called the Sea of Tiberias). The term *Galilee* derives from a Hebrew word meaning "ring." There were many more villages ringing the lake in ancient times than today. For Peter and the others, the lure of their previous vocation would not have been inconsequential after Jesus was gone.

John tells us that the apostles toiled all night on the Sea of Galilee but caught nothing. As dawn broke, they saw a man standing on the shore, though they did not know it was their Master. He asked them about their success and told them to cast their nets on the starboard side of the boat. Their catch turned out to be phenomenal, so great that they could not pull in the net, all because they were willing to listen to One wiser than they. John was the first to recognize Jesus and announced to Peter, "It is the Lord" (John 21:7). So excited was Peter to see his Master that he jumped into the water and made his way to shore. The others also came in the "little ship," dragging the fish-laden net in the water behind the boat (John 21:8).

Living in the Holy Land myself, I came to appreciate John's

account so much more. It has come alive for me because of images still to be seen on the Sea of Galilee, images that provide windows to the past. Fishing companies headquartered on the shores of Galilee still send their boats out at night, and they fish till dawn. Some fishermen still partially strip, as Peter did, when they're working their catch. And a first-century boat can now be seen in a museum built close to the western shore of the sea.

In one of the more spectacular finds of the late twentieth century, archaeologists in 1986 recovered from the muddy bottom of the northwestern sector of the Sea of Galilee a boat from the first century after Christ. Indeed, it seems "little," to use John's term, for a commercial fishing vessel; however, it was well-made and gives us a good idea of what the fishing and ship-building industries were like in the days of Jesus. Shipwrights in antiquity went about building their ships differently from the way wooden ships were built in more recent times. In modern construction the keel was laid down, the ribs attached, and then the hull planking nailed to the ribs ("skeleton-first" construction). In Jesus' time, however, the keel was laid down first and then the hull built around it with the ribs affixed afterward ("shell-first" construction). Such was the construction of the boat found in 1986 dating from the general time period of the Savior and the apostles. The excavation and preservation of this boat, which had been under water for approximately two millennia, constitute a remarkable story. It is wonderfully illuminating to see this boat. It helps us to better visualize the events and feel closer to the people described in John's Gospel (Wachsman, *Sea of Galilee Boat*). It reminds us that the scene described by John really did happen.

## LESSONS IN SERVANT LEADERSHIP

As soon as all the apostles had reached the shore, they found that a bed of hot coals had been prepared and fish were cooking thereon, with fresh bread ready. Jesus then treated his friends to a hot meal (John 21:9, 12–13). Though the Savior would yet use the occasion to teach powerful lessons, the story up to this point is full of profound meaning. From his suggestion to these brethren to cast their nets in a certain location, we see that Jesus did indeed care about their temporal well-being, just as he cares about the temporal well-being of his disciples and Saints today (John 21:5–6). And like the ancient apostles, we have to be willing to listen to him.

Just as it was heartwarming for the apostles then to realize that their Master had not stopped caring about their temporal needs, it is heartwarming now to realize that he cares about our having sufficient for our needs. Just as he knew where the fish were located in the sea, so he knows how we can be happy and what we must do to take advantage of his wisdom. It is important to note that Jesus did *not* do the fishing for his apostles. But he helped them focus their energy so they could be successful.

Ever the servant, Jesus prepared a warm place of rest for his apostles and then cooked a meal for them (John 21:9, 12–13). He cooked for them! What a stunning image this presented—the King of the Jews, the Savior of the World, the Master of the Universe, the very Son of God, the Great Jehovah—prepared a fire and cooked some food for his disciples because they were cold and tired and hungry. We must be clear about this. Jesus was God! He was the Redeemer of all. He had already performed the most significant and profound act of service in the history of Creation: the Atonement. He had already opened the door to an eternity's worth of possibilities for the whole human family, and yet he wanted to make dinner, to make his disciples happy, because they were cold and tired and hungry! It was not beneath his dignity to care for their personal needs, to warm them and make them feel comfortable and valued. He truly modeled what he taught; he who was the greatest made himself to be the least and the servant of all (Matthew 23:11).

Having shown by his actions the way of perfect servant-leadership, Jesus was ready to teach with words. In this atmosphere of total service, and against the backdrop of his personal example of selfless concern for others, Jesus instructed the chief apostle, Peter, as to what he must do for the rest of his life. Using the draft of fish as the object lesson, fish he had helped Peter catch, Jesus taught Peter that he was to leave fishing, leave economic pursuits, and feed the Savior's sheep just as the Savior had fed him that morning (John 21:9–17). Jesus would take care of Peter as he had that morning, but Peter was to take care of the Church. The rest of the New Testament record shows us that this lesson was not lost on the chief apostle.

As if to confirm in Peter's mind that his was now a call to imitate the totally selfless life of his Master, Jesus next foretold of Peter's own death. "Verily, verily, I say unto thee, When thou wast young, thou girdedst thyself, and walkedst whither thou wouldest: but when thou shalt be old, thou shalt stretch forth thy hands, and another shall gird thee, and carry thee whither thou wouldest not" (John 21:18). Of this verse Elder Talmage notes, "John informs us that the Lord so spake signifying the death by which Peter should find a place among the martyrs; the analogy points to crucifixion, and traditional history is without contradiction as to this being the death by which Peter sealed his testimony of the Christ" (*Jesus the Christ*, 693).

Finally, Jesus put the capstone on the morning's instruction. He simply but bluntly commanded Peter, "Follow me" (John 21:19). According to reputable tradition, recorded in the statements of various early authorities of the Christian Church, Peter did follow Jesus. His death fulfilled the prophecy of the Savior. The chief apostle died in Rome—martyred in the last years of the reign of Emperor Nero (A.D. 67–68). In a nonbiblical text, 1 Clement 5:4, it is said of Peter that he suffered not one or two but many trials, and having given his testimony, he went to the place which was his due. Ignatius, bishop of Antioch, refers to the deaths of Peter and Paul in Rome, as does Eusebius of Caesarea. Tertullian refers to three martyrdoms at Rome: Peter, Paul, and John. And, finally, Origen reported that Peter "at the end . . . came to Rome and was crucified head downwards" (Eusebius, *Ecclesiastical History*, 3.1.2). To the very end, Peter followed his Lord and Master in both word and deed. He acted like him, taught like him, was rejected like him, and in the end suffered the same kind of ignominious death.

The last exchange between Jesus and Peter during this, the third visitation of the Savior to an assembled group of disciples in the Holy Land (John 21:14), concerned the destiny of the apostle John. As Jesus and Peter walked together, and Peter contemplated his Master's prophecy that he, the chief apostle, would follow Jesus to a cross, he looked back and saw John following. "Peter seeing him saith to Jesus, Lord, and what shall this man do?" (John 21:21). That Peter's question may have derived from motives not entirely pure seems evident in Jesus' mild rebuke. "If I will that he tarry till I come, what is that to thee? Follow thou me" (John 21:22).

This exhortation that Peter should follow the course outlined for him and stop worrying about what others might be asked to do, or *get* to do, or to experience, is important counsel for modern disciples as well. We should quit measuring what the Lord gives to us by comparing our circumstances to others. Such behavior is almost always motivated by pride. C. S. Lewis reminds us: "Pride gets no pleasure out of having something, only out of having more of it than the next man. . . . It is the comparison that makes you proud: the pleasure of being above the rest. Once the element of competition has gone, pride has gone" (*Mere Christianity*, 110).

From information not known through any biblical texts but revealed only to the Prophet Joseph Smith, we learn that Jesus had earlier spoken to the apostle John about what he most desired in the future. And the beloved disciple asked to have power over death so he could remain on earth until the second coming of Christ in glory and bring souls unto him. It was on account of this previous arrangement that Peter asked the Lord about John's future activities (D&C 7:1–8).

John was granted his desire, and he became a translated being, like the Three Nephites. Of those individuals Elder McConkie stated:

> A change is wrought in their bodies so they cannot die at this time, but when the Lord comes again they "shall be changed in the twinkling of an eye from mortality to immortality," and thus they "shall never taste of death" (3 Nephi 28:1–10, 36–40). They will be like a person who lives during the millennium. Of such the revelation says: "It is appointed to him to die at the age of man. Wherefore, children shall grow up until they become old; old men shall die; but they shall not sleep in the dust, but they shall be changed in the twinkling

of an eye" (D&C 63:50–51). Thus they shall die, in the sense indicated, but they shall not taste of death. (*Doctrinal New Testament Commentary*, 1:865).

Interestingly, the Prophet Joseph Smith said, "John the Revelator [is] among the ten tribes of Israel who had been led away by Shalmaneser, king of Assyria, to prepare them for their return from their long dispersion, to again possess the land of their fathers" (Jackson, *Joseph Smith's Commentary on the Bible*, 142).

## A MOUNTAIN IN GALILEE

After Jesus appeared to seven of his apostles at the Sea of Tiberias, all eleven surviving members of the Quorum of the Twelve met together and went "into a mountain where Jesus had appointed them" (Matthew 28:16). There the Savior met with these brethren and gave them important instructions regarding their divine commission to lead the kingdom after he was gone.

Apparently, other disciples were also present at the preappointed mountain conference because Matthew records that "they worshipped him: but some doubted" (Matthew 28:17). Surely the doubters were not the apostles but others who had not yet seen their Master and did not yet comprehend the literal physical, bodily nature of his resurrection. Elder McConkie writes that this "is likely the occasion of which, as Paul wrote later, 'he was seen of above five hundred brethren at once' (1 Cor. 15:6). If so, the seventies and leading brethren of the Church would have been present, as also perhaps the faithful women who are inheritors of like rewards with obedient priesthood holders" (*Doctrinal New Testament Commentary*, 1:866).

To his special witnesses, Jesus explained the all-encompassing authority and power he possessed but was now delegating to them and expecting them to uphold: "All power is given unto me in heaven and in earth," he said. "Go ye therefore, and teach all nations, baptizing them in the name of the Father, and of the Son, and of the Holy Ghost: Teaching them to observe all things whatsoever I have commanded you: and, lo, I am with you alway, even unto the end of the world. Amen" (Matthew 28:18–20). The Gospel of Mark reports that Jesus also spoke to the apostles about the powerful and distinctive signs that would follow or attend all of those who believed on his name and were baptized: "In my name shall they cast out devils; they shall speak with new tongues; they shall take up serpents; and if they drink any deadly thing, it shall not hurt them: they shall lay hands on the sick, and they shall recover" (Mark 16:17–18). These remarkable promises were realized by many later on, as the book of Acts indicates.

The instructions that the Savior gave to his apostles on the mountain in Galilee serve to reinforce to modern disciples the mission and message of the Lord's true Church in every age. Those instructions clarify and emphasize that *the apostles are the Church's foundation*. They hold the keys in every age or dispensation when the Lord's Church is on the earth. All things in the Lord's Church—power, authority, general instructions, ordinances, and the like—come from Jesus Christ through his authorized representatives, the apostles. Regarding this last dispensation, President Brigham Young summarized the role of apostles when he said: "The keys of the eternal Priesthood, which is after the order of the Son of God, are comprehended by being an apostle. All the Priesthood, all the keys, all the gifts, all the endowments, and everything preparatory to entering into the presence of the Father and of the Son, are in, composed of, circumscribed by, or I might say incorporated within the circumference of, the Apostleship" (*Journal of Discourses*, 1:134–35).

With the convening of this mountain conference in Galilee, the Savior had now given the great missionary charge to his earthly leaders. By this point he had appeared several times to his apostles and disciples to confirm his living reality. This was the essence of his forty-day ministry. The foundation was firmly in place. Many came to know that the resurrection is real, and this gave them the strength to live the gospel of Jesus Christ and preach it to others. Because the ancient disciples knew with certainty that Jesus was the Christ, that he had in reality come back to life, that the promises of resurrection and eternal life were unequivocally true, they could face anything—and many did.

This conviction of the reality of the resurrection is alive and well in our day; it is the linchpin of our faith. With glad hearts Latter-day Saints proclaim the good news: Jesus is alive today and resides in yonder heavens with his divine Father, who is also a glorified man of flesh and bone and who has promised each of us that we can join them and be like them if we commit our lives to them. It is up to us.

---

And there are also many other things which Jesus did, the which, if they should be written every one, I suppose that even the world itself could not contain the books that should be written. Amen.

JOHN 21:25

And when he had spoken these things, while they beheld, he was taken up; and a cloud received him out of their sight.

And while they looked stedfastly toward heaven as he went up, behold, two men stood by them in white apparel;

Which also said, Ye men of Galilee, why stand ye gazing up into heaven? this same Jesus, which is taken up from you into heaven, shall so come in like manner as ye have seen him go into heaven.

ACTS 1:9–11

---

CHAPTER 8

# Concluding His Earthly Ministry

We do not know a great deal about the rest of the Savior's postresurrection ministry among his disciples in the Holy Land, but from clues in biblical and nonbiblical texts, we understand that other instruction he gave during his forty-day ministry had a temple orientation.

In the concluding verses of Luke's Gospel, which report Jesus' last instructions to the disciples just before his ascension, we read:

> And, behold, I send the promise of my Father upon you: but tarry ye in the city of Jerusalem, until ye be endued with power from on high.
>
> And he led them out as far as to Bethany, and he lifted up his hands, and blessed them.
>
> And it came to pass, while he blessed them, he was parted from them, and carried up into heaven.
>
> And they worshipped him, and returned to Jerusalem with great joy:
>
> And were continually in the temple, praising and blessing God. Amen. (Luke 24:49–53)

I do not think it coincidental that Luke reports that Jesus told his disciple-leaders to wait in Jerusalem until they "be endued with power from on high," and then Luke concludes his record by telling us emphatically that they were "continually in the temple" (Luke 24:49, 53). Of these verses, Elder Bruce R. McConkie wrote:

> It is common in Christendom to suppose that Jesus here commanded his apostles to tarry in Jerusalem until the promised gift of the Holy Ghost was received, which gift would constitute an endowment of power from on high. Perhaps the statement can be so used, for certainly the disciples were marvelously and powerfully endowed when the Holy Spirit came into their lives on the day of Pentecost (Acts 2).
>
> But from latter-day revelation we learn that the Lord had something more in mind in issuing this instruction. In this dispensation, after the elders had received the gift of the Holy Ghost and as early as January, 1831, the Lord began to reveal unto them that he had an endowment in store for the faithful (D&C 38:22; 43:16), "a blessing such as is not known among the children of men" (D&C 39:15). In June, 1833, he said: "I gave unto you a commandment that you should build a house, in the which house I design to endow those whom I have chosen with power from on high; For this is the promise of the Father unto you; therefore I command you to tarry, even as mine apostles at Jerusalem" (D&C 95:8–9; 105:11–12, 18, 33).
>
> Thus the apostles—or any ministers or missionaries in any age—are not fully qualified to go forth, preach the

gospel, and build up the kingdom, unless they have the gift of the Holy Ghost and also are endowed with power from on high, meaning have received certain knowledge, powers, and special blessings, normally given only in the Lord's Temple. (*Doctrinal New Testament Commentary*, 1:859)

Even more impressive than the way Luke concludes his Gospel is the way he begins his sequel, the Acts of the Apostles:

The former treatise have I made, O Theophilus, of all that Jesus began both to do and teach.

Until the day in which he was taken up, after that he through the Holy Ghost had given commandments unto the apostles whom he had chosen:

To whom also he shewed himself alive after his *passion* by many *infallible proofs*, being seen of them forty days, and speaking of the things pertaining to the kingdom of God. (Acts 1:1–3; emphasis added)

The word *passion* in this text derives from the Latin *passus* and means "sufferings," as the Joseph Smith Translation also denotes. The phrase "infallible proofs" is much more vivid in the original Greek from which the English is translated. The Greek word here, *tekmeriois*, means "sure signs or tokens" (*Greek-English Lexicon*, 695). In other words, Jesus instructed his disciples during his forty-day ministry using many "sure signs or tokens" and spoke of things pertaining to the kingdom of God. Indeed! The Prophet Joseph Smith taught that in order to obtain eternal life all individuals, no matter the dispensation in which they lived, must follow the same plan of salvation, obey the same principles and ordinances, that were instituted *before* the world was created, and full salvation cannot be obtained without these ordinances. Furthermore, the only place where these ordinances can be obtained is in the house of the Lord, or a like place designated by the Lord when, for example, a temple has not yet been constructed.

This important doctrine is found in many of the Prophet Joseph Smith's sermons and was summarized very powerfully in a discourse given in June 1843. At that time the Prophet declared:

> It was the design of the councils of heaven before the world was, that the principles and laws of the priesthood should be predicated upon the gathering of the people in every age of the world. Jesus did everything to gather the people, and they would not be gathered. . . . Ordinances instituted in the heavens before the foundation of the world, in the priesthood, for the salvation of men, are not to be altered or changed. All must be saved on the same principles.

> It is for the same purpose that God gathers together His people in the last days, to build unto the Lord a house to prepare them for the ordinances and endowments, washings and anointings, etc. (*History of the Church*, 5:423–24)

And then the Prophet made this significant comment:

> If a man gets a fullness of the priesthood of God, he has to get it in the same way that Jesus Christ obtained it, and that was by keeping all the commandments and obeying all the ordinances of the house of the Lord. . . .

> All men who become heirs of God and joint-heirs with Jesus Christ will have to receive the fulness of

the ordinances of his kingdom; and those who will not receive all the ordinances will come short of the fullness of that glory, if they do not lose the whole. (*History of the Church*, 5:424)

It becomes clear to us from nonbiblical sources that the ordinances of exaltation were available to the Lord's disciples in the meridian of time. President Heber C. Kimball taught that the temple endowment available to us in our present dispensation is the same, in principle, as was available in the ancient Church of Jesus Christ. He also said that Jesus "was the one that inducted his Apostles into these ordinances" (*Journal of Discourses*, 10:241). President Joseph Fielding Smith and Elder Bruce R. McConkie stated their belief that Peter, James, and John received the endowment on the Mount of Transfiguration (*Doctrines of Salvation*, 2:165, 170; *Doctrinal New Testament Commentary*, 1:400). Because the chief apostles were commanded by the Savior not to discuss what happened on the Mount of Transfiguration until after Jesus was "risen again from the dead" (Matthew 17:9), it is thought by some gospel scholars that temple ordinances were not administered to the rest of the Twelve, or other worthy members of the Church, until *after* the resurrection of Jesus Christ (Pace, "What It Means to Know Christ," 51).

This view is supported both by certain apocryphal texts that describe Jesus' forty-day postresurrection ministry as a time when our Lord taught the mysteries of the kingdom and established a sacred ritual among his disciples and also by writings that detail the history of the ancient Church. The fourth-century historian Eusebius of Caesarea (260–340) included this stunning statement in his work entitled *Ecclesiastical History*: "After the

187

resurrection, the Lord imparted the higher knowledge to James the Just, John, and Peter. They gave it to the other apostles, and the other apostles to the Seventy" (Maier, *Eusebius*, 58).

Of all the texts in the New Testament itself, the writings of the apostle John are the most transparent in divulging temple teachings and connections, which Jesus taught to the eleven apostles as well as other disciples during his forty-day ministry. John alone speaks of the following:

1. The ordinance of the washing of the feet (John 13)

2. The Second Comforter (John 14)

3. Becoming kings and priests (Revelation 1)

4. The crown of life (Revelation 2)

5. A white stone and a new name (Revelation 2)

6. Power over the nations (Revelation 2)

7. White raiment and the book of life (Revelation 3)

8. Becoming a pillar in God's temple (Revelation 3)

9. Being granted the privilege of sitting with the Lord in his throne (Revelation 4)

We usually say that John wrote for members of the Church of Jesus Christ. It would, perhaps, be more accurate to say that he wrote for members of Christ's Church who knew about the principles and ordinances of the temple and the endowments of knowledge and power received in them.

It should not surprise us that so many independent sources, both those within the Church and those outside it, link the instruction Jesus gave to his disciples after his resurrection with the temple, higher knowledge, and endowments of power.

Resurrection and the temple go together. In the temple the priesthood ordinance of resurrection is prefigured; we are presented with a pattern of how the resurrection will occur. In the temple we are taught the reasons that resurrection is so important. In the temple we are taught the destiny of resurrected beings. In the temple we are given the covenants and powers that exalted resurrected beings will use. In the temple we are taught the same concepts that the Messiah, the first to be resurrected, taught to his followers anciently. The temple is the home of resurrected beings, specifically the Lord himself. The temple is literally his earthly house. It is truly exciting to belong to the Lord's Church and to see how consistent it has been in its operation and teachings from dispensation to dispensation.

## THE DOCTRINE OF RESURRECTION ACCORDING TO PAUL

In addition to instructing his disciples regarding the mysteries of the kingdom, the scriptures tell us that Jesus made other appearances to individuals and groups both before and after his ascension. He confirmed the reality of his bodily resurrection and showed to those he visited what resurrected bodies are like. One of those Jesus visited and instructed was the apostle Paul (1 Corinthians 15:8), who, in turn, helped others understand the doctrine of resurrection by discussing it in one of his major epistles (1 Corinthians 15). Paul began his discussion by listing many of those to whom the Savior appeared before his ascension. Notable among these was James, the half-brother of Jesus. James did not believe that his half-brother was the Messiah while Jesus lived among them before his crucifixion (Matthew 13:55; John 7:1–5). But after the Resurrection, James was found among the community of believers (Acts 1:14) and even became a stalwart in the Jerusalem branch of the Church (Acts 15:13).

Though we do not know exactly when or where Jesus appeared to his half-brother, we believe it was the likely turning point in James's life, the time when he came to know that his half-brother, Jesus, really was who he said he was all along. It is heartwarming to think of Jesus taking special spiritual care of the members of his own family, ministering to them and nurturing their faith after they had endured what must have been very challenging circumstances. I think it could not have been easy for even fundamentally good people to live in the shadow of Jesus in a family setting, to witness his exceptional life, to watch his perfect behavior, and to experience his unique perceptions of the world without developing both positive and negative feelings. In addition, as Jesus grew older he undoubtedly began to draw ridicule and persecution. This would have affected the family. Jesus blessed his half-brother's life eternally by visiting him as the resurrected Messiah, and we appreciate Paul's note about this.

Paul's unparalleled contribution to our understanding of the resurrection is to be found in his comprehensive explanation of it in 1 Corinthians 15. Paul certifies that Jesus was the first to be resurrected, making it possible for all to follow (1 Corinthians 15:15–16, 20). Paul also explains that resurrection itself is redemption, for "if Christ be not raised . . . ye are yet in your sins" (1 Corinthians 15:17). This is so, as the Book of Mormon explains, because without the resurrection our spirits after physical death would increasingly come under the influence and control of Satan who is a spirit, until, without the regeneration that resurrection brings, we would "become like unto him, and we become devils, angels to a devil, to be shut out from the presence of our God" (2 Nephi 9:9). Hence, as Joseph Smith knew, "the resurrection from the dead is the redemption of the soul" (D&C 88:16). The resurrection works in tandem with Christ's infinite and incomprehensible suffering to redeem and rescue us from the lasting effects of sin. These different aspects of the Atonement fit together in perfect, cohesive harmony.

Paul also knew and taught that the resurrection is so powerful and all-encompassing in its redemptive effects that it overcomes and makes right *all* the negative effects of the fall of Adam: "As in Adam all die [physically and spiritually], even so in Christ shall all be made alive [physically and spiritually]" (1 Corinthians 15:22). That is, the resurrection overcomes physical death by giving us immortal physical bodies; it overcomes spiritual death by bringing *every* soul back into the presence of the Lord to be judged, even if only for a short period. Whether or not we will remain in the presence of the Lord is determined by what our own actions were in mortality. But Christ's resurrection, which makes possible our own resurrection, overcomes the spiritual effects of Adam's transgression, which transmitted spiritual death (separation from God) to all the posterity of Adam and Eve—all of us! Thus, the resurrection is inextricably tied to the Fall. President Ezra Taft Benson said:

> The plan of redemption must start with the account of the fall of Adam. In the words of Moroni, "By Adam came the fall of man. And because of the fall of man came Jesus Christ. . . . and because of Jesus Christ came the redemption of man" (Mormon 9:12).
>
> Just as man does not really desire food until he is hungry, so he does not desire the salvation of Christ until he knows why he needs Christ.

No one adequately and properly knows why he needs Christ until he understands and accepts the doctrine of the Fall and its effect upon all mankind. (Conference Report, April 1987, 106)

I make a point of this principle because as a new missionary years ago, I used to teach the doctrine incorrectly by saying that only those who kept the commandments would overcome the effects of spiritual death and that only the righteous would be brought back into the presence of the Lord. Perhaps this came about through a misreading of Alma 11:41: "The wicked remain as though there had been no redemption made, except it be the loosing of the bands of death." The great prophet, Samuel the Lamanite, set me straight. Spiritual death is overcome for all; however, whether or not an individual will suffer a second spiritual death depends upon that individual's repentance and the fruits that flow from it:

> For behold, he [Christ] surely must die that salvation may come; yea, it behooveth him and becometh expedient that he dieth, to bring to pass the resurrection of the dead, that thereby men may be brought into the presence of the Lord.
>
> Yea, behold, this death bringeth to pass the resurrection, and redeemeth all mankind from the first death—that spiritual death; for all mankind, by the fall of Adam being cut off from the presence of the Lord, are considered as dead, both as to things temporal and to things spiritual.
>
> But behold, the resurrection of Christ redeemeth mankind, yea, even all mankind, and bringeth them back into the presence of the Lord.

Yea, and it bringeth to pass the condition of repentance, that whosoever repenteth the same is not hewn down and cast into the fire; but whosoever repenteth not is hewn down and cast into the fire; and there cometh upon them again a spiritual death, yea, a second death, for they are cut off again as to things pertaining to righteousness.

Therefore repent ye, repent ye, lest by knowing these things and not doing them ye shall suffer yourselves to come under condemnation, and ye are brought down unto this second death. (Helaman 14:15–19)

Another important aspect that comes out of Paul's discussion concerns the different times and degrees of the resurrection. Our Heavenly Father's sons and daughters are not all resurrected at the same time. Every individual is made alive "in his own order: Christ the firstfruits; afterward they that are Christ's at his coming" (1 Corinthians 15:23).

In the resurrection, celestial bodies will come forth first, in the "morning" of the first resurrection. Their graves will be opened, and they will be caught up to meet the Savior at his second coming. They will descend with him to rule and reign as kings and queens. Those with terrestrial bodies will come forth next, in the "afternoon" of the first resurrection, after the Savior has ushered in the Millennium. At the end of the Millennium, those with telestial bodies will begin to come forth. The last to be resurrected will be those possessing bodies fit for no kingdom of glory—sons of perdition (McConkie, *Mormon Doctrine*, 640; JST 1 Corinthians 15:40–42).

Each of these kinds of resurrected bodies possesses a different glory, power, and potential. Those raised with celestial bodies overcome all things and dwell with God and Christ forever. They can become like God. But those not raised with celestial bodies cannot dwell with God and Christ, cannot become exactly like them, "worlds without end" (D&C 76:112; see also vv. 50–62). As the Prophet Joseph Smith explained, "In the resurrection, some are raised to be angels, others are raised to become Gods" (*Teachings of the Prophet Joseph Smith*, 312).

Thus, at the time of resurrection there is a judgment and separation, just as there is at the time of physical death. (The righteous go to paradise; the unrighteous, to prison.) This is not the final judgment but preparatory to it. There will be no surprises at the time of the final judgment. Individuals will already possess immortal bodies of varying powers and capabilities, which determine their destiny for eternity. Judgment and resurrection are linked together. Resurrection does not occur without the rendering of a verdict. Elder McConkie stated:

> It is very evident that men will not have to await the day of final judgment—the formal occasion when every living soul will stand before the judgment bar, an event that will not take place until the last soul has been resurrected—to learn their status and the degree of glory they are to receive in eternity. Those who are living a telestial law will be swept off the earth at the Second Coming. (D&C 101:24; Mal. 3:4.) Those who come forth in the morning of the first resurrection, who "are Christ's, the firstfruits," will have celestial bodies and go to a celestial kingdom. "Those who are Christ's at his coming" will come forth with terrestrial bodies and go to a terrestrial kingdom. Similarly those coming forth in the beginning of the second resurrection will have

telestial bodies and go to a telestial kingdom, while the sons of perdition, the last to be resurrected, will have bodies capable of receiving no glory and will be cast out with the devil and his angels forever (D&C 88:98–102).

No one has yet been resurrected with any kind of a body except a celestial. Those who were with Christ in his resurrection will all have eternal inheritance in his celestial presence (D&C 133:54–56). Though there is yet to be a day of formal judgment for all men, yet there is no question, for instance, of the reward that Abraham, Isaac, and Jacob will receive in that day. "They have entered into their exaltation, according to the promises, and sit upon thrones, and are not angels but are gods," the revelation records. (D&C 132:29–37.) The same is true of Adam, Enoch, Noah, Moses, and the faithful saints from the beginning to the day of Christ. (*Mormon Doctrine,* 404)

## THE RESTORATION OF THE EARTH

Truly, resurrection is part of the great law of restoration. The law of restoration dictates that all things created by our Father in Heaven or by Jesus Christ (under his Father's direction) will be redeemed and restored by Jesus Christ—all things! Restoration *is* the redemptive work of Christ. The earth and every living thing on it will be restored to its proper and perfect frame. For mortals, not even a hair of our heads will be lost in the resurrection (Alma 40:23).

What Adam's fall took away, Jesus' atonement restores. All things will be renewed. Even this earth will be restored to its original, created position in the presence of God (Abraham 5:13). When Adam fell, this earth also fell and took up its present position. Resurrection will rectify this aspect of the Fall. President Joseph Fielding Smith said: "When this earth was created, it was not according to our present time, but it was created according to Kolob's time, for the Lord has said it was created on celestial time which is Kolob's time. Then he revealed to Abraham that Adam was subject to Kolob's time before his transgression" (*Doctrines of Salvation*, 1:79).

President Brigham Young presents an even clearer picture of the destiny of this earth owing to Christ's atonement and resurrection:

> When the earth was framed and brought into existence and man was placed upon it, it was near the throne of our Father in heaven. . . . but when man fell, the earth fell into space, and took up its abode in this planetary system, and the sun became our light. When the Lord said—"Let there be light," there was light, for the earth was brought near the sun that it might reflect upon it so as to give us light by day, and the moon to give us light by night. This is the glory the earth came from, and when it is glorified it will return again unto the presence of the Father, and it will dwell there, and these intelligent beings that I am looking at, if they live worthy of it, will dwell upon this earth. (*Journal of Discourses*, 17:143)

## THE ASCENSION

Having finished the work of his forty-day ministry, the Savior was ready to bid farewell to his beloved associates, the apostles. He led them as far as Bethany, on the eastern slope of the Mount of Olives, and gave them final instructions.

Luke records that Jesus commanded the apostles to remain

in Jerusalem until the promised arrival of and immersion in the powers of the Holy Ghost were realized (Acts 1:4–5). The brethren then queried the Lord about the restoration of the great religious and political kingdom that will attend the second coming and millennial reign of Christ on earth, just as the pre-meridian prophets foresaw. Was it to happen during their lifetime? Jesus told them that it was not for them to know the exact timing of these events. They needed to be patient and pursue their commission as special witnesses of the Resurrection, starting in Jerusalem and Judea and spreading out to the uttermost parts of the earth (Acts 1:8).

As the apostles contemplated these instructions, as well as their future, Jesus ascended in a cloud of glory and was gone. But two angelic witnesses appeared and provided important commentary on this experience, which is also for all disciples of this dispensation. Jesus' ascension is a model for his glorious second coming. He will descend from his heavenly throne to appear on the Mount of Olives and reign on the earth as King of Israel, King of Kings. Thus, Jesus' ascension brings us back full circle to the beginning of his atoning experience, forty-three days earlier, and propels us forward to the start of a new era. "The Mount of Olives, 'the olive-orchard'—hallowed spot! On this Mount is the Garden called Gethsemane where Jesus in agony took upon himself the sins of the world . . . here he now ascends in triumphant glory; and here he shall return in that same glory to begin his reign as Israel's King. (D. & C. 133:19–20.)" (McConkie, *Doctrinal New Testament Commentary*, 2:28).

## SPECIAL WITNESSES

After witnessing their Master's ascension from Olivet and thus fulfilling another aspect of their role as special witnesses, the apostles returned to Jerusalem to await the coming of the Comforter in power and then begin teaching the world the gospel of the living God. The core of this gospel message was and is and forever will be the atonement and resurrection of Jesus Christ. The apostles, as well as the other disciples in the meridian dispensation, now knew with eyewitness-certainty that Jesus had risen from the grave and opened a way for all to follow. So impressive are the number of encounters with the risen Lord, and so credible the documentation of these episodes, that one non-Latter-day Saint expert on the New Testament stated categorically:

> The evidence for the resurrection of Jesus Christ is overwhelming. Nothing in history is more certain than that the disciples believed that, after being crucified, dead, and buried, Christ rose again from the tomb on the third day, and that at intervals thereafter he met and conversed with them. The most obvious proof that they believed this is the existence of the Christian church. . . .
>
> It is a commonplace that every event in history must have an adequate cause. Never were hopes more desolate than when Jesus of Nazareth was taken down from the cross and laid in the tomb. Stricken with grief at the death of their Master, the disciples were dazed and bewildered. Their mood was one of dejection and defeat, reflected in the spiritless words of the Emmaus travelers, "We had hoped that he was the one to redeem Israel" (Luke 24:21). A short time later the same group of disciples was aglow with supreme confidence and fearless in the face of persecution. Their message was one of

joy and triumph. What caused such a radical change in these men's lives? The explanation is that something unprecedented had occurred: Jesus Christ was raised from the dead! Fifty-some days after the crucifixion the apostolic preaching of Christ's resurrection began in Jerusalem with such power and persuasion that the evidence convinced thousands. (Metzger, *New Testament*, 126–27)

We may summarize the impressive list of witnesses to the Lord's resurrection (witnesses as well to the empty Garden Tomb) as they have been recorded in scripture. These are arranged in approximate chronological order, as nearly as we can tell.

1. Mary Magdalene (John 20:1–18), outside the Garden Tomb on the morning of Jesus' resurrection

2. Other women (Matthew 28:1–9), somewhere between the Garden Tomb and Jerusalem on Resurrection morning

3. Cleopas and another disciple (Mark 16:12–13; Luke 24:13–32), on the road to Emmaus on Resurrection day

4. Simon Peter (Luke 24:34; 1 Corinthians 15:5), on Resurrection day

5. Ten of the Twelve (Luke 24:36–53; John 20:19–24), in a closed room somewhere in Jerusalem on Resurrection night

6. Eleven of the Twelve (Mark 16:14; John 20:26–31), in a closed room in Jerusalem one week after the Resurrection

7. Seven of the Twelve (John 21:1–14), at the Sea of Galilee (Tiberias), the third visit to the group

8. Eleven of the Twelve (Matthew 28:16–20), on a mountain in Galilee by previous appointment of the Savior

9. More than five hundred brethren at once (1 Corinthians 15:6), probably on the mountain in Galilee with the eleven apostles

10. James (1 Corinthians 15:7)

11. Eleven apostles at Jesus' ascension (Mark 16:14, 19; Luke 24: 50–51; Acts 1:3–11), near Bethany forty days after the Resurrection

12. Saul of Tarsus (1 Corinthians 9:1; 15:8), on the road to Damascus, Syria

13. The Nephites (3 Nephi 11:1–18:39; 19:2, 15–26:15), in the land Bountiful in America near the temple about A.D. 34

14. John the Revelator (Revelation 1:9–18), on the Isle of Patmos sometime between 81 A.D. and 96

15. The Nephite Twelve (3 Nephi 27:1–28:12)

16. Lost tribes of Israel (3 Nephi 16:1–4; 17:4), soon after the Savior's visitation to the Nephite people

17. Mormon (Mormon 1:15)

18. Moroni (Ether 12:39)

19. Joseph Smith (Joseph Smith–History 1:14–20), in the Sacred Grove near Palmyra, New York, in the spring of 1820

Many of these witnesses were visited by the resurrected Lord more than once. But it does not end there. The chain of witnesses to the Lord's resurrection and living reality continues. Many are the accounts and testimonies that tell of individuals since 1820 who have come to *know* that Jesus of Nazareth lives as a resurrected Being. One of the better-known accounts of the resurrected Lord appearing in these latter days comes from Allie Young Pond, granddaughter of Church president Lorenzo Snow. She related this episode:

> One evening while I was visiting Grandpa Snow in his room in the Salt Lake Temple, I remained until the door keepers had gone and the night-watchmen had not yet come in, so grandpa said he would take me to the main front entrance and let me out that way. He got this bunch of keys from his dresser. After we left his room, and while we were still in the large corridor leading into the celestial room, I was walking several steps ahead of grandpa when he stopped me and said: "Wait a moment, Allie, I want to tell you something. It was right here that the Lord Jesus Christ appeared to me at the time of the death of President Woodruff. He instructed me to go right ahead and reorganize the First Presidency of the Church at once and not wait as had been done after the death of the previous presidents, and that I was to succeed President Woodruff."
>
> Then grandpa came a step nearer and held out his left hand and said: "He stood right here, about three feet above the floor. It looked as though He stood on a plate of solid gold."
>
> Grandpa told me what a glorious personage the Savior is and described His hands, feet, countenance and beautiful white robes, all of which were of such a glory of whiteness and brightness that he could hardly gaze upon Him.

Then he came another step nearer and put his right hand on my head and said: "Now granddaughter, I want you to remember that this is the testimony of your grandfather, that he told you with his own lips that he actually saw the Savior, here in the Temple, and talked with him face to face. (*Best-Loved Stories of the LDS People*, 239–40)

Closer to our day, President Harold B. Lee, eleventh president of The Church of Jesus Christ of Latter-day Saints, presented his powerful and thought-provoking witness:

Some years ago two missionaries came to me with what seemed to them to be a very difficult question. A young . . . minister had laughed at them when they had said that Apostles were necessary today in order for the true Church to be upon the earth. They said that the minister said, "Do you realize that when the Apostles met to choose one to fill the vacancy caused by the death of Judas, they said it had to be one who companied with them and had been a witness of all things pertaining to the mission and resurrection of the Lord? How can you say you have Apostles, if that be the measure of an Apostle?"

And so these young men said, "What shall we answer?"

I said to them, "Go back and ask your minister friend two questions. First, how did the Apostle Paul gain what was necessary to be called an Apostle? He didn't know the Lord, had no personal acquaintance. He hadn't accompanied the Apostles. He hadn't been a witness of the ministry nor of the resurrection of the Lord. How did he gain his testimony sufficient to be an Apostle? And the second question you ask him is, How does he know that all who are today Apostles have not likewise received that witness?"

I bear witness to you that those who hold the apostolic calling may, and do, know of the reality of the mission of the Lord. (*Teachings of Harold B. Lee,* 546–47)

And finally, President Ezra Taft Benson, twelfth president of The Church of Jesus Christ of Latter-day Saints, offered this testimony that serves as a fitting summary of all such witnesses:

> Since the day of resurrection when Jesus became the "firstfruits of them that slept," there have been those who disbelieve and scoff. They maintain there is no life beyond mortal existence. Some have even written books which contain their fanciful heresies to suggest how Jesus' disciples perpetrated the hoax of His resurrection.
>
> But I say unto you, the resurrection of Jesus Christ is the greatest historical event in the world to date.
>
> In this dispensation, commencing with the Prophet Joseph Smith, the witnesses are legion. As one of those called as special witnesses, I add my testimony to those fellow Apostles: He lives! He lives with resurrected body. There is no truth or fact of which I am more assured, or *know better by personal experience,* than the truth of the literal resurrection of our Lord. ("Five Marks of the Divinity of Jesus Christ," 48; emphasis added)

God be thanked for such witnesses as these in our own day.

## FINAL THOUGHTS

The story of the Garden Tomb is the culmination of the story of Gethsemane and the story of Golgotha. Its effect is powerful and unforgettable. It describes the foundation of our future. It is a story for all humanity.

For every soul who carries a burden, for every soul who faces a challenge, for every soul who harbors a heartache, for every soul who perseveres through pain, for every soul who is plagued by fears, for every soul who seeks comfort, for every soul who has faced death, for every soul who has lost a loved one, for every soul who has seen horror, for every soul—the message of the Garden Tomb is intended. The message is this: the tomb is empty; Jesus is alive today; he is the literal Son of God, our Heavenly Father; he was resurrected; he alone made it possible and inevitable for every human being who has ever lived to live again; he has guaranteed that we will see our loved ones again; he has all power; he paid for every sin; he knows all suffering; he knows the name of each one of us; he and his Father hear our every prayer. If the Atonement is not for everyone, it will not be for anyone! All Creation is affected by the resurrection of Jesus Christ.

When all is said and done, there has never been nor ever will be anything so powerful, so majestic, so wondrous, so merciful as the atonement of Jesus Christ. There are no words capable of describing the infinite goodness and omnipotence of Jesus. As the apostle John testified, the time is coming for the followers of the Lord when "God shall wipe away all tears from their eyes; and there shall be no more death, neither sorrow, nor crying, neither shall there be any more pain: for the former things are passed away" (Revelation 21:4). The power by which all this is accomplished is the infinite atonement of Jesus Christ. The grace he extends to us is freely given, but it did not come free. Its cost was infinite, and yet he asks no price. All that he wants from us is our loyalty and love and gratitude.

God be thanked for his matchless gift.

# Sources

Aldous, Edwin W. "A Reflection on the Atonement's Healing Power." *Ensign*, April 1987.

Allen, James B. *Trials of Discipleship: The Story of William Clayton, a Mormon*. Urbana: University of Illinois Press, 1987.

*Anchor Bible Dictionary*. Edited by David Noel Freedman. 6 vols. New York: Doubleday, 1992.

Andrus, Hyrum L. *God, Man, and the Universe*. Vol. 1 of *Foundations of the Millennial Kingdom of Christ Series*. Salt Lake City: Deseret Book, 1968.

Avigad, Nahman. *Discovering Jerusalem*. Nashville: Thomas Nelson, 1983.

Benson, Ezra Taft. "Civic Standards for the Faithful Saints." *Ensign*, July 1972.

———. "Five Marks of the Divinity of Jesus Christ." Address to Latter-day Saint Student Association (LDSSA) fireside, University of Utah, Salt Lake City, December 9, 1979.

———. *The Teachings of Ezra Taft Benson*. Salt Lake City: Bookcraft, 1988.

*Best-Loved Stories of the LDS People*. Edited by Jack M. Lyon et al. Salt Lake City: Deseret Book, 1992.

Brown, Raymond E. *The Death of the Messiah*. Garden City, N.Y.: Doubleday, 1994.

Bruce, F. F. *New Testament History*. Garden City, N.Y.: Doubleday, 1980.

Burton, Theodore M. "The Meaning of Repentance." In *Devotional and Fireside Speeches*. Provo, Utah: Brigham Young University Press, 1985.

Cannon, George Q. *Gospel Truth*. Edited by Jerreld L. Newquist. 2 vols. in 1. Salt Lake City: Deseret Book, 1987.

Chadwick, Jeffrey R. "Revisiting Golgotha and the Garden Tomb." *Religious Educator 4*, no. 1 (2003): 16.

Clark, J. Reuben, Jr. *As Ye Sow*. Brigham Young University Speeches of the Year, Provo, Utah, May 3, 1955.

———. *Behold the Lamb of God*. Salt Lake City: Deseret Book, 1962.

*Collected Discourses of the First Presidency and the Twelve*. Edited by Brian H. Stuy. 5 vols. Sandy, Utah: B.H.S. Publishing, 1992.

Davis, C. Truman. "A Physician Testifies about Crucifixion." *Review of the News*, April 14, 1976.

Dibble, Jonathan A. "Delivered by the Power of God." *Ensign*, October 1987.

Doxey, Roy W. *The Doctrine and Covenants Speaks*. 2 vols. Salt Lake City: Deseret Book, 1970.

Edwards, William D., Wesley J. Gabel, and Floyd E. Hosmer. "On the Physical Death of Jesus Christ." *Journal of the American Medical Association [JAMA]* 225, no. 11 (March 21, 1986): 1455.

Ehat, Andrew F., and Lyndon W. Cook, eds. *The Words of Joseph Smith*. Orem, Utah: Grandin Book, 1991.

Eusebius. *The Ecclesiastical History*. Vol. 1. Translated by Kirsopp Lake. Cambridge: Harvard University Press, 1992.

Farrar, Frederic W. *The Life of Christ*. New York: Cassell and Company, 1902.

Faust, James E. "The Atonement: Our Greatest Hope." *Ensign*, November 2001.

Galbraith, David B., D. Kelly Ogden, and Andrew C. Skinner. *Jerusalem, the Eternal City*. Salt Lake City: Deseret Book, 1996.

Ginzberg, Louis. *Legends of the Jews*. Philadelphia: Jewish Publication Society of America, 1937–66.

Haight, David B. "The Sacrament—and the Sacrifice." *Ensign*, November 1989.

Hales, Robert D. "Behold, We Count Them Happy Which Endure." *Ensign*, May 1998.

———. "Faith through Tribulation Brings Peace and Joy." *Ensign*, May 2003.

Hall, John F. *New Testament Witnesses of Christ*. American Fork, Utah: Covenant Communications, 2002.

Hareuveni, Nogah. *Nature in Our Biblical Heritage*. Kiryat Ono, Israel: Neot Kedumim Ltd., 1981.

*Harper's Bible Dictionary*. Edited by Paul J. Achtemeier et al. San Francisco: Harper and Row, 1985.

Hinckley, Bryant S. *Sermons and Missionary Services of Melvin Joseph Ballard*. Salt Lake City: Deseret Book, 1949.

Hinckley, Gordon B. *Teachings of Gordon B. Hinckley*. Salt Lake City: Deseret Book, 1997.

———. "The Symbol of Christ." *Ensign*, May 1975.

Holland, Jeffrey R. *"Therefore, What?"* Address delivered at Brigham Young University, Provo, Utah, 8 August 2000.

Hunter, Howard W. "Eternal Investments." Address to Church Educational System personnel, Salt Lake City, February 10, 1989.

———. Conference Report, April 1986.

*Hymns of The Church of Jesus Christ of Latter-day Saints*. Salt Lake City: The Church of Jesus Christ of Latter-day Saints, 1985.

*Interpreter's Dictionary of the Bible: An Illustrated Encyclopedia*. Nashville, Tenn.: Abingdon Press, 1962.

Jackson, Kent P. *Joseph Smith's Commentary on the Bible*. Salt Lake City: Deseret Book, 1994.

Jackson, Kent P., ed. *1 Nephi to Alma 29*. Vol. 7 of *Studies in Scripture Series*. Salt Lake City: Deseret Book, 1987.

Josephus, Flavius. *The Antiquities of the Jews* and *The Wars of the Jews*. In *Josephus: Complete Works*. Translated by William Whiston. Grand Rapids, Mich.: Kregel Publications, 1960.

*Journal of Discourses*. 26 vols. London: Latter-day Saints' Book Depot, 1854–86.

Keller, W. Phillip. *Rabboni, Which Is to Say, Master*. Grand Rapids, Mich.: Kregel Publications, 1997.

Kimball, Spencer W. *The Miracle of Forgiveness*. Salt Lake City: Bookcraft, 1969.

———. *Faith Precedes the Miracle*. Salt Lake City: Deseret Book, 1972.

———. *Peter, My Brother*. Brigham Young University Speeches of the Year, Provo, 13 July 1971, cited in *Life and Teachings of Jesus and His Apostles* [manual], 2d ed.

———. *Tragedy or Destiny?* Salt Lake City: Deseret Book, 1977.

Klein, Mina C., and H. Arthur Klein. *Temple beyond Time: The Story of the Site of Solomon's Temple at Jerusalem*. New York: Van Nostrand Reinhold, 1970.

Kloner, Amos. "Did a Rolling Stone Close Jesus' Tomb?" *Biblical Archaeology Review*, September/October 1999, 23.

Kofford, Cree-L. "The Trial of Christ." In *Clark Memorandum*. Provo, Utah: Brigham Young University, J. Reuben Clark Law School, Fall 2003.

*Lectures on Faith*. Salt Lake City: Deseret Book, 1985.

Lee, Harold B. Conference Report, October 1973.

———. *Divine Revelation*. Brigham Young University Speeches of the Year, Provo, Utah, 1952, cited in *Life and Teachings of Jesus and His Apostles* [manual], 2d ed.

———. "I Walked Today Where Jesus Walked." *Ensign*, April 1972, 3.

———. "Qualities of Leadership." Address to Latter-day Saint Student Association (LDSSA) Convention, Salt Lake City, August 1970.

———. *Stand Ye in Holy Places*. Salt Lake City: Deseret Book, 1974.

———. *The Teachings of Harold B. Lee*. Edited by Clyde J. Williams. Salt Lake City: Bookcraft, 1996.

Lewis, C. S. *A Grief Observed*. San Francisco: HarperCollins, 1961.

———. *Mere Christianity*. New York: Touchstone, 1980.

*A Lexicon, Abridged from Liddell and Scott's Greek-English Lexicon.*
Oxford: Clarendon Press, 1871.

*The Life and Teachings of Jesus and His Apostles [manual].* 2d ed. Salt
Lake City: The Church of Jesus Christ of Latter-day Saints, 1979.

Littlefield, Lyman Omer. *Reminiscences of Latter-day Saints.* Logan,
Utah: Utah Journal Co., 1888.

MacArthur, John F., Jr. *The Murder of Jesus.* Nashville: Word
Publishing, 2000.

Mace, Wandle. "Journal of Wandle Mace." Typescript, Harold B. Lee
Library, Brigham Young University, Provo, Utah.

Maier, Paul L. *Eusebius—The Church History: A New Translation with
Commentary.* Grand Rapids, Mich.: Kregel Publications, 1999.

———. *In the Fullness of Time: A Historian Looks at Christmas, Easter,
and the Early Church.* New York: HarperCollins, 1991.

Matthews, Robert J. "Resurrection: The Ultimate Triumph." In
*Jesus Christ, Son of God, Savior.* Provo, Utah: Religious Studies
Center, 2002.

Matthews, Victor H. *Manners and Customs of the Bible.* Rev. ed.
Peabody, Mass.: Hendrickson, 1988, 1991.

Maxwell, Neal A. *All These Things Shall Give Thee Experience.* Salt
Lake City: Deseret Book, 1979.

———. *Deposition of a Disciple.* Salt Lake City: Deseret Book, 1976.

———. *Lord, Increase Our Faith.* Salt Lake City: Bookcraft, 1994.

———. "Why Not Now?" *Ensign*, November 1974.

———. "Yet Thou Art There." *Ensign*, November 1987.

McConkie, Bruce R. *Doctrinal New Testament Commentary.* 3 vols.
Salt Lake City: Bookcraft, 1965–73.

———. *Mormon Doctrine.* 2d ed. Salt Lake City: Bookcraft, 1966.

———. *The Mortal Messiah.* 4 vols. Salt Lake City: Deseret Book,
1981.

———. "Probationary Test of Mortality." Address at Salt Lake Institute of Religion, Salt Lake City, Utah, 10 January 1982.

———. *The Promised Messiah.* Salt Lake City: Deseret Book, 1978.

———. "The Purifying Power of Gethsemane." *Ensign*, May 1985.

———. "The Salvation of Little Children." *Ensign*, April 1977.

Metzger, Bruce Manning. *The New Testament: Its Background, Growth, and Content*. Nashville: Abingdon Press, 1965.

Millet, Robert L., and Joseph Fielding McConkie. *The Life Beyond*. Salt Lake City: Bookcraft, 1986.

Mouw, Richard J. "Christian Responses to a World in Crisis." *Fuller Focus*, Spring 2002.

Mumford, Thomas. *Horizontal Harmony of the Four Gospels in Parallel Columns*. Salt Lake City: Deseret Book, 1976.

Murphy-O'Connor, Jerome. "Fishers of Fish, Fishers of Men." *Bible Review*, June 1999, 23.

———. *The Holy Land: An Oxford Archaeological Guide from Earliest Times to 1700*. Oxford: Oxford University Press, 1998.

———. "What Really Happened in Gethsemane." *Bible Review* 14 (April 1998): 28–39, 52.

Nelson, Russell M. *From Heart to Heart: An Autobiography*. Salt Lake City, 1979.

Pace, George W. "What It Means to Know Christ." *Ensign*, September 1974.

Packer, Boyd K. Conference Report, April 1988.

———. "We Honor Now His Journey." *Ensign*, July 1994.

Peterson, H. Donl, and Charles D. Tate Jr., eds. *The Pearl of Great Price: Revelations from God*. Provo, Utah: Brigham Young University, Religious Studies Center, 1989.

*Philonis Alexandrini: Legatio ad Gaium*. Translated by E. Mary Smallwood. Leiden: E. J. Brill, 1970.

Plautus, Titus Maccius. *The Braggart Warrior*. Translated by Paul Nixon. New York: G. P. Putnam's Sons, 1916.

Powers, Tom. "Treasures in the Storeroom." *Biblical Archaeology Review*, July-August 2003.

Pratt, Parley P. *Autobiography of Parley P. Pratt*. Rev. ed. Edited by Scot Facer Proctor and Maurine Jensen Proctor. Salt Lake City: Deseret Book, 2000.

———. *Key to the Science of Theology*. Classics in Mormon Literature Series. Salt Lake City: Deseret Book, 1978.

Robinson, Stephen E. Address to Religious Education prayer meeting, Brigham Young University, Provo, Utah, February 12, 1992.

Rosen, Ceil, and Moishe Rosen. *Christ in the Passover: Why Is This Night Different?* Chicago, Ill.: Moody Press, 1978.

Rousseau, John J., and Rami Arav. *Jesus and His World: An Archaeological and Cultural Dictionary.* Minneapolis: Augsburg Fortress, 1995.

Sloan, Robert, Jr. "The Character of Leadership." *BYU Magazine,* Winter 2003.

Smith, Joseph. *History of The Church of Jesus Christ of Latter-day Saints.* Edited by B. H. Roberts. 2d ed. rev. 7 vols. Salt Lake City: The Church of Jesus Christ of Latter-day Saints, 1932–51

———. *Teachings of the Prophet Joseph Smith.* Selected by Joseph Fielding Smith. Salt Lake City: Deseret Book, 1976.

Smith, Joseph F. *Gospel Doctrine.* Salt Lake City: Deseret Book, 1966.

———. "The Resurrection." *Liahona, the Elders Journal* (August 8, 1908): 178.

Smith, Joseph Fielding. *Answers to Gospel Questions.* Compiled by Joseph Fielding Smith, Jr. 5 vols. Salt Lake City: Deseret Book, 1957–66.

———. *Doctrines of Salvation.* Compiled by Bruce R. McConkie. 3 vols. Salt Lake City: Bookcraft, 1954–56.

Smith, Lucy Mack. *History of Joseph Smith by His Mother.* Edited by Preston Nibley. Salt Lake City: Bookcraft, 1954.

*Special Witnesses of Christ* [videotape]. Salt Lake City: The Church of Jesus Christ of Latter-day Saints, 2000.

*St. Peter "in Gallicantu" "at the Cockcrow"* [leaflet]. Jerusalem: Augustinian Fathers of the Assumption (Assumptionists), n.d.

Talmage, James E. *The Articles of Faith.* Salt Lake City: The Church of Jesus Christ of Latter-day Saints, 1924.

———. *Jesus the Christ.* Salt Lake City: Deseret Book, 1916

Taylor, John. *John Taylor. Teachings of Presidents of the Church* Series. Salt Lake City: The Church of Jesus Christ of Latter-day Saints, 2001.

*The Interpreter's Bible.* 12 vols. Nashville: Abingdon, 1951.

*Tractate Sanhedrin, Chapters 9–11*. Vol. 23c of *The Talmud of Babylonia: An American Translation*. Translated by Jacob Neusner. Chico, Calif.: Scholars Press, 1985.

"Visit Leads Prophet to Walk in Holy Places." *Church News*, 3 November 1979, 4.

Wachsman, Shelley. *The Sea of Galilee Boat: A 2000-Year-Old Discovery from the Sea of Legends*. Cambridge, Mass.: Perseus, 2000.

Walker, Peter. *The Weekend That Changed the World: The Mystery of Jerusalem's Empty Tomb*. Louisville, Ky.: Westminster John Knox Press, 2000.

Weaver, Sarah Jane. "God Will Protect Us in These Perilous Times." *Church News*, February 22, 2003.

Whitney, Orson F. *Improvement Era*, November 1918.

———. *Through Memory's Halls*. Independence, Mo.: Zion's Printing and Publishing, 1930.

Wilkinson, John. *Jerusalem As Jesus Knew It*. London: Thames and Hudson, 1978.

Woodruff, Wilford. *The Discourses of Wilford Woodruff*. Selected and edited by G. Homer Durham. Salt Lake City: Bookcraft, 1969.

Young, Brigham. *Discourses of Brigham Young*. Selected by John A. Widtsoe. Salt Lake City: Deseret Book, 1971.

Zias, Joseph, and Eliezer Sekeles. "The Crucified Man from Giv'at ha-Mitvar—A Reappraisal." *Biblical Archaeologist*, September 1985.

# Index

# About the Author

Andrew C. Skinner, a professor of ancient scripture and Near Eastern studies, is a Richard L. Evans Professor of Religious Understanding at BYU, where he served as dean of Religious Education and as the first executive director of the Neal A. Maxwell Institute for Religious Scholarship. A member of the international editorial group that translated the Dead Sea Scrolls and author or coauthor of more than two hundred articles and books on religious and historical topics, Dr. Skinner taught at the BYU Jerusalem Center and was its associate director. He has served in the Church as a bishop, a counselor in a district presidency in Israel, a member of the Correlation Evaluation Committee, and a member of the Sunday School General Board. He and his wife, Janet Corbridge Skinner, are the parents of six children.